Mendicants, Military Orders, and Regionalism in Medieval Europe

Mendicants, Military Orders,
and Regionalism
in Medieval Europe

Edited by

JÜRGEN SARNOWSKY

Ashgate

Aldershot • Brookfield USA • Singapore • Sydney

Published by
Ashgate Publishing Limited
Gower House
Croft Road
Aldershot
Hants GU11 3HR
England

Ashgate Publishing Company
Old Post Road
Brookfield
Vermont 05036–9704
USA

British Library Cataloguing in Publication Data

Sarnowsky, Jürgen
    Mendicants, Military Orders, and Regionalism in Medieval
    Europe
    1. Friars—Europe—History. 2. Military religious orders—
    Europe—History.
    I. Sarnowsky, Jürgen.
    271'.06'04

Library of Congress Catalog Card Number: 99–C72564

ISBN 1 84014 623 0

This book is printed on acid free paper

Printed in Great Britain by Antony Rowe Ltd., Chippenham, Wiltshire

Contents

List of Illustrations

List of Contributors

KARL BORCHARDT works in the Department of History at the University of Würzburg and researches into the religious orders, for example, the Celestinians, and German regional history. His publications include a book on medieval ecclesiastical institutions at Rothenburg ob der Tauber (1988). He is currently preparing a study on the Hospitallers in central Europe in collaboration with Dr Anthony Luttrell.

DIETER HECKMANN studied at the universities of Saarbrücken and St Etienne sur Loire, and is Archivist at the Geheimes Staatsarchiv, Berlin. He researches into town history and the regional history of Lorraine, Prussia, and Livonia. His publications include *Von Königsberg an die Loire. Quellen zur Handelsreise des herzoglich-preußischen Faktors Antoine Maillet nach Frankreich in den Jahren 1562 bis 1564* (1993).

LIBOR JAN is Lecturer in History at the Department of History in the Faculty of Philosophy, University of Masaryk, Brno, Czech Republic. He researches into the military orders in Bohemia and the history of Moravia in the thirteenth and fourteenth centuries, and is currently preparing a book on the administrative history of Moravia. His publications include a history of the cathedral chapter of Brno.

NIKOLAS JASPERT is Lecturer in Medieval History at the Friedrich-Alexander-Universität in Erlangen-Nürnberg. He is the author of *Stift und Stadt. Das Heiliggrabpriorat von Santa Anna und das Regularkanonikerstift Santa Eulàlia del Camp im mittelalterlichen Barcelona, 1145-1423* (1996) and articles on the medieval history of Spain, the Crusader States and the Kingdom of Sicily.

ANTHONY LUTTRELL studied at Oxford, Madrid, Rome and Pisa, taught at Swarthmore College in Pennsylvania, Edinburgh, Malta and Padua, and was Assistant Director and Librarian of the British School at Rome. He works and publishes extensively on the Hospitallers of Rhodes, on medieval Malta, on the English in the Levant, and on various archaeological projects.

KLAUS MILITZER is Professor of Medieval History at the University of Bochum. His publications on the military orders centre particularly upon the history of the Teutonic Order in Germany, Prussia and Livonia, and include *Die Entstehung der Deutschordensballeien im Deutschen Reich* (1981) and *Ritter-*

brüder im livländischen Zweig des Deutschen Ordens (1993) (with Lutz Fenske).

JOHANNES A. MOL is Research Fellow at the Fryske Akademy in Leeuwarden. His works on the medieval history of Frisia set aside, he published a monograph and several articles on the military orders in the Netherlands. He is currently preparing a book on monasteries and society in medieval Frisia.

BERNHARD NEIDIGER is Archivist at the Stadtarchiv, Stuttgart, and works on the history of religious orders, especially the Observant movement and its intellectual history. His articles and books include *Das Dominikanerkloster Stuttgart, die Kanoniker vom gemeinsamen Leben in Urach und die Gründung der Universität Tübingen. Konkurrierende Reformansätze in der württembergischen Kirchenpolitik am Ausgang des Mittelalters* (1993).

HELEN NICHOLSON is Lecturer in Medieval History at the University of Wales, Cardiff, and works on the military orders and various related subjects. Her most recent book is *Chronicle of the Third Crusade: a Translation of the* Itinerarium Peregrinorum et Gesta Regis Ricardi (1997).

ANNELI RANDLA studied at Cambridge and is currently Academic Secretary of the Institute of Art History of the Estonian Academy of Arts, and Researcher in the Estonian Art Museum. She works on the architecture of the mendicant orders in Northern Europe; her most recent publication is an article on the Dominicans in Livonia.

JENS RÖHRKASTEN is Lecturer in History in the Department of Medieval History at the University of Birmingham. His areas of research are criminal law in the Middle Ages and the history of the mendicant orders in England. Among his publications are *Die englischen Kronzeugen, 1130-1330* (1990) and various articles on mendicants.

ANDREAS RÜTHER is Lecturer in Medieval History at the Justus-Liebig-Universität Gießen. He currently works on politics, society and church in Silesia in the later Middle Ages. His publications include *Bettelorden in Stadt und Land. Die Straßburger Mendikanten und das Elsaß im Spätmittelalter* (1997).

JÜRGEN SARNOWSKY is Professor of Medieval History at the University of Hamburg. His main fields of study are the military orders, the history of medieval Prussia and scholastic thought, and he is now editor of the journal *Beiträge zur Geschichte Westpreußens*. He is currently preparing a book on the administrative and constitutional history of the Hospitallers on fifteenth-century Rhodes.

Editor's Preface

The idea of investigating the problems implicit in the regional and local settings of the mendicant and military orders was conceived during a visit to London in 1996, where I met my friend Jens Röhrkasten from the University of Birmingham. We decided to organize two sessions for the 1997 International Medieval Conference in Leeds, one on mendicants and one on military orders. Most of the papers collected in this volume originally were presented at that conference: those of Bernhard Neidiger, Andreas Rüther, Anthony Luttrell, Karl Borchardt, Jens Röhrkasten, and myself in the sessions mentioned above; those of Klaus Militzer, Libor Jan, and Johannes Mol in a session on the Teutonic Knights organized by Klaus Militzer, and that of Helen Nicholson in another session. Due to organizational problems there were two additional papers for the session on military orders which are also printed here, those of Nikolas Jaspert and Dieter Heckmann; and I asked Anneli Randla for her paper in order to have one more article on mendicants and at least one contribution on art history. I wish to thank all of the contributors as well as the organizers of the sessions for agreeing to publish their respective papers in this collection; their contributions made it possible to examine a wide range of problems.

Concerning the production of the book my personal thanks go to Jens Röhrkasten, who also helped me with the translation of Bernhard Neidiger's paper, and especially to Edith Pawlik, who translated Libor Jan's contribution and helped to revise the introduction, my own paper, and the conclusion. I also wish to thank John Smedley, Ruth Peters and Caroline Cornish of Ashgate Publishing for their support and helpful suggestions.

Jürgen Sarnowsky

Abbreviations

APJC	*Actes de les primeres jornades sobre els ordes religioso-militars als països catalans, segles XII-XIX. Montblanc, 8-10 de novembre de 1985* (Tarragona, 1994).
ARDOU	Archief van de Ridderlijke Duitsche Orde Balije van Utrecht, Utrecht.
CCR	Calendar of the Close Rolls preserved in the Public Record Office.
CDB	*Codex diplomaticus et epistolaris Regni Bohemiae*, vols 4-5, eds J. Šebánek, S. Dušková (Prague, 1962-1993).
CGOH	*Cartulaire Général de l'Ordre des Hospitaliers de S. Jean de Jérusalem, 1100-1310*, ed. J. Delaville le Roulx, 4 vols (Paris, 1894-1906).
CPR	Calendar of the Patent Rolls preserved in the Public Record Office.
FUB	*Fürstenbergisches Urkundenbuch. Sammlung der Quellen zur Geschichte des Hauses Fürstenberg und seiner Lande in Schwaben*, ed. S. Riezler et al., 7 vols (Tübingen, 1877-1891).
GL	Guildhall Library, London.
MC	*Militia Christi e Crociata nei secoli XI-XIII. Atti della undecima Settimana internazionale di studio Mendola, 28 agosto-1 settembre 1989.* Miscellanea del Centro di Studi medioevali 23 (Milano, 1992).
MO	*Military Orders, The. Fighting for the Faith and Caring for the Sick*, ed. M. Barber (Aldershot, 1994).
MS	*Militia Sacra. Gli ordini militari tra Europa e Terrasanta*, eds E. Coli, M. De Marco, F. Tommasi (Perugia, 1994).
NLM	National Library of Malta, Valletta [Libr. = Library Manuscripts] / Archives of the Order of St. John [Arch. = Archives].
OMVR	*Les Ordres militaires, la vie rurale et le peuplement en Europe occidentale, xiie-xviiie siècles. VIe journées internationales d'histoire, 21-23 Septembre 1984, Centre culturel de l'Abbaye de Flaran* (Auch, 1986).
PRO	Public Record Office, London.
QStGDO	Quellen und Studien zur Geschichte des Deutschen Ordens.

RB   *Regesta sive rerum Boicarum autographa usque ad annum 1300*, eds K. H. Ritter von Lang, M. Freiherr von Freyberg, T. Rudhart, 13 vols (Munich, 1822-1854).

RBM   *Regesta diplomatica necnon epistolaria Bohemiae et Moraviae*, ed. J. Emler et al., 7 vols (Prague, 1882-1963).

RCAHMS   Royal Commission on the Ancient and Historical Monuments of Scotland.

RM   *Die Ritterorden zwischen geistlicher und weltlicher Macht im Mittelalter*, ed. Z. H. Nowak. Ordines Militares. Colloquia Torunensia Historica V (Toruń, 1990).

RR   *Ritterorden und Region – Politische, soziale und wirtschaftliche Verbindungen im Mittelalter*, ed. Z. H. Nowak. Ordines Militares. Colloquia Torunensia Historica VIII (Toruń, 1995).

SO   *Stadt und Orden. Das Verhältnis des Deutschen Ordens zu den Städten in Livland, Preußen und im Deutschen Reich*, ed. U. Arnold. QStGDO 44 (Marburg, 1993).

StAW   Staatsarchiv Würzburg.

SWB   *Stellung und Wirksamkeit der Bettelorden in der städtischen Gesellschaft*, ed. K. Elm. Berliner Historische Studien 3, Ordensstudien 2 (Berlin, 1981).

1

Regional Problems in the History of the Mendicant and Military Orders

Jürgen Sarnowsky

In the first age of church reform leading up to the Investiture Contest – roughly the tenth to the twelfth centuries – the old, established monastic institutions underwent a process of reformation and reorganization aimed at renewing the Benedictine ideal and establishing new methods to control observance of the rule in individual monasteries, as may be seen in the foundation and spread of the Cluniac community in the tenth century as well as in that of the Cistercian Order in the twelfth.[1] In the twelfth and thirteenth centuries, new forms of orders developed whose aims and goals required more complex internal organization, namely the military and the mendicant orders.

The military orders were founded in the course of the crusades to improve the security of pilgrims in the Holy Land as in the case, for example, of the Templars, who are thought to have been knights in the service, or at least the entourage, of the Patriarch of Jerusalem before they formed a separate community in about 1119.[2] Their distinguishing characteristic was their synthesis of the monastic vows of obedience, poverty, and chastity with a commitment to the

---

[1] For a general introduction see e.g. C. H. Lawrence, *Medieval Monasticism. Forms of Religious Life in Western Europe in the Middle Ages* (2nd edn, London-New York, 1989); J. Wollasch, *Cluny – Licht der Welt. Aufstieg und Niedergang der klösterlichen Gemeinschaft* (Zürich, 1996); B. Pennington (ed.), *The Last of the Fathers. The Cistercian Fathers of the Twelfth-Century* (Still River, 1983). I wish to thank Edith Pawlik, Hamburg, for correcting the first English version of this paper. The faults that remain are mine.

[2] See M. Barber, *The New Knighthood. A History of the Order of the Temple* (Cambridge, 1994), pp. 1-18; F. Tommasi, '*Pauperes commilitones Christi*. Aspetti i problemi delle origini gerosolimitane', *MC*, pp. 465-75.

From *Mendicants, Military Orders, and Regionalism in Medieval Europe*, ed. Jürgen Sarnowsky. Copyright © 1999 by Jürgen Sarnowsky. Published by Ashgate Publishing Ltd, Gower House, Croft Road, Aldershot, Hampshire, GU11 3HR, Great Britain.

defence of Christianity against the infidel. Other orders were originally founded in conjunction with hospitals, and the brethren of these orders, including the Hospitallers and the Teutonic Knights, undertook not only the defence of Christians and their property in the Holy Land but also the care of sick, poor, or elderly pilgrims.[3] In contrast, the mendicant orders developed in response to the twelfth-century criticism of the wealth and moral decline of ecclesiastical institutions which had led to discontent and the spread of heresy, particularly in southern France and northern Italy, where the Dominicans and the Franciscans originated. The mendicant ideal was a life of poverty and the imitation of Christ and the Apostles; preaching, missionary work, and the cure of souls were their main objectives. From their inception, and in contrast to other orders, the mendicants focused their work on towns and intended to support themselves through begging and the collection of alms. A special study-system designed to provide younger brethren with the skills and knowledge necessary to fulfil their tasks was soon developed and became an essential element of the orders' identity.[4]

In the mendicant and military orders, brethren from all over Christian Europe were working together to reach their orders' aims and goals, and everyone could be sent anywhere in accordance with their superior's orders. While the older monastic orders, in accordance with the ideal of *stabilitas loci*,[5] normally required their members to remain at the monastery which they had originally entered, the brethren of the military orders and the mendicant friars

---

[3] For the military orders cf. e.g. A. J. Forey, *The Military Orders from the Twelfth to the Early Fourteenth Centuries* (Basingstoke, 1992); *The Military Orders. Fighting for the Faith and Caring for the Sick*, ed. M. Barber (Aldershot, 1994) [*MO*]; *Militia Sacra. Gli ordini militari tra Europa e Terrasanta*, eds E. Coli, M. De Marco, F. Tommasi (Perugia, 1994) [*MS*]; *Die geistlichen Ritterorden Europas*, eds J. Fleckenstein, M. Hellmann. Vorträge und Forschungen XXVI (Sigmaringen, 1980).

[4] For the mendicants cf. e.g. J. B. Freed, *The Friars and German Society in the Thirteenth Century* (Cambridge, Mass, 1977); A. Vauchez, *Mouvements Franciscains et société française XIIe-XXe siècles* (Paris, 1984); M. D. Lambert, *Franciscan Poverty. The Doctrine of the Absolute Poverty of Christ and the Apostles in the Franciscan Order 1210-1323* (London, 1961); W. A. Hinnebusch, *The History of the Dominican Order. Origins and Growth to 1500*, 2 vols (Staten Island, NY, 1966-1973); O. Steggink, 'Fraternità e possesso in comune. L'ispirazione presso i Mendicanti', *Carmelus* 15 (1968) 5-35; K. Elm (ed.), *Stellung und Wirksamkeit der Bettelorden in der städtischen Gesellschaft*. Berliner Historische Studien 3. Ordensstudien 2 (Berlin, 1981); D. Berg, *Armut und Wissenschaft. Beiträge zur Geschichte des Studienwesens der Bettelorden im 13. Jahrhundert*. Geschichte und Gesellschaft 15 (Düsseldorf, 1977).

[5] A. Rüther, 'Stabilitas loci', *Lexikon des Mittelalters*, vol. 7 (Munich, 1995), col. 2162-63.

thus moved frequently from one place to another. For the military orders, who had to secure the supply of men and materials for the struggle against the infidel when and wherever necessary, this was primarily a question of logistics,[6] whereas for the mendicants, with a hierarchy of educational institutions ranging from local centres to 'general studies' most often associated with the universities,[7] it took the form of rotation among the various houses according to the needs of the community and the abilities of the brethren in question.

The co-ordination of the orders' aims thus required highly developed internal structures with strong central elements. While the military orders had their headquarters first in the Holy Land (and Spain) and later on Cyprus, Rhodes, and in Prussia, the mendicants placed themselves in or near the sphere of action of their founders or at the Roman curia. Unlike the organizational structures of older monastic institutions with their essentially monarchic character – the Cistercians, who formed an association of monasteries under the authority of the abbots of Cîteaux and the four oldest daughter houses are a good example of the type – those of the military and mendicant orders contained both oligarchic and representative elements. Although these orders were led by a master, grand master, master-general, prior-general, or general minister, there were other brethren in office who influenced the orders' policies as well, and all of these were overseen by the chapters general. These met regularly and – at least partially – consisted not only of officials, but of 'simple brethren' from the orders' houses and provinces as well. These houses formed the lowest administrative level and served as the orders' bases of operations, and were themselves divided into provinces governed by provincial officials and provincial chapters which also exhibited representative elements, while central institutions at least partially, and sometimes regularly, controlled the admission of brethren, promotion to office, and the policies of the orders as a whole.[8]

---

[6] See e.g. the chapter on the Templars' 'network' in Barber, pp. 229-79.

[7] Berg, esp. pp. 142-44; see also e.g. M. O'Carroll, 'The Educational Organization of the Dominicans in England and Wales, 1221-1348', *Archivum Fratrum Praedicatorum* 50 (1980) 23-62; W. J. Courtenay, 'Franciscan *studia* in Southern Germany in the Fourteenth Century', *Gesellschaftsgeschichte. Festschrift für Karl Bosl,* ed. F. Seibt (Munich, 1988), pp. 81-90; J. Kłoczowski, 'Studium generalne dominikanów w Krakowie w XV wieku', *Roczniki Filosoficzne* 27 (1979) 239-43.

[8] In addition to the literature cited in n. 3 and 4 cf. e.g. L. Moulin, 'Les formes du gouvernement local et provincial dans les ordres religieux', *Revue international des sciences administratives* 21 (1955) 31-57; P. Dinzelbacher, J. L. Hogg (eds), *Kulturgeschichte der christlichen Orden* (Stuttgart, 1997); G. R. Galbraith, *The Constitution of the Dominican Order (1226-1360)* (Manchester, 1925); P. Mortier, *Histoire des maitres*

The complex internal structures of the mendicant and the military orders made them more 'international' than the older orders, a tendency which was further reinforced by the fact that the orders were in most cases under papal protection (and control) and thus exempted from episcopal jurisdiction. While such exemption was first granted to the Cluniac community, its implications in the case of the more powerful military and mendicant orders was much further-reaching. In theory and – though not always effectively – in practice, these orders acted as military and spiritual arms of the papacy, the only one of the two universal powers of the Middle Ages which succeeded in maintaining its position until the beginning of the sixteenth century.[9]

---

généraux de l'ordre des Frères Prêcheurs, 8 vols (Paris, 1903-1920); K. Eßer, 'Die endgültige Regel der Minderbrüder im Lichte der neueren Forschung', *Franziskanisches Leben. Gesammelte Dokumente*, eds K. Eßer, E. Grau. Bücher franziskanischer Geistigkeit 13 (Werl, 1968), pp. 31-96; R. B. Brooke, *Early Franciscan Government. Elias to Bonaventura*. Cambridge Studies in Medieval Life and Thought 7 (Cambridge, 1959); H. Dedieu, 'Les ministres provinciaux d'Aquitaine des origines à la division de l'Ordre', *Archivum Franciscanum Historicum* 76 (1983) 129-214; F. F. Lopes, 'Franciscanos de Portugal antes de formarem Provincia independiente. Ministros provinciais a que obedeziam', *Archivo Ibero-Americano* 45 (1985) 349-450; B. Waldstein-Wartenberg, *Rechtsgeschichte des Malteserordens* (Vienna, Munich, 1969) [with some problems]; J. Sarnowsky 'Der Konvent auf Rhodos und die Zungen (*lingue*) im Johanniterorden (1421-1476)', *RR*, pp. 43-65; *idem*, 'The Oligarchy at Work, The Chapters General of the Hospitallers in the XVth Century (1421-1522)', *Autour de la Première Croisade*, ed. M. Balard. Byzantina Sorbonensia 14 (Paris, 1996), pp. 267-76; F. Milthaler, *Die Großgebietiger des Deutschen Ordens bis 1440* (Königsberg-Berlin, 1940); K. Militzer, *Die Entstehung der Deutschordensballeien im Deutschen Reich*. QStGDO 16 (2nd edn, Bonn, 1981); P. G. Thielen, *Die Verwaltung des Ordensstaates Preußen vornehmlich im 15.Jahrhundert*. Ostmitteleuropa in Vergangenheit und Gegenwart 11 (Cologne, Graz, 1965).

[9] For the relationship between popes and orders see e.g. M. d'Alatri, *L'inquisizione francescana nell'Italia centrale nel secolo XIII* (Rome, 1954); C. Schmitt, *Un pape réformateur et un défenseur de l'unité de l'Eglise. Benoît XII et l'ordre des Frères Mineurs (1334-1342)* (Quaracchi, 1959); L. Garcia-Guijarro Ramos, *Papado, cruzadas y órdenes militares XI-XII s.* (Madrid, 1995); R. Iorio, *L'Inchiesta di Papa Gregorio XI sugli Ospedalieri della Diocesi di Trani* (Taranto, 1996); A. Luttrell, 'The Hospitallers and the Papacy, 1305-1314', *Forschungen zur Reichs-, Papst- und Landesgeschichte*, eds K. Borchardt, E. Bünz, vol. 2 (Stuttgart, 1998), pp. 595-622; U. Arnold, 'Der Deutsche Orden zwischen Kaiser und Papst im 13. Jahrhundert', *RM*, pp. 57-70; K. Neitmann, 'Papst und Kaiser in den Staatsverträgen des Deutschen Ordens in Preußen, 1230-1466', *Archiv für Diplomatik* 33 (1988) 293-321; C. Schuchard, 'Rom und die päpstliche Kurie in den Berichten des Deutschordens-Generalprokurators Jodocus Hogenstein (1448-1468)', *Quellen und Forschungen aus italienischen Archiven und Bibliotheken* 72 (1992) 54-122. For the inquisition which was in many cases in the hands of the Dominicans cf. B. Hamilton, *The Medieval Inquisition* (London, 1981); P. Segl (ed.), *Die Anfänge der Inquisition im Mittelalter*. Bayreuther Historische Kolloquien 7 (Cologne, Weimar, Vienna, 1993).

The supranational character of the mendicant and the military orders contrasted with their local, regional, and 'national' foundations. Since they were dependent on the supply of members and donations and on the goodwill and privileges of the ruling classes at the local, regional, and 'national' levels, different channels of influence were opened up. In the early stages of their development, the orders needed the support of local rulers, the nobility, and the townspeople to establish themselves in the various regions of Europe and to create a basis for their operations. Once they had accumulated larger possessions or gained a position of influence, the orders invited interference from local and regional powers, bishops, towns, the nobility, and kings, all of whom sought to strengthen their rule or their standing by gaining control over ecclesiastical institutions and their properties, often by hinting that their ancestors had given large donations. Emperors and popes also tried to use the orders' power to their own advantage in their mutual struggles. While it was not unusual for members of a mendicant or military order to be in the service of kings, nobles, or towns because of their military or intellectual skills, they had to act carefully in order to avoid conflicts of loyalty. The orders' dependence upon local rulers, other ecclesiastical institutions, and social and ethnic groups became especially marked in border regions, where often even the orders' properties were shaped according to local structures and spheres of influence.

But the 'international' character of the mendicant and military orders also led to internal difficulties. Problems arose between members of varying origins living together in the orders' houses and among different regional or 'national' groups within the orders, and it is likely that these increased with the growing 'nationalism' of the later medieval period. Divisions of property which came about accidentally when an order's province boundaries were drawn might necessitate special arrangements. In this respect, external factors played an important role, as well: local traditions, 'national' identities and conflicts, and economic factors, particularly those resulting from the economic difficulties of the later Middle Ages, were influential in moulding the orders' internal structures and in carving out their provinces, and in some cases even contributed to their dissolution. And while custom and to some degree regulations provided norms for the design of the orders' buildings and equipment, regional and 'national' differences resulted in the development of varying styles in the art and architecture commissioned by the orders.

In a recent article, Kaspar Elm described the military orders as a form of 'religious life between universalism and particularism'.[10] The same holds true for the mendicants. It is perhaps due to the complexity of the problems involved that no comparative and systematic approach to this subject yet exists. Nonetheless, historians have explored many aspects of the problem in recent years. Particularly of note here is the Polish-German volume on 'military orders and region', published in 1995,[11] which examines the relationships between the areas of recruiting and operation, between orders and towns, and orders and the regional nobility, and which describes the regional organization of the military orders. And in his brief study on 'Europe and region – conflicting forces in the development of the Teutonic Knights', Udo Arnold advances the hypothesis of a mid fourteenth-century shift in the order's structures: while the rule and extension of the order's houses retained their European character, regional factors played an ever greater role in daily life.[12]

Though generalization is difficult, it is clear that European regionalism was an important factor in the history of all military and mendicant orders. The history of individual houses and provinces and the related aspects of the orders as a whole have been well researched. Numerous articles and monographs have been devoted to the history of the military orders on the Iberian Peninsula,[13] in

---

[10] K. Elm, 'Gli ordini militari. Un ceto di vita religiosa fra universalismo e particolarismo', *MS*, pp. 9-28.

[11] *Ritterorden und Region – Politische, soziale und wirtschaftliche Verbindungen im Mittelalter,* ed. Z. H. Nowak. Ordines Militares. Colloquia Torunensia Historica VIII (Toruń, 1995) [*RR*].

[12] 'Die Norm der Regel, die Verbreitung der Niederlassungen zeigten nach wie vor die europäische Weite, die tägliche Existenz aber engte das Ordensleben auf die Region ein. Die widerstreitenden Kräfte Europa und Region gewannen ab der Mitte des 14.Jahrhunderts eine andere Ausformung, die Schwerpunkte verschoben sich gegeneinander, doch blieben beide auch weiterhin existent', U. Arnold, 'Europa und die Region – widerstreitende Kräfte in der Entwicklung des Deutschen Ordens im Mittelalter', *RR*, pp. 161-72, here p. 169.

[13] See M. de Ayala Martínez, C. Barquero Goñi, J. V. Matellanes Merchán et al., 'Las Ordenes Militares en la Edad Media peninsular. Historiografía 1976-1992, I: Reinos de Castilla y León', *Medievalismo* 2 (1992) 119-69; M. de Ayala Martínez, F. Andrés Robres, J. V. Matellanes Merchán et al., 'Las Ordenes Militares en la Edad Media peninsular. Historiografía 1976-1992, II: Corona de Aragón, Navarra y Portugal', *Medievalismo* 3 (1993) 87-144. Cf. also e.g. E. Rodríguez-Picavea Matilla, 'Frontera, soberanía territorial y órdenes militares en la Península Ibérica durante la Edad Media', *Hispania* 52 (1992) 789-809; J.-L. Martín, 'Ordenes Militares en la Peninsula Ibérica', *MC*, pp. 551-72.

the Spanish kingdoms and regions of Léon and Castile,[14] Aragon and Catalonia,[15] and even Navarre.[16] Similar regional studies can be found for the

---

[14] See e.g. C. de Ayala Martínez, 'Origines de la Orden del Hospital en Castilla y León (1113-1157)', *Hispania sacra* 43 (1991) 775-98; *idem*, 'Possessions and Incomes of the Order of Calatrava in the Kingdom of Léon in the Twelfth and Thirteenth Centuries', *MO*, pp. 283-87; C. Barquero Goñi, 'The Hospitallers and the Castilian-Leonese Monarchy: the Concession of Royal Rights, Twelfth to Fourteenth Centuries', *MO*, pp. 28-33; J. M. Escobar Camacho, 'Las Órdenes Militares en el reino de Córdoba durante el siglo XIII', *Andalucía entre Oriente y Occidente (1236-1492). Actas del V Coloquio de Historia medieval de Andalucía, celebrado en el Salón de Actos de la Exma, Diputación Provincial de Córdoba durante los días 27 al 30 de noviembre de 1986*, ed. E. Cabrera (Cordoba, 1988), pp. 113-21; C. Estepa Diez, 'La disolución de la orden del temple en Castilla y León', *Cuadernos de Historia* 6 (1975) 121-86; J. M. Molero García, 'Participación de la Orden del Hospital en el avance de la frontera castellana (1144-1224)', *Alarcos 1195. Congreso internacional del VIII centenario de la batalla de Alarcos* (Cuenca, 1996), pp. 331-51. For the mendicants cf. e.g. J. Fernandez Conde, 'La orden franciscana en Asturias: origenes y primera época', *Archivum Franciscanum Historicum* 82 (1989) 306-59; M. de Mar Grana Cid, 'Franciscanos y domenicanos en la Galicia medieval: aspectos de una poscion de privilego', *Archivo Ibero-Americano* 53 (1993) 230-70; J. Garcia Oro, 'Páginas mindonenses de espiritualidad jacobea y franciscana. Los primitivos "freires" de la Tercerea Orden Regular en Galicia', *Estudios Mindonienses* 1 (1985) 159-84; J. M. Miura Andrades, 'Conventos y organización social del espacio. Fundatores y fundaciones dominicas en la Andalucia medieval', *Historia Urbana* 2 (1993) 83-111.

[15] See e.g. P. Bertran i Roigé, 'L' Ordre de l' Hospital a Catalunya: els inicis', *L' Avenc* 179 (1994) 22-27; M. Bonet Donato, *La Orden del Hospital en la Corona de Aragón* (Madrid, 1994); A. J. Forey, 'Sources for the History of the Templars in Aragon, Catalonia and Valencia', *Archives* 21 (1994) 16-24; *idem*, 'Els Templers de la Corona d'Aragó i la reconquesta', *L'Avenc* 161 (1992) 24-27; *idem*, *The Templars in the Corona de Aragón* (London, 1973); C. Laliena Corbera, 'Les ordres militaires et le repeuplement dans le sud de l'Aragon (XIIIe siècle)', *OMVR*, pp. 225-32; A. Luttrell, 'The Economy of the Fourteenth-Century Aragonese Hospital', *Estudis Castellonencs* 6 (1994-1995) 759-66; *idem*, 'The Structure of the Aragonese Hospital: 1349-1352', *APJC*, pp. 315-28; J. Miret i Sans, *Les cases de templers i hospitalers en Catalunya. Aplech de noves i documents historichs* (Barcelona, 1910-1913); J. M. Sans i Travé, *Els Templers a Catalunya. De la rosa a la creu*. Els ordes militars 4 (Lleida, 1996); P. Schickl, 'Die Entstehung und Entwicklung des Templerordens in Katalonien und Aragón', *Gesammelte Aufsätze zur Kulturgeschichte Spaniens. Spanische Forschungen der Görresgesellschaft* 28 (1975) 91-229. For the mendicants cf. e.g. T. Echarte, 'Huesca. Convento de predicatores (1254-1835)', *Argensola* 27 (1984) 315-32; J. R. Webster, 'La Barcelona franciscana', *Estudi d'historia medieval* 6 (1990) 1-10.

[16] See e.g. S. García Larragueta, *El gran priorado de Navarra de la Orden de San Juan de Jerusalén, siglos XII-XIII*, 2 vols (Pamplona, 1957); *idem*, 'Orden de San Juan de Jerusalén en Navarra (siglo XIV)', *Las Órdenes militares en el Mediterráneo occidental s. XII-XVIII. Coloquio celebrado los días 4, 5 y 6 de mayo de 1983* (Madrid, 1989), pp. 103-38.

military and mendicant orders in the British Isles,[17] in the regions of France[18] and Italy,[19] in the different parts of the empire[20] and of east central and

---

[17] For the mendicants see e.g. W. A. Hinnebusch, *The Early English Friars Preachers*. Dissertationes Historicae, 14 (Rome, 1951); J. R. H. Moorman, *The Franciscans in England* (London, 1974); *idem*, 'Some Franciscans in England', *Archivum Franciscanum Historicum* 83 (1990) 405-20; A. G. Little, 'Introduction of the Observant Friars into England', *Proceedings of the British Academy* 11 (1923) 455-71; E. Barker, *The Dominican Order and Convocation* (Oxford, 1913); A. F. C. Bourdillon, *The Order of Minoresses in England* (Manchester, 1926); H. F. Chettle, 'The Friars of the Holy Cross in England,' *History* 34 (1949) 204-20; D. D. C. P. Mould, *The Irish Dominicans: The Friars Preachers in the History of Catholic Ireland* (Dublin, 1957); P. Conlan, *Franciscan Ireland* (Gigginstown, 1988); R. N. Hadcock, 'The Order of the Holy Cross in Ireland', *Medieval Studies Presented to Aubrey Gwynn S. J.*, eds J. A. Watt, J. B. Morrall, F. X. Martin (Dublin, 1961), pp. 44-53; W. M. Bryce, *The Scottish Grey Friars*, 2 vols (Edinburgh, London, 1909); A. Ross, *Dogs of the Lord: The Story of the Dominican Order in Scotland* (Edinburgh, 1981); for the military orders cf. J. E. Burton, 'The Knights Templar in Yorkshire in the twelfth century: a reassessment', *Northern History* 27 (1991) 26-40; E. King, *The Knights of St. John in the British Realm*, 3rd edn by H. Luke (London, 1967); C. Tipton, 'The English and Scottish Hospitallers during the Great Schism', *Catholic Historical Review* 52 (1966), 240-45; J. P. C. Field, 'Sir Robert Malory, Prior of the Hospital of St John of Jerusalem in England (1432-1439/40)', *Journal of Ecclesiastical History* 28 (1977) 249-64; W. Rees, *A History of the Order of St John of Jerusalem in Wales and on the Welsh Border, including an Account of the Templars* (Cardiff, 1947).

[18] For the mendicants see e.g. M. Parisse, 'L'implantation des ordres mendiants en Lorraine', *Annales de l'Est* 37 (1985) 132-38; M. Fontette, 'Les Dominicaines en France au XIIIe siècle', *Les religieuses en France au XIIIe siècle*, ed. M. Parisse (Nancy, 1985), pp. 97-106; C. Schmitt, 'Les Franciscains en Alsace du XIIIe au XVIIe siècle', *Archives de l'Église d'Alsace* 44 (1985) 25-61; J.-L. Biget, 'Autour de Bernard Délicieux: franciscanisme et société en Languedoc entre 1295 et 1330', *Revue d'histoire de l'Église de France* 70 (1984) 75-93; H. Martin, 'Les prédicateurs franciscaines dans les provinces septentrionales de la France au XVe siècle', *I Frati Minori tra '400 e '500. Atti de XII convegno internationale, Assisi, 18-20 ottobre 1984*, ed. R. Rusconi (Assisi, 1986), pp. 229-56; M. Richards, 'The conflict between observant and conventual reformed Franciscans in fifteenth-century France and Flanders', *Franciscan Studies* 50 (1992) 263-81; for the military orders cf. R. Fossier, 'Les Hospitaliers et les Templiers au nord de la Seine et en Bourgogne (XIIe-XIVe siècles)', *OMVR*, pp. 13-36; C. Higounet, 'Hospitaliers et Templiers: peuplement et exploitation rurale dans le sud-ouest de la France au Moyen Age', *OMVR*, pp. 61-78; D. Selwood, *Knights of the Cloister. Templars and Hospitallers in central-southern Occitania c. 1100 - c. 1300* (Ph.Diss., Oxford, 1997); P. Vial, 'Les Templiers en Velay aux XIIe et XIIIe siècles', *Actes du 98e congrès national des Sociétés savantes, Reims 1970. Section de philologie et d'histoire jusqu'à 1610*, vol. 2: *Champagne et pays de la Meuse* (Paris, 1975), pp. 63-83; J. Raybaud, *Histoire des Grands Prieurs et du Prieur de Saint-Gilles*, vol. 1 (Nîmes, 1904); J. Brassens, 'Toulouse sous les Hospitaliers de Saint-Jean. De la Commanderie de Saint-Jean (1121) au Grand Prieuré de Toulouse 1315-1790', *Annales de l'Ordre Souverain militaire de Malte* 32 (1974) 87-95.

[19] For the mendicants see e.g. M. Sensi, 'Gli ordini mendicanti a Spoleto', *Atti del 9o congresso internazionale di studi sull alto medioevo*, vol. 1 (Spoleto, 1981), pp. 429-

85; N. Terpstra, 'Confraternities and mendicant orders. The dynamics of lay and clerical brotherhood in Renaissance Bologna', *Catholic Historical Review* 82 (1996) 1-22; G. Cioffari, *Storia dei Domenicani in Puglia, 1221-1350* (Bari, 1986); A. d'Amato, *I Domenicani a Bologna*, vol. 1: *1218-1600* (Bologna, 1988); V. Ferrua, 'I frate predicatori a Torino. Dall'insediamento a tutto il secolo XIV', *Bulletino storica-bibliografico subalpino* 90 (1992) 111-65; B. Paton, *Preaching Friars and the Civic Ethos: Siena 1380-1480*. Westfield Publications in Medieval Studies 7 (London, 1992); F. Sorelli, 'Predicatori a Venezia (fine secolo XIV - metà secolo XV)', *Le Venezie Francescane* 6 (1989) 131-58; L. Pellegrini, *Insediamenti francescani nell'Italia del Duecento* (Rome, 1984); M. de Angelis, 'I conventi franciscani della custodia viterbese fondati nei secoli XIII-XIV', *Laurentianum* 34 (1993), 227-43; M. d'Alatri, 'A proposito dei piú antichi insediamenti francescani in Sicilia', *Schede medievali* 12-13 (1987) 25-35; M. P. Albersoni, *Francescanesimo a Milano nel duecento*. Fonti e ricerche 1 (Milano, 1991); A. Marini, 'Le fondazioni francescane feminali nel Lazio nel Duecento', *Collectanea Franciscana* 63 (1993) 71-96; K. Walsh, 'The Augustinian observance in Siena in the age of S. Caterina and S. Bernardino', *Atti del Simposio internazionale Cateriniano-Bernardiniano, 17-20 Aprile 1980*, eds D. Maffei, P. Nardi (Siena, 1982) pp. 939-50; for the military orders cf. L. d'Arienza, 'Gli Ordini Militari in Sardegna nel Basso Medioevo', *APJC*; F. Bramato, 'L'ordine dei Templari in Italia. Dalle origini al pontificato di Innocenzo III (1135-1216)', *Nicolaus* 12 (1988) 183-221; D. Capolongo, 'Alife: un nuovo Insediamento templare in Terra di Lavoro', *Atti del XV Congresso di Ricerche Templari* (Latina, 1997); A. Gilmour-Bryson, *The Trial of the Templars in the Papal State and the Abbruzzi* (Città del Vaticano, 1982); M. Gattini, *I Priorati, i Baliaggi e le Commende del Sovrano Militare Ordine di S. Giovanni di Gerusalemme nelle Province Meridionali d'Italia prima della Caduta di Malta* (Naples, 1928); A. Luttrell, 'The Hospitaller Priory of Venice in 1331', *MS*, pp. 101-43; A. Miceli di Serradileo, 'L'Ordine di San Giovanni di Gerusalemme in Calabria dal XII al XV secolo', *Studi Meridionali* 10 (1977).

[20] For the mendicants see e.g. B. Neidiger, 'Die Bettelorden im spätmittelalterlichen Rheinland', *Rheinische Vierteljahrsblätter* 57 (1993) 50-74; T. Berger, *Die Bettelorden in der Erzdiözese Mainz und in den Diözesen Worms und Speyer im 13.Jahrhundert. Ausbreitung, Förderung und Funktion*. Quellen und Abhandlungen zur mittelrheinischen Kirchengeschichte (Mainz, 1995); I. Ulpts, *Die Bettelorden in Mecklenburg: ein Beitrag zur Geschichte der Franziskaner, Klarissen, Dominikaner und Augustiner-Eremiten im Mittelalter* (Werl, 1995); H.-J. Schmidt, 'Die Bettelorden und ihre Niederlassungen in der Mark Brandenburg', *Beiträge zur Entstehung Entwicklung der Mark Brandenburg im Mittelalter*, ed. W. Schich. Veröffentlichungen der Historischen Kommission zu Berlin 84 (Berlin 1993), pp. 203-25; idem, *Bettelorden in Trier. Wirksamkeit und Umfeld im hohen und späten Mittelalter*. Trierer Historische Forschungen 10 (Trier, 1986); A. H. Evertse, 'De stad Utrecht en de Franciscanen en de Dominicanen in de vijftiende eeuw', *Jaarboek Oud-Utrecht* (1986) 9-32; E. Börner, *Dritter Orden und Bruderschaften der Franziskaner in Kurbayern*. Franziskanische Forschungen 33 (Werl, 1988); E. Englisch, 'Zur Geschichte der franziskanischen Ordensfamilie in Österreich von den Anfängen bis zum Einsetzen der Observanz', *800 Jahre Franz von Assisi. Franziskanische Kunst und Kultur des Mittelalters* (Krems, 1982), pp. 289-306; *Helvetia Sacra*. Part V, vol. 1: *Die Franziskaner, die Klarissen und die regulierten Franziskaner-Terziarinnen in der Schweiz*, eds K. Arnold, G. Boner et al. (Bern, 1978); *Franziskanisches Leben im Mittelalter. Studien zur Geschichte der rheinischen und sächsischen Ordensprovinz*, ed. D. Berg. Saxonia Franciscana 3 (Werl, 1994); R. Nickel, 'Minoriten und Franziskaner in Westfalen vom 13. bis 17. Jahrhundert. Darstel-

south-eastern Europe.[21] The tendency towards a regional perspective is reinforced by the fact that available sources for the history of the orders themselves

---

lung und Bibliographie', *Franziskanische Studien* 69 (1987) 232-360, 70 (1988) 3-43, and 71 (1989) 235-325; D. J. Baetens, 'Minderbroeders in de zuiderlijke Nederlanden', *Franciscana* 44 (1989) 3-62; H. Ewe, 'Die Franziskaner in der mittelalterlichen Ostseestadt Stralsund', *Recht und Alltag im Hanseraum. Festschrift für Gerhard Theuerkauf,* eds S. Urbanski, C. Lamschus, J. Ellermeyer (Lüneburg, 1993), 145-62; J. Kadlec, 'Die Klöster der Eremiten des hl. Augustinus in Böhmen und Mähren', *Analecta Augustiniana* 56 (1993) 161-218; P. Pfotenhauer, 'Die Kreuzherren mit dem rothen Stern in Schlesien', *Zeitschrift des Vereins für Geschichte und Alterthum Schlesiens* 14 (1878) 52-78; K. Elm, 'Entstehung und Reform des belgisch-niederländischen Kreuzherrenordens', *Zeitschrift für Kirchengeschichte* 82 (1971) 292-313; for the military orders see e.g. M. Nuyttens, 'De Tempeliers in Vlaanderen', *Handelingen der Maatschappij voor Geschiedenis en Oudheidkunde te Gent,* n. s. 28 (1974) 47-57; A. Luttrell, 'The Hospitaller Province of Alamania to 1428', *RR,* pp. 21-41; W. G. Rödel, *Das Großpriorat Deutschland des Johanniter-Ordens im Übergang vom Mittelalter zur Neuzeit* (2nd edn, Cologne, 1972); R. L. Dauber, *Der Johanniter-Malteser Orden in Österreich und Mitteleuropa,* vol. 1 (Vienna, 1996); B. Demel, 'Zur Geschichte der Johanniter und des Deutschen Ordens in Kärnten', *Symposium zur Geschichte von Millstatt und Kärnten (19.-20. Juni 1992),* ed. F. Nikolasch (Millstatt, 1993), pp. 76-99; U. Arnold, 'Die Ballei und das Land: Mittelalter', *Der Deutsche Orden in Tirol. Die Ballei an der Etsch und im Gebirge,* ed. H. Noflatscher. QStGDO 43. (Bozen, 1991), pp. 125-70; D. Heckmann, 'Wirtschaftliche Auswirkungen des Armagnakenkrieges von 1444 bis 1445 auf die Deutschordensballeien Lothringen und Elsaß-Burgund', *Zeitschrift für die Geschichte des Oberrheins* 140 (1992) 101-25; H. Limburg, *Die Hochmeister des Deutschen Ordens und die Ballei Koblenz.* QStGDO 8 (Bad Godesberg, 1969); B. Klück, *De landcommanderij van de Duitse Orde te Utrecht* (Utrecht, 1995); J. A. Mol, *De Friese huizen van de Duitse Orde. Nes, Schoten en Steenkerk en hun plaats in het middeleeuwse Friese kloosterlandschap* (Leeuwarden 1991); U. Braasch-Schwersmann, 'Das Deutschordenshaus Marburg und seine Niederlassungen in hessischen Städten im Mittelalter', *Hessisches Jahrbuch für Landesgeschichte* 42 (1992) 49-85; D. J. Weiss, *Die Geschichte der Deutschordens-Ballei Franken im Mittelalter* (Neustadt a.d. Aisch 1991); B. Sommerlad, *Der Deutsche Orden in Thüringen* (Halle, 1931); J. Voigt, 'Geschichte der Ballei des Deutschen Ordens in Böhmen aus urkundlichen Quellen', *Denkschriften der kaiserlichen Akademie der Wissenschaften. Phil.-hist. Klasse* 12 (Vienna, 1861), pp. 87-146 (also separate: Vienna, 1863).

[21] For the mendicants see e.g. J. Kłoczowski, 'Dominicans of the Polish Province in the Middle Ages', *The Christian Community in Medieval Poland. Anthologies,* ed. J. Kłoczowski. Polish Historical Library 2 (Warszawa, 1981), pp. 73-113; *Franciszkanie w polsce sredniowiecznej,* ed. J. Kłoczowski, vol. 1: *Franciszkanie na ziemiach polskich* (Kraków, 1983); W. Irgang, 'Beiträge zur *Silesia Franciscana* im 13. Jahrhundert', *Archiv für schlesische Kirchengeschichte* 47-48 (1989-1990) 218-47; J. Tandecki, 'Założenie i początki klasztori franciszkanów toruńskich w XIII-XIV w.', *Zapiski Historyczne* 54 (1989) 7-21; G. Mody, 'Franziskaner und Dominikaner in Debrecen bis zur Reformationszeit', Debreceni Déri Múzeum Erkönye (1992-1993; appeared 1994) 101-10; V. Kapitanovic, 'Die Rolle der Franziskaner von Visovac in der kroatischen Geschichte', *Archivum Franciscanum Historicum* 77 (1984) 421-34; J. Dzambo, *Die Franziskaner im mittelalterlichen Bosnien.* Franziskanische Forschungen 35 (Werl, 1991); for the military orders cf. K. Borchardt, 'Military Orders in East Central Europe:

often reflect situations specific to a particular region or province. Thus, for example, chapter acts of the Dominicans in Germany and collections of documents from the French province of the order have been edited,[22] as have documents from the inquests of the Templars in England and of the Hospitallers in France.[23] And the same holds true for documents generated by or concerning the Teutonic Knights in the empire and in Prussia.[24]

The first hundred years', *Autour de la première croisade: Actes du Colloque de la Society for the Study of the Crusades and the Latin East*, ed. M. Balard. Byzantina Sorbonensia 14 (Paris, 1996), pp. 247-54; *idem*, 'The Hospitallers in Pomerania: between the Priories of Bohemia and Alamania', *The Military Orders*, vol.2: *Warfare and Welfare*, ed. H. Nicholson (Aldershot, 1998), pp. 295-306; A. Czacharowski, 'Die politische Rolle der Johanniter im pommerschen Grenzgebiet im Mittelalter', *RM*, pp. 143-52; H. Boockmann, 'Der Deutsche Orden in der Geschichte des spätmittelalterlichen Osteuropa', *Deutscher Orden, 1190-1990*, ed. U. Arnold. Tagungsberichte der Historischen Kommission für ost- und westpreußische Landesforschung 11 (Lüneburg, 1997), pp. 11-32; L. Dobronič, 'The Military Orders in Croatia', *The Meeting of Two Worlds. Cultural Exchange between East and West during the Period of the Crusades*, ed. V. P. Goss (Kalamazoo, 1986), pp. 431-38.

[22] 'Akten der Provinzkapitel der Dominikanerprovinz Teutonia aus den Jahren 1398, 1400, 1401 und 1402', ed. B. M. Reichert, *Römische Quartalschrift* 11 (1897) 287-331; 'Aus den Akten des Rottweiler Provinzkapitels der Dominikaner vom Jahr 1396', ed. B. Altaner, *Zeitschrift für Kirchengeschichte* 48 (1929) 1-15; 'Kapitelsakten der Dominikanerprovinz Teutonia (c. 1349, 1407)', ed. T. Kaeppeli, *Archivum Fratrum Praedicatorum* 22 (1952) 186-95; A. Dondaine (ed.), 'Documents pour servir à l'histoire de la Provence France', *Archivum Fratrum Praedicatorum* 22 (1952) 381-439. Cf. also e.g. E. Ypma, 'Les statuts pour le couvent des Augustins de Paris promulgués au XVe siècle', *Augustiniana* 33 (1983) 283-329; G. Casagrande (ed.), *Chiese e conventi degli ordini mendicanti in Umbria nei secoli XII-XIV. Inventario delle fonti archivistiche e catalogo delle informazioni documentari*. Archivi dell'Umbria. Inventari e ricerche 14 (Perugia, 1989); C. Longo, 'I Domenicani a Cipro. Documenti (1451-1587)', *Archivum Fratrum Praedicatorum* 59 (1989) 149-211.

[23] *Records of the Templars in England in the Twelfth Century: the Inquest of 1185*, ed. B. A. Lees. British Academy, Records of the Social and Economic History of England and Wales 9 (London, 1935); *L'Enquête Pontificale de 1373 sur l'Ordre des Hospitaliers de Saint-Jean de Jérusalem*, ed. J. Glénisson, vol. 1: *L'Enquête dans le Prieuré de France*, ed. A.-M. Legras (Paris, 1987); cf. also B. Beaucage, *Visites générales des Commanderies de l'Ordre des Hospitaliers dépendantes du Grand Prieur de Saint-Gilles: 1338* (Aix-en-Provence, 1982). For the Hospitallers in the British Isles cf. M. Gervers (ed.), *The Cartulary of the Knights of St John of Jerusalem in England*, 2 parts, Oxford 1982-1996; *The Knights Hospitallers in England: being the report of Prior Philip de Thame to the Grand Master Elyan de Villanova for AD 1338*, eds K. B. Larking, J. M. Kemble. Camden Society first series 65 (London, 1857); *Registrum de Kilmainham: Register of Chapter Acts of the Hospital of St. John of Jerusalem in Ireland, 1326-1339 under the Grand Prior, Sir Roger Outlawe, with additions for the times of his successors ...*, ed. C. McNeill (Dublin, 1932).

[24] See the list of printed sources in J. Sarnowsky, *Die Wirtschaftsführung des Deutschen Ordens in Preußen (1382-1454)* (Cologne, 1993), pp. 862-64; cf. also M. Biskup, I.

The sources, the more general works, and the many articles and monographs aside, various other problems resulting from the regionalism of Christian Europe have been examined, including the orders' relationships with kings and emperors[25] and with the leading dynasties and nobility of various European

---

Janosz-Biskupowa (eds), *Protokolle der Kapitel und Gespräche des Deutschen Ordens im Reich (1499-1525)*. QStGDO 41 (Marburg 1991); J. J. de Geer tot Oudegein, *Excerpten uit de oude rekeningen der Ridderlijke Duitsche Orde, balye van Utrecht, vóór de kerkhervorming* (Utrecht, 1895); *Urkundenbuch der Deutschordensballei Thüringen*, vol. 1, ed. K. H. Lampe. Thüringische Geschichtsquellen N. F. 7 (Jena, 1936).

[25] For the mendicants see e.g. A. G. Little, 'A Royal Inquiry into Property Held by the Mendicant Friars in England in 1349 and 1350', *Historical Essays in Honour of James Tait*, eds J. G. Edwards, V. H. Galbraith, E. F. Jacob (Manchester, 1933), pp. 179-88; D. Berg, 'Staufische Herrschaftsideologie und Mendikantenspiritualität. Studien zum Verhältnis Kaiser Friedrichs II. zu den Bettelorden', *Wissenschaft und Weisheit* 26 (1972) 26-51, 185-209; F. Machilek, 'Die Přemysliden, Piasten und Arpaden und der Klarissenorden im 13. und frühen 14. Jahrhundert', *Westmitteleuropa, Ostmitteleuropa. Vergleiche und Beziehungen. Festschrift für Ferdinand Seibt zum 65. Geburtstag*. Veröffentlichungen des Collegium Carolinum 70 (Munich, 1992), pp. 293-306; for the military orders see e.g. E. Albert i Corp, 'Els templers i la política de la Corona d'Aragó', *APJC*, pp. 219-26; M. González Jiménez, 'Relaciones de las Órdenes Militares castellanas con la Corona', *Historia – Instituciones – Documentos* 18 (1991) 209-22; A. J. Forey, 'The Will of Alfonso I of Aragón and Navarre', *Durham University Journal* 73 (1980) 59-65; C. de Ayala Martínez, 'Alfonso X y la Orden de San Juan de Jerusalén', *Estudios de historia medieval: Homenaje a Luis Suárez*, ed. Vicente Alvarez Palenzuela et al. Historia y Sociedad 18 (Valladolid, 1991) pp. 29-50; A. Pladevall i Font, *Guillem de Montrodon. Mestre del Temple i tutor de Jaume I* (Lleida, 1993); M. D.-C. Morales Muniz, 'Documentacion acerca de la administración de la Orden de Santiago por el príncipe-rey Alfonso de Castilla (1465-1468)', *Hidalguía* 36 (1988) 839-68; H. Nicholson, 'The Military Orders and the Kings of England in the Twelfth and Thirteenth Centuries', *From Clermont to Jerusalem: the Crusades and Crusader Societies, 1095-1500*, ed. A. V. Murray (Turnhout, 1998); H. Cleve, 'Kaiser Friedrich II. und die Ritterorden', *Deutsches Archiv für Erforschung des Mittelalters* 49 (1993) 39-73; H. Kluger, *Hochmeister Hermann von Salza und Kaiser Friedrich II. Ein Beitrag zur Frühgeschichte des Deutschen Ordens*. QStGDO 37 (Marburg, 1987); M. Dygo, 'The German Empire and the Grand Master of the Teutonic Order in the Light of the Golden Bull of Rimini', *Acta Poloniae Historica* 61 (1990) 33-61; D. Wojtecki, 'Der Deutsche Orden unter Friedrich II.', *Probleme um Friedrich II.*, ed. J. Fleckenstein. Vorträge und Forschungen XVI (Sigmaringen, 1974), pp. 187-224; J. M. Powell, 'Frederick II, the Hohenstaufen, and the Teutonic Order in the Kingdom of Sicily', *MO*, pp. 236-44; U. Arnold, 'Preußen, Böhmen und das Reich – Karl IV. und der Deutsche Orden', *Kaiser Karl IV. Staatsmann und Mäzen*, ed. F. Seibt (Munich, 1978), pp. 167-73; M. Hellmann, 'Karl IV. und der Deutsche Orden in den Jahren 1346-1360', *Folia diplomatica* 1 (1971) 103-12; H. Vetter, *Die Beziehungen Wenzels zum Deutschen Orden von 1381 bis 1411* (Ph.Diss., Halle, 1912); Z. H. Nowak, 'Die imperialen Vorstellungen Siegmunds von Luxemburg und der Deutsche Orden', *RM*, pp. 87-98; M. Biskup, 'Der Deutsche Orden im Reich, in Preußen und Livland im Banne habsburgischer Politik in der zweiten Hälfte des 15. und zu Beginn des 16. Jahrhunderts', *RM*, pp. 101-25; M. Hellmann, 'König Manfred von Sizilien und der Deutsche Orden', *Acht Jahrhunderte Deutscher Orden*, ed. K. Wieser. QStGDO 1 (Bad Godesberg, 1967), pp. 65-72; I. Hla-

regions.[26] The importance of bishops[27] and towns has also been a subject of study. While it was primarily the mendicants who were most closely connected with town life,[28] the military orders also came to exert some influence on the

---

vácek, 'Zur Rolle der geistlichen und ritterlichen Orden am Hofe der böhmischen Luxemburger', *RM*, pp. 153-60; L. Jan, 'Die Würdenträger der geistlichen Ritterorden an dem Hof der letzten Přemysliden', *Böhmisch-österreichische Beziehungen im 13. Jahrhundert: Österreich (einschließlich Steiermark, Kärnten und Krain) im slawischen Großreichsprojekt Ottokars II. Přemysl, König von Böhmen*, eds M. Bláhová, I. Hlaváček (Prague, 1998), pp. 285-300.

[26] For the military orders see e.g. A. Demurger, 'L'aristocrazia laica e gli ordini militari in Francia nel Duecento: l'esempio della Bassa Borgogna', *MS*, pp. 55-84; E. Magnou, 'Oblature, classe chevaleresque et servage dans les maisons méridionales du Temple au XIIe siècle', *Annales du Midi* 73 (1961) 378-97; K. Militzer, 'Die Aufnahme von Ritterbrüdern in den Deutschen Orden. Ausbildungsstand und Aufnahmevoraussetzungen', *Das Kriegswesen der Ritterorden im Mittelalter*, ed. Z. H. Nowak. Ordines Militares, Colloquia Toronensia Historica VI (Toruń 1991), pp. 7-18; *idem*, 'Die Einbindung des Deutschen Ordens in die süddeutsche Adelswelt', *RR*, pp. 141-60; J. A. Mol, 'Nederlandse ridderbroeders van de Duitse Orde in Lijfland: herkomst, afkomst en carrières', *Bijdragen en Mededelingen voor de Geschiedenis der Nederlanden* 111 (1996) 1-29; for the monastic orders in general see e.g. D. Stievermann, *Landesherrschaft und Klosterwesen im spätmittelalterlichen Württemberg* (Sigmaringen, 1989); E. Koch, *De kloosterpoort als sluitpost? Adellijke vrouwen langs Maas en Rijn tussen huwelijk en convent, 1200-1600*. Maaslandse monografieën 54 (Leeuwarden, Mechelen, 1994); E. Walter, 'Franziskanische Armutsbewegung in Schlesien. War die Herzogin Anna († 1265), die Schwiegertochter der hl. Hedwig, eine Terziarin des Franziskanerordens?', *Archiv für schlesische Kirchengeschichte* 40 (1982) 207-21.

[27] See e.g. A. Murray, 'Archbishop and Mendicants in Thirteenth-Century Pisa', *Stellung und Wirksamkeit der Bettelorden in der städtischen Gesellschaft*, ed. K. Elm. Berliner Historische Studien 3, Ordensstudien 2 (Berlin, 1981), pp. 19-75; *Bürger, Bettelmönche und Bischöfe in Halberstadt. Studien zur Geschichte der Stadt, der Mendikanten und des Bistums vom Mittelalter bis zur frühen Neuzeit*, ed. D. Berg. Saxonia Franciscana 9 (Werl, 1997); M. Sehi, *Die Bettelorden in der Seelsorgegeschichte der Stadt und des Bistums Würzburg bis zum Konzil von Trient*. Forschungen zur fränkischen Kirchen- und Theologiegeschichte 8 (Würzburg, 1981); A. Virgili i Colet, 'Les relacions entre la Catedral de Tortosa i els Ordes Religioso-Militars durant el segle XII, segons el "Cartulari de la Catedral de Tortosa"', *APJC*, pp. 67-79; F. Castillon Cortada, 'Discusiones entre los obispos de Lérida y los templarios de Monzón', *Ilerda* 36 (1975) 41-96; R. Farrero Isus, *Disputas entre los templarios y la mitra ilerdense en la diócesis de Lérida durante los siglos XII y XIII* (Tesis de Licenciatura, Universitat de Barcelona 1982); L. Vones, '... *contra episcopalem auctoritatem multa praesumunt* ... Die Entwicklung des Verhältnisses des Templer- und des Johanniterordens zur Bischofsgewalt in den Ländern der Krone Aragón bis zum Ende des 12. Jahrhunderts', *Ritterorden und Kirche im Mittelalter*, ed. Z. H. Nowak. Ordines Militares, Colloquia Toronensia Historica IX (Toruń, 1997), pp. 163-92.

[28] Cf. *SWB*; D. Berg (ed.), *Bettelorden und Stadt. Bettelorden und städtisches Leben im Mittelalter und in der Neuzeit*. Saxonia Franciscana 1 (Werl, 1992); J. Raspi Serra (ed.), *Gli ordini mendicanti e la città* (Milano, 1990); *Les Ordres Mendiants et la Ville en Italie centrale (v. 1220 - v. 1350)*. Melanges de l'École française de Rome, Moyen

development of the medieval town.[29] As insight into the structures and daily life of the orders is also possible through knowledge of their art and architecture, these aspects have been taken into consideration in a number of studies,[30]

Age-Temps Modernes 89 (1977); D. Postles, 'The Austin canons in English towns, c. 1100-1350', *Historical Research* 66 (1993) 1-20; P. Müller, *Bettelorden und Stadtgemeinde in Hildesheim im Mittelalter* (Hannover, 1994); B. Neidiger, 'Stadtregiment und Klosterreform in Basel', *Reformbemühungen und Observanzbestrebungen im spätmittelalterlichen Ordenswesen*, ed. K. Elm. Berliner Historische Studien 14, Ordensstudien 6 (Berlin, 1989), pp. 539-67; idem, *Mendikanten zwischen Ordensideal und städtischer Realität. Untersuchungen zum wirtschaftlichen Verhalten der Bettelorden in Basel*. Berliner Historische Studien 5, Ordensstudien 3 (Berlin, 1981); B. E. J. Stüdeli, *Minoritenniederlassungen und mittelalterliche Stadt. Beiträge zur Bedeutung von Minoriten- und Mendikantenanlagen im öffentlichen Leben der mittelalterlichen Stadtgemeinde, insbesondere der deutschen Schweiz*. Franziskanische Forschungen 21 (Werl, 1969); H. Hageneder, 'Die Minoriten in den österreichischen Städten', *Stadt und Kirche*, ed. F.-H. Heye. Beiträge zur Geschichte der Städte 13 (Linz, 1995), pp. 57-68; J. Röhrkasten, 'Mendicants in the Metropolis: the Londoners and the Development of the London Friaries', *Thirteenth Century England* VI, ed. M. Prestwich (Woodbridge, 1997), pp. 61-75; idem, 'The Londoners and the London Mendicants in the Late Middle Ages', *Journal of Ecclesiastical History* 47 (1996) 466-77. For the relationship between town and surrounding region see e.g. L. Pellegrini, 'Territorio e città nell'organizzazione insediativa degli ordini mendicanti in Campania', *Ressegna storica salernitana* 5 (1986) 9-41; W. Simons, *Stad en apostolaat. De vestiging van de bedelorden in het graafschap Vlaanderen c. 1225-1350* (Brussels, 1987); A. Rüther, *Bettelorden in Stadt und Land: die Straßburger Mendikantenkonvente und das Elsaß im Spätmittelalter* (Berlin, 1997).

[29] See e.g. *Stadt und Orden. Das Verhältnis des Deutschen Ordens zu den Städten in Livland, Preußen und im Deutschen Reich*, ed. U. Arnold. QStGDO 44 (Marburg, 1993) [*SO*]; U. Arnold, 'Der Deutsche Orden und Venedig', *MS*, pp. 145-65; Braasch-Schwersmann; Brassens; A. Luttrell, 'Emphyteutic Grants in Rhodes Town: 1347-1348', *Papers in European Legal History: Trabajos de Derecho Histórico en Homenaje a Ferran Valls i Taberner*, ed. M. Peláez, vol. 5 (Barcelona, 1992), pp. 1409-16.

[30] For the mendicants see e.g. W. Braunfels, *Monasteries of Western Europe: The Architecture of the Orders* (London, 1972); R. A. Sundt, '*Mediocres domos et humiles habeant fratres nostri*: Dominican Legislation on Architecture and Architectural Decoration in the 13th Century', *Journal of the Society of Architectural Historians* 46 (1987) 394-407; G. Binding, 'Die mittelalterliche Ordensbaukunst der Franziskaner im deutschen Sprachraum', *Franziskanische Studien* 67 (1985) 287-316; A. G. Little (ed.), *Franciscan History and Legend in English Medieval Art*. British Society of Franciscan Studies 19 (Manchester, 1937); R. Piper, *Die Kirchen der Bettelorden in Westfalen: Baukunst im Spannungsfeld zwischen Landespolitik, Stadt und Orden im 13. und frühen 14.Jahrhundert*. Franziskanische Forschungen 39 (Werl, 1993); J. Raspi Serra, 'Influenze arabe nella cultura architettonica degli ordini in Italia', *The Meeting of Two Worlds. Cultural Exchange between East and West during the Period of the Crusades*, ed. V. P. Goss (Kalamazoo, 1986), pp. 277-84; for the military orders see e.g. P. Ritoók, 'The Architecture of the Knights Templar in England', *MO*, pp. 167-78; J. Fuguet i Sans, *L'arquitectura dels Templers a Catalunya* (Barcelona, 1995); H.-J. Mrusek, 'Zur Baugeschichte der Johanniterburg Kühndorf in der ehemaligen Grafschaft Henneberg', *Wissenschaftliche Zeitschrift der Martin-Luther-Universität Halle-Witten-

and last but not least the 'internationality' of some of the orders' houses has also received some attention.[31]

This survey of research on the military and mendicant orders is far from comprehensive, and, accordingly, it will not be possible to investigate all of the problems caused by the different aspects of European regionalism in a single book. The following contributions are therefore intended only to examine some examples of the developments which have been outlined here. The essays in the first section are devoted to border regions where elements of local and regional influence are particularly evident; those in the second section of the book will examine different levels of influence, starting with that of popes and emperors and continuing down to that of nobles, bishops, and towns. Finally, the essays in the last section will explore the internal consequences of local and regional influences: the 'international' character of some of the orders' houses, changes in internal structure, and the architecture employed by the orders.

---

berg 12 (1963) 663-92; B. Aarts, 'Bouw en verbouw van het kasteel van de Duitse Orde', *Commanderij Gemert. Beeldend Verleden*, ed. T. Thelen (Gemert, 1990) 43-64; M. Arszyński, 'Der Deutsche Orden als Bauherr und Kunstmäzen', *Die Rolle der Ritterorden in der mittelalterlichen Kultur*, ed. Z. H. Nowak. Ordines militares, Colloquia Tornunensia Historica III (Toruń, 1985), pp. 145-67; J. Domasłowski, 'Die gotische Malerei im Dienste des Deutschen Ordens', ibid., pp. 169-93. For other aspects of culture see e.g. P. Camao, 'Francescanesimo e cultura in Sicilia', *Quaderni medievali* 14 (1982), 169-96; *Zur geistigen Welt der Franziskaner im 14. und 15. Jahrhundert. Die Bibliothek des Franziskanerklosters in Freiburg / Schweiz*, ed. R. Imbach (Fribourg, 1995); E. Onorati, 'Die franziskanische Bewegung in Italien (1200-1500)', *800 Jahre Franz von Assisi. Franziskanische Kunst und Kultur des Mittelalters* (Krems, 1982), pp. 232-69.

[31] See e.g. J. R. H. Moorman, 'The Foreign Element among the English Franciscans', *English Historical Review* 62 (1947) 289-303; Sarnowsky, 'Konvent'.

I

Religious Orders in Border Regions

2

Bonds and Tensions on the Frontier: the Templars in Twelfth-Century Western Catalonia

Nikolas Jaspert

The emergence of new religious orders sparked wide-ranging changes in the areas where they were established – economic, social, religious, cultural, ecclesiastical, sometimes political, even technological or artistic changes. Young foundations had to struggle to find their place in pre-existing ecclesiastical contexts, both among the ruling groups and their feudal overlords. They also broke into established economic structures, often with significant consequences. Whilst this is true for religious orders in general, the type of institution under examination here, the international military orders, also had to define their position in other respects. First, they played an active role in the military field; second, they were institutionally subordinate to the needs and interests of their mother-houses in a way unequalled by most other religious institutions, which made it particularly difficult to incorporate them into political and ecclesiastical structures. The impact of the military orders on medieval society was consequently especially broad.

But does this finding also hold true for the fringes of Christendom, for border and frontier areas?[1] Here, civil and ecclesiastical structures were often poorly

---

[1] H. J. Karp, *Grenzen in Ostmitteleuropa während des Mittelalters. Ein Beitrag zur Entstehungsgeschichte der Grenzlinie aus dem Grenzsaum* (Cologne, Vienna, 1972); D. Hay, 'England, Scotland and Europe: The Problem of the Frontier', *Transactions of the Royal Historical Society* 5th ser. 25 (1975) 77-93; P. J. Duffy, 'The Nature of the Medieval Frontier in Ireland', *Studia Hibernica* 22-23 (1982-1983) 21-38; C. Halperin, 'The Ideology of Silence: Prejudice and Pragmatism on the Medieval Religious Frontier', *Comparative Studies in Society and History* 26 (1984) 442-66; L. McCrank, 'Cistercians as Frontiersmen', *Estudios en homenaje a don Claudio Sánchez Albornoz*

From *Mendicants, Military Orders, and Regionalism in Medieval Europe*, ed. Jürgen Sarnowsky. Copyright © 1999 by Jürgen Sarnowsky. Published by Ashgate Publishing Ltd, Gower House, Croft Road, Aldershot, Hampshire, GU11 3HR, Great Britain.

developed, and antagonism between newcomers and those already established was less likely. One could expect that on the frontier – with its frequent military conflicts and its ample means for expansion – the bonds that tied the medieval military orders to other institutions and powers were less rigid, tensions amongst Christians less frequent. One such border region where the *Ordines militares* in general and the Order of the Temple in particular took action was the Iberian Peninsula,[2] the only part of Europe where the Templars exercised functions similar to those in the Levant.

West of the Pyrenees, particularly in Aragon and Catalonia, the knights not only possessed extensive landed property, a series of preceptories and important fortresses, but also held lordship over towns and participated actively in campaigns against the Muslims of al-Andalus. They were essential to the Hispanic frontiers. As areas of contact and confrontation alike, these *zonas fronterizas* were not only defined by their function of political and military borders, but also by their character as areas of settlement and of social, cultural, and economic interaction.[3] In all these fields, the military orders, and more specifically

---

en sus 90 años. Cuadernos de Historia de España, Anexos, 3 vols (Buenos Aires, 1983), II, pp. 313-60; R. Schneider, 'Grenzen und Grenzsicherung im Mittelalter. Zu ihrer begrifflichen, rechtlichen und politischen Problematik', *Probleme von Grenzregionen: das Beispiel SAAR-LOR-LUX-Raum. Beiträge zum Forschungsschwerpunkt der Philosophischen Fakultät der Universität des Saarlandes* (Saarbrücken, 1987), pp. 9-27; M. T. Ferrer i Mallol, *La frontera amb l'Islam en el segle XIV: cristians i sarraïns al País Valencià*. Anuario de Estudios Medievales, anexo 18 (Barcelona, 1988); *Medieval Frontier Societies*, eds R. Bartlett, A. MacKay (Oxford, 1989); A. MacKay, 'Sociedades fronterizas', *Almería entre culturas, siglos XII-XVI* (Almería, 1990), pp. 3-12; J. M. Piskorski, 'Die deutsche Ostsiedlung des Mittelalters in der Entwicklung des östlichen Mitteleuropa. Zum Stand der Forschung aus polnischer Sicht', *Jahrbuch für die Geschichte Mittel- und Ostdeutschlands* 40 (1991) 26-84; P. Tyszka, 'O metodzie badan nad średniowiecznymi granicami lokalnymi', *Kwartalnik historii kultury materialney* 43 (1995) 423-30.

[2] An overview of the extensive research on the medieval Hispanic frontiers can be found in: J. A. Fernández Ortal, 'Anexo bibliográfico', *Las sociedades de frontera en la España medieval. IIo seminario de Historia Medieval* (Zaragoza, 1993), pp. 125-87; cf. P. Sénac, 'La frontière d'Al-Andalus au haut Moyen Age', *Le Moyen Age* 100 (1994) 249-54; M. Martínez Martínez, 'Organización y evolución de una sociedad de frontera. El reino de Murcia (ss. XIII-XV)', *Medievalismo* 5 (1995) 31-88; J.-P. Molénat, 'Les divers notions de "frontiere" dans la region de Castilla-La Mancha aux temps des Almoravides at Almohades', *Alarcos 1195. Congreso internacional del VIII centenario de la batalla de Alarcos* (Cuenca, 1996), pp. 105-23; C. Stalls, *Possessing the Land. Aragon's Expansion into Islam's Ebro Frontier under Alfonso the Battler, 1104-1134*. The Medieval Mediterranean 7 (Leiden, New York, Cologne, 1995).

[3] A. MacKay, *Spain in the Middle Ages. From Frontier to Empire, 1000-1500* (London, 1983), pp. 15-57; R. I. Burns, 'The Significance of the Frontier in the Middle Ages', *Medieval Frontier Societies*, pp. 307-31; E. Rodríguez-Picavea Matilla, 'Frontera,

the Knights Templar, played their part.[4] Not surprisingly, by the beginning of
the thirteenth century, the order had become a major military and political
factor in the Arago-Catalan Crown. After Peter I's untimely death on the bat-
tlefield of Muret on 13 September 1213, Prince Jaume, the future *Conqueridor*,
grew up in the Templar castle of Monzón, in the care of Guillem de Montrodon, the local Templar master, and during the beginning of his reign, the order
held the realm's finances firmly in its hands.[5] Such close ties were the result of
a long-standing precedent, not just due to Jaume's personal ties to the Templars.

Unlike most newly-founded religious orders of the high Middle Ages, the
order of the Temple was actively supported by local rulers right from the beginning.[6] This was not only the case for the order in the Holy Land, but also in

soberanía territorial y órdenes militares en la Península Ibérica durante la Edad Media',
Hispania 52 (1992) 789-809; Molénat, 'Divers notions'.

[4] Rodríguez-Picavea Matilla, 'Frontera, soberanía territorial'; D. Rodríguez Blanco,
'Las órdenes militares en la Frontera', *La banda morisca durante los siglos XIII, XIV y
XV. IIas Jornadas de Temas Moronenses* (Morón de la Frontera, 1994), pp. 149-56; J.
M. Molero García, 'Participación de la Orden del Hospital en el avance de la frontera
castellana (1144-1224)', *Alarcos 1195*. Congreso internacional del VIII centenario de la
batalla de Alarcos (Cuenca, 1996), pp. 331-51. Cf. the overviews on the recent research
about the military orders: C. de Ayala Martínez, C. Barquero Goñi, J. V. Matellanes
Merchán et al., 'Las Ordenes Militares en la Edad Media peninsular. Historiografia
1976-1992, I: Reinos de Castilla y León', *Medievalismo* 2 (1992) 119-69; C. de Ayala
Martínez, F. Andrés Robres, J. V. Matellanes Merchán et al., 'Las Ordenes Militares
en la Edad Media peninsular. Historiografia 1976-1992, II: Corona de Aragón, Navarra
y Portugal', ibid. 3 (1993) 87-144; N. Jaspert, 'Die Ritterorden und der Orden vom
Heiligen Grab auf der Iberischen Halbinsel', *Militia Sancti Sepulcri. Idea e Istituzioni*,
eds K. Elm, C. D. Fonseca (Rome, 1998), pp. 381-410.

[5] M. Vilar Bonet, 'Actividades financieras de la orden del Temple en la Corona de
Aragón', *VII Congreso de Historia de la Corona de Aragón* (Barcelona, 1962), II, pp.
577-85; T. N. Bisson, 'Las finanzas del joven Jaime I (1213-1228)', *X Congreso de
Historia de la Corona de Aragón, Comunicaciones I-II* (Zaragoza, 1980), pp. 161-208;
A. Pladevall i Font, *Guillem de Montrodon. Mestre del Temple i tutor de Jaume I*
(Lleida, 1993), pp. 36-52. The Templars were in fact explicitly ordered to reform the
crown finances by Innocent III (Arxiu de la Corona d'Aragó, Collecció de butlles. Inno-
cenci III, lligall 3, doc. 25 – cf. Pladevall, 45). J. M. Sans i Travé, *Els Templers a
Catalunya. De la rosa a la creu*, Els ordes militars 4 (Lleida, 1996), pp. 183-89. On the
years immediately preceding his reign see T. N. Bisson, *Fiscal Accounts in Catalonia
under the Early Count-Kings (1156-1213)*, 2 vols (Berkeley, Los Angeles, 1984), pp.
125-29, 143-46.

[6] R. Hiestand, 'Templer- und Johanniterbistümer und -bischöfe im Heiligen Land',
Ritterorden und Kirche im Mittelalter, ed. Z. H. Nowak. Ordines Militares 9 (Toruń,
1997), pp. 143-61, at 146; A. Demurger, *Die Templer. Aufstieg und Untergang, 1120-
1314* (Munich, 1994; translation of 2nd edn, Paris, 1989), pp. 25-26, 51-55; M. Barber,

north-eastern Spain where co-operation between the knights and the Arago-Catalan rulers began in the first half of the twelfth century, soon after the Templars first set foot in the Iberian Peninsula.[7] Immediately after their participation at the Council of Troyes in January 1129, representatives of the young *societas* crossed the Pyrenees in order to mobilize the local aristocracy in its favour.[8] They received donations in both Aragon and Catalonia and established confraternal ties with a series of local barons, including the Count of Barcelona. Ramon Berenguer III endowed the Templars with the castle of Granyena in 1130 and died shortly thereafter in the order's habit and house.[9] In 1134, in an effort to win the knights for the Reconquista, his son not only swore to serve the order for a year, together with twenty-four of his realm's *optimes*, but also bestowed exemptions from comital jurisdiction and fiscal control upon the order.[10] The generosity of the counts of Barcelona towards the order was truly extraordinary, but it was surpassed by King Alfonso I of Aragon, *el Batallador*. The king's will, drawn up during the siege of Bayonne in 1131 and corroborated after his defeat at Fraga in 1134,[11] laid the foundations for the order of the Temple's considerable wealth in north-eastern Spain. In an act of cunning diplomacy or fervent religiosity – the king's motives have been the object of

---

The New Knighthood. A History of the Order of the Temple (Cambridge, 1994), pp. 8-13.

[7] P. Schickl, 'Die Entstehung und Entwicklung des Templerordens in Katalonien und Aragón', *Gesammelte Aufsätze zur Kulturgeschichte Spaniens. Spanische Forschungen der Görresgesellschaft* 28 (1975) 91-229, at 154, summarizes quite rightly: 'Nirgends war die Beziehung der Landesherren zum Tempel so eng wie in Katalonien-Aragon'. Cf. the rather irregular overview by E. Albert i Corp, 'Els templers i la política de la Corona d'Aragó', *APJC*, pp. 219-26.

[8] On the early history of the order in Catalonia see Schickl, 'Entstehung und Entwicklung', 101-35; A. Forey, *The Templars in the Corona de Aragón* (London, 1973), pp. 15-30; Barber, *The New Knighthood*, pp. 26-32; Sans i Travé, *Templers*, pp. 73-98.

[9] *Cartulaire général de l'Ordre du Temple 1119?-1150*, ed. M. d'Albon (Paris, 1913), doc. 33; *Gesta Comitum Barcinonensium*, ed. J. Massó Torrents, Chròniques Catalanes II (Barcelona, 1925), chap. XVI.

[10] *Cartulaire général*, doc. 71, 72; Schickl, pp. 111-15; O. Engels, 'Das Schutzprivileg in Katalonien (12.-13. Jahrhundert)', *Homenaje a Johannes Vincke*, 2 vols (Madrid, 1962-1963), I, pp. 153-83, at 154-57.

[11] S. García Larragueta, *El gran priorato de Navarra de la Orden de San Juan de Jerusalén, siglos XII-XIII*, 2 vols (Pamplona, 1957), I, doc. 10; J. A. Lema Pueyo, *Colección diplomática de Alfonso I de Aragón y Pamplona*. Fuentes documentales medievales del País Vasco 27 (San Sebastián, 1990), doc. 241, 242, 284. On Alfonso el Batallador see J. M. Lacarra, *Alfonso el Batallador* (Zaragoza, 1978); Stalls, *Possessing the Land*.

much heated discussion[12] – Alfonso bequeathed *totum regnum meum ..., totam terram meam quantum ego habeo et quantum mihi remansit ab antecessoribus meis et quantum ego adquisivi vel in futurum auxiliante Deo adquiram et quicquid ego presens do vel inantea iuste dare potero* to three institutions in the Holy Land: the Templars, the Hospitallers and the Canons of the Holy Sepulchre of Jerusalem. All three quickly realized that they would find it impossible to fulfil the will, for neither were they able to exercise power effectively over an expanding and distant realm nor were the local barons willing to accept the foreign religious as their new lords. The orders therefore remained silent when Ramiro, the deceased king's brother, left the monastery of which he had been abbot, was crowned king, married Agnes of Poitou, and fathered the much-awaited heiress to the throne, Petronilla of Aragon.[13] At the tender age of one, the princess was married to Count Ramon Berenguer IV of Barcelona, thus laying the foundations for a political federation which would mark the history of the western Mediterranean: the Arago-Catalan Crown. The orders apparently regarded the developments as a *fait accompli* and endeavoured to reap what benefit they could. The Hospitallers and Canons of the Holy Sepulchre reached an agreement with Ramon Berenguer in 1140 and 1141, renouncing their claims to the realm in return for donations and the prospect of further acquisitions in newly-conquered territories.[14] A similar solution was reached with the Templars in 1143: the knights were given a series of castles, an annual pension of 1000 *sous*, and the tithes of their estates; furthermore, they were assured that one fifth of all further conquests made by the counts would be theirs.[15] The agreement was complemented by further privileges including the right to appoint their own bailiffs and exert jurisdiction in the

---

[12] Schickl, pp. 115-23; E. Lourie, 'The Will of Alfonso I el Batallador, King of Aragón and Navarre. A Reassessment', *Speculum* 50 (1975) 635-51; A. J. Forey, 'The Will of Alfonso I of Aragón and Navarre', *Durham University Journal* 73 (1980) 59-65; E. Lourie, 'The Will of Alfonso I of Aragon and Navarre: A Reply to Dr Forey', *Durham University Journal* 77/2 (1984-1985) 165-72, cf. E. Lourie, *Crusade and Colonisation* (London, 1990), IV.

[13] A. Ubieto Arteta, *Historia de Aragón: Creación de la Corona de Aragón* (Zaragoza, 1987), pp. 69-93; S. Claramunt Rodriguez, J. F. Utrilla Utrilla, *La génesis de la Corona de Aragón*. La Corona de Aragón 2 (Barcelona, Zaragoza, 1988).

[14] *Liber Feudorum Maior. Cartulario real que se conserva en el Archivo de la Corona de Aragón*, ed. F. Miquel Rosell. Textos y estudios de la Corona de Aragón 1-2, 2 vols (Barcelona, 1945-1947), I, doc. 10, 11; J. Alturo i Perucho, *L'arxiu antic de Santa Anna de Barcelona del 942 al 1200. Aproximació històrico-lingüística*, 3 vols. Fundació Noguera, Textos i Documents 8-10, (Barcelona, 1985), II, doc. 228, 233, 235.

[15] *Cartulaire général*, doc. 314.

areas they possessed.[16] The rights granted to the young institution were such as
to provide the basis for an extensive and largely independent territorial lordship.[17] The first test as to the implementation of the agreement of 1143 came
four years later.

In late spring of 1147, the local and international political conjuncture could
hardly have been more favourable for the Christians to break the power of the
Muslim lordships in north-eastern Spain: papal propaganda had whipped up
crusading fervour in Europe and explicitly extended the field of action to the
Iberian Peninsula.[18] A fleet of crusaders, under way from Germany, the Low
Countries, and England, had already participated in the conquest of Lisbon and
was still in the western Mediterranean.[19] The Almoravid empire and with it the
taifas of Tortosa and Lleida were in a state of crisis, due to the Almohad
threat.[20] The period of uncertainty in Aragon following Alfonso's death was

[16] *Cartulaire général*, doc. 415; Schickl, pp. 126-29, 160-62.

[17] Schickl, pp. 113-14, 160-62; R. Hiestand, 'Reconquista, Kreuzzug und Heiliges Grab.
Die Eroberung von Tortosa 1148 im Lichte eines neuen Zeugnisses', *Gesammelte Aufsätze zur Kulturgeschichte Spaniens. Spanische Forschungen der Görresgesellschaft* 31
(1984) 136-58; L. Vones, '... *Contra episcopalem auctoritatem multa praesumunt ...*
Die Entwicklung des Verhältnisses des Templer- und des Johanniterordens zur Bischofsgewalt in den Ländern der Krone Aragón bis zum Ende des 12. Jahrhunderts',
Ritterorden und Kirche im Mittelalter, ed. Z. H. Nowak. Ordines Militares 9 (Toruń,
1997), pp. 163-92, at pp. 169-71.

[18] H. Gleber, *Papst Eugen III. unter besonderer Berücksichtigung seiner politischen
Tätigkeit*. Beiträge zur mittelalterlichen und neueren Geschichte 6 (Jena, 1936), pp. 35-
61; G. Constable, 'The Second Crusade as Seen by Contemporaries', *Traditio* 9 (1953)
213-79; H. D. Kahl, 'Die weltweite Bereinigung der Heidenfrage – ein übersehenes
Kriegsziel des Zweiten Kreuzzugs', *Spannungen und Widersprüche: Gedenkschrift für
František Graus*, ed. S. Burghartz (Sigmaringen, 1992), pp. 63-89; U. Vones-Liebenstein, *Saint Ruf und Spanien. Studien zur Verbreitung und zum Wirken der Regularka-
noniker von Saint Ruf in Avignon auf der Iberischen Halbinsel (11. und 12. Jahrhundert)*, 2 vols. Bibliotheca Victorina 6 (Paris, Turnhout, 1996), I, p. 336.

[19] Hiestand, 'Reconquista', pp. 138-39; H. Livermore, 'The Conquest of Lisbon and its
Author', *Portuguese Studies* 6 (1990) 1-16; S. Edgington, 'The Lisbon Letter of the
Second Crusade', *Historical Research* 69 (1996) 328-39; J. Phillips, 'St Bernard of
Clairvaux, the Low Countries and the Lisbon Letter of the Second Crusade', *The Jour-
nal of Ecclesiastical History* 48 (1997) 485-98.

[20] R. Pita, *Lérida árabe* (Lleida 1974); P. Guichard, *Les musulmans de Valence et la
reconquête (XIe-XIIIe siècles)*, 2 vols (Damascus, 1990), pp. 101-07, 116-18; M. J.
Viguera, *Los reinos de taifas y las invasiones magrebíes (Al-Andalus, del siglo XI al
XIII)* (Madrid, 1992), pp. 189-201; P. Balañà, *Crónica política de la pre-Catalunya
islàmica* (Barcelona, 1992), pp. 67-71; F. Sabaté i Curull, *El territori de la Catalunya
Medieval. Percepció de l'espai i divisio territorial al llarg de l'Edat Mitjana* (Barce-
lona, 1997), pp. 123-24, 380-85; *Catalunya Romànica 24: el Segrià, les Garrigues, el
Pla d'Urgell, la Segarra, L'Urgell* (Barcelona, 1997), pp. 29-37; *Catalunya Romànica*

over, and the Aragonese and Catalans were under the united command of a determined warrior and politician who had succeeded in gaining the support of the powerful Genoese fleet.[21] While some of these advantages may be seen as a happy coincidence, others were the result of international diplomacy and arduous negotiations. Only after having gained substantial foreign support and having neutralized potential enemies did Ramon Berenguer IV embark on the conquest of the two powerful Muslim centres.[22] The Templars actively participated in both campaigns, thus entering the Reconquista for the first time. In a *tour de force* of considerable logistic and organizational skill, the Christian forces encircled Tortosa, the strategically-important port at the mouth of the Ebro, which capitulated after a seven-month siege on 30 December 1148.[23] They then rolled up the Ebro valley from the south, to subdue the town of Lleida, the heart of the extensive Muslim taifa (24 October 1149). Here was the moment the agreement with the Templars had anticipated, and the count proved to be true to his word: in Tortosa, a fifth of the town, plus a tenth of Count Ramon Berenguer's possessions, was handed over to the Temple together with three nearby castles. In Lleida, the order received the same percentage of the houses as well as the strategically crucial castle of Gardeny, perched on a hilltop just south of the town.[24]

26: *Tortosa i les terres de l'Ebre. La Llitera i el Baix Cinca. Obra no arquitectònica, dispersa i restaurada* (Barcelona, 1997), 34-39.

[21] P. E. Schramm, 'Die Entstehung eines Doppelreiches: Die Vereinigung von Aragon und Katalonien durch Ramon Berenguer IV. (1137-1162)', *Vom Mittelalter zur Neuzeit, Festschrift für Heinrich Sproemberg*, ed. H. Kretschmar (Berlin, 1956), pp. 19-50; Caffaro, 'Ystoria captionis Almerie et Tortuose', *Annali Genovesi*, ed. L. T. Belgrano. Fonti per la Storia d'Italia 11 (Genoa, 1980), pp. 77-91; Hiestand, 'Reconquista', pp. 141-43, 155-56.

[22] E. Bayerri y Bertomeu, *Historia de Tortosa y su comarca*, (Tortosa, 1954), VI, pp. 761-67, 768-70; L. Pagarolas, *La comanda del Temple de Tortosa: primer període, 1148-1213* (Tortosa, 1984), pp. 51-58.

[23] Bayerri, VI, pp. 772-85; Forey, *Templars*, pp. 24-25, 68-71; W. Rogers, *Latin Siege Warfare in the Twelfth Century* (Oxford, 1992), pp. 179-82; A. Virgili i Colet, 'Conquesta i feudalització de la regió de Tortosa (1148-1200)', *Les darreres investigacions arxivístiques de la història de Tortosa* (Tortosa, 1995), pp. 36-49; Sabaté i Curull, *Territori de la Catalunya medieval*, pp. 380-85; N. Jaspert, '*Capta est Dertosa, clavis Christianorum*: Tortosa and the Crusades': The Second Crusade, Scope and Consequences, eds M. Hoch, J. Phillips (Manchester, 1999), to appear.

[24] *Diplomatari de la catedral de Tortosa (1062-1193)*. Fundació Noguera, diplomataris 11, ed. A. Virgili (Barcelona, 1997), doc. 18; Pagarolas, *Comanda*, doc. 54, 56; *Liber Feudorum Maior*, I, doc. 161; *Alfonso II Rey de Aragón, Conde de Barcelona y Marqués de Provenza. Documentos (1162-1196)*, ed. A. I. Sánchez Casabón. Fuentes Históricas Aragonesas 23 (Zaragoza, 1995), doc. 443.

The donations formed the nucleus of two Templar houses founded in 1156 which existed right up to the order's dissolution.[25] Created under similar auspices and circumstances, Gardeny and Tortosa are excellent case-studies of the military orders' role and position in a border region of medieval Christianity. The order itself, not the area in which it settled, is this study's main focus. Military and cultural interaction between the Templars and the Muslims, and its specific impact in Catalonia are therefore beyond the scope of this paper, which will limit itself to the establishment of the order and the support and resistance it encountered among fellow Christians, and the comparison of this process with other frontier zones. Coincidentally, both Tortosa and Gardeny produced cartularies in the twelfth century, both of which are still extant, though unpublished.[26] Together with the substantial documentation housed in Catalan archives, they form a solid base for examining the interactions between the Catalan Templars on the one hand and both lay and ecclesiastical powers on the other.

The struggle for lordship: Tortosa

Turtusha, the ancient Roman port of Dertosa and capital of an independent taifa, had long been one of the Pyrenean counts' most sought-after prizes.[27] Under Muslim rule it had maintained its economic, political and cultural importance, and its strategic position at the mouth of the Ebro delta converted its ruler into the master of any sea-trade the river generated.[28] During the siege of

---

[25] Sans i Travé, *Templers*, pp. 355-64; L. Pagarolas, *Comanda*; L. Pagarolas, 'Els senyorius templers de les Terres de l'Ebre. Significació i síntesi', *APJC*, pp. 54-66. Schickl, pp. 141-42, argues in favour of an earlier foundation date for the house in Lleida.

[26] Barcelona, Arxiu de la Corona d'Aragó, Arxiu del Gran Priorat de Catalunya, Ms. 197, Cartulari de Gardeny (= Cart. Gardeny); ibid., Ms. 115, Cartulari de Tortosa (= Cart. Tortosa); J. Miret i Sans, *Cartoral dels Templers de les comandes de Gardeny y Barbens* (Barcelona, 1899), only includes very few transcriptions. Cf. Forey, *Templars*, pp. 58, 146, 158, 457; A. Forey, 'Sources for the History of the Templars in Aragon, Catalonia and Valencia', *Archives* 21 (1994) 16-24; D. Le Blévec, A. Venturini, 'Cartulaires des ordres militaires, XIIe-XVe siècles (Provence occidentale, basse vallée du Rhône)', *Les cartulaires. Actes de la Table ronde, 5-7 décembre 1991*, eds O. Guyotjeannin, L. Morelle, M. Parisse (Paris, 1993), pp. 451-67.

[27] Bayerri, VI, pp. 692-756 offers a summary of authentic and fictitious Christian attempts to conquer the town. On the importance of the town's conquest for the house of Barcelona see Sabaté i Curull, *Territori de la Catalunya Medieval*, pp. 30-32. On the crusading context of the attack see Jaspert, *'Capta est Dertosa'*.

[28] On Muslim Tortosa see Bayerri, VI, pp. 319-689; M. de Epalza, 'Tortosa, un lloc etratègic a Al-Andalus', *T(D). Revista d'Arts i Lletres* 2 (1987) 13-14; P. Balaña i

1148 the Templars controlled Tortosa's northern side together with the Anglo-Flemish crusader contingents, so the order was present when the defenders surrendered the castle, or Suda, on 30 December.[29] One may suppose that individual knights remained in the newly-conquered town, but the first reference to a representative (a *procurator*) dates from 1156, and a *comendator* can be traced back to 1174.[30] The Templar presence in the Ebro valley was in no way limited to Tortosa, since by taking an active role in the conquest they became fully involved in large-scale military and colonizing operations, in the Reconquista and the *repoblación*. They received parish churches, were entrusted with the defence and settlement of an extensive frontier area on the banks of the Ebro and acquired both the land and network of fortifications necessary to do so, while other possessions were purchased from the count-kings over the course of the twelfth century.[31] The order's estates in the Ebro area were of such importance that a new territorial administrative district was created, the 'preceptory of the Ribera', which comprised all houses of the lower Ebro valley and can best be characterized as an intermediate entity between a fully-fledged province and a preceptory.[32] The Templars seemed to be in the process of creating a territorial lordship of their own. Its military centre, the castle of Miravet, was firmly in their hands by 1153.[33] However, gaining control of the major urban centre, Tortosa itself, was a far more complex undertaking.

Even before its conquest, Tortosa had been promised to a series of Christian barons. In 1097, Ramon Berenguer III had pledged it to his ally, Count Artau of Pallars. Alfonso el Batallador had done the same to the Hospitallers. And Ramon Berenguer IV had made similar promises to Guillem VI de Montpel-

---

Abadia, 'Reivindicació del passat islàmic de Tortosa (713-1148)', *Sharq Al-Andalus* 6 (1989) 241-46; X. Ballestin, 'Tortosa, al-Andalus, Magrib, Orient. Relacions culturals', *Les darreres investigacions arxivístiques de la història de Tortosa* (Tortosa, 1995), pp. 9-31; *Catalunya Romànica 26*, pp. 34-39. On the importance of the Ebro and its trade in the later middle ages see F. Zulaica Palacios, 'Mercados y vias fluviales: el Ebro como eje organizador del territorio e integrador de la economia aragonesa en los circuitos europeos', *Aragón en la edad media* 13 (Zaragoza, 1997), pp. 65-104.

[29] Rogers, *Latin Siege Warfare*, pp. 179-80; Virgili i Colet, *Conquesta*, p. 39.

[30] Pagarolas, *Comanda*, pp. 58-59; Forey, *Templars*, pp. 92-93, 105, notes 36-39.

[31] *Liber Feudorum Maior*, doc. 467; Virgili i Colet, *Conquesta*, pp. 42-44; Pagarolas, *Comanda*, pp. 67-73; *Alfonso II*, doc. 63, 72, 74, 98, 149, 171, 214, 316, 341, 503, 628.

[32] Pagarolas, 'Senyorius', p. 56.

[33] A. Bladé i Desumvila, *El castell de Miravet* (Barcelona, 1994); Sans i Travé, *Templers*, pp. 336-48; J. Fuguet i Sans, *L'arquitectura dels Templers a Catalunya* (Barcelona, 1995), pp. 78-90; *Catalunya Romànica 26*, p. 190.

lier, the Republic of Genoa, and to Guillem Ramon de Montcada.[34] Such
seemingly rash donations during the Reconquista were in fact an important and
often-used way to assert future suzerainty over a particular area against com-
peting Christian rulers.[35] But this meant that even before border regions in
medieval Spain actually fell into Christian hands, they were already marked by
a series of claims – overlapping or contradictory, often vague and sometimes
hypothetical. This system of divided authority ultimately favoured the count's
position as feudal overlord of the entire town, ensuring that none of the baronial families from Old Catalonia established a predominant position in the
newly-conquered centres. This guaranteed the house of Barcelona's authority
in the frontier region.[36] In the case of Tortosa, four parties finally succeeded in
acquiring seigneurial rights over the town: Count Ramon Berenguer IV retained two thirds of the area, of which he gave the Templars one fifth of the
dominium with its respective income. One third of the area was handed to the
Genoese, while one third of the count's remaining revenues was given to the
Catalan Baron Guillem Ramon de Montcada.[37] In a breach of his pledge, and
despite complaints before the comital curia, Ramon Berenguer IV handed
Guillem Ramon only one third of his own rights, not one third of the entire
town.[38] The Genoese in turn sold their portion to the count as early as 1153,[39]
which further strengthened his position. Ramon Berenguer IV thus maintained
his hold over Tortosa. It was with him more than anyone else that the Templars
had to deal.

The knights had become firmly established as holders of large urban property, an area which was centred around their fortress on the banks of the Ebro,

---

[34] Bayerri, VI, pp. 751-60; *Colección de documentos inéditos del Archivo general de la
Corona de Aragón*, 47 vols (Barcelona, 1847-1985), IV, doc. 22, 51; *Liber Feudorum
Maior*, I, doc. 462, 463; J. C. Shideler, *A Medieval Catalan Noble Family: the Montca-
das, 1000-1230* (Berkeley, Los Angeles, London, 1983), pp. 96-98; Pagarolas,
Comanda, pp. 47-51; Cart. Tortosa, fol. 27r-28r.

[35] O. Engels, 'Die Reconquista', idem, *Reconquista und Landesherrschaft. Studien zur
Rechts- und Verfassungsgeschichte Spaniens im Mittelalter*. Rechts- und staatswissen-
schaftliche Veröffentlichungen der Görres-Gesellschaft, N.F. 53 (Paderborn, 1989), pp.
279-300, at 285-86.

[36] Shideler, pp. 98-99.

[37] *Diplomatari de la catedral*, doc. 19.

[38] *Colección de documentos inéditos*, IV, doc. 51; Bayerri, VII, pp. 81-84; Shideler, pp.
102-03.

[39] *Liber Feudorum Maior*, I, doc. 463.

in the south-western corner of the town.[40] During the decades following the conquest, especially from 1165 to 1182, they succeeded in augmenting and concentrating their possessions substantially by donations and a series of purchases and exchanges.[41] The specific situation in the newly-conquered town made it especially suited for such a process of agglomeration: in an nascent urban society, based on recently-established rights and possessions, mobility was high and changes in property were less questionable than in the established centres of Old Catalonia with centenarian and at times contradictory titles. During the century and a half that they were present in Tortosa, the Templars actively contributed to urban resettlement and growth by the construction of *villae novae* in the north and west of the town.[42] But urban property, despite its value, was not the Templars' ultimate aim. They wanted lordship. This was an unusual, but hardly unheard-of goal. In certain towns and areas of the Holy Land military orders held seigneurial positions long before the Hospitallers and Teutonic Knights achieved territorial lordships of their own in the thirteenth and fourteenth centuries. Examples include Margat, Sidon, and Tortosa in the Holy Land, as well as the island of Cyprus.[43] It appears as a strange historical coincidence that the Order of the Temple acquired such rights in the mid-twelfth century in two towns that now bear the same name, Tortosa. One was in Catalonia, the other on the shores of the Levant, thirty miles north of Tripoli. In both cases they had to share power with other lay and ecclesiastical lords, so that the acquisition and maintenance of seigneurial rights was a matter of paramount importance. In the Iberian Tortosa the order was extraordinarily successful at this. During the second half of the twelfth century the Templars acquired virtually all of the count-king's titles, largely by taking advantage of his constant need for money. In 1153, the knights purchased one

---

[40] It seems that their urban property did not comprise one fifth of the total area, i.e. that the donation of 1149 was limited to the count's revenues, not to property itself. P. Izquierdo Tugas, 'Excavacions al Portal del Temple. Una aproximació a l'evolució del recinte emmurallat de Tortosa', *Acta arqueológica de Tarragona* 3 (1989-1990) 9-20. On the order's convent and church (which was constructed in the thirteenth century) see Fuguet i Sans, *L'arquitectura*, pp. 74-76; *Catalunya Romànica 26*, pp. 56-70, 107-68.

[41] Pagarolas, *Comanda*, pp. 77-114; Forey, *Templars*, p. 49.

[42] Fuguet i Sans, *L'arquitectura*, p. 73.

[43] J. Riley Smith, *The Knights of Saint John in Jerusalem and Cyprus c. 1050-1310* (London, 1967), pp. 410-13; J. Riley-Smith, 'The Templars and the Castle of Tortosa in Syria. An Unknown Document concerning the Acquisition of the Fortress', *English Historical Review* 84 (1969) 278-88; B. Hamilton, *The Latin Church in the Crusader States. The Secular Church* (London, 1980), pp. 47, 108, 111; Hiestand, 'Templer- und Johanniterbistümer'.

fifth of the portion which the Genoese had sold Ramon Berenguer IV. In 1175, they received another fifth of the royal possessions through a donation by Alfonso el Casto, and in 1182, the king handed over his remaining possessions and rights in the town, reserving for himself only certain demesnes and half his revenues which were administered by a *baiulius regis*.[44] For a brief period, these seigneurial rights were maintained first by Queen Sancia, Alfonso el Casto's wife, and later by a baronial representative of the king's, Guillem IV de Cervera, before being finally acquired by the Templars in 1215.[45] By then, the order had accumulated the lordship of around two-thirds of the town and virtually ruled Tortosa. Its only major competitors were the heirs of Guillem Ramon de Montcada.[46]

Guillem Ramon de Montcada had been one of the first Catalans to establish ties with the Knights of the Temple. In one of the earliest charters signed in the young institution's favour, the baron and his brother pledged their personal service and material support, promising to remain in the order as *fratres ad terminum* for a year and to finance the equipment of a further knight.[47] After the conquest of Tortosa, Guillem Ramon may have served as the count's right-hand man and as *castlà*, i.e. the castellan of the Suda.[48] His presence there is well documented from 1148 to 1154, when he subscribed most of the count's charters, including those establishing and endowing the new bishop.[49] In the course of his lifetime de Montcada repeatedly came into contact with the Templars of Tortosa, sometimes in his position as a major landholder, sometimes in

---

[44] *Liber Feudorum Maior*, doc. 466; Pagarolas, *Comanda*, doc. 57, 75; *Alfonso II*, doc. 339, 347, 382; *Diplomatari de la catedral*, doc. 18, 335.

[45] *Liber Feudorum Maior*, doc. 466; Bayerri, VII, pp. 118-22; Forey, *Templars*, pp. 30, 71; Shideler, pp. 200-201; Bisson, *Fiscal Accounts*, I, pp. 230-31; *Alfonso II*, doc. 161. According to Lluis Pagarolas, the main authority on Templar Tortosa, the complicated transition of rights between Peter I, his mother Sancia, and Guillem de Cervera 'no ha estat gens estudiada' (Pagarolas, 'Senyorius', p. 60, note 36).

[46] On him and his relations to the Templars see Shideler, pp. 87-114; Pagarolas, *Comanda*, pp. 149-50.

[47] *Cartulaire général*, doc. 72. Cf. G. Ligato, 'Fra ordini cavallereschi e crociata: *milites ad terminum* e *confraternitates armata*', *MC*, pp. 645-99; F. Tommasi, '*Pauperes commilitones Christi*. Aspetti i problemi delle origini gerosolimitane', *MC*, pp. 465-75.

[48] Shideler (pp. 100-101) claims he in fact acted as the count's representative; however, de Montcada may have only accompanied the count, for he hardly ever appears without Ramon Berenguer IV, who in turn was represented from 1156 by a *baiulius comitis in Tortosa*, Guillem de Copons (*Diplomatari de la catedral*, doc. 70, 75, 191).

[49] *Diplomatari de la catedral*, doc. 12, 13, 14, 15, 16, 17, 19, 20, 21, 22, 23, 24, 26, 28, 30, 36, 41, 45, 46, 47, 48, 50, 51, 57; Shideler, pp. 99-103.

his role as a representative of the count.[50] He had vigorously – although unsuccessfully – contested having been apportioned his share of the town after the Templars had received theirs,[51] and one might have expected the two co-lords to have battled for power, but this was not the case. In two conflicts with the local bishop to which we will return later, Guillem Ramon, the Great Seneschal, acted as an arbitrator, and his successors donated their rights over several estates to the order.[52]

That serious discord did not mar the relations between the barons and the Templars may have been partially due to personal ties between the family and the order: for example, when Ramon Berenguer IV was obliged to provide high-ranking hostages to the Genoese in 1153, he chose a son of Guillem Ramon de Montcada as well as Arnau de Torroja, the future Templar master of the Iberian Peninsula with whom the de Montcadas were to have so much contact in years to come.[53] But the situation changed in 1182: when Alfonso el Casto donated the greater part of his rights in Tortosa to the Templars, they outstripped the de Montcadas in possessions and rights. Guillem de Cervera, the comital representative after 1208, became the de Montcadas' natural ally against the Templars, and indeed both signed a series of charters together and even appear to have acted as co-lords in 1209 and 1210, a period during which Guillem de Cervera resisted paying homage to the order.[54] After he gave up his claims in 1215, and in spite of temporary disagreements about the extent of their respective rights,[55] co-operation between the de Montcadas and the Templars increased once again. Matters of administration were often jointly executed, both defended their common interests against the local *probi homines*, and the barons are even known to have used the Templar house at Tortosa as a *depositorium* for their documents.[56]

---

[50] *Alfonso II*, doc. 131; *Diplomatari de la catedral*, doc. 34, 70.

[51] *Colección de documentos inéditos*, IV, doc. 51; Shideler, pp. 87-114.

[52] Pagarolas, *Comanda*, doc. 54, 55, 56, 63, 78, 110, 122, pp. 149-52.

[53] *Colección de documentos inéditos*, IV, doc. 78; Forey, *Templars*, pp. 477-78.

[54] Forey, *Templars*, pp. 30, 71, note 101; Shideler, pp. 200-201; Pagarolas, *Comanda*, pp. 149-52.

[55] Forey, *Templars*, p. 190.

[56] Cart. Gardeny, fol. 99v; Schickl, p. 147, note 68 and 69; Forey, *Templars*, pp. 57, 347 – who also refers to the house in Gardeny as a depository. Cf. R. I. Burns, 'Religious Houses as Archives / Depositories. A "Letter of Credence" from the Majorcan to the Barcelonan Templars (1244)', *Estudis Castellonencs* 6 (1994-1995) 235-42.

If there were reasons for strife between the Templars and other lay powers in Tortosa, there were many more for dissension between the knights and the local church.[57] Since Innocent II's path-breaking bull *Omne datum optimum* (1139) and a series of further grants, the Templars enjoyed far-reaching privileges, including exemption from tithes on mobile goods, permission to ordain their own priests and the right of burial.[58] These were precisely the points over which the bishops and the knights quarrelled. The more property the Templars acquired in Tortosa, the more devastating the economic consequences threatened to become for the local clergy. An extension of Templar possessions meant a loss of diocesan revenue, and the order's considerable popularity deprived the secular church of important burial spoils. Furthermore, the bishops could not tolerate the concentration of independent parish churches in the hands of an order which held an extensive lordship of its own. While these points of friction between the secular clergy and the military orders were not unique to the Iberian Peninsula,[59] they acquired particular virulence west of the Pyrenees due to the number of Templar parishes and the extent of their possessions and temporal rights on the eastern Hispanic frontier.

Despite such military and economic weight, the Templars never succeeded in extending their ecclesiastical privileges. The secular church of the Iberian frontier had received far-reaching privileges from the count-kings, who actively supported it against local powers. The church's resistance against the Templars' exemptions was not only quick to be felt, but was also highly effective. In spite of much debate, the military orders were not able to push their claims on the Catalan frontier as far as the early papal privileges permitted in principle.[60] In this respect, a marked difference can be discerned between Catalonia and the Holy Land: in the crusader states, tensions between the order and the church

---

[57] On the church of Tortosa in the twelfth century see R. Miravall, *Gaufred d'Avinyó, bisbe dels tortosins* (Barcelona, 1970); Virgili, *Relacions*; Pagarolas, *Comanda*, pp. 134-39; Vones-Liebenstein, *Saint Ruf*, I, pp. 426-46; *Diplomatari de la catedral*.

[58] *Papsturkunden für Templer und Johanniter,* ed. R. Hiestand, 2 vols. Vorarbeiten zum Oriens Pontificius 1-2 (Göttingen, 1972-1984), I, doc. 3, 6, 7; II, 67-103; A. Forey, *The Military Orders from the Twelfth to the Early Fourteenth Centuries* (Basingstoke, 1992), pp. 113-15; Barber, *New Knighthood*, pp. 56-63; Vones, pp. 167-68.

[59] J. Richard, 'Le paiement des dîmes dans les Etats des croisés', *Bibliothèque de l'École des Chartes* 150 (1992) 71-92; Forey, *Military Orders*, pp. 115, 123; Barber, *New Knighthood*, pp. 57-59.

[60] Forey, *Templars*, pp. 172-81; Vones, pp. 171-73.

were rare and privileges generally respected,[61] while the contrary seems to have held true for the western frontier. The existence of local military orders, the relatively stable situation on the Catalan frontier, the count-kings' power and the latter's influence over the local church were important reasons for the Templars' relatively weak stand in western Catalonia with respect to the church. The conflicts which arose on the Hispanic fringes of Christendom may even have been the spark which led to a tighter definition of the military orders' exemptions during the Third Lateran Council of 1179, as Ludwig Vones has suggested.[62]

The restrictions laid upon the order can be clearly discerned in the case of the Ebro region. As early as 1158 the Templars were only allowed to freely ordain a priest in the chapel of their castle in Miravet if he belonged to the order. Otherwise, as in all other churches the knights were to erect in the area, the priests had to formally swear obedience to the bishop.[63] Rules were also laid down in the matter of burial rights: seventeen years after the knights took over the castle of Tortosa in 1182, the bishop granted them the adjacent cemetery stipulating exactly who was allowed to be buried there, namely the brethren, three individually named inhabitants of Tortosa and those healthy enough to walk or ride up the hill to the Suda without aid – a rule which excluded the last-minute *fratres ad sucurrendum*.[64] Only in 1281 did the knights receive the freedom to bury whoever they wished in their cemetery.[65] The most controversial issue was the Templars' exemption from paying tithes. A solution was found in 1182 and 1185. In Tortosa, the order's original possessions remained exempt, while it paid a fixed sum for later acquisitions.[66] The rural estates were subject to payment according to the degree in which the order colonized the land. Where the Templars actively pursued the *repoblación*, they were partially

---

[61] Hamilton, *Latin Church*, pp. 108-9, 111, 148-49; Barber, *New Knighthood*, pp. 58-59.

[62] Vones, *passim*.

[63] *Diplomatari de la catedral*, doc. 34, 35; Schickl, pp. 216-17; A. Virgili i Colet, 'Les relacions entre la Catedral de Tortosa i els Ordes Religioso-Militars durant el segle XII, segons el "Cartulari de la Catedral de Tortosa"', *APJC*, pp. 67-79, 75-76, doc. 1 and 2.

[64] *Viaje literario a las iglesias de España*, ed. J. Villanueva, 22 vols (Madrid, Valencia 1803-1852), V, pp. 277-80; Forey, *Templars,* p. 172; Pagarolas, *Comanda*, doc. 112; Virgili i Colet, 'Relacions', p. 78, doc. 18. Cf. contemporary papal legislation on this point: *Papsturkunden*, I, doc. 160, 208, 213.

[65] Sans i Travé, *Templers*, pp. 118-19.

[66] *Diplomatari de la catedral*, doc. 18, 383.

relieved from paying their dues.[67] Similar solutions had already been implemented in a dispute between the Bishop of Zaragoza and the order in 1147, but
in spite of being in accordance with contemporary papal decrees, neither in
Zaragoza nor in Tortosa did they guarantee a lasting settlement of the question,
as later documents demonstrate.[68]

The church may have had strong reasons to complain about the Templars in
the Catalan border areas, but the points of friction themselves were not unusual. However, the rather unusual situation existed of a military order with
extensive seigneurial rights which in turn were weakened by the church's prerogatives. One might expect the order to have reacted to this conjuncture by
trying to influence the choice of Tortosa's bishop – as the Hospitallers seem to
have done in their urban lordship of Valenia in the Holy Land – or the clergy to
have been subordinated to the Templars, as in the case of Tortosa in the Levant.[69] But nothing of this sort is recorded nor did any member of the order
ever hold the see of the town on the Ebro. Consequently, the typical conflicts
between lay lords and the church over clerical privileges, particularly over
exemption from tax payments, broke out between the Tortosan Templars and
the local church. For instance, the Templars had a natural interest in distrib-
uting the expenses for the upkeep of the town wall on all landholders. The
cathedral of Tortosa possessed important estates, which it even augmented by
acquiring further property in the Camp de Sant Joan,[70] but it was exempt from
local taxes and levies and successfully defended this privilege against the lords
of the city.[71] The same may be said of local jurisdiction. The clergy was effec-

---

[67] J. Miret i Sans, *Les cases de templers i hospitalers en Catalunya. Aplech de noves i documents historichs* (Barcelona, 1910-1913), p. 184; Pagarolas, *Comanda*, doc. 77, 87, 88; Virgili i Colet, 'Relacions', pp. 77-78, doc. 3, 13, 14, 15; *Diplomatari de la catedral*, doc. 341, 381. On the *repoblación* in the area: Bayerri, VII, pp. 95-96, 103-5, 115-16; Forey, *Templars*, pp. 52, 174, 215-16, 237; Schickl, pp. 163-67; Pagarolas, *Comanda*, pp. 154-67; A. Virgili i Colet, 'Conquesta, colonització i feudalització de Tortosa (segle XII) segons el Cartulari de la Catedral', *La formació i expansió del feudalisme català. Actes del colloqui, 8-11 gener 1985*, ed. J. Portella i Comas. Estudi General 5-6 (Girona, Barcelona, 1985-1986), pp. 275-89. Comparable examples from other European border areas: Forey, *Military Orders*, pp. 114-15.

[68] *Cartulaire général*, doc. 460; Forey, *Templars*, pp. 174-76, 381-84, doc. 15; Vones, p. 172.

[69] Hiestand, 'Templer- und Johanniterbistümer'.

[70] Bayerri, VII, 71-73, 77-79; *CGOH*, 1, doc. 164; *Papsturkunden* I, doc. 240; Virgili i Colet, *Relacions*, pp. 76-77, doc. 4-9, 16.

[71] *Diplomatari de la catedral*, doc. 332; Virgili i Colet, Relacions, p. 70.

tively freed from being cited at the local courts, which were in turn presided over in part by the Templars' officials.[72]

The other members of the local *curia* were the de Montcadas or their representatives, and the citizens, with whom the Templars also shared power in Tortosa. As an incentive to repopulate the conquered town, and possibly in a further effort to curb the power of local lords, Ramon Berenguer IV had given far-reaching privileges to Tortosa's Christian and Jewish inhabitants in 1148 and 1149.[73] Once again, the specific situation of the Arago-Catalan border areas had an effect upon the relations between the Templars and their surroundings. When the order acquired the royal rights over Tortosa in 1182 they had to come to grips with a developed and self-confident urban élite with legal and economic prerogatives dating from the time of the reconquest. So developed was this élite, that it intervened in the Templars' legal matters: in 1179, a disagreement between the knights and a local landholder was solved by the representatives of Tortosa's leading families, the *probi homines*.[74] A clear indication of how vexed the Templars were by this self-assured group and its long-standing privileges is provided by the extant copies of the inhabitants' foundation rights, the *carta pobla de Tortosa*. Jesus Massip has identified a group of nine charters which he termed the *versió templària*, their common trait being several interpolations which enhance the knights' position with respect to the citizens.[75] It is no coincidence that the changes to the text were introduced in 1182. Conflicts ensued about the inhabitants' right to appoint jurats of their own, and although the cases not involving the lords of the town were heard before the city court, the selection of the jurats as well as the location of the court remained a matter of dispute until well into the thirteenth century.[76] Finally, the town's *prohoms* were to form an alliance with the count-

---

[72] Pagarolas, *Comanda*, doc. 116; Virgili i Colet, *Relacions*, p. 79, doc. 20; *Diplomatari de la catedral*, doc. 365.

[73] J. M. Font i Rius, 'La comarca de Tortosa a raiz de la reconquista cristiana (1148)', *Cuadernos de Historia de España* 19 (1953) 104-28; *Cartas de población y franquicia de Cataluña*, ed. J. M. Font i Rius, 2 vols (Madrid, 1969-1983), I, doc. 75, 76; Shideler, pp. 202-03. On the Tortosan Jews see the overview by E. Casanova Querol, 'Estado de la cuestión sobre los judíos de Tortosa (XII-XIV)', *Actes del primer colloqui d'història dels jueus a la Corona d'Aragó* (Lleida, 1991), pp. 393-401.

[74] Pagarolas, *Comanda*, doc. 68, cf. doc. 77, 101, 107.

[75] *Diplomatari de la catedral*, doc. 20; J. Massip, 'La carta de població del territori de Tortosa, i el Temple', *APJC*, pp. 42-66.

[76] Pagarolas, *Comanda*, pp. 144-49, doc. 116; Virgili i Colet, *Relacions*, p. 79, doc. 20; Forey, *Templars*, pp. 193-96; Shideler, pp. 203-04.

king which enabled him to regain partial control of the town and gave the citizens more say in its affairs. The climax of this development was the compilation of the famous *costums de Tortosa* in 1277 and the sale of the Templars' rights over the town to Jaume II in 1294.[77] Ultimately, it was the commune and the count-king that ousted the knights from power, not the local barons or the church. In doing so they put an end to a long struggle for power and lordship.

Between the counts: Gardeny

After a seven-month siege, Lleida surrendered to Ramon Berenguer IV and his allies on 24 October 1149.[78] This feat may not have found as strong a reflection in contemporary documentation as the conquest of Tortosa,[79] but was of no lesser strategic importance. It eliminated a wedge which effectively separated the two halves of the future Arago-Catalan Crown. The year before the conquest, the Count of Barcelona reached an agreement with the Count of Urgell, Ermengol VI, over Lleida's future division: the lordship with the Suda or castle of the town was to be held by Ermengol in fief from the Count of Barcelona, while the town was to be split, one third of the *dominium* going to the Count of Urgell, two thirds to Ramon Berenguer. One fifth of the town's *dominium* – taken from the Count of Barcelona's two thirds – was to be handed over to the Templars.[80] At that time, Ermengol was already in possession of all the mili-

---

[77] R. Miravall, *Fonaments de l'autodeterminació medieval de Tortosa* (Barcelona, 1973); J. M. Font i Rius, 'El procés de formació de les Costums de Tortosa', *Revista Jurídica de Catalunya* 62 (1973) 155-78; also *idem, Estudis sobre els drets i institucions locals en la Catalunya medieval* (Barcelona, 1985), pp. 141-62; C. Duarte i Montserrat, *El vocabulari jurídic del Llibre dels Costums de Tortosa (Ms. De 1272)*. Collecció estudis 4 (Barcelona, 1985); J. Massip i Fonollosa, *Inventari de l'Arxiu Històric de Tortosa*, 2 vols (Tortosa, 1995); doc. 118, 129, 137, 141, 281; *Costums de Tortosa*. Fundació Noguera, textos i documents 32, ed. J. Massip i Fonollosa (Barcelona, 1996).

[78] J. M. Font i Rius, *La reconquista de Lérida y su proyección en el orden jurídico* (Lleida, 1949); J. Tortosa Durán, 'La conquista de la ciudad Lérida por Ramon Berenguer IV, conde de Barcelona', *Ilerda* 17 (1953) 27-66; J. Lladonosa i Pujol, *La conquesta de Lleida* (Barcelona, 1961), pp. 28-46; J. Lladonosa i Pujol, *Història de Lleida*, 2 vols (Tàrrega, 1972), I, pp. 119-24. On the Templar's participation: Schickl, pp. 140-41, 171-72. On Muslim Lleida see Lladonosa i Pujol, *Conquesta*, pp. 3-27; J. Mutgé i Vives, *L'aljama sarraïna de Lleida a l edat mitjana. Aproximació a la seva història*. Anuario de Estudios Medievales, Annex 26 (Barcelona, 1992).

[79] M. D. Cabanes Pecourt, 'Datos históricos en la documentación de Veruela (siglo XII)', *Aragón en la Edad Media* 12 (1995) 13-29, 18-20. Cf. *Cartulaire général*, doc. 532, 534, 549.

[80] *Liber Feudorum Maior*, I, doc. 161.

tary strongholds in Lleida's immediate surroundings, which he had apparently wrested from the Muslims in 1147 and 1148 while Ramon Berenguer was campaigning in Almería and Tortosa.[81] One of the castles was Gardeny. The fortress was probably built under Alfonso el Batallador in 1122 or 1123 during a first, fruitless attack on Lleida and was now in the count's hands while he awaited Ramon Berenguer IV's arrival.[82] The Count of Barcelona seems to have camped there during the siege of Lleida, for he issued a series of charters within its walls in the spring and early summer of 1149, including one signed by a Templar named Peter.[83] After the conquest, the fortress was transferred to the Templars, along with a large suburb leading from the town walls up to their castle together with the seigneurial rights over their urban possessions.[84]

The first mention of a *comendator* is in 1156, although probably by then the house had been in existence for some time.[85] It soon became not only the administrative centre of important urban properties in Lleida, but also of several mills and bakeries.[86] It was also the focal point of extensive rural possessions in the *territorium Ilerde*,[87] where the knights owned large herds of sheep and bred horses – with such success that the latter were not only destined for service in the Holy Land, but also repeatedly used as means of payment.[88]

---

[81] Lladonosa, *Història*, I, pp. 119-21.

[82] J. M. Lacarra y de Miguel, 'Documentos para el estudio de la reconquista y repoblación del Valle del Ebro', *Estudios de la Edad Media de la Corona de Aragón* 2 (1946) 469-574, doc. 29, 30, 31; ibid. 3 (1949) 499-727, doc. 117; Lladonosa i Pujol, *Història*, I, 93-94, 121; Stalls, *Possessing the Land*, pp. 46-48.

[83] *Diplomatari de la catedral*, doc. 15, 16, 17, 18.

[84] *Alfonso II*, doc. 443; Lladonosa i Pujol, *Història*, I, p. 130; Forey, *Templars*, p. 26. The suburb was razed in 1468 during the Catalan Civil War (Sabaté i Curull, *Territori de la Catalunya Medieval*, p. 156).

[85] Schickl, pp. 141-42; Forey, *Templars*, pp. 92, 105; P. Bertran i Roigé, 'Gardeny, els Templers de Lleida', *Lleida, la ciutat dels dos turrons* (Lleida, 1992), pp. 11-42, at p. 14.

[86] Cart. Gardeny, fol. 15v, 69r-v, 94v-95r. Lladonosa i Pujol, *Història*, I, pp. 272, 282; cf. for the immediate surroundings D. Pifarré Torres, 'L'esplotació dels bens territorials de la comanda templera de Gardeny', *APJC*, pp. 111-16.

[87] Cart. Gardeny, fol. 16r, 19v-21r, On the extent of Lleida's *territori*: J. E. García i Biosca, *Els orígens del terme de Lleida. La formació d'un territori urbà, segles XI-XII* (Lleida, 1995); Sabaté i Curull, *Territori de la Catalunya Medieval*, pp. 45, 55, 96; *Catalunya Romànica 24*, pp. 49-61. On the possessions see the overview in Bertran, 'Gardeny', pp. 34-35.

[88] Cart. Gardeny, fol. 27v, 54v, 103v-104r, 104r, 104v, 105v, 106r, 107v. Bertran, 'Gardeny', p. 30; Sans i Travé, *Templers*, pp. 324-26. On horse- and cattlebreeding see M.-C. Gerbet, 'Les ordres militaires et l'élevage dans l'Espagne médiévale (jusqu'à la

In order to work their estates effectively, the knights undertook several projects to settle inhabitants in and around the town, and also endeavoured to draw settlers into the barren areas just east of Lleida and in the Segrià, thus participating actively in the *repoblación*.[89] At the same time, and as a typical response to the Arago-Catalan border situation, they relied heavily on Muslim tenants and, to a lesser degree, on slaves, just as their brothers did on the banks of the Ebro.[90] The Templars of Gardeny also played an important role in the area of ecclesiastical reorganization through the number of parish churches they administered. In their work as major temporal and spiritual colonizers of the eastern Hispanic frontier, the Templars often acted jointly with the secular church and local noble families. But these relations were not always productive and cordial. Like Tortosa, the history of the house of Gardeny is one of both co-operation and strife with local lay and ecclesiastical powers. In fact, the order's supporters and adversaries were not only the same institutions, but to some extent even the same individuals. Local nobles, the bishops of Lleida and particularly the ruling lords – counts and count-kings – figure prominently among them.

Conflicts between the bishops and the Templars were every bit as virulent in Lleida as in Tortosa. A long series of charters bears witness to the constant quarrels which poisoned relations between both parties and to their futile

---

fin du XVe siècle)', *OMVR*, pp. 79-106; X. Eritja i Ciuró, 'Habitat i espai ramader a la regió de Lleida (segle XII)', *Béns comunals als Països Catalans i a l'Europa contemporània. Sistemes agraris, organització social i poder local als Països Catalans* (Lleida, 1996), pp. 75-90. Not all the Templars' horses remained in Catalonia or were sent to the Holy Land: Alfonso el Casto is known to have purchased one from Gardeny which was given to Emperor Frederick Barbarossa as a present (*Alfonso II*, doc. 192). Horses were also used as payment in Tortosa (Pagarolas, *Comanda*, doc. 32, 72, 79, 83).

[89] Cart. Gardeny, fol. 16r, 19v, 29r-30r, 30v-31r, 32r, 33r, 34v-35v, 36v-37r, 37v-38r, 38v-40v, 42r, 43r-44v, 45r-v, 46v-47r, 48v-49v, 50r-v, 51r-v, 52v-53r, 58v, 71v, 77v-81r, 87v-88r, 88v-89r, 94v-95v, 109v. Lladonosa i Pujol, *Història*, I, pp. 150-51, 192-95, 221-31; Forey, *Templars*, 214-15, 225; Sans i Travé, *Templers*, pp. 321-22; Font i Rius, *Cartas*, I, doc. 87, 108, 256; J. Bolós i Masclans, 'Paisatge i societat al "Segrià" al segle XIII', *Paisatge i societat a la Plana de Lleida a l'Edat Mitjana*, ed. J. Bolós i Masclans (Lleida, 1993), pp. 45-81, at 51-52. On similar activities in the Holy Land see M. Amouroux, 'L'Église réguliere, outil de la colonisation de la Syrie par les croisés aux XIIe-XIIIe siècles', *Coloniser au Moyen Age*, eds M. Balard, A. Ducellier (Paris, 1995), pp. 119-26.

[90] Lladonosa i Pujol, *Història*, I, pp. 254-59; Forey, *Templars*, pp. 285-86; Bertran, Gardeny, pp. 33-34; Mutgé i Vives, pp. 78, 89. Cf. J. Massip, 'Els moriscos de Tortosa i la Ribera de l'Ebre a l'Arxiu de Tortosa', *L'expulsió dels moriscos: conseqüencies en el món islàmic i el mon cristià* (Barcelona, 1994) pp. 225-34.

efforts to reach lasting agreement.[91] Contemporary *narrationes* reveal the extent and duration of the conflicts: *Propter maximas et difficiles conquestiones atque contentiones quae inter episcopum ilerdensem et fratres Militiae Templi diutius agitatae fuerunt* (1154), ... *de querelis quae habebant* (1160), *maximae et difficiles conquestiones atque contentiones* ... (1173), *cum multae controversiae sive contentiones existentes inter ilerdenses et rotenses ecclesias et Domum Militiae Templi* ... (1192).[92] A later *concordia* between the Bishop of Lleida and the Templars of the nearby castle of Monzón dating from 1264 vividly shows how violent these quarrels could become. In the document, the bishop accuses the knights of having attacked his houses, stolen goods, kidnapped one serf, killed a second, and injured two more. The Templars were even charged with having murdered a priest. The counter-accusation was equally horrendous. The order claimed the bishop's men had destroyed an aqueduct, injured many serfs and tenants, and stolen herds as well as property. One of the Templars' serfs and a slave had been killed, and a *frater* had been stripped naked and injured.[93] The Archbishop of Tarragona and the Abbot of the Cistercian monastery of Poblet had to intervene on behalf of the pope to put an end to the violence.

Both parties' intransigence is understandable. There was much at stake. In 1245, the bishop of Lleida calculated the loss in revenue that local parish churches had suffered by the decision of twenty citizens to be buried in the cemetery of Gardeny at 500 pieces of gold.[94] This was all the more irritating as Gardeny was one of the few Templar houses which enjoyed free burial rights. These rights were usually restrained by the local bishops, but in an agreement signed in 1192, Monzón, Calavera, and Gardeny were singled out as houses where brethren and laymen alike were explicitly permitted to be buried.[95] The knights defended this prerogative ruthlessly, even if it meant having a corpse dug up and transferred to their grounds, as in the case of the nobleman Guillem

---

[91] F. Castillon Cortada, 'Discusiones entre los obispos de Lérida y los templarios de Monzón', *Ilerda* 36 (1975) 41-96, doc. II-IX; R. Farrero Isus, *Disputas entre los templarios y la mitra ilerdense en la diócesis de Lérida durante los siglos XII y XIII* (Tesis de Licenciatura, Universitat de Barcelona, 1982); Vones, pp. 175, 178; *Alfonso II*, Apéndice, doc. 65.

[92] Cart. Gardeny, fol. 9v-10r, 42v; Castillon Cortada, *Discusiones*, doc. 3, 4, 5, 6. Cf. *Papsturkunden*, I, doc. 103.

[93] Castillon Cortada, *Discusiones*, doc. 8, 9.

[94] Bertran, 'Gardeny', pp. 31-32.

[95] Castillon Cortada, *Discusiones*, doc. 6; *Papsturkunden*, I, doc. 244.

de Cardona.[96] Only on rare occasions did the order's burial rights fully comply with papal privileges. The same can be said of the Templars' other exemptions. For example, the knights of Gardeny were expected to pay tithes on demesne *labores* as well as on demesne *novales* on their estates in the Segrià, and in most other cases, tithes had to be paid in part.[97] They were similarly not exempt for possessions they had acquired in Lleida's territory after the immediate post-conquest period,[98] and their parish clergy were also under close scrutiny. Priests were presented by the order, but subordinate to and controlled by the local bishop.[99] These restrictions effectively curtailed the Templars' income and independence, and ensured conflicts with the church until the order's abolition.

In Lleida, just as in Tortosa, nobles were charged with representing the counts as castellans on a local level. But the similarities between the towns do not end here. The baron that Count Ramon Berenguer IV probably invested as *castlà* of the newly-conquered Suda in Lleida was none other than Guillem Ramon de Montcada, who already had close ties with the Templars.[100] While Guillem Ramon and later his son and grandson, Ramon de Montcada I and II, acted as the Count of Barcelona's castellans, members of a second family with which the Templars shared their lordship in Tortosa were entrusted with representing the Count of Urgell. From 1179 onwards, Guillem IV de Cervera acted together with Ramon I de Montcada as Lleida's *castlani maiores*.[101] Both had some share of the town's lordship, and both were major landholders.[102] Some of these urban possessions were eventually to end up in the hands of the Templars. From 1167 the order and the de Montcadas jointly possessed a mill in Lleida, the full rights over which were finally purchased by the knights in 1202, and even portions of the de Montcada's harvest shares are known to have fallen to the order.[103] The latter's seigneurial rights might otherwise have sewn the seeds of strife with the *castlani*, but in fact there are very few references to

---

[96] Bertran, 'Gardeny', p. 22.

[97] Castillon Cortada, *Discusiones*, doc. 3-8; cf. the explicit papal orders against this practice: *Papsturkunden*, I, doc. 110, 111, 155, 185, 201.

[98] Castillon Cortada, *Discusiones*, doc. 3.

[99] Castillon Cortada, *Discusiones*, doc. 6.

[100] Shideler, pp. 100-102.

[101] *Liber Feudorum Maior*, I, doc. 188; *Alfonso II*, doc. 276.

[102] Shideler, pp. 102, 212-14; *Liber Feudorum Maior*, I, doc. 188; *Alfonso II*, doc. 183, 276.

[103] Shideler, p. 215.

conflicts between the Templars, the de Cerveras and the de Montcadas. One reason for these comparatively good relations lay in the ties which the nobles' respective overlords – the counts of Barcelona and Urgell – maintained with the order.

Lleida formed a border area in more than one respect. It not only lay on the inter-confessional frontier between Christendom and Islam and on the political border between the kingdom of Aragon and the county of Barcelona, but also on the dividing line between the counties of Barcelona and Urgell. For the rulers of both counties gaining control of Lleida was a matter of vital importance. The Arago-Catalan Crown with its 'rural-parochial, stock-raising, and feudal-warrior upland' in the west[104] and its 'urban commune, commercial society'[105] in the east had no hope of becoming an effective entity if it was geographically split. Urgell could only continue playing a role in the reconquest if it maintained its option of expanding south.[106] The agreement reached by Ramon Berenguer IV and Ermengol VI in 1148 is a reflection of this conjuncture: the town's lordship was neatly divided between both lords, the Count of Barcelona maintaining the greater part of the rights, the Count of Urgell gaining the *de facto* possession of the town.[107] But the Barcelonese had not the slightest intention of loosening their grip on Lleida. Their *baiulii* continued to represent their interests in the town, and Alfonso I's itinerary shows just how strongly the count-kings made their presence felt in Lleida.[108] Regular visits were just one way of underlining one's overlordship, well-directed and openly propagated support of local religious houses was another.[109] Both the house of Barcelona and the house of Urgell strove to strengthen their hold over Lleida and its territory by such extra-feudal means. Several institutions became enmeshed in the houses' struggle for dominion, and the Templars were among them.

---

[104] Burns, 'Significance of the Frontier', p. 319.

[105] Ibid.

[106] Lladonosa i Pujol , *Història*, I, pp. 104-07; Sabaté i Curull, *Territori de la Catalunya Medieval*, p. 378; idem, 'Organització administrativa i territorial del Comtat d'Urgell', *El Comtat d'Urgell* (Lleida, 1995), pp. 17-71; *Catalunya Romànica 24*, pp. 65-67.

[107] *Liber Feudorum Maior*, I, doc. 161.

[108] J. Caruana Gómez de Barreda, 'Itinerario de Alfonso II de Aragón', *Estudios de la Edad Media de la Corona de Aragón* 7 (1962) 73-298; cf. *Alfonso II*.

[109] As demonstrated for Ramon Berenguer IV's relations to the house of Sant Ruf in Lleida: Vones-Liebenstein, *Saint Ruf*, I, pp. 346-66. Similar mechanisms can also be observed on the frontier between Germans and Slavs: W. Kuhn, 'Kirchliche Siedlung als Grenzschutz 1200 bis 1250 (am Beispiel des mittleren Oderraumes)', *Ostdeutsche Wissenschaft* 9 (1962) 6-55.

Even before Lleida's conquest, the counts of Urgell held the castle of Gardeny, and they probably participated in its donation to the Knights Templar. After the foundation of the preceptory they actively supported it through a series of gifts which both tied them to the Templars and the order to their house. In 1161 Ermengol VII founded a chapel in Gardeny, endowing it with a substantial annual rent.[110] He and his wife Dolça donated half of the castle of Pedrís and the entire fortress of Alcabès to the house in 1185.[111] But despite such support, other religious institutions with less strong ties to rival powers, such as the Praemonstratensian monastery of Bellpuig de les Avellanes, became the centres for the counts' dynastic *memoria*.[112] This change can also be traced by the way the counts of Urgell used the Templars in their struggle against the house of Barcelona. After the conquest of 1149, Ramon Berenguer IV had acquired Ermengol VI's part of the lordship rights he had given the Templars in Lleida.[113] Ermengol's grandson, Ermengol VIII, reclaimed these rights from Alfonso el Casto, Ramon Berenguer IV's son. In 1192, an agreement was reached, according to which the Count of Urgell not only accepted the sale, but also underlined his status as the count-king's *homo solidus* in Lleida.[114]

Originally, the counts of Barcelona supported the Templars of Gardeny less than their rivals. Following the donations of 1149, which were simply a fulfilment of the treaty of 1143, the knights only received possessions in nearby Fontanet through Ramon Berenguer IV's will in 1162.[115] However, Ramon Berenguer's son and successor, Alfonso el Casto, began endowing the house extensively with privileges and estates.[116] Although the count-kings did not attempt to establish any form of family *memoria* in Gardeny, their hold on the

---

[110] Cart. Gardeny, fol. 15r; cf. other donations to the order: Cart. Gardeny, fol. 61r-v.

[111] Cart. Gardeny, fol. 103r-104r; 108r-109r. P. Bertran i Roigé, 'Donacions de la comtessa Dolça d'Urgell als ordes religiosos (1184-1210)', *Analecta Sacra Tarraconensia* 49-50 (1976-1977) 41-50, doc. 1 and 2; Bertran, 'Gardeny', p. 30.

[112] E. Corredera, 'Santa María de Bellpuig de les Avellanes i los condes de Urgel', *Ilerda* 31 (1971) 115-41; P. Bertran i Roigé, 'Per un diplomatari d'Ermengol VII. Els ordres militars al Comtat d'Urgell', *Ilerda* 45 (1984) 147-74; F. Español Bertan, 'Els comtes d'Urgell i el seu panteó dinàstic', *El Comtat d'Urgell* (Lleida, 1995), pp. 149-83.

[113] *Alfonso II*, doc. 443.

[114] *Alfonso II*, doc. 553.

[115] *Liber feudorum maior*, I, p. 494.

[116] Cart. Gardeny, fol. 69v-70r, 89r-v; *Alfonso II*, doc. 328, 624; Miret i Sans, *Cases*, p. 151; Bertran, 'Gardeny', p. 29.

house became stronger than that of the counts of Urgell. One reason for this was the house of Barcelona's position as Lleida's feudal overlord. As such, the Barcelonese counts played a decisive role in legal disputes such as the conflicts between the Templars and the local bishops. Agreements were reached with the count's *consilium et voluntas* or at least in his presence. Ultimately, this circumstance, and above all the general rise of the house of Barcelona, ensured that the heirs of Ramon Berenguer IV, not those of Ermengol VI, became the true patrons of the Templars of Gardeny. Jaume I's marriage with Aurembaix, Ermengol VIII's only child, in 1228 put an end to any hopes the house of Urgell might have had of controlling Gardeny. Urgell's rights and titles in Lleida passed on to the count-kings: the Templars stood between the counts no more.

The rivalry of the ruling houses was one of the reasons for Gardeny's considerable wealth; it may also explain why such a high percentage of the middling Catalan nobility tied itself to Gardeny by means of the *confraternitas*. Ninety individuals have been identified as having entered the Templars' confraternity in the twelfth century alone, over half of whom belonged to the local aristocracy:[117] ... *Hi consten totes les famílies de la baixa i mitjana noblesa de la Catalunya de ponent.*[118] This is quite different to Tortosa, where *confratres*, *donati, familiares,* etc. appear far less often in the documentation.[119] The convent's wealth, popularity and its favoured position with respect to the count-kings during the latter's frequent sojourns in Lleida converted it into one of the order's most important centres which presided over a series of dependencies.[120] The Aragonese and Catalan preceptors often met in the castle over the Segre, and important accords were discussed within its walls.[121] Possibly due to

---

[117] Cf. the list in Bertran, 'Gardeny', pp. 26-27. To it must be added: Carbonell Guerreta and his wife Ales (s. d.), Guillem, son of Arnau Ramon (1158), Berenguer d'Artesa (1168), Berenguer de Calders (1170), Ramon de Vernet and his wife Estefania (1175), Bernat d'Aguilella (1179), Gombau de Ribelles (1179), Arnau d'Anglesola (1179), Bernat Bofarull and his wife Garsiona (1182), P(ere) de ça Aguda (1192) (Cart. Gardeny, fol. 55v-56r; 58r, 59r, 71r, 71v-72r, 72v-73r; 98v-99r, 104v; Barcelona, Arxiu Diocesà, Codex Llibre Negre, fol. 43v); Schickl, pp. 216-19; Forey, *Templars*, pp. 45-46; Bertran, *Gardeny*, pp. 22, 25-29; cf. E. Magnou, 'Oblature, classe chevaleresque et servage dans les maisons méridionales du Temple au XIIe siècle', *Annales du Midi* 73 (1961) 378-97; A. Demurger, 'L'aristocrazia laica e gli ordini militari in Francia nel Duecento: l'esempio della Bassa Borgogna', *MS*, pp. 55-84.

[118] Bertran, 'Gardeny', p. 26.

[119] Pagarolas, *Comanda*, pp. 128-32.

[120] Forey, *Templars*, p. 450; Fuguet, *Arquitectura*, pp. 158-60.

[121] *Alfonso II*, doc. 328; Forey, *Templars*, p. 316. On the monument see Bertran, *Gardeny*; R. Alcoy Pedrós, 'El castell de Gardeny', *Lleida, la ciutat dels dos turrons*

its ties to the count-kings, the position as a preceptor of Gardeny also seems to have been an excellent stepping-stone for a successful career in the Templar hierarchy: many a future provincial master and even one grand master led the house for a time.[122]

For several decades after the conquest, Tortosa and Lleida – the former on the frontier with Islam, the latter on the border with Aragon – marked Catalonia's southern and western limits.[123] In Alfonso el Casto's words, Catalonia in 1173 reached *a Salsis usque ad Dertusam et Ilerdam, cum finibus suis*.[124] But as the count-kings' dominions extended south, the houses slowly became part of the hinterland, and new, local military orders now reaped the rulers' patronage. The situation seemed to change in 1196, when the Templars incorporated the titles of the *Ordo Sancti Redemptoris*,[125] thus taking up the defence of the frontier in southern Aragon. But the following conquests of the Balearic Islands and the kingdom of Valencia did not bring substantial gains to the order. Its role in these new areas was limited to participation in the conquest, whereas other tasks that it had fulfilled on the frontier during the twelfth century such as colonization or the extension of the parochial system were entrusted to other orders. With the conquest of Valencia in 1238 the Templars ceased to regard the areas under discussion here as frontier regions, as the disappearance of the 'preceptory of the Ribera' as an entity in its own right demonstrates.[126] The knights had acted as a part of the Catalan border for a century and a half. They had served the specific needs of a frontier society in the military, economic, and spiritual field: they had fought, propagated the Christian faith, colonized, and had resisted acculturation by the high Islamic culture in which they were embedded.[127] But unlike the Hospitallers and the Teutonic Knights on Rhodes

---

(Lleida, 1992), pp. 44-52; J. García, J.-R. Gonzàlez, J. Markalain, 'La comanda templera de Gardeny', *APJC*, pp. 154-65.

[122] Schickl, pp. 197-98.

[123] Sabaté i Curull, *Territori de la Catalunya Medieval*, pp. 281-312, 485-87.

[124] *Les constitucions de pau i treva a Catalunya (segles XI-XIII)*, Textos jurídics catalans. Lleis i costums II,3, ed. G. Gonzalvo i Bou (Barcelona, 1994), doc. 15; *Alfonso II*, doc. 149.

[125] *Alfonso II*, doc. 658.

[126] Sans i Travé, *Templers*, pp. 358-59.

[127] Cf. Burns, 'Significance', p. 326; E. Rodríguez-Picavea Matilla, 'Un ejemplo de aculturación cristiano-feudal en la frontera nazarí: la Orden de Calatrava en Alcaudete', *Actas del II Congreso de Historia de Andalucia* (Córdoba, 1994), pp. 49-61; F. Cardini, 'Ordine templare e mondo islamico', *I Templari. Mito e storia*. Atti del convegno inter-

and Malta and in Prussia respectively, the Templars had not been able to take advantage of the most important opportunity border regions had to offer: the count-kings' strength and foresight had prevented them from creating a stable territorial lordship. When the Order of the Temple lost its place of origin and its spiritual centre, when criticism and enmity against it grew,[128] the consequences of this omission were to become all too apparent.

nazionale di studi alla Magione Templare di Poggibonsi-Siena, 29-31 Maggio, eds G. Minucci, F. Sardi (Siena, 1989), pp. 9-15.

[128] P. A. Throop, *Criticism of the Crusades: a Study of Public Opinion and Crusade Propaganda* (Amsterdam, 1940); E. Siberry, *Criticism of Crusading, 1095-1274* (Oxford, 1985); H. Nicholson, *Templars, Hospitallers and Teutonic Knights: Images of the Military Orders, 1128-1291* (Leicester, 1993).

3

The Knights Hospitaller on the Frontiers
of the British Isles

In this article I shall discuss the problem of why the Knights Hospitaller, the brothers of the Hospital of St John of Jerusalem, were established on the frontiers of the British Isles and what they did there.

Although the Hospital of St John of Jerusalem was founded as a hospice in Jerusalem for poor and sick pilgrims, during the course of the twelfth century it became involved in the military protection of pilgrims and undertook military functions in the Holy Land, being entrusted with the custody of castles and endowed with border territory to defend.[1] In making these grants patrons not only made provision for their immortal souls but also surrendered frontier territory which they lacked the resources to defend to an organisation which had growing international resources to draw upon; they gave the order their claim to territory which they had not yet conquered, encouraging the order to bring its extensive military resources to bear in their support; they encouraged the order to bring in colonists to populate frontier territory with their own people (European Christians), supplementing the indigenous peoples whose loyalty could not be depended upon; or, by colonizing an underpopulated area, established their authority over it.

---

[1] *CGOH*, 1, nos 116, 144, 313, 391, 411, 585, 596, 676, 783, 801, 804; and see J. Riley-Smith, *The Knights of St John in Jerusalem and Cyprus, c. 1050-1310* (London, 1967), pp. 52-53, 55-57, 65-69; and A. Forey, 'The Militarisation of the Hospital of St John', *Studia Monastica* 26 (1984) 75-89; republished in his *Military Orders and Crusades* (Aldershot, 1994), IX.

From *Mendicants, Military Orders, and Regionalism in Medieval Europe*, ed. Jürgen Sarnowsky. Copyright © 1999 by Jürgen Sarnowsky. Published by Ashgate Publishing Ltd, Gower House, Croft Road, Aldershot, Hampshire, GU11 3HR, Great Britain.

In Europe in the twelfth and thirteenth centuries the Hospital was given frontier territory for these same reasons, in Spain and in Hungary. In north-eastern Europe the brothers' military function seems to have been less important, but they were valued as colonizers, and were given many donations of unpopulated or underpopulated land in frontier territory. Here their function was clearly to assist a landowner in establishing authority over a disputed area. It should be stressed that although in these cases the frontier was with non-Christians, in fact throughout Europe we can see landowners giving the Hospital territory – as all religious orders were given territory – which was unproductive, or disputed with neighbours, in order to have it made productive and brought firmly into their ambit.[2]

So to the frontiers of the British Isles. For the purpose of this article, the 'frontiers' will be regarded as Ireland, Wales, and Scotland, for from the Anglo-Norman point of view these areas were frontiers from the late eleventh century onwards. These were areas where land was available for colonization, and into which those hungry for land and power were moving. In Scotland, the movement was largely peaceful – until the late thirteenth century – and 'the frontier' was the frontier between the Highlands and the Lowlands, and between central Scotland and the outlying regions such as Galloway, rather than the frontier between England and Scotland. In Wales, the Anglo-Norman colonists were established in south Wales by the end of the twelfth century, although there was still strong Welsh authority in Deheubarth (south-west Wales, but not the extreme south-west). Central Wales was Anglo-Normanized in the early twelfth century; then there was a Welsh recovery. Central east Wales, the kingdom of Powys, became Anglo-Normanized more smoothly; during the final war between the Prince of Gwynedd and King Edward I, the Prince of Powys supported King Edward I. North Wales was forcibly conquered in the late thirteenth century.

Passing on to Ireland: the Anglo-Norman, English and Welsh colonists became established there in the latter half of the twelfth century, and the eastern lowlands came under the control of the incomers, governed by a justiciar appointed by the King of England and based at Dublin. By the end of the thirteenth century in theory all the Irish were the subjects of the King of England. Yet in practice the royal administration did not control the highlands of Leinster (in the south-east). Much of Ulster, in the north, and west Ireland were

---

[2] For this, see my *Templars, Hospitallers and Teutonic Knights: images of the military orders, 1128-1291* (Leicester and London, 1993), pp. 17-18, 64, 68, 155, n. 42, 43, 44, 45, pp. 156-57, n. 67.

ruled by Irish kings and by the end of the thirteenth century the English royal administration in Ireland was becoming less effective. This was partly because too many of the great Anglo-Norman lordships were now governed by absentee lords, or their lord was under age; and partly because too much money and too many military resources had been taken out of Ireland to fight wars in Wales, Scotland, and France.

The foregoing is, of course, an extremely simplified summary of the situation, to form an introduction to the discussion which follows.[3]

Wales, Ireland, and Scotland were also frontiers in the sense of being on the edge of the civilized world, from the viewpoint of the central administration of the Hospital, which was based in the Middle East: initially in the Holy Land, after 1291 on Cyprus, and after 1310 on Rhodes. The grand master and convent considered all of the Hospitallers in the British Isles to be under the authority of the Prior of England – Ireland had its own prior, but subject to England. the lands in Scotland continued to be subject to the English prior even during the Anglo-Scottish wars of the first three decades of the fourteenth century, although later in the century both the English prior and the grand master on Rhodes had problems keeping control of the Scottish part of the order.[4]

The traditional view on why the Knights Hospitaller were brought into Wales and Ireland has been that they were to act as a defensive military force for their Anglo-Norman patrons.[5] As the kings of Scotland were expanding their area of authority from the eleventh century onwards into the Highlands and Islands

---

[3] There is a vast amount of secondary literature on the frontiers of the British Isles in the Middle Ages. There are numerous references in R. Bartlett, *The Making of Europe: Conquest, Colonization and Cultural Change, 950-1350* (Harmondsworth, 1993); see also, for instance, R. R. Davies, *Domination and Conquest: the Experience of Ireland, Scotland and Wales* (Cambridge, 1990); R. Frame, *The Political Development of the British Isles, 1100-1400* (Oxford, 1990); D. Walker, *The Normans in Britain* (Oxford, 1995). See also the articles in R. Bartlett, A. Mackay (eds), *Medieval Frontier Societies* (Oxford, 1989).

[4] See, for example, NLM Arch. 323, fol. 138r (new foliation 146r), 321, fol. 136r (new foliation 145r); *CCR, Edward III*, 14 (1374-1377) (London, 1913), pp. 297-98; I. B. Cowan, P. H. R. Mackay, A. Macquarrie (eds), *The Knights of St John of Jerusalem in Scotland*. Scottish History Society, fourth series 19 (Edinburgh, 1983), pp. xxxiv-xxxvi; C. Tipton, 'The English and Scottish Hospitallers during the Great Schism', *Catholic Historical Review* 52 (1966) 240-45, at p. 241.

[5] J. Rogers Rees, 'Slebech Commandery and the Knights of St John', *Archaeologia Cambrensis*, 14 (1897), 85-107, 197-228, 261-84; 15 (1898), 33-53; 16 (1899), 220-34, 283-98, at pp. 218-26; A. Gwynn, R. N. Hadcock, *Medieval Religious Houses in Ireland* (London, 1970), pp. 332-33.

and into Galloway, it could be argued that the Hospitallers could have performed a similar function in Scotland.

So the first question to ask is: what properties did the Knights Hospitaller hold in these areas, and were they on the frontiers?

In Scotland, they were granted only one major house, or preceptory, which was at Torphichen in central Scotland, near Edinburgh,[6] and not at all near the frontiers! By the sixteenth century the Hospitallers also had a vast number of small properties, especially rentals, scattered across Scotland; but it is not clear when they obtained these. More research is needed on this subject.[7]

In Wales, the Hospitallers had property in south Wales, especially in the Gower, and west Wales, given by both Anglo-Norman and Welsh lords; in west and south-west Wales their headquarters or preceptory was at Slebech, but the properties in south-east Wales were governed from the preceptory at Dinmore in Herefordshire.[8] This was all frontier country. In Gwynedd, north-west Wales, they had a preceptory at Dolgynwal, now Yspytty Ifan, granted to them by a local Welsh magnate[9] in the early thirteenth century. This was not frontier country – at least, not a frontier with the Anglo-Normans.

In Ireland, quoting from Aubrey Gwynn and R. N. Hadcock:[10] 'The order was richly endowed with Irish lands by Anglo-Normans, and there were soon preceptories in every Irish province except Connacht'. Yet, given that Connacht was very much frontier country, it is interesting that the Hospitallers had no preceptory there. Much of their property was in or near the large towns where the incomers settled, but some of their preceptories were clearly in frontier country when they were originally founded; such as Castleboy in Ulster and Mourne, north-west of Cork.

Who gave the Hospitallers these possessions? According to an English Hospitaller (John Stillingflete) writing in the fifteenth century, their preceptory in Scotland, Torphichen, was given to them by King David I of Scotland.[11] In north Wales, Dolgynwal was given by a local Welsh magnate, but confirmed

---

[6] D. E. Easson, *Medieval Religious Houses in Scotland* (London, 1957), p. 133.

[7] Cowan-Mackay-Macquarrie, pp. 202-32.

[8] W. Rees, *A History of the Order of St John of Jerusalem in Wales and on the Welsh Border, including an account of the Templars* (Cardiff, 1947), p 19; see maps, pp. 30, 62.

[9] William Rees identified the donor as Ifan ap Rhys of Trebys, p. 63. 'Yspytty Ifan' means 'John's Hospital', i.e., the Hospital of St John.

[10] Gwynn-Hadcock, p. 332.

[11] Easson, p. 133; Cowan-Mackay-Macquarrie, p. xxvii.

and added to by Prince Llywelyn the Great of Gwynedd between 1221 and 1224.[12] In south and south-west Wales, they received property from Anglo-Normans and Flemings, and from Welsh lords. Donations came mainly from particular families: the Marcher families of de Braose, de Clare, and de New-burgh and the royal house of Deheubarth.[13] As the de Clares and their allies led the Anglo-Norman invasion and colonization of Ireland, it is perhaps hardly surprising that the Hospitallers did well in Ireland. Their chief house of Kil-mainham was founded by Richard fitz Gilbert de Clare, Earl of Pembroke and Striguil, in around 1174; their house at Wexford was founded by William Mar-shal, who married Isabel de Clare, heiress of Richard de Clare and Eva of Leinster.[14] Two other houses were founded by the de Lacys, who were linked by marriage to the de Braoses[15] and who in the late twelfth and early thirteenth century were making donations to the Hospitallers in Herefordshire.[16] Other donations came from other Anglo-Norman lords.

Why were these donations made? I said above that Hospitallers were often given land to colonize, in order to make undercultivated land profitable and to enforce the donor's claim to the land given. There is no doubt that they were performing this function in Wales and Ireland; in Scotland, their property seems to have been central, in an area which was already well cultivated. So I shall put the question of Scotland aside for the moment.

In Wales and Ireland, some historians have assumed that the Hospitallers not only colonized their land but also played an active military role in its defence. Hospitallers certainly did fight non-Christians elsewhere on the frontiers of Europe; against Muslims in Spain, and Mongols in the East. But the Welsh

---

[12] Rees, p. 63.

[13] Rees, p. 34.

[14] Gwynn-Hadcock, pp. 334, 339. For the genealogy of the de Clares see the genealogi-cal tables in M. Altschul, *A Baronial Family in Medieval England: the Clares, 1217-1314* (Baltimore, 1965).

[15] Ibid., pp. 335, 337; Walter de Lacy, founder of the Hospitaller's preceptory of Kil-mainhambeg (Gwynn-Hadcock, p. 337), was married to Margaret, daughter of the Wil-liam de Braose who confirmed a gift to the Hospitallers *c.* 1176-1177, Rogers Rees, 14 (1897), p. 263.

[16] Walter de Langley and Emma de Lacy gave the Hospitallers the church of Siddington and three virgates between 1189 and 1213: the charter is preserved in the Nelthorpe Collection, Gloucs. Record Office (I am grateful to Professor Peter Coss for this infor-mation); Margaret de Braose and Walter de Lacy gave the Hospitallers a religious house for women which they had founded at Aconbury, Herefordshire, in 1216: *CGOH*, 2, nos 2047, 2059; *Rotuli litterarum patentium in turri Londinensi asservati*, ed. T. M. Hardy, vol. 1, part 1, 1201-1216 (London, 1835), p. 199b.

and the Irish were Christians; and the Welsh were patrons of the Hospitallers. In any case, the international military orders usually tried to avoid becoming involved in wars between Christians,[17] for they could not spare the necessary military resources, which were needed for their true vocation of defending Christendom against non-Christians. Even where their houses were built like fortresses, as they were in Ireland, this does not mean that they set out to fight the Irish; only that the area was insecure and they needed to make their houses defensible.

All over Europe, Hospitallers certainly did need defence against Christians; in 1235 Pope Gregory IX allowed the brothers in Europe to defend themselves when they were attacked, which indicates that hitherto they had followed the usual monastic practice of not bearing arms (except, as their order commanded, against Muslims).[18] In the report which the English priory sent to Rhodes in 1338, the brothers complained that the preceptory of Slebech in west Wales had a great deal of expense from 'many coming over from Wales; many come each day, and they do a great deal of destruction'.[19] The brothers at Slebech had to pay 40 shillings (£2) a year each to two local magnates to protect their property against their attackers and malefactors in Welsh parts. Likewise, Halston in Shropshire and Dolgynwal (Yspytty Ifan) in north Wales had to give many gifts to various lords and their seneschals and representatives, so that the Hospitallers could have and retain their rightful liberties and have these lords' aid, favour and friendship: 100 shillings (£5) a year. 'Ditto, to the servants of the lord king and other lords and to have their favour and friendship, 100 shillings a year'.[20] Dinmore in Herefordshire also suffered because it was in the March of Wales[21] – and this was in a time of peace! In Scotland, all of the order's

---

[17] A. Forey, 'Military Orders and Holy War against Christians in the thirteenth century', *English Historical Review*, 104 (1989) 1-24, reprinted in his *Military Orders and Crusades*, VII. However, in the thirteenth century the English government did make limited use of Templar naval expertise during the war with France; see H. Nicholson, 'The Military Orders and the kings of England in the Twelfth and Thirteenth Centuries', *From Clermont to Jerusalem: the Crusades and Crusader Societies, 1095-1500*, ed. A. V. Murray (Turnhout, 1998), pp. 211-15.

[18] *CGOH*, 2, no. 2105.

[19] *The Knights Hospitallers in England: being the report of Prior Philip de Thame to the Grand Master Elyan de Villanova for AD 1338*, eds K. B. Larking, J. M. Kemble. Camden Society, first series 65 (1857), p. 35.

[20] Ibid., pp. 39-40.

[21] Ibid., p. 32.

property had been destroyed and burnt during the war between Scotland and England.[22]

Of course, the English prior would have been inclined to underestimate the income of the Hospital in the British Isles and to exaggerate its problems, in order to prevent the grand master and convent on Rhodes from making unreasonable financial demands. Yet this does not sound like an order which could make an effective military contribution to the protection of the frontiers of the British Isles.

Having said this, there is some evidence that the Hospitallers did become involved in military activity on the frontiers of Ireland. In July 1285 Brother William fitz Roger, Prior of the Hospital of St John of Jerusalem in Ireland and acting in place of the king's justiciar in Ireland, was about to set out with an army against the king's enemies in Connacht.[23] In 1302 payment of £100 was made in wages to men-at-arms in the company of Brother William de Ros, Prior of the Hospital of St John of Jerusalem in Ireland – who had been acting in place of John Wogan, Justiciar of Ireland, who was in Scotland with the king – for the preservation of the king's peace in Leinster. In 1304 the king pardoned a felon because in 1302 he had been with Brother William de Ros fighting against the Irish in the mountains of Glenelory.[24] In August 1318 Roger Outlaw, or Utlagh, Prior of the Hospital of St John of Jerusalem in Ireland, on account of his good service against the Scots who had invaded Ireland with Edward Bruce, and in compensation for the losses inflicted on him, was given licence with his brothers to acquire lands, tenements, and rents in mortmain and advowsons to the value of 100 shillings a year.[25] In July 1338 Roger Outlaw, now ex-Chancellor of Ireland, was petitioning the king for payment of his wages from the time he stood in place of the justiciar and was Chancellor of Ireland, and for the fees and wages of his men from the time he was in the king's service; the request for payment of his men suggests that he had been performing military service.[26] In June 1360 an entry in the Close Rolls recorded that the Hospitallers in Ireland 'hold there a good position for the repulse

---

[22] Ibid., p. 129.

[23] *Calendar of Documents relating to Ireland preserved in her majesty's Public Record Office*, ed. H. S. Sweetman, 5 vols (London, 1875-1886), 3, 1285-1293 (1879), p. 369, no. 814.

[24] *Calendar of Documents relating to Ireland*, 5, p. 5; *CPR, Edward I*, AD 1302-1307 (London, 1898), p. 291.

[25] *CPR, Edward II*, AD 1313-1317 (London, 1898), p. 197.

[26] *CCR, Edward III*, AD 1337-1339 (London, 1900), p. 437.

of the king's enemies daily warring upon his liege people'.[27] In April 1388 Brother Thomas Mercamston of the Order of the Hospital of St John of Jerusalem in Ireland was appointed keeper of the castle of Carrickfergus in Ulster.[28]

However, these duties did not indicate that the order in Ireland was expected to do anything out of the ordinary for the Hospital or for a religious order.[29] The king expected religious orders to take their share of responsibility for the defence of the realm, the Hospital included.

On the other hand, the Hospitallers could also be given more peaceful duties which were more in conformity with their religious vocation. In 1332 Brother Roger Outlaw, Prior of the Hospital of St John of Jerusalem in Ireland, was given authority to treat with the English and Irish who wished to return to the king's peace after the recent war.[30]

Yet this duty, and the Hospitallers' fighting, stemmed more from their service as loyal servants of the king than from their military-religious vocation. What is most noticeable about the Hospitallers in Ireland is not that they were involved in fighting, as all the colonists must have been involved in fighting, but that they were closely involved in the English royal administration. I have already mentioned two priors of the order in Ireland who acted in place of the royal justiciar during his absence. In the fourteenth century priors of the Hospital in Ireland regularly served as chancellor, from the appointment of Brother Roger Outlaw as chancellor in January 1322 to the retirement of Brother William Tany as chancellor in March 1383. In April 1388 Brother Richard White was appointed Treasurer of Ireland.[31] Although Robert Hales, Prior of the Hospital in England, held the office of treasurer in the first part of 1381,[32] it was not usual for priors of the Hospital to hold this office in England

---

[27] *CCR, Edward III*, AD 1360-1364 (London, 1909), p. 39.

[28] *CPR, Richard II*, AD 1385-1389 (London, 1900), p. 438.

[29] For examples of the King of England commanding the Hospitallers in England to assist with the defence of the realm, see, for instance: *CCR, Edward III*, AD 1339-1341 (London, 1901), pp. 124-25; *CPR, Edward III*, AD 1345-1348 (London, 1903) p. 211; *CCR, Edward III*, 13, AD 1369-1374 (London, 1911), p. 568; in 1377 Robert Hales, Prior of England, was made Admiral of the Royal Fleet to the Westward: ibid., 14, AD 1374-1377 (London, 1913), p. 495.

[30] *CCR, Edward III*, AD 1330-1333 (London, 1898), p. 484; *CPR, Edward III*, AD 1330-1334 (London, 1893), p. 325.

[31] *CPR, Edward II*, 4, AD 1321-1324 (London, 1904) p. 46; ibid, *Richard II*, AD 1381-1385 (London, 1897), p. 292; ibid., AD 1385-1389 (London, 1900), p. 441.

[32] Appointed *CPR, Richard II AD 1377-1381* (London, 1895), p. 589; he was murdered during the Peasant's Revolt: *CCR, Richard II*, 2, AD 1381-1385 (London, 1920), p. 21.

in the fourteenth century. I suggest that the priors of the Hospital were used in this way by the English royal administration in Ireland because they were known to be loyal and efficient officials. However, this does not explain why they were given their lands in the first place, although it does help to explain why the order flourished in Ireland.

Again, if the order was introduced to the frontiers to fight 'the enemy' in Wales and Ireland, we would expect that it would not have had friendly relations with the Celtic peoples of those areas. In fact, Lord Rhys, Prince of Deheubarth, did patronise the order, as did other Welsh magnates. In Ireland, matters are less clear. The surviving records of the chapter acts of the Irish Hospitallers for 1326 to 1348 do show the Hospitallers giving concessions in respect of good service to a few people with Irish-sounding names, although most of the concessionees are English, Welsh, Scottish, or French. Charles Tipton has pointed out that there was a division within the Irish priory between English and Anglo-Irish brothers; perhaps this was as important as the division between the Irish and the Anglo-Irish. More research is needed on this subject.[33]

In sum, I suggest that the Hospitallers were not given land in order to gain their military support. Certainly they could give military support, but no more than any great abbot or bishop.

Another possibility is that land was given to show the donor's support for the order's work in the Holy Land. This is a very likely motive for all these donors. According to Ailred of Rievaulx, King David I of Scotland had a great interest in crusading, and would have gone on crusade if he had not been dissuaded by his subjects.[34] This may have been exaggeration, but it was true that by the mid-twelfth century the true Christian monarch was expected to go on crusade, or at least to support the crusade. This was also true for all Christian magnates. Those who could not go because of commitments at home should at least aid

---

[33] *Registrum de Kilmainham: Register of Chapter Acts of the Hospital of St John of Jerusalem in Ireland, 1326-1339 under the Grand Prior, Sir Roger Outlawe, with additions for the times of his successors ...*, ed. C. McNeill (Dublin, 1932), p. 36 Nesta Inyndonull, p. 49 Richard McColaghty, p. 66 Robert Carrig, p. 78 William and John Ocorcran, p. 88 Thomas O'Malawyll, p. 111 Richard Ogloeryn; C. Tipton, 'The Irish Hospitallers during the Great Schism', *Proceedings of the Royal Irish Academy* 69 C (1970) 33-43.

[34] A. Macquarrie, *Scotland and the Crusades, 1095-1510* (Edinburgh, 1985), p. 17; quoting Ailred's lament over King David, which was written for Henry II, son of Empress Matilda (David's niece), and included in John of Fordun, *Chronica Gentis Scotorum*, ed. W. F. Skerne. Historians of Scotland, 1 (Edinburgh, 1871), book 5, ch. 41, p. 242.

those who did labour to defend the holy places. And those who were seeking to establish themselves on the international stage as rulers of authority and prestige must be seen to support the crusade. King David of Scotland was a donor to the Knights Templar and Hospitaller at the same time as King Stephen of England and his queen, Matilda, were giving generously to the Templars; these were also monarchs who were intent on building up their prestige.[35] Later in the century, the royal family of Deheubarth were giving to the Hospitallers. Gerald of Wales tells us that Lord Rhys of Deheubarth had intended to go on crusade, but was persuaded out of it; perhaps this was only an excuse for his failure to fulfil his vow, but he attempted to compensate for this failure by making a donation to the Hospital.[36] In the early 1220s Prince Llywelyn the Great of Gwynedd confirmed the Hospitallers' possession at Dolgynwal and added a church.[37] Llywelyn claimed overlordship over the whole of Wales; this gesture in favour of a great crusading order could not do his claims any harm, and might reinforce them.

The great lords of the Welsh Marches and Ireland, the de Lacys, the de Clares, and the de Braoses, did not normally go on crusade because their involvement in the Marches and in the conquest of Ireland took all of their resources; and perhaps patronage of this military order was intended to compensate for this failing. The de Lacys also patronised the Order of the Temple.[38]

So I would suggest that the influence of the crusade was a more important factor in donations than the Hospitallers' ability to fight.

I have tried to explain why the Hospitallers' patrons wanted them in the frontiers of the British Isles. They colonised newly-acquired land and helped to ensure that newly-conquered land did not revert to the enemy; and they represented the defence of the Holy Land, thus boosting their patron's prestige. What did the order get out of this?

---

[35] *Regesta Regum Anglo-Normannorum*, eds H. W. C. Davis, H. A. Cronne, R. H. C. Davis, 4 vols (Oxford, 1913-1969), 3, pp. 310-18.

[36] Gerald of Wales, 'Itinerarium Cambriae', ed. J. F. Dimock (London, 1868) = *Giraldi Cambrensis Opera*, ed. J. Brewer et al., 8 vols. Rolls Series 21 (London, 1861-1891), 6, p. 15; Rees, pp. 113, 28. Possibly Lord Rhys was also influenced by his alliance with King Henry II of England, a donor to the order.

[37] Rees, p. 63.

[38] W. E. Wightman, *The Lacy Family in England and Normandy, 1066-1194* (Oxford, 1966), pp. 188-89, 207.

Not as much as it would have liked, for the brothers and their money fell under the control of the king, who could prevent essential officials or money from leaving the realm. Often the officials of the order in the British Isles seemed to be serving their secular king or their own interests rather than the grand master. On 27 June 1275 King Edward I ordered Brother William fitz Roger, Prior of the Hospital in Ireland, to go to Ireland; the prior was refusing to go on the grounds that he had been summoned to the east by the master of the order, Hugh Revel.[39] Edward, however, required his services in Ireland as vice-justiciar. In 1338 Roger Outlaw was forbidden to send anything out of the realm – effectively preventing the Irish priory from paying its dues (responsions) to the master and convent on Rhodes. The same problem occurred again in 1348.[40] In 1374 to 1376 the grand master discovered that he could not deal as he wished with his order's lands in Scotland, because Edward III supported the English prior's rights to control it.[41] The King of England also expected the grand master to respect his wishes regarding the appointment of the prior in England.[42] It is, therefore, questionable how much benefit these frontier lands actually brought to the order.

---

[39] *Calendar of Documents relating to Ireland*, 2, 1252-1284 (London, 1877), p. 200, no. 1146.

[40] *CCR, Edward III*, AD 1337-1339 (London, 1900), p. 290; ibid., 8, AD 1346-1349 (London, 1905), pp. 554, 558.

[41] *CCR, Edward III*, 14 (1374-1377) (London, 1913), pp. 297-98; Tipton, 'English and Scottish Hospitallers during the Great Schism', p. 241; Cowan-Mackay-Macquarrie, p. xxxvi.

[42] *CCR, Edward III*, 7, AD 1347-1346 (London, 1904), p. 219; *CPR, Edward III*, 13, AD 1364-1367 (London, 1912), p. 404.

4

Quelques aspects de comparaison entre les commanderies de l'Ordre teutonique à Metz et à Liège au moyen-âge

Dieter Heckmann

Pour essayer d'accomplir cette tâche, il semble avant tout être utile de se rappeler les points communs justifiant les comparaisons. Dans ce contexte-ci, il suffit peut-être d'en mentionner les plus évidents. Ce sont d'abord les deux villes de l'ancienne Lotharingie qui ont des racines gallo-romaines.[1] Ensuite, Metz et Liège sont depuis l'époque franque des sièges épiscopaux. Et finalement, les deux villes sont situées très près de la frontière linguistique qui s'est établie depuis les VIIe et VIIIe siècles.[2] Là, elles ont pu former des cercles de protection de la langue romane à l'aide de villages et autres petites habitations autour d'elles. C'est en tout cas le fait pour Metz, ainsi que Wolfgang Haubrichs l'a montré il y a quelques années.[3] Maurits Gysseling a décrit un

---

[1] G. Kurth, *La cité de Liège au moyen-âge*, t. 1 (Bruxelles, Liège, 1909), pp. 1-52; J. Schneider, *La ville de Metz aux XIIIe et XIVe siècles* (Nancy, 1950), p. 27. L'auteur remercie cordialement Mme Christiane Kohser-Spohn, Berlin, d'avoir fait la révision linguistique de ce texte.

[2] M. Gysseling, 'La genèse de la frontière linguistique dans le nord de la Gaule', *Revue du Nord* 44 (1962) 5-37, ici p. 30.

[3] W. Haubrichs, 'Warndtkorridor und Metzer Romanenring. Überlegungen zur siedlungsgeschichtlichen und sprachgeschichtlichen Bedeutung der Doppelnamen und des Namenswechsels in Lothringen', *Ortsnamenwechsel. Bamberger Symposion*, ed. R. Schützeichel. Beiträge zur Namenforschung N. F. 24 (Heidelberg, 1986), pp. 264-300.

From *Mendicants, Military Orders, and Regionalism in Medieval Europe*, ed. Jürgen Sarnowsky. Copyright © 1999 by Jürgen Sarnowsky. Published by Ashgate Publishing Ltd, Gower House, Croft Road, Aldershot, Hampshire, GU11 3HR, Great Britain.

phénomène semblable à ce 'Romanenring' messin en remarquant que, dans son essor, la ville de Liège a peut-être ... été le centre de dispersion d'une vague de dégermanisation, comme ce fut le cas à l'ouest pour Arras et Tournai'.[4] Si Liège et Metz avaient joué ce rôle protecteur de la langue et même de la civilisation romane sur le sol de l'Empire médiéval, on peut se demander si les implantations teutoniques dans ces deux villes avaient développé des formes d'adaptation ou non. Ce cadre inclut non seulement le problème de recrutement (surtout devant la tendance croissante d'exclure des frères non-allemands de l'ordre),[5] mais aussi de l'usage de la langue par l'administration des commanderies, notamment quant aux besoins internes. Cet usage porte également le regard sur la clientèle des commanderies dans la ville et à la campagne. Mais, comme les deux commanderies ne sont pas encore bien étudiées,[6] les observations suivantes ne peuvent être que provisoires.

Pour trouver des réponses, il semble d'abord nécessaire de se souvenir des circonstances de la fondation des deux établissements religieux.

Remarques sur la maison teutonique à Metz

A Metz, les Teutoniques construisirent leur commanderie entre 1210 et 1241 à l'est de la nouvelle enceinte, en construction à cette époque-là. Elisabeth d'Hongrie, la célèbre sainte de leur ordre, prêta son nom à l'agglomération qui fut le noyau du faubourg de Sainte-Elisabeth démoli après l'occupation de Metz en 1552 par les troupes du roi de France Henri II.[7] Faute de preuves directs, les noms du fondateur et des premiers bienfaiteurs restent inconnus. Malgré cela, il est certain que le comte Albert de Dabo (Dagsburg) et de Metz ainsi que le chapitre de la grande église possédèrent des droits et des terroirs dans les environs.[8] En outre, il faut ajouter que ce fut soit le comte Albert, soit son père

---

[4] Gysseling, p. 31.

[5] K. Forstreuter, *Der Deutsche Orden am Mittelmeer*. QStGDO 2 (Bad Godesberg, 1967), pp. 214-16; J. Voigt, *Geschichte des Deutschen Ritter-Ordens in seinen zwölf Balleien in Deutschland*, vol. 1 (Berlin, 1857), pp. 266 seq. et 274.

[6] Voir H. Lempfrid, *Die Deutschordenscomturei Metz* (Beilage zu dem Jahresberichte des Gymnasiums zu Saargemünd 1887) (Saargemünd, 1887); N. Laguesse-Plumier, 'Vestiging van de Duitse Orde in Luik (13de eeuw)', *De Duitse Orde in Luik (1254-1794)*, ed. M. Van der Eycken (Bilzen-Rijkhoven, 1991), pp. 21-25.

[7] D. Heckmann, 'Die Deutschordensniederlassung Metz (1210 / vor 1241-1552) zwischen Germania und Romania' (article prévu pour 1999).

[8] V. Chatelain, 'Le comté de Metz et la vouerie épiscopale du VIIIe au XIIIe siècle', *Jahrbuch der Gesellschaft für Lothringische Geschichte und Altertumskunde* 10 (1898)

Hugues qui fonda déjà en 1173 l'hôpital à Sarrebourg (Saarburg) lequel devint en 1222 le siège d'une commanderie teutonique.[9] Ajoutons encore que Conrad de Scharfenberg, à la fois évêque de Spire et chancelier impérial, monta également sur le trône épiscopal de Metz en 1213. C'est la raison pour laquelle Lempfrid propose le comte Albert et l'evêque comme les principaux donateurs de la maison teutonique à Metz.[10] Si la fondation de la commanderie teutonique remonte en fait jusqu'à l'an 1210, comme le suppose Lempfrid,[11] la présence de l'Ordre teutonique à Metz promit alors d'être un support pour les adhérents du roi Romain Frédéric II de Hohenstaufen contre ses adversaires guelfes. Il est donc possible que les frères teutoniques s'étaient engagés à côté des paraiges ou lignages messin d'Outre-Seille et Porte-Moselle contre le paraige de Porte-Sailly. Le conflit ne se termina qu'après l'intervention de Frédéric II en 1215 par la défaite du paraige de Porte-Sailly dont plusieurs chefs de famille avaient quitté la ville.[12] Cet engagement présumé des Teutoniques semble avoir serré les liens entre les paraiges d'Outre-Seille et de Porte-Moselle et la commanderie. En plus, il donnerait une réponse possible au fait qu'on ne trouve aucune mention des possessions teutoniques dans le comté et futur duché de Bar. Car, le lignage de Porte-Sailly comptait, selon une hypothèse de Jean Schneider,[13] au nombre des alliés du comte de Bar.

Si ces suppositions se vérifient, les premières années de l'installation de la commanderie auraient préformé le futur destin de l'ordre à Metz. Un coup d'oeil sur la répartition des biens de la commanderie semble confirmer ces observations. C'est possible grâce à un censier de l'établissement qui est conservé dans les Archives Départementales de la Moselle.[14] Ce régistre, écrit en allemand, a été dressé en 1404 par le commandeur teutonique Jean de Brandenburg probablement pour donner une briève orientation à son successeur. Jean de Brandenburg avait composé le censier pendant une période où l'Ordre teutonique se trouvait au sommet de son influence et où il comptait parmi les

---

72-129, et 13 (1901) 245-311, ici pp. 277 seq.; Schneider, pp. 31, 49 n. 92, 95, 107, 119 n. 23 et 121.

[9] E. Ewig, 'Die Deutschordenskommende Saarburg', *Elsaß-Lothringisches Jahrbuch* 21 (1943) 81-126, ici p. 82.

[10] Lempfrid, pp. 1 seq., 4-8 et 14.

[11] Lempfrid, pp. 5 seq. et 37 seq.

[12] Schneider, pp. 119 seq. et 122.

[13] Schneider, p. 122.

[14] Archives Départementales de la Moselle, H 4768/2.

grands puissances de l'Europe.[15] C'est ainsi que le censier reflète sans doute l'état de la plus grande prospérité de la commanderie teutonique à Metz. L'analyse montre que les possessions, les censes et d'autres droits dont les frères teutoniques jouissaient, se cumulaient dans le quartier d'Outre-Seille et dans le faubourg de Sainte-Elisabeth, tandis que les Teutoniques, à une exception près,[16] n'avaient pas de revenues dans les quartiers de l'ancienne cité gallo-romaine. C'est dans le quartier d'Outre-Seille qu'habitaient la plupart des familles du paraige du même nom et que le paraige d'Outre-Seille avait son lieu de réunion en l'église paroissiale de Saint-Maximin.[17] Là, l'Ordre teutonique trouvait son plus grand soutien parmi la population messine. Malgré cela, la commanderie semble avoir mobilisé en 1399 des membres de tous les six paraiges pour participer au voyage de Prusse en compagnie du duc Charles de Lorraine.[18] Grâce à un rôle de 1404,[19] il est en tout cas possible d'établir l'appartenance de Jacques Dex au paraige de Porte-Moselle, de Jehan Noiron et Jehan Faulquenel dit Crowelet au paraige de Porte-Sailly, de Guerciriat Boulay au paraige de Jurue, de Jehan de Vy au paraige du Commun et de Morixat de La Tour au paraige d'Oultre-Seille. Faute de renseignements, les appartenances de Lowy Paillat, de Jehan de Waldrewange et de Parrain Grounaix restent inconnus. Mais, il est vraisemblable qu'au moins un de ces trois patriciens fut membre du paraige de Saint-Martin.

A la campagne, les possessions de la maison teutonique se concentraient surtout dans le territoire de la ville libre impériale, le pays messin, et quelques kilomètres à l'est de celui-ci. Là, entre la seigneurie de Boulay (Bolchen) et le pays messin, l'ordre réussit à former un petit territoire immédiat vis-à-vis de l'Empire autour de Narbéfontaine (Memmersbronn) et Breuchlingen.[20] Au cours du moyen-âge, la frontière linguistique se forma entre ces deux groupes

---

[15] B. Schumacher, *Geschichte Ost- und Westpreußens* (6e edn, Würzburg, 1977), pp. 122-27; M. Biskup, 'Wendepunkt der Deutschordensgeschichte', *Beiträge zur Geschichte des Deutschen Ordens*, vol. 1, ed. U. Arnold. QStGDO 36 (Marburg, 1986), pp. 1-18.

[16] *An der Porten Serpenotze* (Porte Serpenoise), Mos. H 4768/2, fol. 6r.

[17] Schneider, p. 125, n. 51.

[18] *Die Metzer Chronik des Jaique Dex (Jacques D'Esch) über die Kaiser und Könige aus dem Luxemburger Hause*, ed. G. Wolfram. Quellen zur lothringischen Geschichte 4 (Metz, 1906), pp. 336-40.

[19] J. François / N. Tabouillot, *Histoire générale de Metz par les religieux Bénédictins*, vol. 1-7 (Metz, 1768-1790; réimp. Paris, 1974-1975), vol. 2, pp. 546-50.

[20] R. Schmidt, *Die Deutschordenskommenden Trier und Beckingen 1242-1794*. QStGDO 9 (Marburg, 1979), p. 226.

de possessions. Son existence d'ailleurs n'a pas laissé de traces dans le censier de Jean de Brandenburg. Donc, pour l'administration des biens, il semble que la frontière linguistique propre ne comptait pas ou peu. Ce qui est plus important, par contre, c'est le témoignage sur la collaboration avec des germano-phones dans le pays de langue romane, le pays messin. Le censier permet par exemple de découvrir la tendance à préférer comme payeurs de cens des gens qui habitaient au-delà de la frontière linguistique ou qui venaient des régions germanophones du voisinage.[21] La collaboration avec les gens parlant la langue allemande paraît avoir été moins le résultat d'une conscience prénationale quelconque que celui d'une réflexion économique. A cet égard, l'ordre n'a fait qu'imiter d'autres grands possesseurs de biens de la région, comme par exemple l'abbaye de Saint-Arnoul.[22]

En ce qui concerne le recrutement, il n'y a que peu de témoignages. On sait par exemple que Henke Schampell avait été maïeur (meiger).[23] Son nom est dérivé du toponyme du quartier messin Outre-Seille Champel ou Champé. Sur une liste de conscription de 1404 Hennequin de Champel compte parmi les paroissiens de Saint-Euchaire.[24] Il est donc très évident que l'ordre avait recruté Henke parmi les germanophones de la ville épiscopale. Un cas semblable représente le commandeur de la maison teutonique de Beauvoir en 1395, Arnold,[25] dont le nom 'de Sailly' se rapporte au quartier messin 'Port-Sailly' et au fleuve 'Seille'.

Remarques sur la maison teutonique à Liège

A Liège, l'Ordre teutonique s'installa en 1254[26] ou au début de l'année 1255. Ce fut l'évêque élu Henri de Gueldre qui, le 13 janvier 1255, autorisa les frères teutoniques à s'établir, aussi longtemps qu'il vivrait, dans sa maison de Beaurepart sur l'Ile, incluse par la nouvelle enceinte du début du XIIIe siècle.[27]

---

[21] Des preuves sont receuillis dans Heckmann: 'Die Deutschordensniederlassung Metz'.

[22] M. Müller, *Am Schnittpunkt von Stadt und Land. Die Benediktinerabtei St. Arnulf zu Metz im hohen und späten Mittelalter*. Trierer Historische Forschungen 21 (Trier, 1993), pp. 261 seq.

[23] Mos., H 4768/2, fol. 18v.

[24] *Histoire de Metz*, vol. 4, p. 558.

[25] Lempfrid, p. 30, n. 4.

[26] J. Daris, 'Notes historiques sur les commanderies de l'Ordre teutonique au diocèse de Liège', *Bulletin de l'Institut Archéologique Liègeois* 17 (1883) 13-40, ici p. 35.

[27] Laguesse-Plumier, p. 22.

Comme à Metz, les circonstances précises de leur implantation ne sont pas connues. Mais, il est certain qu'après le bannissement et la destitution de l'empereur Frédéric II par le pape, l'ordre – ou la plus grande partie de celui-ci – se rangea du côté du contre-roi Guillaume d'Hollande, au plus tard en 1245, par crainte de perdre ses biens dans l'Empire.[28] En Prusse surtout, où les Teutoniques venaient de commencer leur lutte contre les païens, les frères avaient besoin de renfort sans interruption de l'Empire et de sa noblesse. C'est sans doute la raison pour laquelle le landmeister de Prusse Dietrich de Grüningen s'efforça de soutenir le pape et tous les contre-rois à l'époque de Frédéric II.[29] Il semble d'ailleurs que l'appui de l'ordre à la maison de Hohenstaufen portât plus ou moins des emprunts personnels du Maître Général Hermann de Salza, décédé en 1239,[30] et que l'ordre fût strictement fidèle non pas à une dynastie particulière, mais à l'institution impériale elle-même.[31] Dans ce cadre politique, l'invitation à s'installer à Liège faite par le cousin germain du roi Guillaume, Henri de Gueldre, à l'adresse de l'ordre s'explique aisément, notamment, si l'on considère que l'élu avait besoin d'un allié sûr pour sauver sa position dans la ville.[32] Cette position fut fort troublée en 1253 par le mouvement communal sous le tribun Henri de Dinant. L'événement eut lieu à une époque où les mouvements communaux en Flandre et sur le Rhin s'étaient déjà apaisés.[33] Bien qu'une paix fût conclu sous l'intermédiaire du légat papal, Pierre Capocci, à Maestricht le 11 décembre 1253 entre Liège et le prince qui lui permit de rentrer, deux jours après, dans sa ville épiscopale, la paix ne porta que le caractère d'une trêve.[34] La mise à disposition de sa maison de Beaurepart par Henri de

---

[28] M. Hellmann, 'König Manfred von Sizilien und der Deutsche Orden', *Acht Jahrhunderte Deutscher Orden*, ed. K. Wieser. QStGDO 1 (Bad Godesberg, 1967), pp. 65-72, ici p. 69.

[29] *Die Berichte der Generalprokuratoren des Deutschen Ordens an der Kurie*, vol. 1, ed. K. Forstreuter. Veröffentlichungen der Niedersächsischen Archivverwaltung 12 (Göttingen, 1961), p. 54.

[30] H. Kluger, *Hochmeister Hermann von Salza und Kaiser Friedrich II.* QStGDO 37 (Marburg, 1987), p. 192.

[31] Kluger, p. 6 seq., mentionne des exemples anticipés, où l'Ordre teutonique montra des attitudes semblables.

[32] Laguesse-Plumier, p. 22, est plus sceptique: 'Er bestaat echter geen bewijs dat Hendrik van Gelre erover gedacht heeft de orde in het bestuur van het prinsbisdom te gebruiken'.

[33] Voir K. Schulz, *'Denn sie lieben die Freiheit so sehr ...' - Kommunale Aufstände und Entstehung des europäischen Bürgertums im Hochmittelalter* (Darmstadt, 1992), pp. 6-9.

[34] Kurth, pp. 179-215, notamment p. 200.

Gueldre au profit des frères teutoniques n'est peut-être qu'une expression de ce caractère provisoire. Peu après, la guerre éclata de nouveau. A l'aide des princes voisins, Henri de Gueldre parvint pourtant à mater la ville en révolte qui fut obligée à se rendre par la paix de Bierset, le 17 octobre 1255.[35] Pendant la période où la défaite commençait à se dessiner, l'ordre reçut une donation importante dans la ville. Par la charte du 6 juillet 1255 le chevalier Jacques de Celles confirma la donation de sa maison *dictam de Cheles*, le droit de collation de l'église paroissiale de Saint-André *et aliis quibuscunque appendiciis spiritualibus et secularibus*.[36] Selon une charte du 5 avril 1262, l'ordre parvint à acquérir la deuxième moitié de la maison de Celles (avec des terres à Waremme) qui avait appartenu à Jean Hustin de Thynes.[37] Grâce aux largesses du chevalier de Celles, de Jean Hustin de Thynes et d'autres ministériaux de l'église de Liège,[38] l'ordre cumula des droits et des biens qui garantissaient sa subsistance à Liège. Parmi ces droits, celui de collation des églises de Saint-André et de Saint-Gangulphe – le dernier fut probablement acquis avec la deuxième moitié de la maison de Celles[39] – comptait beaucoup, car il permettait à l'ordre non seulement d'y installer ses propres prêtres, mais aussi à jouir des revenues des paroisses. C'est le cas des deux paroisses, puisque depuis leur acquisition, la paroisse de Saint-Gangulphe fut administrée par le curé de Saint-André qui employait souvent des vicaires pour subvenir aux besoins des fidèles.[40] L'administration des deux paroisses par un curé permit sans doute à l'ordre de réduire les frais sur les revenues.

C'est probablement à cause de ces bonnes conditions de départ qu'Henri de Gueldre consentit, à deux reprises par les chartes du 25 janvier 1256[41] et du 20 juillet 1259,[42] à ce que l'ordre transfère son siège provincial de Bilzen à Liège.

---

[35] Kurth, p. 210.

[36] *Urkundenbuch des Deutschen Ordens*, ed. J. H. Hennes, vol. 2 (Mainz, 1861), no. 111, pp. 107 seq.

[37] *Regestenlijst der oorkonden van de landkommanderij Oudenbiezen en onderhorige kommanderijen*, part 3, ed. J. Grauwels. Rijksarchief te Hasselt (Brussels, 1967), no. 1846, pp. 642 seq.

[38] Laguesse-Plumier, p. 23.

[39] Laguesse-Plumier, 'De Sint-Gangulfuskerk', *De Duitse Orde in Luik*, pp. 32-36, ici p. 32.

[40] Sint-Gangulfuskerk, p. 32.

[41] Hennes, no. 117, p. 111.

[42] La datation de Grauwels, *Regestenlijst*, no. 1845, p. 642, diffère avec celle de Hennes, no. 142, pp. 131 seq., où Henri de Gueldre dispose le transfert de la maison de Bernissem à Saint-Trond.

Ce déménagement, d'ailleurs, n'eut peut-être jamais lieu, comme le suppose à bonnes raisons Laguesse-Plumier.[43]

Un autre transfert n'était pas moins important, puisqu'il se déroula dans la ville même. Entre 1294 et 1300, Guillaume de Brusthem, curé de Saint-André et de Saint-Gangulphe, abondonna l'hôtel de Celles dans la rue de la Wache pour installer la commanderie près de l'église de Saint-André dans le quartier du Marché. Cela semble avoir eu pour effet que la plupart des paroissiens suivirent les frères teutoniques dans les environs du marché.[44] Cette action est unique dans l'histoire de Liège. Elle ne s'explique guère autrement que par les liens entre le curé et les paroissiens et par les avantages économiques que la clientèle liégeoise de l'ordre espérait trouver dans le coeur de la cité.[45] L'installation de la commanderie et de sa clientèle dans le centre économique, administratif, culturel et religieux de la ville mosane exige une attitude ouverte de tous les participants, particulièrement dans le domaine de la langue. Comme signe de cette ouverture, l'on peut mentionner la bilingualité des documents de l'administration interne malgré la préponderance du bas allemand. Quant aux documents de caractère publique, ainsi qu' à Metz d'ailleurs, comme par exemple les chartes, ils sont écrit en général dans la langue officielle de la ville. C'est-à-dire que les plus anciens sont écrits en latin et ceux qui suivent en wallon. Par rapport à la bilingualité, le censier du curé de Saint-André et de Saint-Gangulphe du XVe siècle[46] représente un bon exemple. Grâce à leur connaissance des langues, les frères teutoniques à Liège disposaient d'un avantage considérable pour l'administration effective de leurs possessions aussi bien dans le pays de la langue wallone que dans celui de la langue allemande.[47] Cette observation est confirmée par le trésorier des chartes de la commanderie,

---

[43] Laguesse-Plumier, p. 25, n. 7.

[44] Laguesse-Plumier, p. 23 seq.

[45] E. Poncelet, *Les domaines urbains de Liège*. Documents et mémoires sur le pays de Liège 2 (Liège, 1947), p. 188.

[46] Archives d'Etat de Liège, E 29.

[47] Selon les chartes de la commanderie, l'Ordre n'avait pas seulement des possession à Liège, mais aussi dans les environs de la ville, comme par exemple à Vottem et à Flémalle. Dans le pays de langue allemande, les biens se concentraient à et autour de Tongres, comme par exemple à Millen, à Widooie et à Wintershoven; voir aussi M. Van der Eycken, *Inventaris van het Archief van de Balije Biesen van de Duitse Orde*, part II. Bijdragen tot de geschiedenis van de Duitse Orde in de Balije Biesen 3b (Bilzen, 1996), pp. 546-71.

où se trouve des documents en latin, en wallon et en allemand.[48] Par consé-
quent, il n'est pas étonnant que dans les documents, l'on rencontre des membres de la commanderie dont les noms et dont les témoignages écrits déclinent
une identité romane. Robiens de Waremme, qui fut curé de Saint-André en
1335 et premier représentant de la commanderie,[49] est un de ces exemples.

La fuite des capitaux comme en 1333 'en tiech pays' fut sans aucun doute
une exception. Sinon, l'ordre n'eût guère veillé à transformer en hôtel[50] sa
maison 'en Pierreuse', acheté en 1294 par Guillaume de Brusthem, et non plus
à élargir ses droits et ses biens en Wallonie comme à Flémalle, au sud-ouest de
Liège.[51]

Résumé

En conclusion, on peut dire que durant la première moitié du XIIIe siècle
l'Ordre teutonique fut invité à s'installer dans les deux villes épiscopales probablement pour porter du renfort aux seigneurs des villes, menacés par des
forces adverses. A Metz, les frères teutoniques s'établirent dans le quartier
Outre-Seille et dans le faubourg de Sainte-Elisabeth où la concentration de la
population germanophone était très dense. Là, les Teutoniques cumulaient la
plupart de leurs biens et de leurs droits dans la ville mosellane. Tandis qu'à
Liège l'ordre réussit à s'implanter pas à pas dans le centre de la ville épiscopale jusqu'à la fin du XIIIe siècle. Ces conditions de départ exigeaient des
formes d'adaptation différentes. La concentration de la commanderie messine
dans la partie Est de la ville et de la population germanophone qui y habitait
entraîna une étroite collaboration avec les gens parlant la langue allemande. La
tendance à accepter plutôt des germanophones que des romans comme preneurs
de bail dans le pays messin ne semble être qu'un signe de cette collaboration.
Cette mesure fut avant tout dictée par le besoin d'administrer les biens à peu de
frais et moins par une sorte de sentiment prénationale. Cela n'exclut pourtant

---

[48] Quant au tracé de la frontière linguistique, ces documents peuvent servir à une première orientation, parce qu'ils permettent à observer qu'en général depuis la première
moitié du XIVe siècle les documents en latin ou en allemand s'adressent de préférence
aux germanophones.

[49] *Regestenlijst*, no. 1857, p. 646.

[50] Laguesse-Plumier, p. 24; Poncelet, p. 183.

[51] *Regestenlijst*, nos 1848 seqq.

pas un renfort de l'élément germanique à Metz qui semble avoir atteint le sommet de son développement autour de l'an 1522.[52]

Malgré la majorité des frères aux noms germanophones parmi les membres de la commanderie liégeoise, l'élément roman était tellement présent que parfois un wallon fut choisi comme curé de Saint-André et de Saint-Gangulphe, donc comme chef de la commanderie. Cette répartition ethnique est reflétée entre autre dans les archives de la commanderie, surtout en ce qui concerne l'usage des deux langues par l'administration interne. A condition que ces observations se confirment, on peut se poser la question de savoir si la commanderie teutonique à Liège faisait une exception ou non parmi les autres grands possesseurs de biens. Cela entamerait le problème de la bilingualité des groupes sociaux de la ville en particulier et celle de la population urbaine en général. Mais, cela est un sujet propre qui dépasserait largement le cadre de cette étude.

---

[52] D. Heckmann, 'Zum Persönlichkeitsbild des Metzer Patriziers Andre Voey de Ryneck (1444-1525/29)', *Jahrbuch für westdeutsche Landesgeschichte* 15 (1989) 43-66, ici p. 58.

II

Different Levels of Regional Influence

5

From the Holy Land to Prussia:

the Teutonic Knights between Emperors and

Popes and their Policies until 1309

Klaus Militzer

The Teutonic Order was founded in 1190. During the siege of Acre by a Christian army, crusaders of Bremen and perhaps of Lübeck established a hospital for wounded and sick German pilgrims.[1] They stretched a sail to protect the patients against the sun and gave the administration of the hospital to a brotherhood, directed by a master. Duke Frederick of Suevia, a son of the Emperor Frederick I Barbarossa, transformed the brotherhood into a hospitaller order in 1190 and asked his brother, King Henry VI, for confirmation and for confirmation by the pope. Both happened in 1191, and Pope Clement III took the order under the protection of the Holy See. At that time a cleric, perhaps a priest, had the leading position in the order.[2]

In 1198 the new corporation was transformed into a military order by German crusaders. These crusaders acted in agreement with the King and Emperor, Henry VI, because he needed the order for his policy in the eastern Mediterranean. Not much is known about his aims because the emperor died in

---

[1] H. St. Brünjes, *Die Deutschordenskomturei in Bremen*. QStGDO 53 (Marburg, 1997) p. 212. The first English version of this paper was revised by Jürgen Sarnowsky, Ruth Peters and Caroline Cornish.

[2] M.-L. Favreau, *Studien zur Frühgeschichte des Deutschen Ordens*. Kieler Historische Studien 21 (Stuttgart, [1974]), pp. 35-63; U. Arnold, 'Entstehung und Frühzeit des Deutschen Ordens', *Die geistlichen Ritterorden*, eds J. Fleckenstein, M. Hellmann. Vorträge und Forschungen XXVI (Sigmaringen, 1980), pp. 81-96.

From *Mendicants, Military Orders, and Regionalism in Medieval Europe*, ed. Jürgen Sarnowsky. Copyright © 1999 by Jürgen Sarnowsky. Published by Ashgate Publishing Ltd, Gower House, Croft Road, Aldershot, Hampshire, GU11 3HR, Great Britain.

September 1197, before the order was militarized. The transformation was confirmed by Pope Innocent III who bestowed on the order the rule of the Templars with regards to its military activities, and that of the Hospitallers in regards to its charitable activities. Between 1218 and 1221 the order achieved an equal status with Templars and Hospitallers as a result of privileges invested upon it by Pope Honorius III. Since 1198 the order was governed by knightly brethren,[3] and the priest-brethren became more and more of secondary importance.

The popes did not initiate the militarization of the order, yet they did not prevent it. For the popes it was essential to keep a supreme authority over the order, indeed, it was subordinate to the popes according to canon law. However, in reality the situation was more complex. After the militarization in 1198, the order recruited the knights of the lower nobility, the so-called *ministeriales*, the sergeants of the princes, the emperors and the German empire. Most of the members of this noble class were loyal to the emperor and the German empire. The order got most of its goods and estates from the emperor or his loyal nobility. Because of the recruitment and the donations, the Teutonic Knights became an order of the noble Hohenstaufen family, and of the empire itself, as the Hohenstaufen were the royal or imperial family at the end of the twelfth and in the first half of the thirteenth century.[4] The Hohenstaufen depended on the order in implementing their Mediterranean policies, and for this purpose it had been endowed with estates. On the other hand, the order depended on the Hohenstaufen and the emperors from this family, because without their help it would not have emerged so quickly that even contemporaries were astonished by its achievements. According to canon law the pope was the supreme authority of the order, but in reality, especially in cases of conflict, the knightly brethren were more loyal to the emperor and the empire than to the pope.

It was especially Hermann von Salza, the order's master in the time of Frederick II, who experienced these problems, never able to join sides openly with the pope as the masters of the Templars and Hospitallers did, although he could negotiate compromises between emperor and pope since he enjoyed the confidence of both parties. However, throughout these negotiations Hermann von

---

[3] Arnold, 'Entstehung', pp. 98-107; Favreau, pp. 64-94.

[4] D. Wojtecki, 'Der Deutsche Orden unter Friedrich II.', *Probleme um Friedrich II.*, ed. J. Fleckenstein. Vorträge und Forschungen XVI (Sigmaringen, 1974), pp. 187-224.

Salza never forgot the interests of his order and reaped many benefits from them.[5]

Hermann's successor, Konrad von Thüringen, tried to continue the order's friendly policy towards the Hohenstaufen, but he died in 1240, a short time after his election, and never had the chance to negotiate between emperor and pope as his predecessor had done. Subsequently, the newly elected master, Gerhard von Malberg, tried to change the order's policies in siding with the pope more strongly than before. The pope invested him with a ring in 1143 and let him swear an oath of allegiance.[6] Such an act was unusual and remained an exception, and in 1244, one year after this act of investiture, Gerhard was forced to abdicate, having been accused of financial irregularities.[7] However, this was probably not the main reason, which was rather his friendly relationship with the pope. Nevertheless Gerhard, who remained in the order, had found several supporters for his attitude.

Gerhard's successor, Heinrich von Hohenlohe, soon became aware of the opposition. Heinrich was a member of a Frankish family traditionally friendly to the Hohenstaufen.[8] He was faced with difficulties when he tried to resume the order's former policies and had to tolerate officials of high rank who were adherents of the pro-papal party.[9] Consequently, he was not in a position to support the emperor without reservation and this resulted in irritating the emperor Frederick II who confiscated all the order's estates in Sicily. Only on his deathbed, in 1250, did he return the confiscated estates.[10]

Heinrich von Hohenlohe died in 1249, approximately one year before Frederick. When the next election was to take place, the brethren could not agree on one candidate and so elected two masters. The pro-papal party elected Wilhelm von Urenbach while the faction that wished to retain friendly relations

---

[5] H. Kluger, *Hochmeister Hermann von Salza und Kaiser Friedrich II. Ein Beitrag zur Frühgeschichte des Deutschen Ordens.* QStGDO 37 (Marburg, 1987), *passim.*

[6] *Preußisches Urkundenbuch*, ed. R. Philippi et al., vol. 1, 1 (Königsberg, 1882; repr. Aalen, 1961), no. 147; I. Matison, 'Die Lehnsexemtion des Deutschen Ordens und dessen staatsrechtliche Stellung in Preußen', *Deutsches Archiv* 21 (1965), p. 219.

[7] *Tabulae Ordinis Theutonici*, ed. E. Strehlke (Berlin, 1869), no. 483-486, 488; *Regestenlijst der oorkonden van de landkommanderij Oudenbiezen en onderhorige kommanderijen*, ed. J. Grauwels, 1 (Brussels, 1966), no. 25, 48-49, 51-52.

[8] *Hohenlohisches Urkundenbuch*, ed. K. Weller, vol. 1 (Stuttgart, 1899), no. 236.

[9] K. Militzer, *Die Entstehung der Deutschordensballeien im Deutschen Reich.* QStGDO 16 (Marburg, 1981), pp. 46-47.

[10] M. Hellmann, 'König Manfred von Sizilien und der Deutsche Orden', *Acht Jahrhunderte Deutscher Orden*, ed. K. Wieser. QStGDO 1 (Bad Godesberg, 1967), pp. 67-70.

with the emperor choose Gunther von Wüllersleben. Since the two masters blocked each other in their activities nothing came out of it; therefore, the official tradition of the order ignored both.[11]

The supporters of the Hohenstaufen family lost their backing after the death of Frederick in 1250. When Gunther von Wüllersleben died in 1252, his successor no longer had any problems with the earlier factions. The order remained an order of the empire, and in the following years it mostly supported the king or the emperor in case of a conflict with the pope. But the close contacts with the Hohenstaufen family in the early years of the thirteenth century could not be transferred to the other ruling families of the empire: the ties to the successors of the Hohenstaufen kings were not as close as before. With the end of the Hohenstaufen family the inner conflicts ceased to exist, and its officials gained more freedom. After 1250 the splitting into factions – the partisans of the emperor on one side and those of the pope on the other side – belonged to the past.

Although the Teutonic Order had become an order of the Hohenstaufen family or of the empire, it remained an offshoot of the crusade movement. The order originated in the Holy Land and had its headquarters in Acre or Montfort, the castle near Acre, but its spiritual centre was Jerusalem. The Holy City was part of the order's title: *domus hospitalis Theutonicorum sancte Marie in Jerusalem.* The order never did establish its headquarters in Jerusalem except in an allegorical sense. In the *Narratio de primordiis ordinis Theutonici* which was written in about 1250 by a priest-brother at a time when the rule of the order was compiled, it states that the order included Jerusalem in its full title because everyone was hoping that the town would be regained.[12] In fact, in one phase of the order's development it was planned to move its headquarters into the Holy City. In 1229 Master Hermann von Salza entered the town with Emperor Frederick II and occupied the old hospital of the Germans, dependent on the Hospitallers before the fall of Jerusalem in 1187. In 1229 the Teutonic Order also received the *curia regia* near the Gate of David in Jerusalem.[13] This gift by Frederick II allowed the order to establish for itself a relationship with the kingdom of David. The order placed itself in the tradition of David's kingship, and members of the order have reflected this in its chronicles and

---

[11] K. Forstreuter, *Der Deutsche Orden am Mittelmeer.* QStGDO 2 (Bonn, 1967), pp. 207-10.

[12] *Die Statuten des Deutschen Ordens nach seinen ältesten Handschriften,* ed. M. Perlbach (Halle, 1890), p. 159.

[13] *Tabulae,* no. 69; Kluger, pp. 131-40.

imagery. But the order was not able to keep the hospital of St Mary and the *curia regia* in Jerusalem for long; it lost both soon after the retreat of Frederick II. Nevertheless, the reference to Jerusalem and King David allowed the order to claim equal rank with the two other important military orders, and therefore it could also stress its rank *vis-à-vis* the German nobility within the empire.

In an allegorical sense, Jerusalem could be understood to be the Christian church. Wherever the order built a church or fought for the faith, it served the church and also – in an allegorical sense – Jerusalem, that is, the celestial Jerusalem.[14] But I doubt whether the simple knights would have understood the fine allegories which were devised by clerics. Most of the knights when speaking about Jerusalem may have thought of the real town and of its reconquest. Christ had lived in the Holy Land and in Jerusalem. Many knights believed that the Holy Land was the *patrimonium Christi*. They saw themselves as vassals of Jesus Christ, and therefore they had to protect the *patrimonium* of their Lord and to reconquer all of it. Thus, the order was obliged to fight for the Lord against the Saracens,[15] and according to the mentality of its brethren the reconquest of Jerusalem was the foremost task of the order. Moreover, Hermann von Salza considered the fight against the Muslims in the Holy Land as the order's most important mission, since the centre of the order was situated there. The popes had supported the conquest of the Holy Land by proclaiming the crusades, and therefore its defence depended on the Holy See. But it became increasingly more difficult to find courageous crusaders who were willing to follow the widespread idea of the *patrimonium Christi*. The popes had no other option than to support the military orders and therefore also the Teutonic Knights since they had the best organized troops in Palestine.

Furthermore, under Hermann von Salza's mastership another development had already begun. In 1230, the master sent Hermann Balk together with some knights to Prussia, who finally succeeded in conquering the territory and in building up an own administration of the order.[16] When, in 1237, the pope incorporated the Sword Brethren in Livonia – who had been defeated by their enemies – with the Teutonic Order, Hermann von Salza also entrusted the consolidation of Livonia to Hermann Balk. Balk and his successors gained

---

[14] F. Ohly, *Schriften zur mittelalterlichen Bedeutungsforschung* (Darmstadt, 1977), pp. 14-15.

[15] M. Keen, *Das Rittertum* (1984, translation by H. Ehrhard: Munich, Zürich, 1987), pp. 81-99.

[16] H. Boockmann, *Der Deutsche Orden* (Munich, 1981), pp. 66-92; *idem, Deutsche Geschichte im Osten Europas: Ostpreußen und Westpreußen* (Berlin, 1992), pp. 116-28.

supremacy for the order in Livonia, although its position there was not so dominant as eventually in Prussia.[17] In the Baltic the order was involved in the struggle against the pagan Prussians, Lithuanians, and against the schismatics, which meant the Orthodox Russians, and the order served the church in the Baltic as well. Its brethren fought for the faith there, as they did in the Holy Land. The popes themselves had put the fight against the pagans in the Baltic on the same level as the crusades in the Latin East. This view had a long tradition and was widespread in the German nobility.[18]

Nevertheless, in the eyes of contemporaries the engagement in the Holy Land and the reconquest of Jerusalem was more meritorious than the fight against the pagans in the Baltic. Thus, for Hermann von Salza and his immediate successors, the defence of the Holy Land took precedence over the conquest of the Baltic. Until the middle of the thirteenth century the difference between the two factions in the order – the papal and the imperial – took precedence over all other arguments. After the death of Frederick II in 1250, when the conflict between the popes and the emperors became less important, members of the order reflected on the operations in the Latin East and the Baltic. The engagement in both regions demanded the mobilization of knights, with men and supplies to support them. In the Latin East, after Jerusalem had been lost in 1244, the castle of Montfort was threatened. It was attacked in 1266, but not conquered, and was finally taken by Baibars in 1271. His army appeared before the walls of Acre within the same year, but retreated.[19] The situation of the Christians and the Teutonic Knights in the Latin East was critical. In Prussia, native tribes revolted against the order for the first time from 1243 to 1249. In 1260, the order suffered a defeat against the Lithuanians near Durben, and during that year Curonians and Semigallians rebelled in the south of Livonia. Simultaneously the order had to face another rebellion of the Prussians: in Prussia the last tribes were not subjugated until 1283.[20] The fights in the Latin East and in the Baltic were a very expensive burden on the order's resources; many knights lost their lives and had to be replaced. It became necessary to set

---

[17] H. von zur Mühlen, 'Livland von der Christianisierung bis zum Ende der Selbständigkeit (etwa 1180-1561)', *Deutsche Geschichte im Osten Europas: Baltische Länder*, ed. G. von Pistohlkors (Berlin, 1994), pp. 90-101.

[18] H.-D. Kahl, 'Zum Ergebnis des Wendenkreuzzugs von 1147', *Wichmann Jahrbuch* 11/12 (1957/58) 99-120; H. E. Mayer, *Geschichte der Kreuzzüge* (8th edn, Stuttgart, 1995), pp. 93-94.

[19] Forstreuter, pp. 47-49, 232-33.

[20] Boockmann, *Deutsche Geschichte*, pp. 113-15; von zur Mühlen, pp. 67-68.

priorities. In the conflict about the distribution of resources, the supporters of the Holy Land were at first successful. The order was and still remained an offspring of the crusade movement and felt therefore more responsible for the defence of the Latin East than for the conquest of the Baltic. The headquarters of the order were still in Acre, and not in Prussia as in the later period. The most important officers such as the grand commander (Großkomtur), the supreme marshal (Oberster Marschall), the supreme hospitaller (Oberster Spittler), the supreme draper (Oberster Trappier) and the treasurer (Treßler) lived in the headquarters. From this group of leading brethren only the master was often absent though most of the chapters general took place in Acre. The master and the chapter general appointed the Deutschmeister (the master over the bailiwicks in Germany), the masters of Prussia and Livonia and the most important officers in the Latin East.[21]

Only the master and the chapter general together could change or modify the rules. Therefore, one of the most important tasks of the master and his officers was to watch over the rule and to preserve a uniform standard of life for the whole order. It was in this context that the master, perhaps Heinrich von Hohenlohe, sent Grand Commander Eberhard of Sayn as his representative to the brethren in Prussia and Livonia in the middle of the thirteenth century. Eberhard of Sayn decreed that no office-holder should promulgate new rules without the consent of the master and the chapter general in the Holy Land. On the contrary the brethren in the Baltic were referred to the rules in the Latin East again and again. Once a year the masters of Prussia and Livonia had to send a written report on the order's situation in their regions to the master and his chapter in Acre, and every second or third year one brother had to render account personally.[22] Eberhard of Sayn left no doubt that the order's headquarters were in the Latin East.

After the death of master Heinrich von Hohenlohe in 1249, the brethren in the Holy Land succeeded in inserting a new provision into the order's rules: the master was forbidden to go to the West on his own responsibility; in future he had to ask for permission from the headquarters' chapter. He had to account for the necessity of the journey and to appoint a representative for the time of his absence with the consent of the chapter. The chapter could dismiss the representative and replace him by another brother.[23] The new provision corre-

---

[21] *Statuten*, p. 97.

[22] *Statuten*, pp. 161-62.

[23] *Statuten*, pp. 99-100, 'Gewohnheit' 12.

sponded well with Eberhard of Sayn's instructions for Prussia and Livonia. Since the headquarters and the centre of the order were supposed to be in the Holy Land, the master had to stay and live there and could leave it only on rare occasions.

The new regulation could not tie the master to the headquarters. Nevertheless the chapter general had probably already reinforced the provision during the mastership of Anno von Sangerhausen between 1256 and 1273. According to this decision, the chapter had to examine the master's request, to decide whether he was allowed to go or not and to fix the period of his absence. If the master exceeded the temporal limits he was automatically deposed. Thus, he could no longer take his own decision whether a journey to the West was necessary.[24] The chapter's decision was taken by the most important brethren living in the Holy Land.

In the order's branch in the Holy Land a faction had been established that wanted to keep the master in the headquarters in Acre. This faction stressed the pre-eminence of the defence of the Holy Land against the fight for the faith in the Baltic and insisted on the new regulation even when Montfort Castle was taken by Baibars and the order was thrown back on Acre and its surroundings. Even after 1271, the order bought estates of the Frankish nobility in the Latin East and thereby spent a lot of money. Consequently, it was able to expand within the surroundings of Acre and to build up its own territory. Some of the new estates, in fact, never came into the hands of the order since they remained under Muslim control.[25] The order's branch in the Holy Land needed a lot of money and laid claim to a great part of the resources of the bailiwicks in the German empire. The money and goods invested in Palestine were thus not available in Prussia and Livonia where the brethren fought for their survival. In consequence, the brethren in the Baltic began to protest against the policies of the pro-Palestine faction and its claims, but could not yet succeed because the headquarters were still in the Holy Land and where most of the chapters general took place as well. These chapters were dominated by brethren from Palestine, most of them belonging to the faction stressing the importance of the defence of the Holy Land. Neither the pope nor the emperor intervened to support one or the other of these factions; they kept out and left the decision to the brethren's discretion.

---

[24] *Statuten*, p. 135.

[25] *Tabulae*, nos 113, 119, 120, 121, 122.

When the situation for the Christians in Palestine became hopeless the influence of the Baltic faction grew, and already the last master living in the headquarters in Acre, Burchard von Schwanden, was confronted with this development. When he returned to Palestine in 1290, he was accompanied by forty knights and about 400 crusaders, but this contingent was not strong enough to attack the Muslim armies or even to keep the Muslims from attacking the Christian strongholds.[26] Burchard resigned, left the order, and entered the Hospitallers. He went back to Switzerland, his homeland, and became a commander of one of the Hospitallers' houses there.[27]

Burchard's counterpart in the Teutonic Order was Konrad von Feuchtwangen, an important representative or even the leader of the Baltic faction. He rejected measures for an effective support of the Holy Land and did not follow Burchard in defending Acre and the Holy Land.[28] After the fall of Acre in 1291, he was elected master of the order. Even after his election, he opposed any further engagement in the Holy Land and did everything to support the struggle against the pagans in the Baltic. Under his direction the order began to redefine its aims. Its headquarters were established at Venice and not on Cyprus, and the order did not care for the refugees from Acre who came to Cyprus, as the Templars and Hospitallers did.[29] More than the other military orders, it retired from the affairs of the Holy Land. But Konrad von Feuchtwangen could not realize all his plans. He died in 1296, before he had succeeded in transferring the order's headquarters to Prussia.

When Acre fell, the master lost important functions. He no longer had the leading part in the fight for the faith against the Muslims, and he was not able to take over control in the struggle against the pagans in the Baltic, because this was the task of the masters of Prussia and Livonia. Furthermore, the master's attendance was not necessary for the administration of the bailiwicks in

---

[26] T. Hirsch (ed.), 'Nikolaus von Jeroschin, Reimchronik', *Scriptores rerum Prussicarum*, eds T. Hirsch, M. Toeppen, E. Strehlke, vol. 1 (Leipzig, 1861), pp. 513-14; Forstreuter, pp. 51-52.

[27] D. Wojtecki, *Studien zur Personalgeschichte des Deutschen Ordens im 13. Jahrhundert*. Quellen und Studien zur Geschichte des östlichen Europa 3 (Wiesbaden, 1971), pp. 100-101.

[28] U. Arnold, 'Deutschmeister Konrad von Feuchtwangen und die "preußische Partei" im Deutschen Orden am Ende des 13. und zu Beginn des 14. Jahrhunderts', *Aspekte der Geschichte. Festschrift für Peter Gerrit Thielen zu seinem 65. Geburtstag*, eds U. Arnold, J. Schröder, G. Walzik (Göttingen, 1990), pp. 22-42.

[29] M.-L. Favreau-Lilie, 'The military orders and the Escape of the Christian Population from the Holy Land in 1291', *Journal of Medieval History* 19 (1993) 201-17, at p. 223.

the German empire, since this task pertained to the Deutschmeister. Moreover, many regulations in the statutes were designed for a situation when the order had its headquarters in the Holy Land, and this held true especially for the masters' election.[30] Normally, the masters had to be elected in the headquarters. The grand commander (Großkomtur) invited the electors, among them the Deutschmeister and the masters of Prussia and Livonia as the most important officers outside the headquarters, but it was left to them to decide if they deemed it necessary to attend. The grand commander (Großkomtur) also invited the leaders of less important bailiwicks like those of Greece (Morea), Apulia, Austria, or Armenia because their bailiwicks were located around the Mediterranean. Thus, this procedure was related to having the headquarters in the Holy Land and could not be abolished in a short time. It may have been a good compromise to establish the new headquarters at Venice since this decision enabled the order to maintain the old structures for some time whilst discussing the order's policies.

In Venice, master and treasurer lacked the incomes from the estates in the Holy Land and had no real compensation for these. If the old system had been maintained, the office of the master would have suffered a decline because the master would have lost his main tasks and a part of his incomes. In the long run, the master might even have lost his important position and his prestige as the head of the order, if he were not able to develop a new mission for himself. Konrad von Feuchtwangen had died before achieving substantial changes. Neither pope nor king could help the order in solving its problems. The pope was occupied with his attempts to promote a new crusade, while he also tried to strengthen his supremacy in Christendom. And while King Adolf von Nassau was hardly able to maintain his own position, his successor, Albrecht I von Österreich, was involved in other political affairs and did not care much for the order.

When Konrad's successor, Gottfried von Hohenlohe, was elected master in Venice in 1297, he first had to confirm an article by oath which tied him to the headquarters in Venice and which restricted his freedom of movement.[31] The faction which supported a crusade to the Holy Land had again gained the upper hand against the Baltic faction favoured by Konrad von Feuchtwangen. But as a successful crusade against the Muslims in Palestine became more and more illusory, the crusade faction in the headquarters at Venice lost its support

---

[30] *Statuten*, pp. 90-95, 'Gewohnheiten' 2-6.

[31] *Statuten*, pp. 144-45.

within the order, and the influence of the Baltic faction grew. Then, during the last years of the thirteenth century, a new threat arose: after the fall of Acre in 1291, influential clerics proposed a union of the military orders to improve the fighting power of the Christian armies in a crusade against the Muslims. If this had been realized the Teutonic Order would have lost its independence, and, more than that, the Baltic faction would have been deprived of its newly-gained influence, and Prussia and Livonia would again have become peripheral and of little importance. But this was only a danger for the future, another development was more threatening. In the first years of the fourteenth century, it became clear that the Holy See could no longer protect the Templars against attacks by the French king.[32] Accusations like the ones brought forward in the trial of the Templars could easily have been directed at other military orders. When the pope went from Rome to Avignon in 1309 and thus settled in the sphere of influence of the French kings, the danger for the Teutonic Knights became obvious. In this same year, Master Siegfried von Feuchtwangen was forced by the Baltic faction to transfer the order's headquarters to Marienburg castle in Prussia. In taking this decision, the Teutonic Order turned its back on its origins in the Holy Land and gave up any hope of a new successful crusade against the Muslims. It also escaped the threat of abolition or a union with other military orders and became, at least partly, emancipated from the influence of the pope and, even more, that of the emperors. It had moved its headquarters into a territory dominated by itself.

By transferring the order's headquarters to Marienburg castle in Prussia in 1309, Siegfried von Feuchtwangen had not overcome all obstacles; in the following years, other difficulties would arise. Nevertheless, the transfer turned out to be of value for the future and influenced the history of the order until modern times. Finally, the Baltic faction had won against the supporters of the order's engagement in the Holy Land. While the Teutonic Order had withdrawn from the Mediterranean, from fighting for the faith and from the defence of Christendom in this area, it had gained more independence from popes, emperors, and kings. From now, and for a long time to come, the order's development was connected with the Baltic.

---

[32] M. Barber, *The New Knighthood* (Cambridge, 1994), pp. 280-313; M. Barber, *The Trial of the Templars* (Cambridge, 1993), *passim*.

6

Kings and Priors:

the Hospitaller Priory of England in the Later

Fifteenth Century

Jürgen Sarnowsky

The medieval military orders were powerful institutions. Having attracted many donations for the defence of the Holy Land they possessed large estates in and considerable incomes from most European countries. In the later Middle Ages the Spanish military orders dominated large areas in Andalusia, while two of the greater orders, the Hospitallers and the Teutonic Knights, succeeded in building up their own territories in the Aegean and in Prussia, regions where there were no strong Christian rulers to restrain them.[1] Though some of the military orders, the Spanish orders, the Teutonic Knights, and the English order of St Thomas of Acre, were primarily confined to parts of Europe, they were in theory and often in reality 'supranational' and independent of local and regional powers, having been established to defend Christianity as a whole against the 'infidels'. This could lead to conflict, especially where princes sought to strengthen their rule by gaining control over ecclesiastical institutions. Thus the growing military and financial strength of the Templars in

---

[1] For a general history of the military orders up to 1300 see A. Forey, *The Military Orders from the Twelfth to the Early Fourteenth Centuries* (London, 1992); cf. also *Die geistlichen Ritterorden Europas*, eds J. Fleckenstein, M. Hellmann. Vorträge und Forschungen XXVI (Sigmaringen, 1980); *MO*; *MS*. The main body of research for this article has been made possible by a Heisenberg scholarship of the Deutsche Forschungsgemeinschaft. I also wish to thank Edith Pawlik, Hamburg, for revising the first English version of this paper. The faults that remain are mine.

France probably led to the suppression of the order by Philippe le Bel at the beginning of the fourteenth century.[2]

The case of the Templars was an exception, but from time to time the other military orders also ran into difficulties when their policies or even their internal regulations contradicted royal ambitions. This holds true for the Hospitallers in England, where the brethren of the order had been organized in their own priory since the middle of the twelfth century.[3] The priors of England soon became prominent in English politics. One of them, Fr Robert Hales, then Treasurer of England, was a victim of the Peasants' Revolt in 1381.[4] Ninety years later, in 1471, one of his successors, who was also Treasurer of England at that time, Fr John Langstrother, having sided with the reinstated Henry VI, met a similar fate, when he was captured and beheaded after the battle of Tewkesbury.[5] This case makes clear the necessity for English kings of gaining influence upon the nomination of priors, especially in troubled times when they had to seize all opportunities for securing their position. In my paper I will attempt to analyse the relationship between kings and priors in one troubled period of English history, the later fifteenth century, first in terms of the political role of priors (1440 to 1501),[6] then in terms of problems arising from the 'election' of new priors.

---

[2] For the Templars see e.g. M. Barber, *The New Knighthood. A History of the Order of the Temple* (Cambridge, 1994).

[3] J. Riley-Smith, *The Knights of St John in Jerusalem and Cyprus, c. 1050-1310. A History of the Order of the Hospital of St John* 1 (London, 1967), pp. 357-58.

[4] Cf. e.g. M. McKisack, *The Fourteenth Century, 1307-1399.* The Oxford History of England, 5 (Oxford, 1959, reprinted 1988), p. 412. For the history of the English priory in general see e.g. E. King, *The Knights of St John in the British Realm,* 3rd edn by H. Luke (London, 1967); W. K. R. Bedford, R. Holbeche, *The Order of the Hospital of St John of Jerusalem. Being a History of the English Hospitallers of St John, Their Rise and Progress* (London, 1902); C. Tyerman, *England and the Crusades, 1095-1588* (Chicago, London, 1988), esp. pp. 354-58. Here as below 'Fr' is used for *frater,* i.e. Hospitaller brother.

[5] 1471 May 6, for the events see e.g. *Historie of the Arrivall of Edward IV in England and the Finall Recouerye of His Kingdoms from Henry VI. A.D. M.CCCCLXXI,* ed. J. Bruce. Camden first Series 1 (London, 1838), p. 31; John Warkworth, *A Chronicle of the First Thirteen Years of King Edward the Fourth,* ed. J. O. Halliwell. Camden first Series 10 (London, 1839), pp. 18-19. Cf. King-Luke, p. 73, and C. Ross, *Edward IV.* English Monarchs (London, 1974; reprinted 1991), p. 172.

[6] Since there is a already biographical study on Fr Robert Malory (P. J. C. Field, 'Sir Robert Malory, Prior of the Hospital of St John of Jerusalem in England (1432-1439/40)', *Journal of Ecclesiastical History* 28 (1977) 249-64) – though not without mistakes – it is convenient to start with Fr Robert Botyll (prior 1440-1468) and to end with Fr John Kendall (prior 1489-1501) for an analysis of the later fifteenth century.

The Hospitaller priors in English politics

The political role of the Hospitaller priors of England has been characterized by Christopher Tyerman in his book on 'England and the Crusades' as follows: 'The prior was automatically a royal councillor. ... Although a member of a religious order, [he] was also the premier baron of England, ranking above all lay barons and immediately after dukes, earls and marquesses.'[7] This statement is confirmed even by an incomplete survey of the sources. The five legitimate priors from 1440 to 1501, Fr Robert Botyll, Fr John Langstrother, Fr William Tornay, Fr John Weston, and Fr John Kendall, often stayed at the royal court, took part in law suits and inquests or went on diplomatic missions.

Though Fr Robert Botyll, prior since 1440, continued to participate in the affairs of the Hospitallers after his 'election', in 1446 to 1447, by presiding – with others – over the Roman chapter general of the order,[8] from the beginning he was engaged in the royal service.[9] There he witnessed several important events at the English court, as for example in March 1450, when the Duke of Suffolk was condemned to exile,[10] or in April 1454, when Edward, the infant son of Henry VI, was created Prince of Wales.[11] In the 1450s, he was one of the 'intimate councillors'[12] who visited Henry during his mental illness. As was reported to John Paston, Botyll and others wept for joy when, in January 1455, the king 'spoke to them as well as he ever did'.[13] The prior also took part when Henry received oaths of allegiance after the first battle of St Albans in July

---

[7] Tyerman, p. 355 (with reference to the 'contemporary illustration of the 1512 parliament procession, when the prior was Thomas Docwra'); this is confirmed by the rank of the priors in earlier lists, cf. n. 14, 17, and 21 below, and by a royal letter from 7 November 1461, which calls Robert Botyll *primus baronus nostri regni Anglie*, T. Rymer (ed.), *Foedera, Conventiones, Literae, et cujuscunque generis acta publica*, 3rd edn rev. G. Holmes, vol. 5 (Den Haag, 1741), part 2, p. 105a.

[8] Cf. R. Valentini, 'Un capitolo generale degli Ospitalieri di S. Giovanni tenuto in Vaticano nel 1446', *Archivio Storico di Malta* 7 (1936) 133-68, at p. 142.

[9] See below, n. 38-39.

[10] *Rotuli Parliamentorum; ut et petitiones et placita in parliamento*, VI vols (n.p., n.d. [London, 1777-1783]), V, p. 182b.

[11] *Rotuli Parliamentorum* V, p. 249b, and *CPR, Henry VI*, 6, AD 1452-1461 (London, 1911), pp. 171-72; for the events cf. e.g. B. Wolffe, *Henry VI*. English Monarchs (London, 1981), pp. 225-28, and 278.

[12] Wolffe, p. 273.

[13] *The Paston Letters*, ed. J. Gairdner (1904; reprinted Gloucester 1986), vol. 3, p. 13. For a special commission to speak with the king in March 1454 see *Rotuli Parliamentorum* V, p. 240b.

1455 and again in December 1459.[14] But this did not prevent him from changing sides when Edward IV came to power, and he remained in that king's favour until his death in 1468. His successor, Fr John Langstrother, went over to Henry VI and played an important role during his restoration. He probably continued to be in the royal entourage until he was ordered to conduct Queen Margaret and Henry's son, Prince Edward, who arrived too late to prevent the final victory of Edward IV.[15] When Langstrother had been executed in May 1471, the king extracted a fine from the Hospitallers. The new prior, Fr William Tornay, and three other brethren were fined £300 for the order's participation in the rebellion.[16] But Tornay stayed at court, and in July 1471 he was among a group of lords who recognized young Edward, prince of Wales as his father's heir.[17] He was succeeded by Fr John Weston, who was prior in the last decade of the Wars of the Roses and the first years of Henry VII, apparently without being involved in the political unrest of the period. In 1484 he spent some time in Rome, where Innocent VIII appointed him a member of his household and requested safe conduct for his journey to Richard III.[18] At least he was present at Richard's court in the spring of 1485.[19] Only when Weston was succeeded by Fr John Kendall did the Hospitaller prior once more become prominent in English politics.[20] Thus Kendall was present at a tournament when the future Henry VIII was dubbed knight and created Duke of York in the autumn of 1494,[21] and in November 1499, he was a member of the grand jury

---

[14] *Rotuli Parliamentorum* V, pp. 283a and 352a; Tyerman's observations are confirmed by the place of the prior in the two lists of liegemen who swore allegiance to the king.

[15] Langstrother was sent to conduct the queen and her son in February 1471, see Rymer, 5, 2, p. 189b, but Margaret landed only in April, Wolffe, pp. 345-46. For Langstrother's role as a leading opponent of Edward IV during this time see *The Crowland Chronicle Continuations*: 1459-1486, eds N. Pronay, J. Cox (London, 1986), p. 126.

[16] See Ross, *Edward IV*, p. 183.

[17] *Rotuli Parliamentorum* VI, p. 234b; *CCR, Edward IV*, 2, AD 1468-1476 (London, 1953), pp. 229-30; the prior is among the first of the lay barons. The year in the document is '11 Edw IV', though July 1471 is very close to the execution of Langstrother.

[18] *Calendar of the Entries in the Papal Registers relating to Great Britain and Ireland*, XIV, 1484-1492 (London, 1960), p. 5 (1484 Nov. 30 and Dec. 31).

[19] King-Luke, p. 74, assembly of the lords of the realm and the mayor and citizens of London in Clerkenwell; for the context see C. Ross, *Richard III*. English Monarchs (London, 1981), p. 145.

[20] For Kendall cf. my article in the New DNB, forthcoming.

[21] *Letters and Papers illustrative of the reigns of Richard III and Henry VII*, ed. J. Gairdner. Rolls Series 24 (London, 1861-1863), 1, pp. 388-404, esp. p. 402 (the prior again is the first of the lay barons).

which found Edward, earl of Warwick, one of the presumptive heirs of Richard III, guilty of high treason.[22] That the prior took part in these proceedings is a bit odd since he himself may have been accused of a conspiracy against Henry VII three years earlier. According to a document from March 1496, one of his servants, a certain Bernard de Vignolles, confessed that his master, two of his nephews, and others had been looking for 'means and ways to achieve to let die the king of England' and to replace him with the Yorkist pretender Perkin Warbeck.[23] Whatever the truth behind the story, Kendall was granted a general pardon in August 1496 and appears to have remained in the king's favour.[24] The priors continued to form part of the king's entourage until the dissolution of the order in England in April 1540.[25]

When present at court, the priors were involved in the affairs of the realm, especially since they were regularly summoned to parliament by the *premunientes* clause which was also used for other lords spiritual.[26] Therefore they were called upon periodically to inquire into judicial and administrative problems; in February 1452 Fr Robert Botyll, Richard earl of Warwick, and others examined complaints against one of the king's commissaries for the governance of Normandy, and in February 1453 he and others heard an appeal against the

---

[22] *Plumpton Correspondence. A series of letters chiefly domestick, written in the reigns of Edward IV, Richard III, Henry VII and Henry VIII*, ed. T. Stapleton. Camden first Series 4 (London, 1839), p. 143.

[23] Kendal and two others (*estans a Romme firent cherche de trouver*) *moien et faczon de entreprendre faire mourir le roy d'Angleterre ...*; *Letters ... Richard III and Henry VII*, 2, pp. 318-23. Cf. F. Madden, 'Documents relating to Perkin Warbeck, with Remarks on his history', *Archaeologia* 27 (1838) 153-210, esp. pp. 171-74; I. Arthurson, *The Perkin Warbeck Conspiracy, 1491-1499* (Stroud, Glouc., 1991).

[24] *CPR, Henry VII*, 2, AD 1494-1509 (London, 1916), p. 49. Maybe Kendall sought to obtain this general pardon for security; for the practice of general pardons cf. A. L. Brown, *The Governance of Late Medieval England, 1272-1461*. The Governance of England 3 (London, 1989), pp. 48, 106, and 138-39.

[25] Tyerman, pp. 356-58.

[26] For the *premunientes* clause and the summoning of the lords spiritual cf. Brown, pp. 182-83. The priors were summoned e.g. in 1439, 1445-1447, 1449-1450, 1453, 1455, 1459-1463, 1469, 1470, 1472, 1482, 1483, 1487, and 1496, *CCR, Henry VI*, 3, AD 1435-1441 (London, 1937), p. 337; 4, AD 1441-1447 (London, 1937), pp. 279, 454, and 465; 5, AD 1447-1454 (London, 1941), pp.160, 225, and 394; 6, AD 1454-1461 (London, 1939), pp. 25, 421 and 462; *CCR, Edward IV*, 1, AD 1461-1468 (London, 1953), pp. 59, 162-63; 2, pp. 86 (cancelled ibid., p. 115), 176, and 255; *CCR, Edward IV – Edward V – Richard III*, AD 1476-1485 (London, 1954), p. 290 and 340; *CCR, Henry VII*, 1, AD 1485-1500 (London, 1955), pp. 69 and 287.

judgement of the Mayor and aldermen of Calais.[27] During the parliament of
July 1455, the prior joined two committees formed to discuss the financial
problems of Calais and Berwick and the retention of gold and silver in the
realm.[28] In February 1460, he also acted as a local royal justice, when he received the commission of oyer and terminer for London and its suburbs, in which
position he heard and determined cases of treason and other offences.[29] In
1461, 1465, and 1467, he was four times Commissioner of the Peace and of
Array for Middlesex.[30] The important political role of the priors continued
when Fr John Langstrother became prior in 1469. He was created Treasurer of
England, and in October 1470, he and others were commissioned to inquire
into felonies, homicides, and other offences in the county of Middlesex.[31] Finally, in February 1471, he and John Delves were granted the offices of warden
of the exchange and mint in London for life, responsible for England and Calais.[32] His successor, Fr William Tornay, was one of the members of a parlia-
mentary committee which collected the payment of a tenth on all incomes
which had been granted to Edward IV in October 1472.[33] From 1485 to 1488,
Fr John Weston was several times Commissioner of the Peace for Middlesex,
Essex, Kent, and Warwickshire, mainly in areas with landed property of the
order.[34] Finally Fr John Kendall also played a very active role. In 1492 and
from 1495 to 1500, he was Justice of the Peace and Commissioner of the Peace
in Essex and Middlesex,[35] and in 1493, he was nominated Commissioner of the
Peace for several counties.[36] In May 1497, he and others had to control the state

---

[27] *CPR, Henry VI*, 5, AD 1446-1452 (London, 1911), p. 444, and 6, p. 42, cf. J. Ferguson, *English Diplomacy, 1422-1461* (Oxford, 1972), p. 188.

[28] *Rotuli Parliamentorum* V, pp. 279b and 280a, cf. Wolffe, p. 296.

[29] *CPR, Henry VI*, 6, p. 565; for the commission of oyer and terminer cf. Brown, pp. 116
and 118-19.

[30] *CPR, Edward IV*, AD 1461-1467 (London, 1897), p. 567.

[31] *CPR, Edward IV – Henry VI*, AD 1467-1477 (London, 1900), p. 248; for his nomination as Treasurer of England see below. He was also Commissioner of the Peace for
Middlesex, ibid., pp. 621-22.

[32] Rymer, 5, 2, p. 191b; *CPR, Edward IV – Henry VI*, p. 239.

[33] *Rotuli Parliamentorum* VI, pp. 6a-8a and 42a-b; cf. Ross, *Edward IV*, p. 215.

[34] Six times in Middlesex (1485-1487), thrice in Kent (1485 and 1487), and twice in
Essex and Warwickshire (1485, 1487, 1488), *CPR, Henry VII*, 1, AD 1485-1494 (London, 1914), pp. 486, 489-90, 493, and 503.

[35] *CPR, Henry VII*, 1, p. 405, and 2, pp. 49, 638, and 650.

[36] In *CPR, Henry VII*, 1, pp. 481-82, 484, 488-97, 500, and 503-8, he is mentioned as
commissioner of the peace for Buckinghamshire, Derbyshire, Hertfordshire, Hunting-

of fortifications in Lincolnshire, and in the same year in June, he was a member of a committee convened to inquire into the activities of participants in various rebellions in southern England.[37]

Sometimes the priors were required to travel to the Continent on diplomatic missions and were involved in peace negotiations or preparations for war. Though after his election to prior in 1440 Fr Robert Botyll first went to Rhodes, he soon came back and, in 1442, took over an embassy to the German electors.[38] In 1446 to 1449, he was sent to Charles VII of France and to Pope Nicholas V;[39] in 1451, he went to Utrecht to negotiate with representatives of the Hanseatic League, to the pope, and to Alfonso V of Aragon;[40] twice, in 1458 and 1461, he was commissioned with others to negotiate the truce with Burgundy,[41] and in 1466, he was again one of the emissaries sent to Philip of Burgundy.[42] In December 1470, Botyll's unlucky successor, Fr John Langstrother, was a member of the commission inquiring about complaints from Spanish merchants, and in February 1471, he and others had to bring about a truce with France.[43] More than twenty years later, in June 1492, Fr John Kendall took part in peace negotiations, again with France.[44] In February 1496, he was a member of an embassy to the Emperor's son, Archduke Philip, Duke of Burgundy.[45] In June 1500, he went to Calais and met Philip in the company of the king.[46] On a very different level, in 1475, the disputed Prior Fr Robert Multon

---

donshire, Leicestershire, Lincolnshire, Middlesex, Northamptonshire, Nottinghamshire, Oxfordshire, Staffordshire, Warwickshire, Worcestershire, and Yorkshire.

[37] *CPR, Henry VII*, 2, pp. 90 and 118.

[38] Ferguson, pp. 116 and 118, cf. *Memorials of the Reign of King Henry VI. Official Correspondance of Thomas Bekyngton*, ed. G. Williams. Rolls Series, 56 (London 1872), 1, pp. 80-81, 87-90, 210-11.

[39] *CPR, Henry VI*, 5, pp. 284 and 376-77 (concerns the payment of his wages, 1449 April 27, and 1450 Mai 30); *Rotuli Parliamentorum* V, p. 237a; Rymer, 5, 1, pp. 183a-184a (*Inspeximus* of the truce with France, 1447 Nov. 4). For this mission see also Ferguson, pp. 139-40, 179, and 214.

[40] Ferguson, pp. 103-4, 199 and 206; *Hanserecesse, Zweite Abteilung, von 1431-1476*, ed. G. Frhr. von der Ropp, vol. 3 (Leipzig, 1881), no. 709 and 712, esp. pp. 536, 539-41 and 563.

[41] Rymer, 5, 2, p. 80a-b (1458 May 14); ibid., p. 106a, and *CPR, Edward IV*, p. 102 (12 November 1461).

[42] Rymer, 5, 2, p. 143a.

[43] Ibid., pp. 181a-182b and 185a-188a.

[44] Rymer, 5, 4, p. 45a-b.

[45] Ibid., pp. 82b-86b.

[46] *Letters ... Richard III and Henry VII*, 2, p. 87.

took muster of soldiers who were to be sent to France, and was retained as Warden for the Marches towards Scotland, together with the Earl of Northumberland.[47] The wide range of tasks conferred upon the Hospitaller priors of England is an indication of their prominent position in English politics during the later fifteenth century.

The election of the Hospitaller priors of England

The Hospitallers were among the greatest landowners in England and their prior was 'one of the great magnates of the kingdom, given power, money, and access to the king'.[48] In consequence the English kings tried to ensure that the 'election' of new priors took place in England itself, that the new prior would support their policies, and that he would willingly take over the tasks conferred upon him. This conflicted with the internal regulations of the order which required that all priors be 'elected' by the chapters general or – in the periods in between chapters – by the master and his council on Rhodes.[49] The main criteria for this 'election' were how long the brother had been member of the order and how long he had stayed on Rhodes 'at the border of christendom'. Thus, the chapter general of 1433 decreed that no one could be elected prior or bailiff who had not been on Rhodes for more than ten years.[50] This statute was revised in 1446 during the Roman chapter general. From then on, the future prior was required have been a member of the order for fifteen years of which at least five should have been spent on Rhodes.[51] In many cases it was the groupings of brethren in the convent on Rhodes, the 'tongues', which decided who best fulfilled the criteria.[52] But they also had to take into account the situation in the western priories. In fact, there appear to have been many 'elec-

---

[47] *CPR, Edward IV – Henry VI*, pp. 526 and 545 (23 May and 22 July 1475); cf. *CCR, Edward IV*, 2, p. 386.

[48] Field, p. 249.

[49] Riley-Smith, pp. 360-61; cf. the regulations in *CGOH*, 2, nos 1193 and 2213, pp. 34-35 and 109; 3, no. 3396, 7, p. 227.

[50] See e.g. the French version of the statutes in Paris, Bibliothèque Nationale, Franç. 17255, fol. 110v.

[51] Paris, Bibliothèque Nationale, Franç. 17255, fol. 123r; this regulation was renewed in the revised version of the statutes compiled by the Vice-Chancellor Guillaume Caoursin and others in 1489, see the manuscript of the Latin version in NLM Libr. 244, fol. 105v.

[52] Cf. J. Sarnowsky, 'Der Konvent auf Rhodos und die Zungen (*lingue*) im Johanniterorden (1421-1476)', *RR*, pp. 43-65, at p. 55.

tions' of priors which did not conform to the statutes. Thus, for example, in 1440, when Fr Robert Malory died,[53] the English Hospitallers 'elected' Fr Robert Botyll and the king asked the master, Fr Jean de Lastic, to confirm this 'election'.[54] In his letter, Henry pointed out that 'the prior ... according to the customs and laws of our kingdom must be one of the lords of our parliament and our great councils';[55] therefore, he had appealed to the English brethren to 'elect' one who was qualified for these tasks. Though Robert was confirmed by master and convent,[56] it was likely no accident that he decided to go to Rhodes when it was attacked by the Mamluks and only afterwards embarked upon the diplomatic mission which had been imposed on him by the king;[57] perhaps he first had to secure his position by demonstrating his zeal for his order.

When Botyll died in 1468,[58] new problems arose. The English brethren in the convent were probably in favour of Fr John Langstrother, the Bailiff of Eagle and former turcopolier of the order.[59] But it seems that he was known to be a supporter of the Lancastrian cause,[60] which was perhaps the reason why Edward IV was reluctant to confirm him as Prior of England. Since in the meantime the priory was kept vacant, master and convent acted with as much caution as possible. In April 1469, they decided to send Langstrother himself to

---

[53] For the date of his death (after 16 December 1439) cf. Field, p. 257.

[54] See the letters of Henry VI in *Memorials ... Bekyngton*, 1, pp. 78-81, 86-87. There is some confusion concerning the dates of the letters. Since no. LXI renders thanks for the confirmation of Botyll which has been asked for in no. LX, it (and no. LXII) must be dated 29 April 1441, so that '19 Hen VI' is correct. Cf. also n. 57.

[55] *Prior ... juxta regni nostri consuetudines et jura esse debeat unus ex dominis parliamenti nostri et magnorum conciliorum nostrorum ...*, ibid., p. 78.

[56] As is evident from Henry's letter, ibid., p.81; he was confirmed during the Rhodian chapter general in November 1440, cf. NLM Arch.354, fol. 208r.

[57] See n. 38. For this journey to Rhodes, Henry recommended Botyll to the Venetians, *Memorials ... Bekyngton*, 1, pp. 210-11 (12 May 1441). 10-11 February 1442 (again '20 Hen VI' is the correct year), he admonished Botyll who was then staying on Rhodes to go on his mission to the German electors, ibid., pp. 87-90.

[58] In this context, the date of his death is important, but not easy to determine. King-Luke, p. 72, has September 1467; Bedford, p. 188, has 1468, but there is little direct evidence. In *CPR, Edward IV*, p. 507, a certain John Yorke is convicted on 12 October 1467 for not appearing to answer the prior, and in *CPR, Edward IV – Henry VI*, p. 132, dated 15 November 1468, the prior is one of the witnesses for a writ of privy seal. If these dates are correct, Botyll died after November 1468, which reduces the time of the vacancy.

[59] For the office of turcopolier cf. Riley-Smith, p. 325.

[60] King-Luke, p. 72. In May 1440, Henry VI had recommended him and his brother William to the master, Fr Jean de Lastic, cf. *Memorials ... Bekyngton*, 1, p. 85.

England. In his instructions nothing is said regarding his designation as prior. His task was to make an urgent appeal to Edward IV to allow the nomination of a new prior 'according to the form of the statutes'.[61] He had to describe the negative results for England and for other provinces as well if the prior could not be 'elected' that way and had to point to the pressing financial problems of the order. When he arrived in England, the country had entered a period of political instability which it had not experienced since the Norman Conquest,[62] and Langstrother was drawn into the struggle. In August 1469, the Earl of Warwick took over control of the government, and his supporter, John, became Treasurer of England.[63] When Edward resumed power in October, Langstrother was replaced by William, Bishop of Ely,[64] but soon a reconciliation was achieved. In November, the king confirmed all acts made by Langstrother as Treasurer of England, pardoned him for all offences committed by him in his office,[65] and then allowed the 'election' of a new prior. When Langstrother was presented to the king and admitted as prior, he had to swear fealty to Edward, which he did under protest.[66] The affair seemed settled in February 1470, when the king declared that he accepted the 'election' of priors by the English brethren of the order without royal licence as lawful and in no way to his detriment. Edward even confirmed after a examination of records, rolls, and documents that with one exception – an alien brother not born in England – no former priors had pledged fealty, while Langstrother had done so only under protest.[67] Only now was the way clear for the formal 'election' in the convent, which took place in April 1470.[68] The Earl of Warwick had been exiled that same month, but returned to England in October and put Edward to flight.

---

[61] *Secundum formam stabilimentorum* is a standing phrase in Hospitaller documents, here see NLM Arch. 378, fol. 163v-164v (16 April 1469).

[62] Ross, *Edward IV*, p.126.

[63] *CPR, Edward IV – Henry VI*, p. 165 (16 August 1469); cf. Ross, *Edward IV*, p. 133.

[64] *CPR, Edward IV – Henry VI*, p. 176 (25 October 1469); cf. Ross, *Edward IV*, p. 136.

[65] *CPR, Edward IV – Henry VI*, p. 177 (11 November 1469).

[66] Ibid., pp. 231-32 (following a document from 20 December 1470); *CCR, Edward IV*, 2, pp. 101-2; Rymer, 5, 2, p. 172b (and 180a), with the formula for the oath and the addition: ... *sub protestatione tamen quod hujusmodi fidelitas, sic per ipsum facta, non cedat in praejudicium dicti prioris vel successorum suorum in futurum* (18 November 1469).

[67] *CPR Edward IV – Henry VI*, p. 189 (21 February 1470); one other problem was that the prior insisted that all monies coming in during the vacancy pertained to the order for its hospitaller function and for the defence of Christianity.

[68] NLM Arch. 74, fol. 3v (new foliation: 15v) -4(16)r (5 April 1470).

Henry VI was restored, and the prior sided once again with Warwick and the Lancastrians. When he had again been accepted as prior and made fealty to Henry, again under protest,[69] he was as before appointed Treasurer of the Exchequer.[70] He continued in office until his execution following the battle of Tewkesbury in May 1471.

That Langstrother was dead was known in Rhodes by August at the latest, when master and council decided on his successor and Fr William Tornay, the Bailiff of Eagle, was 'elected' Prior of England.[71] Tornay, along with other Hospitallers, was fined by the king,[72] but he received a general pardon in February 1472[73] and probably remained unmolested for the rest of his time in office.[74] Only after his death does Edward seem to have asserted his influence. In August 1474, four Hospitaller brethren, one of these being the future Prior Fr John Kendall, presented to the king within the wardrobe in the Palace of Westminster Fr Robert Multon, whom they had unanimously 'elected' prior, and asked for royal assent. This was granted by the king, and this time the new prior paid him fealty without any sign of protest. He pledged faith and truth to the king and to his heirs, and promised to keep the king's counsel and to be obedient to him and to his commandments.[75] While Multon already acted as prior,[76] he sent his proctor to Rhodes to receive the confirmation of his 'election'. Again, the master and his council proceeded cautiously. In February 1475, when Robert's proctor had arrived at the convent and his case was being discussed in the council, Fr John Weston, the turcopolier, protested that he had a better claim to the priory than Multon because he was a conventual bailiff and had been a member of the order longer than Multon. He expressed his hope that 'the king of England for his justice and equity like as the justest prince would preserve him in his right' and proposed to present himself to Edward to

---

[69] Rymer, 5, 2, p. 178a (and 180b); *CPR, Edward IV – Henry VI*, p. 232 (20 October 1470); *CCR, Edward IV*, 2, p. 161.

[70] Rymer, 5, 2, p. 178a; *CPR, Edward IV – Henry VI*, p. 229.

[71] See NLM Arch. 74, fol. 76(88)v-77(89)r (28 August 1471). In this formal document nothing is said about Langstrother's fate, but in NLM Arch. 379, fol. 149 (8 October 1471), he is rather unusually called *nobis precarissimus frater*.

[72] See n. 16.

[73] *CPR, Edward IV – Henry VI*, p. 306 (18 February 1472).

[74] On 22 December 1472, master and convent decided to sent envoys to Edward, NLM Arch. 74, fol. 140(152)r, but this mission also concerned France and Burgundy.

[75] *CCR, Edward IV*, 2, p. 380 (with the formula for the oath, cf. n. 66).

[76] See n. 47.

avoid damage.[77] The council followed this suggestion and declined to make any decision or provision for either Multon or Weston before the case had been brought before the English king. Weston was declared Lieutenant of Master and Convent for Italy, Germany, and England and received his credential letters and instructions. But it was only in June, that he was allowed to leave the island, and then he was first required to go on a mission to Pope Sixtus IV.[78] Small wonder that nearly another year passed before news of the situation in England reached the convent. In May 1476, proctors of the English tongue appeared before master and council and related that they had received letters from Weston indicating that the king would agree to accept him as prior. But the council remained cautious. Since they had received no written answer to their letters to King Edward, they decided to postpone the matter.[79] Only in July, when Edward's response arrived, leaving the case open, was the discussion in the council resumed. After Multon's and Weston's proctors had again presented their point of view, the master and his council decided to send another mission to England. This time they appointed the draper, Spaniard Fr Nicolau Zaplana, who was instructed to explain to the king that Weston had a better claim to the priory and to take with him the bulls of master and convent. 'Nevertheless', as is explicitly stated in the acts of the council, 'for the honour of his royal majesty, these bulls should not be made out for the same turcopolier without the will and consent of his royal majesty for the preservation of royal prerogative'.[80] Though Zaplana should by all means make plain that, according to the statutes, Weston should have been 'elected', he was also instructed to give in should the king insist upon Multon. Should that be the case, he had only to ensure that all monies pertaining to the convent from the vacancy after the death of Tornay, and from the time when Multon was in office, be paid into

---

[77] (*Ita sperabat quod serenissimus dominus*) *rex Anglie pro sua iustitia et equitate tanquam princeps justissimus eum conservaret in suo iure* ..., NLM Arch. 75, fol. 61(69)v-62(70)r (27 February 1475).

[78] Ibid., fol. 75(83)r (17 June 1475).

[79] Ibid., fol. 109(117)r (27 May 1476).

[80] *Nihilominus pro honore sue regie maiestatis dicte bulle non fuerint consignate eiusdem domino turcupellerio sine voluntate et beneplacito sue regie maiestatis ad conservacionem sue regalis prerogative* ..., ibid., fol. 123(131)r-125(133)r (24 and 29 July 1476), at fol. 123(131)v, see Appendix I.

the treasury. But these precautions proved unnecessary. Weston was finally confirmed as prior[81] and remained in office until his death in 1489.

It appears that the cautious proceeding of master and council in the case of Fr John Weston paved the way for a less strained relationship between the English kings and the Hospitallers in the last decades before the dissolution of the order in England. As with Fr John Weston, succeeding priors were 'elected' in the convent, where they had been turcopoliers, then sent to England to be accepted by the king. Westons immediate successor, Fr John Kendall, was turcopolier and proctor general at the Roman curia, when he was named Prior of England in June 1489.[82] It took him some time to leave Rome,[83] and when he finally arrived in England, he had to ask for royal pardon because he had brought and published the bulls of master and convent nominating him Prior of England without royal assent and the 'election' by the English brethren.[84] In the end, however, he was accepted without further disturbance and pardon was granted in January 1492. His successor, Fr Thomas Docwra, was 'elected' in the convent in August 1501[85] and soon became prominent in English politics.[86]

Although the degree of influence varied with every Hospitaller Prior of England, nearly all the priors of the later fifteenth century played an important role in the politics of their time. Most of them stayed at court and acted as royal councillors and as royal justices. Furthermore, Fr Robert Botyll and Fr John Kendall were employed on several diplomatic missions. Ranking first among the lay barons and with succession dependent upon 'election' by fellow brethren, the office of prior was open to royal ambitions, especially in the troubled times of the Wars of the Roses, when the kings had to secure their standing among the shifting loyalties of their entourage. While the regulations of the statutes excluded any external influence, in reality, for every succession of priors a precarious balance had to be kept, as becomes clear – probably not

---

[81] It is not clear when this did happen, but in April 1477, the news had even reached Rhodes, when – as his successor – Fr John Kendall was elected turcopolier, ibid., fol. 148(156)v-149(157)v.

[82] NLM Arch. 77, fol. 3(18)r (22 June 1489).

[83] In August 1490, he was allowed to leave Rome by bull of master and convent, NLM Arch. 390, fol. 131v-132r, but he was still there in March 1491, when Pope Innocent VIII took him under papal protection, *Calendar of the Entries in the Papal Registers*, XIV, pp. 273-74.

[84] *CPR, Henry VII*, 1, p. 368.

[85] NLM Arch. 79, fol.15(22)v (6 August 1501).

[86] King-Luke, pp. 75, 98-99 and 147-48 (with a 'portrait' from 1602 before p. 73).

accidentially – especially in the cases of Fr John Langstrother and Fr John Weston. While for other priories, for example the priory of Ireland,[87] the Hospitaller master and convent adhered to the order's regulations as closely as possible, they were reluctant to enforce the statutes upon the nomination of English priors, as this might jeopardize their standing with the king. The situation was quite different in France, where there were several priories, or in Germany, where the kings and emperors did not have the means to exercise political pressure. In England, there was a direct, often personal relationship between kings and priors and thus, during the Wars of the Roses, the nomination of priors became a delicate affair. In the end, the order's moderate policy proved successful. Since the troubled succession of Fr John Weston all priors were 'elected' in accordance with the statutes, and the end of the Wars of the Roses contributed to a more peaceful relationship between kings and priors. This ended only with the dissolution of the Hospitallers in England by Henry VIII in April 1540.

---

[87] See e.g. the problems around the 'election' of Thomas Fitzgerot as Prior of Ireland in 1449 to 1450, who had been nominated by the English brethren and sought to be confirmed by master and council, NLM Arch. 362, fol. 120r-127v, edited in Appendix II.

Appendix
I

24-29 July 1476.

Notes concerning the legation to King Edward IV. Everything is to be done to establish the turcopolier Fr John Weston as Prior of England because of his merits and standing in the order, but the envoy has to proceed very carefully not to rouse the king's anger or to cause damage in respect of the order's incomes from England. If the king does not accept the order's decision, the envoy has to give in and to secure the payments to the common treasury.[88] The draper Fr Nicolau Zaplana, the conventual bailiff of the Aragonese-Catalonian tongue, is elected orator and nominated lieutenant of the master.

NLM Arch. 75, fol. 123(131)r-125(133)r.

(123[131]r)[89] *Die 24 mensis Jullii 1476 per reverendissimum dominum magistrum fratrum Petrum dAubusson hospitalis Jherusalem (etc.)[90] ac suum reverendum consilium ordinarium cum scrutinio balotarum secundum formam stabilimentorum fuerunt deliberata / (123[131]v) et ordinata que sequuntur super expedicione et provisione prioratus Anglie vaccantis per obitum quondam fratris Guillelmi Tornay,[91] super hoc prius habita relacione reverendissimi domini magistri prefati ac reverendorum dominorum alias deputatorum super hoc negocio et (presertim) auditis procuratoribus reverendi domini fratris Johannis Weston[92] et fratris Roberti Multon.[93]*

Primo[94] quod de dicto prioratu Anglie expediantur et fiant bulle dicto reverendo domino fratre Johanni Weston turcupellerio tanquam anciano et benemerenti cui secundum formam stabilimentorum religionis Jherusolimitani pertinet dictus prioratus.

---

[88] See above, n. 80. The edition is made according to the following principles: (1) All abbreviations are expanded; (2) if some expansion is uncertain, it is put in brackets; (3) Roman numerals are transcribed in Arabic numerals; (4) the original spelling of the text has been kept, except where 'u' is to be pronounced as 'v'.

[89] In the margin: *Deliberaciones super prioratu Anglie.*

[90] Grand master 1476-1503.

[91] For him see n. 16-17, 33, 71-74.

[92] For him cf. n. 18-19, 34, 77-81.

[93] For him cf. n. 75-81.

[94] In the margin: *Pro prioratu Anglie nota.*

Insuper quod de baiuliatu turcupelleriatus et de preceptoriis quas resignat idem dominus turcupellerius per promocionem ad ipsum prioratum non fiat aliqua provisio et collacio per reverendissimum dominum magistrum et conventum Rhodi donec et quousque dictus reverendissimus magister et reverendum consilium ordinarium fuerint avisati per ambaxiatorem qui pro hoc negocio mittetur in Anglia, quod serenissimus rex Anglie est contentus quod dictus reverendus dominus turchupellerius habeat dictum prioratum.

Preterea ut dicte bulle melius et comodius possint educi ad executionem in favorem et comodum dicti reverendi domini turcupellerii et ut eciam conservetur benevolencia dicti serenissimi regis Anglie ad evitandum damna et scandala est deliberatum et ordinatum quod mittatur ambaxiator in Angliam religiosus condicionis qui secum deferet bullas que fient de dicto prioratu eidem reverendo domini turcupellerio, quiquidem orator significavit dicto serenissimo domino regi Anglie optimum jus et justiciam quam habet in eodem prioratu ipse dominus turcupellerius, et qualiter consideratis eius virtutibus et meritis religio ipsa eum constituit priorem dicti prioratus. Nihilominus pro honore sue regie maiestatis dicte bulle non fuerint consignate eidem domino turcupellerio sine voluntate et beneplacito sue regie maiestatis ad conservacionem sue regalis prerogative. / (124[132]r) Pro (cuius indifferenti) conservacione, considerato quod in electione facta in Anglia dictus dominus turcupellerius unacum dicto domino fratre Roberto Multon fuit per suam regiam maiestatem nominatus prout suis regiis litteris apparet, ideo visum est reverendissimo domino magistri prefato et ipsi religioni, visa tali nominacione facta per ipsam regiam maiestatem, quod dicta prerogativa regalis est observata dando dictum prioratum eidem domino turcupellerio qui secundum formam stabilimentorum et consuetudinum religionis habet jus in eodem prioratu sicuti amplius et diffusius continebitur in instructionibus que expedientur dicto oratori, qui talem operam adhibeat ut dictus reverendus dominus turcupellerius dictum prioratum habere et obtinere possit in vigore bullarum sibi (confectarum). In quibusquidem bullis ad evitandum inconveniencia que sequi possent racione ammissionis dictarum bullarum aut aliter et eciam ad conservandum jura communis thesauri addetur clausula infrascripta ante 'In cuius rei testimonium (etc.)', videlicet quod dicte bulle non ponantur in execucionem nec effectum habeant nisi fuerint signate et subscripte manu propria dicti ambaxiatoris ut sequitur: 'Ego ... [95] *orator reverendissimi domini magistri et reverendi consilii Rhodi sum contentus et placet mihi quod huiusmodi bulle prioratus Anglie ponantur*

---

[95] Blank left for the name of the envoy.

in execucionem atque suum sorciantur effectum in comodum dicti reverendi domini fratris Johannis Weston turcupellerii. Ita est ... manu propria'.

Ulterius adhibita omni diligencia quod dictus reverendus dominus turcupellerius adipiscatur ipsum prioratum, casu quo dictus serenissimus dominus rex Anglie noluerit perperi aliquomodo quod dictus dominus turcupellerius habeat dictum prioratum, sed quod dictus prioratus conferatur eidem fratri Roberto Multon, eodem casu ad evitandum indignacionem dicti serenissimi domini regis et ad conservandum indemnitatem communis thesauri, cum detrimenta insequi possent propter dilacionem temporis et non obtemperando dicte regie maiestati quam super omnia dicta religio observare et colere debet, dictus orator, in vim bullarum plumbearum communium que sibi fient, eidem potestatem hoc agendum tribuendo, / (124[132]v) ex nunc debeat conferre dictum prioratum eidem fratri Roberto Multon cum reservacionibus jurium communis thesauri. Nihilominus antequam faciat dictus oratur talem collacionem sit tutus et cautus de juribus mortuarii et vaccantis per obitum quondam fratris Guillelmi Tornay olim prioris dicti prioratus.

Item quod ex nunc procuratores dicti reverendi domini turcupellerii cedant et renuncient in utilitatem dicti communis thesauri illud debitum quod idem dominus turcupellerius debet habere a spolio quondam fratris B(attiste) de Ursinis olim magistri dicti ordinis,[96] quequidem summa quando dictus thesaurus eam receperit ab eodem spolio, ponetur in computo (scutorum) 900 qui solventur pro dicto mortuario et vaccanti.

Item quod pro resto dicti summe (scutorum) 900 pro jure dicti mortuarii et vaccantis fideiussores presentati nomine dicti domini turcupellerii per ipsos procuratores acceptentur per ipsum thesaurum et quod quilibet sit obligatus tanquam principalis solutor pro quantitate pro qua fideiubet, ita tamen, quod dictus ambaxiator non consignet dictas bullas factas domini turcupellerio prefato donec fuerit tutus et cautus a mercatoribus sufficientibus in Anglia aut per viam cambii de summa pro qua fideiubent fratres religionis nostre.

Die[97] 29 mensis Jullii 1476 per reverendissimum dominum magistrum et suum reverendum consilium cum scrutinio balotarum fuit electus orator ad serenissimum dominum regem Anglie pro negociis prioratus dicti regni reverendus dominus frater Nicolaus Saplana[98] draperius sacri conventus Rhodi qui hoc onus obedienter suscepit et exequi intendit ad honorem et comodum religionis.

---

[96] Master 1467-1476.

[97] In the margin: *Electio oratoris pro Anglia.*

[98] Fr Nicolau Zaplana, draper of the Hospitallers about 1476 to 1478.

(125[133]r) *Insuper reverendissimus dominus magister facta dicta electione ordinavit quod pro honorem dicti reverendi domini draperii et favore rerum Anglie ipse reverendus dominus draperius intituletur locumtenens magistri.*

II

9-10 September 1450.
Master and council at Rhodes discuss the problem of the 'election' of Fr Thomas fitzGerot as Prior of Ireland by the brethren of the Irish priory.[99] Though they have received letters from Henry VI and the brethren of the English priory confirming the 'election' they decide to reject this decision as being contrary to the statutes. Only after some deliberations in the English tongue is fitzGerot finally accepted and formally 'elected'.

NLM Arch. 362, fol. 122(123)v-123(124)v.

(122[123]v) *Postquam die 9a Septembris anni 1450mi, cum esset congregatum consilium in camera paramenti more solito, reverendissimus dominus magnus magister,*[100] *lectis premissis litteris et bene intellectis, vocari fecit prefatum magistrum Henricum Kynk procuratorem prefati domini fratris Thome ffitzGerot coram sua reverendissima dominatione et suo venerando consilio et interrogavit eundem quid petebat. Qui respondit quod petebat confirmari in priorem prioratus Hibernie dictum fratrem Thomam ffitzGerot electum per fratres preceptores et alios fratres conventus Hibernie, prout in ipsorum litteris bullis eorum roboratis coram reverendissima dominatione sua presentatis late demonstratur, quia eligendi priorem habebant auctoritatem virtute cuiusdam privilegii in capitulo Aquensi alias eis concessi. Quo audito et interrogato si aliud dicere volebat et respondente quod non, jussus fuit e camera consilii abire, ut super eius peticionem deliberaretur.*

Deinde immediate examinata diligenter peticione prefata per prefatum reverendissimum dominum magistrum et eius venerandum consilium et quod erat expresse contra formam stabilimentorum[101] *religionis, presertim contra stabilimentum felicis memorie condam reverendissimi domini fratris (Antonii) Fluviani Hospitalis / (123[124]r) Sancti Johannis Jherosolimitani magistri,*[102] *quo cavetur, ne deinceps ellectio baiullivi vel prioris fiat extra conventum, et si*

---

[99] Cf. above, n.87.

[100] Fr Jean de Lastic, master 1437-1454.

[101] It again follows *formam*, this time crossed out.

[102] Master 1421-1437.

facta fuerit huiusmodi ellectio extra conventum sit nulla et nullius valoris. Quorum stabilimentorum virtute et vigore matura consultacione habita, declaratum est, et determinatum concorditer, quod dicta ellectio in Hibernia per fratres dicti prioratus facta nullo modo fieri poterat et quod erat nulla et nullius valoris, et pro nulla haberi voluerunt et declaraverunt. Et per consequens confirmatio similiter dicte ellectionis (est) nulle, fieri non poterat. Qua deliberatione et determinatione habita paulo post, fuit vocatus dictus magister Henricus in consilio et sibi per reverendissimum dominum magistrum relata determinatio sua et sui venerandi consilii super peticione facta per eum confirmando in priorem dictum fratrem Thomam ffitzGerot, ellectum in Hibernia, quia ellectio (erat) nulla et nullius valoris, et confirmatio fieri non poterat de re nulla. Et omnibus displicebat, quod non poterant mayestati serenissimi domini regis Anglie et aliis qui scripserant in favorem ipsius fratri Thome morem gerere et eorum votum satisfacere, quibus auditis dictus magister Henricus recessit.

Et paulo post rediit et se genuflectens exposuit reverendissimo domino magistro et suo prefato venerando consilio, quod in litteris, quas presentaverat, continebant duo capita, unum erat, quod reverendissime dominationes sue confirmarent ellectionem factam de dicto fratre Thoma ffitzGerot in priorem Hibernie, vel si magis vellent dominationes sue et eis placeret, facerent novam provisionem dicto fratri Thome fitzGerot de dicto prioratu Hibernie, et sic humiliter petebat et suplicabat quod dominationes sue facere dignarentur. Quibus auditis dictus reverendissimus dominus magister sumpsit tempus ad deliberandum usque ad diem crastinum, cum suo venerando consilio, super hac secunda peticione de nova provisione ipsius prioratus facienda.

Post hec ut servaretur bona consuetudo conventus ipse reverendissimus dominus magister dedit licentiam venerabili religioso domino fratri Guillelmo Daunnay conventus Rhodi turchupellerio,[103] *ut congregaret fratres venerabilis lingue Anglie in dicto conventu residentes, et ad videndum si aliquid esset que dictum prioratum Hibernie petere vellet pro se vel procuratio nomine aliquorum (fratrum) dicte lingue absentium, an si ipse frater Thomas ffitzGerot esset magis idoneus, ne cui fiat iniuria, sed jus uniuscuiusque custodiatur.*

Die vero decima dicti mensis Septembris anni quo supra coram prefato reverendissimo domino magistro et eius venerando consilio loco quo supra congregato prefatus dominus frater Guillelmus Daunay turcupellerius, presentibus illic procuratoribus venerabilis lingue Anglie existens, retulit se de mandato

---

[103] Fr William Daunay, turcopolier about 1450-1464; perhaps identical with Prior Fr William Tornay (1471-1474), see above.

sue reverendissime dominationis tenuisse linguam super cuiusdam prioris Hibernie faciendi electionem, et quod unanimiter fuerat ellectus et nominatus dictus frater Thomas ffitzGerot, quia erat in scientiis et armis peritus et de magna parentela et potens, et nullus erat aptior ipso ad recuperandum et restaurandum dictum prioratum Hibernie destructum et desolatum ad priorem statum, et ut ipse prioratus ad obedientiam veniret facilius, non obstante quod non fuisset in conventu, neque in dicto conventu fecisset residentiam tanto tempore secundum formam stabilimentorum, non preiudicantes propter hoc alicui vel aliquibus fratri vel fratribus in conventu vel extra conventum existentibus prioratus Anglie in baiuliatibus, preceptoriis, prioratibus et aliis beneficiis vacantibus vel vacaturis in futuram quovismodo. /

(123[124]v) Demum dicta ellectione audita et lingue prefate deliberatione, prefatis reverendissimus dominus magister et suum venerandum consilium ordinatum ad similia in sufficienti numero concorditer fecerunt et creaverunt dictum dominum fratrem Thomam fitzGerot in priorem legitimum dicti prioratus Hibernie. Et eidem de dicto prioratu novam provisionem fecerunt secundum formam stabilimentorum bonorumque morum et consuetudinum religionis. Dictusque reverendissimus dominus magister mandavit michi Ellisseo Delamanna vicecancellario et secretario suo et sacri conventus Rhodi,[104] quod facerem bullas secundum stillum cancellarie dicto domino fratri Thome ffitzGerot de dicto prioratu Hibernie, et sic de mandato sue reverendissime dominationis feci bullas dicti prioratus in modum, que sequitur inferius.[105]

---

[104] Acting as Vice-Chancellor under Fr Melchiore Bandini about 1450-1454.

[105] The magisterial bull of Fr Jean de Lastic dated 10 September 1450 follows on fol. 123(124)v-124(125)v.

7

Between International Horizon
and Regional Boundary:
the Bohemian Crosiers of the Red Star in Silesia

Andreas Rüther

I

To introduce my paper, I would like to explain the usage of the words 'international' and 'regional' in its title: I will not speak about an international order in the strict sense of the word 'international', nor even about an order, really, but rather about an association of hospitallers, whose status as an order in the actual sense of the word is, as is well known, disputed.[1] This community of hospitallers was not even international, much less universal, as we might perhaps describe the case of the knightly orders in Palestine.[2] In the case of the

---

[1] M.-L. Windemuth, *Das Hospital als Träger der Armenfürsorge im Mittelalter.* Sudhoffs Archiv Beiheft 36 (Stuttgart, 1995); *Das Hospital im späten Mittelalter,* ed. W. Moritz. Ausstellung des Hessischen Staatsarchivs (Marburg, 1983); *idem*, 'Das Hospital der hlg. Elisabeth in seinem Verhältnis zum Hospitalwesen des frühen 13. Jahrhunderts', *Sankt Elisabeth: Fürstin, Dienerin, Heilige*, ed. Philipps-Universität Marburg (Marburg, 1981), pp. 101-16; J. Sydow, 'Spital und Stadt in der Kanonistik und Verfassungsgeschichte des 14. Jahrhunderts', *Der deutsche Territorialstaat im 14. Jahrhundert*, vol. 1, ed. H. Patze. Vorträge und Forschungen XII (Sigmaringen, 1970), pp. 175-95; D. Jetter, *Geschichte des Hospitals*, vol. 1: *Westdeutschland von den Anfängen bis 1850.* Sudhoffs Archiv Beiheft 5 (Wiesbaden, 1966), pp. 10-38. For many helpful suggestions in discussing and translating this paper I am cordially obliged to Susan R. Boettcher Ph.D., Lecturer at the University of Wisconsin, Madison (USA).

[2] J. Sarnowsky, 'Hospitalorden', 'Ritterorden', *Eine Kulturgeschichte der christlichen Orden im Mittelalter*, ed. P. Dinzelbacher (Stuttgart, 1996), pp. 193-203 and 329-48; *MO*; K. Elm, 'Gli ordini militari. Un ceto di vita religiosa fra universa lismo e particolarismo', *MS*, pp. 9-28.

From *Mendicants, Military Orders, and Regionalism in Medieval Europe*, ed. Jürgen Sarnowsky. Copyright © 1999 by Jürgen Sarnowsky. Published by Ashgate Publishing Ltd, Gower House, Croft Road, Aldershot, Hampshire, GU11 3HR, Great Britain.

Bohemian Crosiers we are also not speaking of an offshoot of the well-known Belgian or Italian religious orders (Crutched Friars), which count as minor mendicant orders and whose devotion to the cross had its own particular features.[3]

The Crosiers of the Red Star were rather societies of brothers who, although they did share a common *devotio sanctae crucis*, did not originate in western or southern Europe. Instead, they found their beginning in 'younger Europe' – or, more precisely, in the empire's new centre, the capital of Bohemia – and remained for the Roman and German regions of the continent, if not unknown, then at least without an exact opposite number.[4] In any case, it is difficult to place them on the same level as, for example, the mendicant friars of London or Basle, the Italian Templars, or the Knights of St John, even though there are some similarities. Nonetheless a discussion of the Crosiers within the framework of this volume is justified, in my opinion, because they occupied a place between mendicant and military orders and thus offer a comparative perspective.

The Crosiers of the Red Star, endowed in the Přemyslid kingdom, show clearly by their development up to the thirteenth century the ways in which an ecclesiastical and spiritual association of the Middle Ages with very general duties developed a specific identity in a particular setting: in this case, that of

---

[3] J. Jansen, 'Kreuzherren', *Wetzer und Welte's Kirchenlexikon*, VII (1891), pp. 1101-18; Zöckler, 'Kreuzherren (crucigeri, cruciferi)', *Realencyklopädie für protestantische Theologie und Kirche*, XI (1902), pp. 96-97; P. A. Ceyssens, 'Croisiers, Règle des', *Dictionnaire de droit canonique*, IV (1949), pp. 799-814; S. Mattei, 'Crocigeri della stella rossa', *Enciclopedia Cattolica*, IV (1952), pp. 998-99; M. Vincken, 'Croisiers', *Dictionnaire de spiritualité, ascétique et mystique. Doctrine et histoire*, II (1953), pp. 2561-76; M. Vincken, 'Croisiers', *Dictionnaire d'histoire et de géographie ecclésiastiques*, XIII (1956), pp. 1042-62; A. van de Pasch, 'Kreuzherren', *Lexikon für Theologie und Kirche*, 2nd edn, VI (1961), pp. 619-21; K. Elm et al, 'Frati della penitenza dei Beati Martyri', *Dizionario degli Istituti di Perfezione*, VI (1980), pp. 1392-98; S. Bringer, 'Kreuzherren', *Lexikon für Theologie und Kirche*, 3rd edn, VI (1997), pp. 459-60.

[4] K. Elm, 'Les ordres monastiques, canonicaux et militaires en europe du Centre-Est au bas Moyen Age', *L'Eglise et le peuple chrétien dans le pays de l'Europe du Centre-Est et du Nord (XIVe-XVe siècles). Acte du colloque organisé par l'Ecole française de Rome avec la participation de l'Istuto polacco di cultura cristiana (Roma) et du Centre européen de recherches sur les congrégations et ordres religieux (CERCOR), Rome 27-29 janvier 1986*. Collection de l'Ecole Française de Rome 128 (Rome, 1990), pp. 161-80; F. Machilek, 'Reformorden und Ordensreformen in den böhmischen Ländern vom 10. bis 18. Jahrhundert', Bohemia sacra. *Das Christentum in Böhmen 973-1973*, ed. F. Seibt (Düsseldorf, 1974), pp. 63-80, at pp. 70-71. See the other contributions in this volume.

backward eastern central Europe.[5] The community quickly connected the function of poor relief with that of the *cura animarum*, a combination that finds no real counterpart in the developed and long-settled lands of western Europe.[6] The order was international in that it obtained papal approval and followed a commonly-recognized monastic rule. Its expansion was, however, at the same time dynastically bound; that is to say, its organization extended solely to Bohemia and Moravia and the Silesian dukedoms. On the other hand, it was no mere minor order, for its influence extended beyond its regional and local boundaries, which can be concluded from the fact that the courts of sovereigns authorized members of the order in diplomatic and administrative functions.

At this point one might object that in principle, regionally typical features may be observed in all monastic and canonical congregations throughout Christendom.[7] In the case of the Crosiers, however, more is meant by the designation 'regional', namely, the orientation of the order *per se* toward an obligation that is denoted by Christianization, settlement, and the territorialization of the central European countryside.[8] That is to say, we are not speaking of a

---

[5] P. Moraw, 'Mittelalter (bis 1469)', *Schlesien*, ed. N. Conrads. Deutsche Geschichte im Osten Europas 5 (Berlin, 1994), pp. 37-176. Cf. J. G. Pounds, 'The urbanization of East Central and South-East Europe: an historical perspective', *Eastern Europe. Essays in Geographical Problems*, ed. G. W. Hoffmann (London, 1991), p. 59; M. Bogucka, 'The Towns of East-Central Europe from the Fourteenth to the Seventeenth Century', *East-Central Europe in Transition. From the Fourteenth to the Seventeenth Century*, eds A. Mączak, H. Samsonowicz, P. Burke. Studies in Modern Capitalism, Études sur le capitalisme moderne, Past and Present Publications (Cambridge, 1985), pp. 97-108.

[6] W. Sułowski, *The Hospital Orders in Bohemia, Poland and Hungary in the Thirteenth Century* (M.A. Thesis, Central European University, Budapest, 1994); K. Dola, 'Szpitale średniowiecznego Śląska', *Rocznik Teologiczny Śląska Opolskiego* 1 (1968) 239-93; E. Walter, 'Das Hospital zum Hl. Geist in Breslau und die Brüder vom Orden des Hl. Geistes', *Archiv für schlesische Kirchengeschichte* 49 (1991) 219-30; M. Słoń, 'Ludzie z rachunków klasztornych. Przykład szpitala Św. Ducha we Wrocławiu w XV wieku', *Klasztor w społeczeństwie średniowiecznym i nowożytnym*, eds M. Derwich, A. Pobóg-Lenartowicz (Opole, Wrocław, 1996), pp. 445-52.

[7] Cf. U. Arnold, 'Europa und die Region – widerstreitende Kräfte in der Entwicklung des Deutschen Ordens im Mittelalter', *RR*, pp. 161-72; M.-L. Favreau-Lilie, 'Die Bedeutung der geistlichen Ritterorden für die Mission im östlichen Mitteleuropa (13. Jahrhundert)', *Auf den Spuren der Freiheit: Einheit Europas, was ist das?* Trigon: Kunst, Wissenschaft und Glaube im Dialog 7 (Berlin, 1997), pp. 56-69.

[8] J. Kłoczowski, 'Die Entwicklung der Kirchen Mittelost- und Nordeuropas', *Die Zeit der Zerreißproben (1274-1449)*, eds M. Mollat du Jourdin, A. Vauchez, B. Schimmelpfennig. Die Geschichte des Christentums: Religion, Politik und Kultur 6 (Freiburg, Basle, Vienna, 1991), pp. 771-811; A. Rüther, 'Ordensneugründungen und Anpassungsvorgänge im spätmittelalterlichen Klosterwesen Prags, Breslaus und Krakaus', *Wanderungen und Kulturaustausch im nördlichen Ostmitteleuropa des 15. und 16.*

modification of intentions, but about the founding of an order *sui generis* that acquired a unique character within a specific area under its own conditions.[9]

Having said this much about my paper's broader framework, I would now like to turn to the order's endowment and constitution, its state of dependence upon princes or members of the powerful aristocracy in the later Middle Ages. Subsequently, I will depict the development of the Crosiers during the phase of augmentation of lordly authority and the increasing potential for influence on the part of the communal authorities in the period before the Reformation.

II

In spring, 1241, after their conquest of Kievan Russia, the warriors of the Tatar tribes fell upon Poland. The intruders' original destination had been the King of Hungary's territories, but soon the Golden Horde had pushed as far as Silesia. The Duke of Oppeln, the King of Bohemia, and perhaps also the future Grand Master of the Teutonic Knights in Prussia came to the aid of Duke Henry II of Breslau, but the united Christian infantry suffered an annihilating defeat at the hands of the Mongolian raiders: on 9 April 1241, on the plain of Wahlstatt, the Silesian army's commander Duke Henry the Pious met his end.[10] Although the Asian horsemen under the leadership of a grandson of Genghis Khan won the battle, their prince broke off the western offensive in order to resolve a conflict of succession at home.

The inhabitants of Breslau, who had fled behind the ducal defenses before the attack, founded a new settlement on the ruins of their destroyed city as German legal tradition prescribed. Since the succession of Duke Henry I, the Bearded, at the beginning of the thirteenth century, the Piast Court had main-

---

Jahrhunderts. Tagung des Johann Gottfried Herder-Forschungsrates Marburg, 8.-10. Oktober 1997, ed. H. Boockmann † (Munich, 1999) (forthcoming).

[9] Cf. M. Goliński, 'Krzyżany czy Joannici? W sprawie rzekomej obecnosci Joannitów pod Wrocławiem w 1273r.', *Śląski Kwartalnik Historyczny Sobótka* 46 (1991) 341-44; K. Gancarczyk, 'W kwestii początków zakonu joannitów na Śląsku', *Śląski Kwartalnik Historyczny Sobótka* 40 (1985) 191-201; idem, 'Fundacja komendy joannickiej Bożego Ciała w Wrocławiu', *Acta Universitatis Wratislaviensis* 1112, *Historia* 76, pp. 155-63; K. Dola, 'Zakon joannitów na Śląsku do połowy XIV wieku', *Studia Teologiczny-Historyczne Śląska Opolskiego* 3 (1973) 43-86.

[10] J. Strzelczyk, 'Die Schlacht von Liegnitz. Geschichte und Tradition', *Zeitschrift für Ostforschung* 41 (1992) 95-101; M. Cetwiński, 'Co wiemy o bitwie pod Legnicą?', *Acta Universitatis Wratislaviensis* 800, *Historia* 50, pp. 75-94; M. Goliński, 'Templariusze a bitwa pod Legnicą. Próba rewizji poglądów', *Kwartalnik Historyczny* 98 (1990) 3-16; J. Mularczyk, 'Mongolowie pod Legnicą w 1241r.', *Kwartalnik Historyczny* 96 (1988) 3-26.

tained family connections to the great dynasties of the *Sacrum Romanum imperium*; these connections went hand in hand with the intensification of lordly sovereignty and the territory's developing autonomy. This incipient build-up of power broke down, however, with the catastrophe of 1241, so that dynastic weakness resulted in the splintering of Silesia.[11]

Before this background, which had been termed the rescue of the West from the advancing heathens, the foundation of a chivalric order by the Silesian Piasts for the defence of the emerging urban complexes could have been expected. However, instead, Hospitaller friars came from Prague to support the settlement of the defended lands as had been previously done in the West. In Bohemian's main city, Agnes of Bohemia – like Elisabeth of Thuringia, Hedwig of Silesia, or Margaret of Hungary before her – had lived according to an ideal of poverty and penitence that was particularly widespread in noble circles in central Europe[12] and which expressed itself in Bohemia around 1234 via the founding of a Franciscan house and a convent of Poor Clares, as well as a hospice for the poor at the Moldau.[13]

---

[11] U. Schmilewski, 'Schlesien im 13. Jahrhundert vor und nach der Schlacht von Wahlstatt', *Wahlstatt 1241. Beiträge zur Mongolenschlacht bei Liegnitz und zu ihren Nachwirkungen*. Beiträge zur Liegnitzer Geschichte 21 (Würzburg, 1991), pp. 9-34; J. Mularczyk, 'Podziały Śląska między synów Henryka II Pobożnego w połowie XIII wieku', *Przegląd Historyczny* 76 (1985) 481-504.

[12] H. Manikowska, 'Zwischen Askesis und Modestia. Buß- und Armutsideale in polnischen, böhmischen und ungarischen Hofkreisen im 13. Jahrhundert', *Acta Poloniae Historica* 47 (1983) 33-53; B. Sasse, 'Das Doppelkloster der Přemyslidenprinzessin Agnes in Prag', *Agnes von Böhmen 1211-1282. Königstochter – Äbtissin – Heilige*, ed. J. Polc. Lebensbilder zur Geschichte der böhmischen Länder 6 (Munich, 1989), pp. 219-42; A. Skýbová, 'Agnes von Böhmen – Eine Přemysliden-Prinzessin als Verfechterin einer neuen Spiritualität', *Fürstinnen und Städterinnen. Frauen im Mittelalter*, eds G. Beyreuther, B. Pätzold, E. Uitz (Freiburg, Basle, Vienna, 1993), pp. 40-64; F. Machilek, 'Die Přemysliden, Piasten und Arpaden und der Klarissenorden im 13. und frühen 14. Jahrhundert', *Westmitteleuropa, Ostmitteleuropa. Vergleiche und Beziehungen. Festschrift für Ferdinand Seibt zum 65. Geburtstag*. Veröffentlichungen des Collegium Carolinum 70 (Munich, 1992), pp. 293-306; H. Soukupova, *Anežský klášter v Praze* (Prague, 1989).

[13] V. Rudolf, *Křičžovníci s červenou hvěždou do r. 1419, rekonstrukce jejich činnosti*. (Ph.Diss., Prague, 1990); F. Machilek, 'Die selige Agnes von Böhmen und der Orden der Kreuzherren mit dem roten Stern', *Von der alten zur neuen Heimat. Vierzig Jahre Ackermann-Gemeinde in Bamberg*, eds Franz Kubin, Arnulf Rieber (Bamberg, 1986), pp. 23-34; P. V. Bělohlávek, P. J. Hradec, *Dějiny českých křižovniku s červenou hvězdou* (Prague, 1930); V. Sádlo, 'Klášter křizovníků s červenou hvězdou v Praze', *Památky archeologické, skupina historická* 38, new ser. 2 (1932) 33-34; A. Petitova-Bénoliel, *L'église à Prague sous la dynastie des Luxembourg (1310-1419)*. Middeleeuwse Studies en bronnen 52 (Hilversum, 1996), pp. 164-66.

Henry II's widow, Duchess Anne, daughter of the Přemyslid king, brought this ascetic lifestyle to the Silesian court: in 1242 she fulfilled the last wish of her slain husband and founded a hospice on the left bank of the Oder next to the ducal castle in Breslau. This received the *patrocinium* of her cousin, the only recently canonized Elisabeth of Thuringia. Franciscans had already been settled at this point by the duke, and in 1257 a settlement of Poor Clares followed.[14] The *hospitium* or *infirmaria* was occupied by the so-called Crosiers of the Red Star, whose community had been elevated to the status of an order by the pope in 1238.[15] The *crucigeri* observed the rule of St Augustine, and according to their statutes, they were exempt from episcopal visitations and were to practice charitable works. In 1243 the Crosiers took over the *oratorium ad sanctam Matthiam* on the lands of the ducal curia, which had been allocated to them.[16]

---

[14] P. M. Kysk, 'Vita Annae Ducissae Silesiae', *Nasza Przeszłość* 79 (1992) 126-50; E. Walter, 'Zur Gründungsgeschichte des Breslauer Klarenstifts', *Jahrbuch der Schlesischen Friedrich-Wilhelms-Universität zu Breslau* 32 (1991) 21-28; E. Walter, 'Franziskanische Armutsbewegung in Schlesien. War die Herzogin Anna († 1265), die Schwiegertochter der hl. Hedwig, eine Terziarin des Franziskanerordens?', *Archiv für schlesische Kirchengeschichte* 40 (1982) 207-21; *idem*, 'Zu den Anfängen des Franziskanerklosters St. Jakob und des Klarissenklosters St. Klara auf dem Breslauer Ritterplatz', *Archiv für schlesische Kirchengeschichte* 53 (1995) 225-40; W. Irgang, 'Beiträge zur Silesia Franciscana im 13. Jahrhundert', ibid. 47-48 (1989-1990) 218-47; G. Wąs, *Klasztory franciszkanskie w miastach sląskich i łuzyckich XIII-XVI w.* (Ph. D., Wrocław, 1996); *eadem*, 'Franziskanie w społeczenstwie Śląska w średniowieczu i dobie nowożytnej', *Klasztor w społeczenstwie średniowiecznym i nowożytnym*, eds M. Derwich, A. Pobóg-Lenartowicz (Opole, Wrocław, 1996), pp. 105-37.

[15] F. Jaschke, *Die Entstehung, Bestimmung und Ausbreitung des ritterlichen Ordens der Kreuzherren mit dem roten Stern*. Programm des K. K. deutschen Gymnasiums in Kremsier 1902 (Prague, 1904); S. Reicke, *Das deutsche Spital und sein Recht im Mittelalter*, vol. 1: *Das deutsche Spital. Geschichte und Gestalt*. Kirchenrechtliche Abhandlungen, 111-12 (Stuttgart, 1932), pp. 182-89; M. Heimbucher, *Orden und Kongregationen der katholischen Kirche*, 3rd edn, vol. 1 (Paderborn, 1933), pp. 421-22; W. Lorenz, *Die Kreuzherren mit dem roten Stern*. Veröffentlichungen des Königsteiner Instituts für Kirchen- und Geistesgeschichte der Sudetenländer 2 (Königstein im Taunus, 1964); G. Rocca, 'Crocigeri della stella rossa', *Dizionario degli Istituti di Perfezione*, III (1976), pp. 313-14; K. Elm, 'Kreuzherren', *Lexikon des Mittelalters*, V (1992), col. 1500-1502.

[16] N. N., 'Die Kirche und das Fürstliche Hospitalstift St. Matthias des Ordens der Kreutzherren mit dem rothen Stern,' *Topographische Chronik von Breslau. Quarthal IV* (Breslau, 1808); G. A. Stenzel, 'Beiträge zur Geschichte des Ordens der Kreuziger mit dem rothen Sterne in Schlesien und des Hospitals der heiligen Elisabeth des Hauses des heiligen Matthias', *Übersicht der Arbeiten und Veränderungen der schlesischen Gesellschaft für vaterländische Kultur*. Beilage IV (Breslau, 1838); J. Heyme, *Dokumentirte Geschichte des Bisthums und Hochstiftes Breslau. Denkwürdigkeiten aus der Kirchen- und Diöcesan-Geschichte Schlesiens*, vol. 1 (Breslau, 1860-1868), pp. 263-

A 1480 painting located in the sacristy of the Poor Clares' cloister shows the Dowager Duchess Anne, Regent of Silesia, in a mantle and wearing a crown, among the ducal endowments. Along with her burial ground, in St Clare's, and the Minorites' convent of St James, which had been founded by Henry and in which he was buried, the church of St Matthew was included among the three foundations, which had been integrated into the city as an individual spiritual quarter by the construction of defensive fortifications. In close connection with the ducal residence, St Matthew's was responsible for the relief of the poor, as well as for the care of pilgrims and of the sick.[17] This charge changed, however, as early as 1253, when responsibility for the parish of St Elisabeth, along with its equipment and tithes, was given to the hospice in Breslau, thus incorporating the clergy of St Elisabeth into St Matthew's church; the canons named the priests, whom they soon recruited from their brotherhood.

The house received generous donations and numerous privileges, a situation that was facilitated by its physical proximity and organisational connections to the ruling family. The *cruciferi cum stella rubea sub cruce rubea* took over or founded a number of hospices, churches, and commendatories in Silesia and Poland, among them Kreuzburg, Bunzlau, Schweidnitz, Glatz, Münsterberg, Liegnitz, Neumarkt, Leslau, and Brest.[18] The leader of the Silesian branches elected the master, the head of the Breslau chapter, who continued to be confirmed by his superior, the general of the order in Prague. But Breslau sought to achieve a certain independence from the Bohemian mother-house, which was eventually permitted in 1404. The temptation to relax the order's bonds to

---

65; 390-92, 518-29, 848-50; II, pp. 581-94, 703-05; III, pp. 943-54; P. Pfotenhauer, 'Die Kreuzherren mit dem rothen Stern in Schlesien', *Zeitschrift des Vereins für Geschichte und Alterthum Schlesiens* 14 (1878) 52-78.

[17] E. Małachowicz, *Książece rezydencje, fundacje i mauzolea w lewobrzeznym Wrocławiu* (Wrocław, 1994); H. Weczerka, 'Die Residenzen der schlesischen Piasten', *Fürstliche Residenzen im spätmittelalterlichen Europa*, eds H. Patze, W. Paravicini. Vorträge und Forschungen XXXVI (Sigmaringen, 1991), pp. 311-47.

[18] P. Dittrich, 'Beiträge zur Geschichte des Fürstentums Breslau II; Die Kreuzherren im Fürstentum Breslau', *Zeitschrift des Vereins für Geschichte und Alterthum Schlesiens* 45 (1911) 201-56; *idem*, 'Beiträge zur Geschichte des Fürstentums Breslau III; Die Kreuzherren im Landkreise Breslau', ibid. 46 (1912) 124-58; *idem*, 'Die Besitzungen und wirtschaftlichen Verhältnisse des Matthiasstiftes bzw. der Kreuzherren mit dem Roten Stern', *Festschrift des Kgl. St. Matthiasgymnasiums zur Jahrhundertfeier 1811-1911*, pp. 5-95; B. Pohl-Resl, *Rechnen mit der Ewigkeit. Das Wiener Bürgerspital im Mittelalter*. Mitteilungen des Instituts für österreichische Geschichtsforschung 33 (Munich, 1996), pp. 16-19; M. Starnawska, 'Krzyżowcy z czerwoną gwiazdą w Legnicy średniowieczu', *Dzieje klasztorów i życia zakonnego w Legnicy*, eds M. Derwich, A. Niedzielenko (Legnica, 1998).

Prague, or even to break them, grew with increasing autonomy. After 1417, the Silesian commendatories were subordinate to the master in Breslau and no longer to the *supremus vel summus Magister* who resided near Charles's Bridge in Prague.

According to the statutes of 1292, the master was responsible for secular leadership, while the prior was in charge of the spiritual office. The membership was divided into priest-monks, serving brothers, and sisters. But not only the outward constitution changed; pastoral engagement increased in the wake of the favourable development under the Bohemian crown, closer settlement, and the general consolidation of the area. The Crosiers turned away from the care of the hospices and, because of a shortage of clergy, exerted themselves more intensely in the field of spiritual welfare among the well-dispersed citizens of Silesia. Their obligations in the hospices were increasingly fulfilled by nurses from the ranks of the beneficed sisters. All of the patronage churches were occupied by *domini* or *patres* from the order itself and safeguarded the necessary distribution of the sacraments to the towns, some of which had been founded only shortly before.[19]

In the period after 1400 the situation of the Crosiers deteriorated rapidly: wars against the Hussites, frequent outbreaks of the plague, poor management of resources, and lordly interventions increasingly threatened their position. The financial administration of their settlements was transferred to the respective communes in Schweidnitz, Liegnitz, Münsterberg, Bunzlau, Neumarkt, and Kreuzburg. This precarious situation remained unaltered until the surrender of St Elisabeth's clerical privilege to the Breslau city council in the course of the reformation. In 1525, after the cession of the patronage to a reform-minded preacher, its clerical district was transferred to St Matthew's church, which remained catholic.

---

[19] E. Frhr. v. Kleist, 'Das Breslauer Matthiasstift des Ordens der Kreuzherren mit dem roten Stern', *Festschrift des Kgl. St. Matthiasgymnasiums zur Jahrhundertfeier 1811-1911*, pp. 96-145; idem, *Beiträge zur Geschichte des Kreuzherrenordens mit dem roten Stern, besonders in Schlesien* (Theol. Diss., Breslau, 1911); J. Sossalla, *Die Säkularisation der Matthias-Stiftskommende Neuhof bei Kreuzburg OS. Ein Beitrag zur Geschichte der Säkularisation in Schlesien* (Theol. Diss., Breslau, 1936; Ohlau, 1937); K. Eistert, 'Beiträge zur Geschichte des Ordens der Kreuzherren mit dem roten Stern vom Breslauer Matthiasstift', *300 Jahre Matthiasgymnasium zu Breslau 1638-1938. Eine Erinnerungsschrift* (Berlin, 1938) pp. 1-51; J. Sossalla, 'Przyczynki do historii krzyżowców z czerwoną gwiasdą', *Nasza Przeszłość* 23 (1966) 199-237.

III

The fraternity which originated in the mendicant milieu of Prague around 1230 had now oriented itself toward the care of the urban hospices, and, after its development into a canonical society before the fourteenth century, had taken over the *cura animarum* in the divided dukedoms of Silesia and the kingdom of Bohemia. The endowments established by the Piast family at the Breslau court reveal its spiritual ties to the territorial sovereigns, whose advisors were the Crosiers. In the proximity of the ducal castle, the chapter of St Matthew had become a spiritual residence on the feudal lord's home ground. In emulation of the western pattern, the dukes had already supported religious houses, such as the abbeys, to which they had entrusted the securing and marking of borders since the twelfth century.[20] Crosiers served as administrative specialists and travelled abroad as diplomats. This type of 'house-monastery' would later be understood as an extension of the area of sovereignty, a sign of westernization in an unfolding civic society.

Interestingly enough, this east central European development provided different solutions to the same problems arising within the empire. A working hypothesis might consequently be: the settlement of the area according to German legal traditions demanded a particular order that did not perpetuate itself in the West, but rather bore in mind the frontier situation of the *Germania slavica*. Although, as compared to southern and western Europe, lordly intervention on the periphery between the 'old' and 'new' world took place rather late, it had been of advantage to the endowments. An impressive corpus of over 800 charters and documents for this period in the State Archives of Wrocław (Breslau) facilitates our understanding of how a society of beneficed priests and commendatories developed from the once-poor hospitaller community into an influential order.[21] This influence of princely power caused, how-

---

[20] W. Irgang, ' "Libertas ecclesiae" und landesherrliche Gewalt. Zur Kirchenpolitik der Piasten im 13. Jahrhundert', *Säkularisation in Ostmitteleuropa. Zur Klärung des Verhältnisses von geistlicher und weltlicher Macht im Mittelalter, von Kirche und Staat in der Neuzeit*, ed. J. Köhler. Forschungen und Quellen zur Kirchen- und Kulturgeschichte Ostdeutschlands 19 (Cologne, Vienna, 1984), pp. 33-58; H. Appelt, 'Klosterpatronat und landesherrliche Kirchenhoheit der schlesischen Herzöge im 13. Jahrhundert', idem, *Kaisertum, Königtum, Landesherrschaft. Gesammelte Studien zur mittelalterlichen Verfassungsgeschichte*. Mitteilungen des Instituts für Österreichische Geschichtsforschung 28 (Vienna, Cologne, Graz, 1988), pp. 331-50.

[21] Archiwum Państwowe we Wrocławiu, Rep. 66: 1253-1335 = Nr. 1-113 (within Polish feudalism = 113); 1336-1468 = Nr. 114-505 (under Bohemian kings = 390); 1469-1525 = Nr. 506-807 (during the Hungarian supremacy = 302); *La vie quotidienne des moines et chanoines réguliers au Moyen Age et Temps modernes*, ed. M. Derwich.

ever, a strong dependence of the canons on the dukes.[22] Further study should give special attention to the question of how an adaptation to the local constellation of Silesia took place, and eventually, differences from the original Bohemian typus may be detected.

The universal ideal of a *militia christi*, as understood by the military and hospitaller orders during the crusades in Palestine and as it lived on subsequently in the self-understanding of these institutions, took on a different form in this region than in others. The relative homogeneity of the *vita monastica*, *vita canonica,* or forms of mendicant religious life stood in contrast to the unique character of the hospitaller and military orders respectively, whose common spirituality cannot really be described, except possibly in a normative sense, by the analysis of privileges.[23]

IV

The role of the Silesian Crosiers was transformed from an involvement in charitable activities to a focus on pastoral care for the inhabitants of the lordly micro-structures that had been created by the local nobility. Lay brothers soon became clergy, who pursued missionary goals as well. The relationship of priests to serving sisters deserves particular consideration, for a male–female role-separation in the convents was the result. As in the case of St Matthew's, economic administration by the master remained separate from the spiritual direction by the prior; the friars of the order continued to fill the position of provost in parish churches and hospices alike. In contrast, the hospices were communalized up to 1370; that is to say, they were subordinated to citizen care exercised through *gubernatores* in the urban communities of Silesia. Consi-

---

Travaux du laboratoire de recherches sur l'histoire des congrégations et ordres religieux, Colloquia 1. Publications de l'Institut de l'Université (Wrocław, 1995), pp. 71-79, 539-53.

[22] Twelve manuscripts have survived: Biblioteka Uniwersitetu Wrocławskiego: I F 266; I F 502; I F 609; I F 658; I F 671; I F 680; I F 735; I F 762; I F 35a; I F 136; I F 139; I F 258 (fourteenth and fifteenth century); Necrologium: rps. IV. Q.198a, fol. 21v-32v; M. Starnawska, ,Nekrolog Krzyżowców z czerwoną gwiazdą: Źródło do Poznania środowiska zakonu i jego kontaktów', *Klasztor w społeczeństwie średniowiecznym i nowożytnym*, eds M. Derwich, A. Pobóg-Lenartowicz (Opole, Wrocław, 1996), pp. 210-19.

[23] K. Elm, 'Die Spiritualität der geistlichen Ritterorden des Mittelalters. Forschungsstand und Forschungsprobleme', *MC*, pp. 477-518; *idem* 'Die Spiritualität der geistlichen Ritterorden des Mittelalters', *Die Spiritualität der Ritterorden im Mittelalter*, ed. Z. H. Nowak. Ordines militares, Colloquia Torunensia Historica 7 (Toruń, 1993), pp. 7-22.

derations of principle imposed themselves on the multifunctionality of the hospice: should it be a hospital, a nursing home, a centre for the distribution of alms, or should benefices be provided or guests lodged?

The ducal support in each and every urban settlement in Silesia is particularly noticeable: nearly every dukedom founded and supported its own hospice. The original contribution of the nobility among the convents is not insignificant; a tendency toward communalization of the formerly princely and then civic foundations can be suspected. An increase in the influence of the bourgeois element may be read from the immense artistic donations for the Breslau St Elisabeth's church under the patronage of St Matthew's by the burghers and families of the city.[24] The progress of clericalization remains unexplained, as well as the role of the priest-monks, who, in the course of eastern settlement, assumed an important function. Did, in the end, the Crosiers become an order concerned with spiritual welfare like every other?

These observations lead us to regard a different context, namely that of the late medieval territories. The Crosiers' spread followed territorial zones of influence; these provincial zones, some of which led the way to national state boundaries, took into consideration commercial, geographical, and political units and criteria. The regional extension of the military orders, which can also be observed in other locations, gave rise to the development of different types of organization that brought expansion into further areas, as well as further deviations from the pattern, as we have seen in the case of Silesia. Each offshoot of the Crosiers dealt with the historical transition differently. Of course, the Hussite secession, as well as the urban development, strengthened an ethnic and linguistic separation that arose from the interaction between central powers and local initiatives to a considerable extent. In the region around the Oder, pragmatic solutions were adopted; that is to say, the modern orders established only traditional relationships with courts, as a result of the east–west phase displacement. This innovative diversification rose to the challenge of territorialization – somewhat similarly to the Iberian Peninsula, but com-

---

[24] H. Weczerka, 'Breslaus Zentralität in ostmitteleuropäischen Raum um 1500', *Metropolen im Wandel. Zentralität in Osteuropa an der Wende vom Mittelalter zur Neuzeit*, eds E. Engel, K. Lambrecht, H. Nagosch. Forschungen zur Geschichte und Kultur im östlichen Mitteleuropa (Berlin, 1995), pp. 245-62; O. Pusch, *Die Breslauer Rats- und Stadtgeschlechter in der Zeit von 1241 bis 1741*. Veröffentlichungen der Forschungsstelle Ostmitteleuropa an der Universität Dortmund, B: 33, 35, 38, 39, 41 (Dortmund, 1986-1991); W. v. Stromer, 'Nürnberg-Breslauer Wirtschaftsbeziehungen im Spätmittelalter', *Jahrbuch für fränkische Landesforschung* 34-35 (1975) [= Festschrift für Gerd Pfeiffer] 1079-1100.

pletely differently to, for example, Prussia, the realm of the Teutonic Knights –
and in any case, in a manner thoroughly appropriate to the specific situation in
developing Silesia.[25]

---

[25] *Ständefreiheit und Staatsgestaltung in Ostmitteleuropa. Übernationale Gemeinsam-
keiten in der politischen Kultur vom 16. bis 18. Jahrhundert*, eds J. Bahlke, H. J. Bö-
melburg, N. Kersken. Forschungen zur Geschichte und Kultur des östlichen Mitteleuropa (Leipzig, 1996); M. Starnawska, 'Crusade Orders on Polish Lands during the
Middle Ages. Adaptation in a Peripheral Environment', *Religious Communities and
Corporations in Central Europe, 10th to 15th centuries*. Quaestiones medii aevi novae
2 (Warszawa, 1997), pp. 121-42; cf. T. Jurek, 'Die Entwicklung eines schlesischen
Regionalbewußtseins im Mittelalter', *Zeitschrift für Ostmitteleuropa-Forschung* 47
(1998) 21-48; *Silesiographie. Stand und Perspektiven der Schlesienforschung. Festschrift für Norbert Conrads zum 60. Geburtstag*, eds M Weber, C Rabe. Wissenschaftliche Schriften des Vereins für die Geschichte Schlesiens 4 (Würzburg, 1998).

8

The 'Hospice of the German Nobility': Changes in the Admission Policy of the Teutonic Knights in the Fifteenth Century

Johannes A. Mol

Introduction

The Teutonic Order has been called an aristocratic corporation in crisis for the period 1410 to 1466.[1] Crisis, decline, and decay are the words that have been used to mark the condition in which the order found itself in the fifteenth century.[2] And indeed this brotherhood whose task it was to protect Christendom against its enemies got into a long series of difficulties in this period, which in the long run threatened to destroy the very foundations of its existence, at least in the Baltic, where the order by then had its main area of operation. Since the Grand Duke of Lithuania had been converted in 1386 there were, formally, no heathen to be fought. From then on, the only object of the order could be to ensure that the crusading state it had founded prevailed against its mighty catholic contending neighbours Poland and Lithuania. The order had to do this on its own, without the help of the west-European nobility, which in the pre-

---

[1] See the subtitle, chosen by M. Burleigh, *Prussian society and the German Order. An aristocratic corporation in crisis c. 1410-1466* (Cambridge, 1984).

[2] J. Voigt, *Geschichte des Deutschen Ritterordens in seinen zwölf Balleien in Deutschland*, 2 vols (Berlin, 1857-1859), here vol. 1, pp. 640-41; S. Ekdahl, 'Die Schlacht von Tannenberg und ihre Bedeutung in der Geschichte des Ordensstaates', *Deutsche Ostkunde* 35 (1989) 63-80, at pp. 68-70; H. Boockmann, *Deutsche Geschichte im Osten Europas. Ostpreussen und Westpreussen* (Berlin, 1992), p. 185.

From *Mendicants, Military Orders, and Regionalism in Medieval Europe*, ed. Jürgen Sarnowsky. Copyright © 1999 by Jürgen Sarnowsky. Published by Ashgate Publishing Ltd, Gower House, Croft Road, Aldershot, Hampshire, GU11 3HR, Great Britain.

ceding century had come to Prussia in great numbers to hunt down heathen Lithuanians. Only the Livonian branch could still serve Christendom after 1400 by continuing its struggle against the schismatic Russians. The smashing defeat at Tannenberg in 1410 and the humiliating second peace-treaty of Thorn in 1466, in which the grand master had to cede more than half of his territory and strongholds to the Polish king and to accept his overlordship for the remainder, had seriously weakened the cohesion of the order – if they did not already mark the end of its universal ambitions. Add to this the fact that the third branch of the order, which was organized in twelve bailiwicks in the German empire at the same time, had to face the consequences of an economic depression and, for some bailiwicks, increasingly had to put up with the control of territorial lords,[3] and the gloomy background of my story is sketched. In this context, the question nearly automatically is to be raised what connections can be established between these developments and the changes that took place in the conditions of access to the order. Before I focus upon these changes, let us first have a look at the figures.

Figures

Many things could be said about the question of how precise our figures are and what they tell us exactly.[4] Especially, the quota of knight-brethren in Prussia and Livonia on the eve of Tannenberg have been subject to discussion for

---

[3] R. ten Haaf, *Deutschordensstaat und Deutschordensballeien. Untersuchungen über Leistung und Sonderung der Deutschordensprovinzen in Deutschland vom 13. bis zum 16. Jahrhundert*. Göttinger Bausteine zur Geschichtswissenschaft 5 (2nd edn, Göttingen, Frankfurt, Berlin, 1954), pp. 52-59.

[4] The numbers in the annexed tables are mainly based on F. Benninghoven, 'Zur Zahl und Standortverteilung der Brüder des Deutschen Ordens in den Balleien um 1400', *Preussenland* 26 (1988) 1-20. See also Voigt, 1, pp. 301-3, Ten Haaf, pp. 38-39, and E. Maschke, 'Die inneren Wandlungen des Deutschen Ritterordens', *Geschichte und Gegenwartsbewußtsein. Festschrift für Hans Rothfels zum 70. Geburtstag dargebracht* (Göttingen, 1973), pp. 247-77 [reprinted in *idem, Domus Hospitalis Theutonicorum. Europäische Verbindungslinien der Deutschordensgeschichte. Gesammelte Aufsätze aus den Jahren 1931-1963*, ed. U. Arnold. QStGDO 10 (Bonn-Bad Godesberg, 1970), pp. 35-59], at pp. 257-58. I have corrected some evident errors and omissions for the bailiwicks of Utrecht and Biesen. As for the date of the first visitation report from the beginning of the fifteenth century, Benninghoven gives two possibilities: either 1400 or 1409 to 1410, of which he takes the former. I have chosen the latter, because of the absence of Ootmarsum under the commanderies of Utrecht (this house was transferred to Westphalia only after 1406: ARDOU, no. 2298).

many years, mainly because they have to be estimated.[5] The figures for the bailiwicks did not get that much attention until now. They are based on visitation reports. The main problem with both groups of figures is that they are not complete: the data for the second half of the fifteenth century are missing, simply because no visitation reports have been preserved for that period. To get some grip on them we can only estimate the development on the basis of sure counts for some groups of commanderies. In doing this we have to leave Prussia and Livonia aside: Prussia because the loss of more than half of its territory in 1466 makes a comparison less useful, and Livonia because there are hardly any numbers available for this branch over the period 1450 to 1550. Our possibilities are thus limited to those bailiwicks in the German empire for which enough source-material has been preserved. As research in this field has not yet made many advances – most studies of individual bailiwicks and houses focus upon regional themes – for the beginning of the sixteenth century some figures can be produced only for the bailiwicks of Franconia, Koblenz, and Utrecht.[6] They seem, however, to mirror tendencies reflected in many houses of other bailiwicks at the same time.

Which conclusions can be drawn from these figures? In the first place, that on the eve of Tannenberg, the order was at full strength in the German empire, compared to the foregoing decades. Secondly, it can be assessed that after Tannenberg – up to the crisis that would lead to the Thirteen Years' War – the order did not succeed in making up the losses in Prussia and Livonia. In the same period the number of knight-brethren in the bailiwicks was on the wane too, rather dramatically. This decrease, however, was largely compensated for

---

[5] B. Jähnig, 'Der Danziger Deutschordenskonvent in der Mitte des 15. Jahrhunderts', *Danzig in acht Jahrhunderten. Beiträge zur Geschichte eines hansischen und preussischen Mittelpunktes*, eds B. Jähnig, P. Letkemann (Münster, 1985), pp. 151-84, at pp. 156-58; Benninghoven, p. 20; K. Militzer, 'Die Ritterbrüder im livländischen Zweig des Deutschen Ordens. Eine Einführung in die Möglichkeiten und Grenzen der Auswertung des Ritterbruderkatalogs', *Ritterbrüder im livländischen Zweig des Deutschen Ordens*, eds L. Fenske, K. Militzer. Quellen und Studien zur baltischen Geschichte 12 (Cologne, 1993), pp. 11-70, at pp. 14-16; S. Neitmann, *Von der Grafschaft Mark nach Livland. Ritterbrüder aus Westfalen im livländischen Deutschen Orden*. Veröffentlichungen aus den Archiven Preussischer Kulturbesitz, Beiheft 3 (Cologne, 1993), pp. 35-37.

[6] The sixteenth century figures in Tables 4.1, 4.2 and 4.3 are respectively based on: D.J. Weiss, *Die Geschichte der Deutschordens-Ballei Franken im Mittelalter* (Neustadt a. d. Aisch, 1991), pp. 337-41; H. Limburg, *Die Hochmeister des Deutschen Ordens und die Ballei Koblenz*. QStGDO 8 (Bad Godesberg, 1969), p. 167; J. A. Mol, *De Friese huizen van de Duitse Orde. Nes, Schoten en Steenkerk en hun plaats in het middeleeuwse Friese kloosterlandschap* (Leeuwarden, 1991), pp. 204-5.

by an increase in the number of priest-brethren. As the figures for Koblenz demonstrate, the diminution in the number of knights was strongest in the four bailiwicks that were under direct control of the grand master, the so-called 'Kammerballeien' or chamber-bailiwicks: apart from Koblenz, these were Alsace-Burgundy, Austria, and Bozen. In the eight bailiwicks under the German master, of which Franconia was by far the greatest, the decrease of knight-brethren was almost totally balanced by an increase of priest-brethren.

When we then try to extend the line up to 1500 we see that the developments in the bailiwicks in the period after 1450 are varying. The chamber-bailiwicks of the grand master – represented in Table 4.2 by Koblenz – did lose both knight-brethren and priests. Between 1410 and 1500 the total strength in this bailiwick fell back to less than a third. In the main bailiwick of the German master, Franconia, on the other hand, the total number of brethren more or less remained stable. The number of knights continued to diminish but this development was nearly balanced by the growth of the priest-brethren staff. For Utrecht the tendency has yet another direction, though it has to be admitted that for this bailiwick the latest survey, in which figures are mentioned, dates only from 1539. From the source-material on individual Utrecht houses, however, it can be deduced that the decrease in figures reached its greatest momentum by the end of the fifteenth century.[7] In the neighbouring bailiwicks of Biesen and Westphalia the number of knight-brethren also continued to fall in the same period, albeit not as sharply as in Utrecht.

Considering these tendencies, if one tries to estimate the total strength of the Teutonic Knights in all the bailiwicks in the German empire about the year 1500, one will probably have to come up with a number of not more than 170 or 180 brethren. All in all, therefore, less than half of their number in 1410.

Recruitment

How, then, can one evaluate this decrease in numbers? The Berlin archivist Friedrich Benninghoven is very clear about it: according to him the main cause is the 'wirtschaftlich-finanzielle Niedergang, der den Lebensunterhalt der Brü-

---

[7] See for example the dates for the commanderies of Leiden, Middelburg, and Schelluinen: L. E. Loopstra, 'De Leidse commanderij van de Duitse Orde in de middeleeuwen', *Leids Jaarboekje* 1984, 33-59, at pp. 50-51; P. Aengenheyster, *Die Kommende des Deutschen Ordens von Middelburg zwischen den Jahren 1248 und 1581* (unpublished M.A. Thesis, Free University, Amsterdam, 1990), pp. 24, 34; and H. Zuidervaart, *Het Duitse huis te Schelluinen* (Schelluinen, 1988), p. 30.

der so stark geschmälert hat, daß ihre Zahl verringert werden mußte'.[8] If I am interpreting correctly, two premises are hidden in this judgement. First, that the established decrease was not a matter of supply, not the consequence of a lessened interest of the German nobility in membership of the order. And secondly, that the cost of living for knights was far higher than for priests – otherwise it could not be explained how in some bailiwicks the number of priest-brethren was growing. That does suggest that the decrease in knights was the deliberate result of a policy of limitation, adopted by the leaders of the order. Was this indeed the case? Before I comment upon that, it seems useful to sketch how and by whom knight-brethren were admitted to the order in the fifteenth century.[9]

In theory it was the grand master who decided on receiving new brethren, though he needed the advice of the chapter general. The statutes leave no doubt about that. The grand master could, however, delegate his authority in these matters to other officials, and so he did. But here we have to discern between his own dominions – Prussia and the chamber-bailiwicks – and those of the Livonian and German masters. The latter already controlled the recruitment for their branches by 1400 – and probably earlier.[10] The German master in turn delegated his power to admit new brethren regularly to the heads of the bailiwicks, called land-commanders. Eberhard von Seinsheim for example authorized the Utrecht Land-Commander Herman van Keppel to receive 'honest men' into the brotherhood of the order in 1426.[11] Probably this authorization was related to one or more individual cases.

The Master of Livonia mostly held the initiative in his own hands. How he received new brethren can be gleaned from a report on a recruiting campaign that the Land-Commander of Westphalia organized for him in 1411, shortly after Tannenberg.[12] The Livonian master himself was a Westphalian, and

---

[8] Benninghoven, p. 18.

[9] For the following, I am leaning heavily on Voigt, vol. 1, pp. 256-79 ('Die Aufnahme im Deutschen Orden'), and K. Militzer, 'Die Aufnahme von Ritterbrüdern in den Deutschen Orden. Ausbildungsstand und Aufnahmevoraussetzungen', *Das Kriegswesen der Ritterorden im Mittelalter*, ed. Z. H. Nowak. Ordines Militares – Colloquia Torunensia Historica 6 (Toruń, 1991), pp. 7-18.

[10] Militzer, 'Ritterbrüder', p. 60.

[11] J.J. de Geer tot Oudegein, *Archieven der Ridderlijke Duitsche Orde, balie van Utrecht*, 2 vols (Utrecht, 1871), no. 348.

[12] Ibid. no. 345; J.A. Mol, 'Nederlandse ridderbroeders van de Duitse Orde in Lijfland: herkomst, afkomst en carrières', *Bijdragen en Mededelingen voor de Geschiedenis der Nederlanden* 111 (1996) 1-29, at pp. 15-16.

Westphalia by then was the most important recruiting region for the Livonian branch of the Teutonic Order. In this report the land-commander who was entrusted with this task tells us how he proceeded, asking his subordinate commanders whether they knew suitable candidates among their kin. Within six weeks he assembled thirty-three men, of whom he demanded admission fees between 0 and 60 Rhenish guilders. He gave them lodgings in his houses till the last one had arrived. After that he had them accompanied to Lübeck, where they departed on a ship to Riga.

It seems as if the grand master recruited his personnel for Prussia and his chamber-bailiwicks in the same way. That is to say, his officials first of all received new brethren for Prussia. Only when brethren had proved themselves to be good administrators – after a military career – could they expect an appointment as commander in one of the chamber-bailiwicks.[13] Thus, in the bailiwick of Koblenz, for example, practically no young knight-brethren could be found.

The grand master in Prussia recruited hardly any more brethren in Prussia itself than the Master of Livonia recruited from the nobility in Livonia. Nineteen out of twenty of all brethren for the Prussian branch were recruited in the German empire.[14] They came not only from the areas that were covered by the chamber-bailiwicks but also from other parts of the empire. The recruitment could be organised in separate campaigns or by individual admissions via the land-commanders. Grand Master Konrad von Jungingen, for example, sent two of his officials to Germany in 1406 to give the habit to new brothers, sending them directly to Prussia.[15] The same was done by Paul von Rusdorf in 1422 and 1428.[16] Apart from such campaigns, the grand master regularly contacted individual land-commanders about receiving new brethren for his territory. The Utrecht and Biesen sources from the first half of the fifteenth century mention a few cases of land-commanders presenting the habit for Prussia.[17]

---

[13] Militzer, 'Aufnahme', p. 12.

[14] H. Boockmann, 'Herkunftsregion und Einsatzgebiet', *RR*, pp. 7-19, at pp. 16-17.

[15] Maschke, p. 260; Geheimes Staatsarchiv Preußischer Kulturbesitz, Berlin, XX. Hauptabteilung, Historisches Staatsarchiv Königsberg, Ordensfoliant 3, p. 278.

[16] 1422: Jähnig, pp. 161-62; 1428: Ten Haaf, p. 40. The recruitment campaign of 1422 was organized in view of the coming war with Poland. Until then, Paul von Rusdorf's predecessor, Michael Küchmeister, had maintained a stop on admissions because the order could not feed newcomers.

[17] ARDOU, no. 340 (Land-Commander Herman van Keppel, before 1444). See also Ten Haaf, p. 40; and Jähnig, pp. 161-63.

Although serious prosopographical studies are still lacking for Prussia and the bailiwicks,[18] we get the impression from the names of the brethren that by 1400 there was hardly any exchange of personnel between the bailiwicks of the German master on the one side and the Prussian and Livonian branches on the other.[19] Apparently their career-circuits were already separated by then. Every brother who took the habit for Prussia or Livonia left at a very young age. As we learn from a report on an incident in Utrecht in 1454, he was expected never to return to his family or bailiwick of origin.[20] The carnal brother of the ruling land-commander, who, after serving in Livonia, had showed up in Utrecht to live on the pocket of the bailiwick, probably frustrated in his career, was supplied with a horse, armour, and a departing bonus of 150 guilders on the express condition that he would leave immediately for Livonia, never to come back again.

On the other hand, every brother who was received for the bailiwick made his career there. He only went to the Baltic if he expressly wished to go there, like Knight-Brother Bernt Schele, who – bored with his administration tasks in a remote Utrecht commandery – applied for a transfer to Prussia or Livonia in 1431.[21] And, of course, brethren of the bailiwick had to go to Prussia if they were called for a common expedition, as happened several times in the years after Tannenberg with the brethren of Biesen.[22] For Utrecht, such a call is

---

[18] Only for the bailiwick of Biesen have names and data been systematically gathered, by Michel van der Eycken ('Ridders, priesters en ambtenaren van de balije Biesen', *De Balije Biesen in het Maas-Rijngebied*, ed. U. Arnold [Gent, 1993], pp. 55-79), though for the fifteenth century his collection is far from complete. Most other bailiwicks have not been studied at all in this respect, the Prussian branch at least for the period after 1350. Apart from Jähnig no one has recently taken the trouble to gather data on the origins, descent, and careers of Prussian brothers, probably because their number is too great for one person to work on. For the Livonian branch, which was far smaller than the Prussian one, an extensive catalogue with prosopographical data on all known knight-brethren was published in 1993 by L. Fenske and K. Militzer (*Ritterbrüder im livländischen Zweig des Deutschen Ordens*): the result of a lengthy international research project that started in 1987. As Militzer and also Neitmann have shown, these data allow us a sharp view of the personal structures of the Teutonic Order. They could tell us even more if they could be compared with the data of Prussia and the bailiwicks. So here there is still a lot of work to do. It almost goes without saying that this can only be done by a research group rather than by one person alone.

[19] Boockmann, 'Herkunftsregion', p. 14; Neitmann, p. 631.

[20] ARDOU, no. 313*.

[21] ARDOU, no. 2198; De Geer, *Archieven*, no. 807.

[22] W. Reese, 'Gesamtdeutsche und territoriale Zusammenhänge in der Geschichte des Deutschritterordens der Niederlande', *Blätter zur Deutschen Landesgeschichte* 83 (1936-1937) 223-72, at p. 243.

recorded for 1453, when the herald of the grand master personally turned up in the Teutonic house of Utrecht to get all hands to go to Prussia.[23] It was in fact the last time such an expedition was organized. It was also the last time personnel were sent to the Baltic from the bailiwick of Utrecht. After 1466 there is no mention of recruitment for Prussia or Livonia in the Utrecht records. By then the bailiwick seems to have been leading its own life, more or less independantly of the needs of the Prussian and Livonian branches, independently too from the German master. Only when a knight-brother had to be punished, was a transfer to the Baltic considered in Utrecht.[24]

Conditions

The conditions for entry into the Teutonic Order are not found in the original statutes. Some requirements are formulated in the *Gesetze*, the laws that were added to the statutes and early laws under Grand Master Dietrich von Altenburg (1335-1341).[25] Klaus Militzer supposes that they already date from the end of the thirteenth century.[26] These requirements are very clear, and seem very similar to what was asked by the Templars.[27] Recruits of the Teutonic Order had to be young (over fourteen years old), healthy, without physical imperfections, not hindered by debts or other worldly obligations. And they had to be of knightly descent. These principles were still in force by 1400, suited as they were to the military practice of the order at that time. On its expeditions in Prussia and Livonia, in its battles and skirmishes, only healthy and hardened young men could be used. As long as knight-brothers were effectively sent into the field – and in Livonia this was the case during the whole of the fifteenth century, whilst in Prussia after Tannenberg the military undertakings were more and more put out to mercenaries – these conditions continued to remain important. The requirement of knightly birth, *rittermassig und geboren zu iren wappen*,[28] guaranteed that candidate brothers were familiar with, and from their early years on well trained in, the handling of horses, swords, and

---

[23] J. J. de Geer tot Oudegein, *Excerpten uit de oude rekeningen der Ridderlijke Duitsche Orde, balye van Utrecht, vóór de kerkhervorming* (Utrecht, 1895), p. 42.

[24] Mol, 'Nederlandse ridderbroeders', p. 17.

[25] Perlbach, p. 149.

[26] Militzer, 'Aufnahme', p. 8.

[27] A. J. Forey, 'Recruitment to the military orders', *Viator* 17 (1986) 139-71, at pp. 141 seqq.

[28] Cf. n. 15.

armour. The grand master could, by the way, revoke this condition. As we know that in the thirteenth and fourteenth centuries many sons of patricians were admitte,[29] the condition cannot have had its decisive class-discriminating character by then.

In the fifteenth century this was to change. Both in the bailiwicks and the Baltic the importance of noble birth came to be stressed. And 'noble' in this context did not mean of high noble descent (*edelfrei*), but of knightly birth. Although high-born noblemen, counts' and dynasts' sons are known to have joined the order, from the beginning most of its brethren had been recruited among what the later Middle Ages called the lesser nobility or gentry.[30] In the German empire this lower nobility originated from an amalgamation of the class of the free knights and that of the *ministeriales,* that is, of men originally not free who were servants of important lords. This orientation on the class of the *ministeriales* is demonstrated by the fact that most grand masters and also most masters of Livonia and Germany had this background.

What then strikes the eye is that, in both the bailiwicks and the Baltic in the fifteenth century, a call resounds for full noble birth to be required of new brothers – at first only for the two halves (that is from both parents) and later for the four parts (grandparents). This requirement had to be met, it seems, whenever a knight-brother wanted to exert a lordship in the name of the order. When, for example, a new land-commander had to be appointed in Utrecht in 1442, the main objection that was raised against the candidate Dirk van Enghuzen was that he was noble only for the eighth part, and even that only by bastardy.[31] Thus, complete knightly descent from both father and mother was already required at that time for the simple membership of the order. In 1440 some discontented brethren in Prussia formulated as one of their demands that every newcomer had to prove his nobility by this criterion before being admitted.[32] Sons of patricians, bastards, and half nobles – however experienced and trained in administration and the use of arms they might be – were not welcome any more. About 1450, noble birth from two parts was explicitly

---

[29] Maschke, p. 258.

[30] M. Hellmann, 'Bemerkungen zur sozialgeschichtlichen Erforschung des Deutschen Ordens', *Historisches Jahrbuch* 80 (1961) 126–42, at pp. 128 seqq.

[31] W*ant he een achtendeel noch geen deel en hadde dat der ritterscap to behoert, dan van verre basterdie*, Geheimes Staatsarchiv Preußischer Kulturbesitz, Berlin, XX. Hauptabteilung, Historisches Staatsarchiv Königsberg, Ordensbriefarchiv (OBA), no. 8306. The complaint was uttered towards the grand master by the old Land-Commander of Westphalia, Sweder Cobbing, who came from the same region as Enghuzen.

[32] Maschke, p. 274.

established in an oath formula of the German master.[33] But by then the tendency was already heading towards a further sharpening of the criterion. In 1451, the visitators of the grand master ordered the Commander of Koblenz to admit only brethren who could demonstrate four noble parts.[34] This criterion was in force throughout the order by about 1500.[35] It must be stressed, however, that this development by no means took place only in the Teutonic Order. It can be observed in cathedral chapters, nunneries, and secular military orders as well, even at earlier dates.[36]

Brethren of German birth: the importance of the region

What changed at the same time was that admission became restricted to what was then called the German nation. At first glance, this may seem strange because of the order's name. But that name, derived from the Hospital of the Germans in Jerusalem that was considered by the order to be its real centre, was not meant to restrict entry only to German-speaking brothers. Quite like the other military orders the Teutonic Knights fostered their universal principles and ambitions.[37] Although in practice most of its members came from the German empire, occasionally men from non German-speaking areas were admitted. Thus, until the end of the fourteenth century Italians, Swedes, Frisians, and even some French, Polish, and Spanish knights could be found in the ranks of the order.[38]

---

[33] According to this formula, at his admission the candidate had to bring two knights of his kin (fründe), not older than forty, who could guarantee that he was ... siner synne, vernunffte, gelieder unn am leybe ungebrechelichen und von vater und muter edel und wappensgenoss, OBA, no. 9447; Jähnig, pp. 161-62.

[34] H. Reimer, 'Verfall der Deutsch-Ordensballei Koblenz im 15. Jahrhundert', Trierisches Archiv 11 (1907) 1-42, at p. 29; Jähnig, p. 162 n. 52, mentions the case of a Heinrich Graf von Schwarzburg, who already in 1432 vouched for Candidate-Brother Hans von Hongede that he had four knightly grandparents.

[35] Militzer, 'Aufnahme', p. 14.

[36] K. Militzer, 'Die Einbindung des Deutschen Ordens in die süddeutsche Adelswelt', RR, pp. 141-60, at pp. 153-54; A. Schulte, Der Adel und die deutsche Kirche im Mittelalter. Studien zur Sozial-, Rechts- und Kirchengeschichte (Stuttgart, 1910), pp. 29 seqq.; E. Koch, De kloosterpoort als sluitpost? Adellijke vrouwen langs Maas en Rijn tussen huwelijk en convent, 1200-1600. Maaslandse monografieën 54 (Leeuwarden, Mechelen, 1994), p. 65.

[37] U. Arnold, 'Europa und die Region – widerstreitende Kräfte in der Entwicklung des Deutschen Ordens im Mittelalter', RR, pp. 161-72, at p. 164.

[38] Maschke, 'Wandlungen', pp. 253-55; Militzer, 'Aufnahme', pp. 9-10.

In the fifteenth century this situation belonged to the past. The call to forbid entry to foreign knights resounded louder and louder. When the Land-Commander of Biesen received a Walloon as knight for Prussia in 1449, the grand master wrote to him – even though this candidate was a son of the Count of Namur – that he should never do this again; and he sent the young man back to Maastricht immediately.[39] In the words of the grand master the order was a real German order, to which no non German-speaking brethren could be admitted.

This definitive expulsion of other nations and languages ran parallel to the growth of regional thinking in the order. Or, perhaps we should better call it regional particularism.[40] The development of this phenomenon can, among other things, be concluded from the quarrels that were fought out in both Livonia and Prussia between brethren of different regional origin in the first half of the fifteenth century.[41] The assignment of desirable offices and posts in the commanderies was the main issue. Brethren high in the hierarchy, who could decide on promotions, first of all tended to favour members of their families and then fellow-countrymen, that is, men from their own regional noble circle. In this way discriminatory tendencies were established which led almost automatically to complaints by men from minority regions. In Prussia discord existed between the south-Germans (Franconians and Swabians) on the one side, and north-Germans (Rhinelanders and Westphalians) on the other. In Livonia the Westphalians contested with the Rhinelanders. In the latter case the opponents could perfectly well understand each other's dialects. Thus, not the language as such was at stake, but the difference between marriage-circles, that apparently did not interfere. In both Prussia and Livonia the complaints were most vehement at the moment when the smaller group was dominating. In both branches the larger group won, with the effect that in the end it monopolized all important offices for its members more completely than ever before.

---

[39] Voigt, vol. 1, pp. 273-74.

[40] Arnold, pp. 165 seqq.

[41] Prussia: C. A. Lückerath, *Paul von Rusdorf. Hochmeister des Deutschen Ordens 1422-1441*. QStGDO 15 (Bad Godesberg, 1969), pp. 184 seqq.; Livonia: Neitmann, pp. 54 seqq.

Financial conditions

As with every other religious order, the canonical rule was in force also for the Teutonic Order that no quid pro quo compensation could be required from candidate members at their entry.[42] But that was theory; in practice this rule was easy to get around for the leaders of the military orders, by presenting the entrance fee as a free gift.[43] In spite of the vow of poverty, the postulant who could not produce such alms was not admitted. Unfortunately not much is known about such simoniacal practices, as they were forbidden in the twelfth century and since then carefully kept out of the records![44]

Thus, for the Teutonic Order not many data are available. We do know that a knight-brother who went to Prussia had to bring one or more horses, a saddle, armour, and a sum of money, enough to cover his travelling expenses; all before he was given the habit with the black cross.[45] We already saw that the official of the Livonian master charged his candidate brethren 60 Rhenish guilders, although only a few of them could afford to pay the sum totally. 60 guilders was exactly the sum that is mentioned in the already quoted oath-formula of the German Master Jobst von Venningen (1447-1454), as the sum new Prussian brethren had to pay for three horses, besides 25 guilders for the cost of travel.[46]

It is not clear whether the knight-brethren who entered the bailiwicks and stayed there had to bring the same equipment or the equivalent in money, but I tend to think so. In the accounts of the bailiwicks an entrance fee is sometimes mentioned, of which it is not clear whether the candidate got his horses and all else for it or not. In 1457 a sum of 100 Rhenish guilders, for example, is noted for the admission of Brother Claes van Malsen as a knight.[47] That was a large

---

[42] On entry-gifts to religious foundations in general see J. Lynch, *Simoniacal entry into religious life from 1000 to 1260. A social, economic and legal study* (Columbus, Ohio, 1976).

[43] Forey, p. 155.

[44] For Frisia, some evidence is available on the payment of entrance fees by Hospitaller and Teutonic Order's priest-brethren and sergeants: Mol, *Friese huizen*, pp. 87, 106.

[45] In 1422 Grand Master Paul von Rusdorf wanted his officials to recruit ... *brudere, die gutin harnisch und hengiste hetten*: Jähnig, p. 161; see also: *Protokolle der Kapitel und Gespräche des Deutschen Ordens im Reich (1499-1525)*, eds M. Biskup, I. Janosz-Biskupowa. QStGDO 41 (Marburg, 1991), p. 42 (1502).

[46] N. 23 above.

[47] '*Item IC rijnsgulden van heren Claes van Malsen als hie ten oirden gecleyt wart*': ARDOU, no. 330:1.

amount of money, at least for a member of the gentry. It probably was the standard fee. When in 1467 the brethren of Biesen had to take measures to consolidate their finances; they established the maximum number both of knights and priests at twenty each, with the express condition that every knight-brother had to pay 130 Rhine guilders at his entry, where priest-brethren had to offer 25 guilders.[48] Considering the necessity of raising their income, it is likely that the brethren had thus raised their earlier fee.

Hospice of the German nobility

Bearing in mind the information gathered above, it is not difficult to answer the question of whether the decrease in the number of knights was a matter of supply or demand. As the interest of the nobility in securing places in the order was growing rather than decreasing, we cannot but choose the latter option. In the different bailiwicks nobles were putting pressure on the leading officials to admit their younger sons into the order. The Land-Commander of Biesen wrote to the grand master in 1449 that he had received a lot of complaints from nobles in the neighbourhood that he had admitted too many foreigners to his bailiwick.[49] What other function could the order possibly have, according to them, than to offer a refuge to the nobility of the region? *Spital und Zuflucht und Aufenthalt des Adels Teutscher Nation* is what the order was by then called,[50] or even, *Spital des armen Adels Teutscher Nation*. In which case, as Manfred Hellmann made clear, *armer Adel* is not to be understood as poor, but as lower nobility, the more so because really impoverished noble families simply could not afford the high entrance fees mentioned earlier. We can assume that in most bailiwicks admission to the very limited number of places came to be reserved to a small group of top families within the gentry.

How then do we have to estimate the weight of the economic decline that Benninghoven gave as his explanation for the diminishing numbers of knights? It is beyond doubt that most bailiwicks did not flourish in the fifteenth century, although the picture for a number of them – especially Franconia – is not as

---

[48] J. Grauwels, *Regestenlijst der oorkonden van de landkommanderij Oudenbiezen en onderhorige kommanderijen*, 4 vols (Brussels, 1966-1969), here vol. 1, no. 428.

[49] Voigt, vol. 1, p. 273.

[50] Hellmann, p. 137; Maschke, pp. 268, 272; H. H. Hofmann, *Der Staat des Deutschmeisters*. Studien zur bayerischen Verfassungs- und Sozialgeschichte 3 (Munich, 1964), p. 199.

gloomy as it has sometimes been sketched.[51] Further research is required in this matter. It is certain that the bailiwick of Thuringia nearly continuously balanced on the verge of bankruptcy.[52] And the sad case of Bohemia will become clear from the article of Libor Jan below.[53]

In this decline the most important factor was not the economic depression. In fact, most bailiwicks did overcome its consequences in the first decades of the fifteenth century.[54] Neither did the help for Prussia exhaust their resources – apart from the chamber-bailiwicks. Most of their material troubles seem to have been caused by war or mismanagement.

Were the incomes of the bailiwicks in the fifteenth century really so much lower than in the fourteenth, that less people could be maintained – Prussia, of course, set aside? The strange phenomenon is, and I take Biesen and Utrecht as examples again, that in this very period of 'decline' a series of extensive and costly building activities were undertaken in some of the bailiwicks which had their share in the general burdens of the order. In Biesen, Land-Commander Iwan van Cortenbach who went three times on expedition to Prussia after Tannenberg to support the grand master with men and money, from 1420 to 1435, erected a completely new castle on the order's territory in Gemert, only to embellish thereafter the commanderies of Bernissem and Bekkevoort and the main house of the bailiwick in Maastricht.[55] In the bailiwick of Utrecht, which fell prey to internal disorder between 1440 and 1465, costing the brethren enormous sums of money,[56] Land-Commander Johan van Drongelen built a new and luxurious aisle for the convent complex in Utrecht in 1475.[57] At the time of

---

[51] Hofmann, pp. 92 seqq.; Weiss, pp. 328-36, 392-94. The latter author states, on the basis of detailed research, that the bailiwick of Franconia experienced a 'wirtschaftliche Aufschwung' under Land-Commander Melchior von Neuneck (1463-1491). It induces him to say that Voigt's thesis of the economic decline of the Teutonic Order in the fifteenth century has been falsified.

[52] B. Sommerlad, Der Deutsche Orden in Thüringen (Halle, 1931), pp. 66 seqq.

[53] Below, pp. 233-42.

[54] K. Militzer, 'Auswirkungen der spätmittelalterlichen Agrardepression auf die Deutschordensballeien', Von Akkon bis Wien. Studien zur Deutschordensgeschichte vom 13. bis zum 20. Jahrhundert, ed. U. Arnold. QStGDO 20 (Marburg, 1978), pp. 62-75, at p. 74.

[55] B. Aarts, 'Bouw en verbouw van het kasteel van de Duitse Orde', Commanderij Gemert. Beeldend Verleden, ed. T. Thelen (Gemert, 1990), pp. 43-64, at pp. 46-51; A. Otten, De vestiging van de Duitse Orde in Gemert 1200-1500 (Gemert, 1987), p. 85.

[56] Reese, pp. 251-60.

[57] B. Klück, De landcommanderij van de Duitse Orde te Utrecht (Utrecht, 1995), pp. 26 seqq.

his appointment, according to the chronicle of the Utrecht bailiwick, he found nothing but empty stores; only the treasury was full, but with letters of debt, up to 3000 Rhenish guilders. How to explain these developments?

The answer, of course, is not that difficult. Both van Cortenbach and van Drongelen, bringing in their family capital, wished to impress. They wanted to show their lordly qualities and demonstrate the honour of the order according to what they thought the tradition of the order was.[58] And – even more important – they were eager to have the luxury and comfort suitable to men of their class. What becomes apparent in their buildings is the raised standard of living to which they and their fellow-brethren had become accustomed. The raising of this standard took priority over maintaining the number of knights or supporting the political ambitions of the grand master. The consequence was that the number of brethren had to be limited, and by the end of the century not more than one knight-brother was residing in most houses of the bailiwicks. Brethren who led a communal or convent life were hardly to be found by about 1500. The less prosperous houses were entrusted to priest-brethren. Then, nearly every knight in the bailiwick was landlord and administrator and had to keep up appearances as such. It has been noted quite often, but it still remains striking, that in this period, members of the Teutonic Order are no longer called *fratres* but *domini* ('Herren').[59] They had become Teutonic lords instead of Teutonic brethren.

If the foregoing may be summarized in two sentences, I would like to conclude that the fifteenth century did not end with the downfall of the Teutonic Order. From the materials collected concerning its admission policy it has become clear, however, that by then the order had undergone a metamorphosis from a universal brotherhood to a confederation of regional corporations of celibate noblemen, whose main function it was to mirror and feed the self-consciousness and class pride of their families and nobility groups.

---

[58] On the person of Johan van Drongelen, see Mol, *Friese huizen*, pp. 145 seqq.

[59] P. Heim, *Die Deutschordenskommende Beuggen und die Anfänge der Ballei Elsass-Burgund*. QStGDO 32 (Bonn-Bad Godesberg, 1977), pp. 148-49; Arnold, p. 167.

Appendix: numbers of brethren in the Teutonic Order

Table 1 Prussia

	Knights
1410	c. 700
1438	c. 350

Table 2 Livonia

	Knights
1410	300-350
1451	c. 200

Table 3 The bailiwicks in the German empire

	Knights	Priests	Sergeants	Total	Others*
1379	-	-	-	701	123
1383	-	-	-	662	123
1394	-	-	-	620	86
1410	362	359	57	778	-
1451	226	402	32	660	-

* Chaplains, sisters, corrodians, schoolmasters, etc.

Single bailiwicks

Table 4.1 Franconia

	Knights	Priests	Total
1410	80	53	133
1451	*52	77	130
1513	41	83	124

* Including one sergeant.

Table 4.2 Koblenz

	Knights	Priests	Total
1410	37	16	53
1451*	**16	23	39
1515	2	13	15

* Excluding the house of Dieren which was sold to Biesen in 1420.
** Including two sergeants.

Table 4.3 Utrecht*

	Knights	Priests	Total
1410	c. 16	31	47
1451**	15	29	44
1539	8	9	17

* Excluding two houses in Frisia.
** Including the house of Dieren which was bought from Biesen in 1434.

9

The Basle Dominicans between
Town and Province

Bernhard Neidiger

Like every mendicant convent the Basle Dominicans were integrated into their province as well as the order as a whole, and these superior levels of administration determined the norms for the friars' conventual life, controlled the observance of rules and regulations and decided which of the brethren was to be transferred to another convent or admitted to the order's studies.[1] Despite the levels of control within the order there was a close relationship between mendicants and towns.[2] The friars had to win over the faithful to be able to fulfil their main tasks, the cure of souls and their duties in papal service. They also had to come to an arrangement with the secular and ecclesiastical authorities regarding preaching and the collection of alms. This did not only apply to the bishops in their double function as temporal and spiritual lords, to the

---

[1] W. A. Hinnebusch, *The History of the Dominican Order. Origins and Growth to 1500*, 2 vols (Staten Island, NY, 1966-1973). This paper was written for the Leeds Conference 1997 and is reproduced here without major changes. The notes are restricted to the most important references. Translation by Jürgen Sarnowsky and Jens Röhrkasten, revised by Ruth Peters.

[2] For Basle cf. B. Neidiger, *Mendikanten zwischen Ordensideal und städtischer Realität. Untersuchungen zum wirtschaftlichen Verhalten der Bettelorden in Basel.* Berliner Historische Studien 5, Ordensstudien 3 (Berlin, 1981) pp. 211-14; B. E. J. Stüdeli, *Minoritenniederlassungen und mittelalterliche Stadt. Beiträge zur Bedeutung von Minoriten- und Mendikantenanlagen im öffentlichen Leben der mittelalterlichen Stadtgemeinde, insbesondere der deutschen Schweiz.* Franziskanische Forschungen 21 (Werl, 1969); see also *SWB*; D. Berg (ed.), *Bettelorden und Stadt. Bettelorden und städtisches Leben im Mittelalter und in der Neuzeit.* Saxonia Franciscana 1 (Werl, 1992).

From *Mendicants, Military Orders, and Regionalism in Medieval Europe*, ed. Jürgen Sarnowsky. Copyright © 1999 by Jürgen Sarnowsky. Published by Ashgate Publishing Ltd, Gower House, Croft Road, Aldershot, Hampshire, GU11 3HR, Great Britain.

nobility and local dynasties, but also to the communal governments of the towns which became increasingly more important.[3] From this network of relationships and conflicts which resulted from the antagonism between the 'international' structure of the mendicant orders and their ties to the pope on the one hand, and the convents' regional spheres of influence on the other hand, three points shall be discussed. In referring mainly to the Dominican convent of Basle, it will be possible to examine the gradual integration of the mendicant convents into town life, the shaping of the convents by their urban surroundings, and, finally, the convents' extensive autonomy from the towns as far as the brethren's mobility in their provinces and the organisation of the orders' study-systems were concerned.

I

The foundation of the Basle Dominican convent in 1233 was primarily promoted by the local bishop who was hoping to improve the cure of souls with the help of the brethren.[4] The citizens were not involved, a feature which reflected the political and constitutional situation as at that time Basle was under the lordship of its bishop.[5] Thus, the Basle convent belongs to the series of earlier Dominican foundations in episcopal towns.[6] From the beginning the brethren wanted to concentrate on pastoral activities, not only in the town, but also in a large area with the bishop's approval. Preaching and collecting alms in the case of the Basle Dominicans not only extended to the Basle diocese, but also included large parts of the diocese of Constance. At first, the convent was supported by the bishops of Constance as well as by those of Basle.

After the Bishop of Basle had published the deposition of Emperor Frederick II by the Council of Lyons in 1245, the Basle citizens who were loyal to the

---

[3] M. Wehrli-Johns, *Geschichte des Zürcher Predigerkonvents (1230-1524). Mendikantentum zwischen Kirche, Adel und Stadt* (Zürich, 1980); B. Neidiger, 'Die Bettelorden im spätmittelalterlichen Rheinland', *Rheinische Vierteljahrsblätter* 57 (1993) 50-74.

[4] G. Boner,'Das Predigerkloster in Basel von der Gründung bis zur Klosterreform 1233-1429', *Basler Zeitschrift für Geschichte und Altertumskunde* 33 (1934) 195-303, 34 (1935) 107-259, here 33 pp. 204-9; R. Wackernagel, *Geschichte der Stadt Basel*, 3 vols (Basle, 1916-1924), here vol. 1, p. 150.

[5] Wackernagel, vol. 1, pp. 15-16; E. Rütimeyer, *Stadtherr und Stadtbürgerschaft in den rheinischen Bischofsstädten. Ihr Kampf um die Hoheitsrechte im Hochmittelalter.* Beihefte der Vierteljahrsschrift für Wirtschafts- und Sozialgeschichte 13 (Stuttgart, 1928) pp. 196-203.

[6] Wehrli-Johns, pp. 8 seqq. For the following cf. Boner, 33, pp. 225-29, 292-94.

emperor stormed the episcopal palace and completely destroyed it in 1247.[7] This may have been caused by their aspiration for independence as well as by the recollection of an earlier clash of interests, when the privilege of a town council granted by Frederick in 1211 was abolished at the bishop's instigation in 1218.[8] Dominicans as well as Franciscans kept the interdict which was inflicted upon Basle, and participated in the propaganda for bishop and pope. In 1249 the bishop, who had earlier supported the brethren against the secular clergy, again gave the mendicants extensive rights concerning the cure of the souls, as if it were a reward.[9] Meanwhile, representatives of the citizens had established contacts with bishop and pope. In 1248, the citizens of Basle changed to the papal side and the bishop gave his consent to a town council which was responsible for the internal affairs of the town.[10] The following close co-operation between town council and bishops had positive consequences for the development of the mendicant convents. The Franciscans were allowed to transfer their house to an area inside the town walls close to the cathedral, a measure agreed to by the town council.[11] The Dominicans made progress in the construction of their church, probably because they received more gifts from the faithful than before.[12] The last joint action of the Bishop of Basle and the town council was the struggle against Rudolph of Habsburg, who besieged Basle. Then the news of his election as German king became known and the town opened its gates to him. In consequence, Rudolph of Habsburg used Basle as a footing for his royal policies, liberated the town from exclusive episcopal domination and put it under the authority of a royal bailiff.[13] The relationship

---

[7] Boner, 34, pp. 192-94; Wackernagel, vol. 1, p. 25-28; cf. J. B. Freed, *The Friars and German Society in the Thirteenth Century* (Cambridge, Mass, 1977) pp. 137-57; D. Berg, 'Staufische Herrschaftsideologie und Mendikantenspiritualität. Studien zum Verhältnis Kaiser Friedrichs II. zu den Bettelorden', *Wissenschaft und Weisheit* 26 (1972) 26-51, 185-209, here esp. p. 206.

[8] Wackernagel, vol. 1, pp. 20-23; Rütimeyer pp. 198-99.

[9] Wackernagel, vol. 1, p. 151; Boner, 33, pp. 293-94.

[10] Wackernagel, vol. 1, pp. 29-32; Rütimeyer p. 202.

[11] Wackernagel, vol. 1, p. 147; Neidiger, *Mendikanten*, pp. 137-38.

[12] Boner, 33, pp. 209-13; Wackernagel, vol. 1, p. 150.

[13] Wackernagel, vol. 1, pp. 34-49; T. M. Martin, *Die Städtepolitik Rudolfs von Habsburg.* Veröffentlichungen des Max-Planck-Instituts für Geschichte 44 (Göttingen, 1976) pp. 28-31; P. Moraw, 'Rudolf von Habsburg. Der "kleine" König im europäischen Vergleich', *Rudolf von Habsburg 1273-1291. Eine Königsherrschaft zwischen Tradition und Wandel*, eds E. Boshof, F.-R. Erkens (Cologne, 1993), pp. 185-208, at p. 197.

between the Dominicans and Franciscans and King Rudolph was good from the beginning because of the papal policies and the correspondingly friendly attitude of the orders' provincial leaders. Rudolph and his wife Agnes were themselves closely connected, especially with the Basle Dominicans. This contributed to the good reputation of the brethren within the town, and in this respect, the interests of the order, the convent, and the town were congruent.[14] The relationship of the mendicants to the Franciscan Henry of Isny, who as one of the closest confidants of King Rudolph became Bishop of Basle by papal nomination in 1274, was also without problem.[15] After Henry of Isny had succeeded to the archbishopric of Mainz in 1287, however, it soon became evident that the situation had changed. The new bishop, or his official, supported the parish clergy against the mendicants,[16] but on the other hand the Dominicans were now enjoying the citizens' support. In a charter of 1289, the town council emphasized explicitly that the brethren served the common welfare of the town.[17] The reorientation of the convent from the bishop to town council and citizens had taken place step by step since 1248, and in 1289 it was finally completed.

The citizens' aspiration for autonomy and the struggles between the popes and the Staufen dynasty also influenced the development of the mendicant convents in other towns. For example, in the imperial town of Zürich, the town council supported the establishment of the Dominicans to further its own independence from the local houses of regular canons which were subordinate to the Bishop of Constance. Accordingly, the town council of Zürich reacted with indignation when the mendicants together with the other members of the clergy observed the interdict imposed in connection with the Staufen controversy.[18] In Cologne, where the citizens were also opposed to the rule of the Staufen family, no problems arose at any time; and the Dominicans were also successfully backing civic autonomy against the archbishop.[19] In Strasbourg, the mendi-

---

[14] Boner, 34, pp. 194-95; O. Redlich, *Rudolf von Habsburg. Das deutsche Reich nach dem Untergang des Kaisertums* (Innsbruck, 1903), pp. 206-7; Freed, pp. 161-65; Martin, pp. 73-75.

[15] For him see *Neue Deutsche Biographie*, vol. 8, pp. 370-71.

[16] Neidiger, *Mendikanten*, p. 146; Boner, 34, p. 295; Wackernagel, vol. 1, pp. 165-66.

[17] Boner, 34, pp. 195-96. *Urkundenbuch der Stadt Basel*, vol. 2 (Basle, 1893), pp. 368-69, no. 659: *apud nos ... residentes propter bonum commune nostre civitatis, quod favorabiliter prosequntur.*

[18] Wehrli-Johns, pp. 18, 78.

[19] Freed, pp. 91-134.

cants were promoted by the bishops in particular. After the town council had succeeded in gaining complete authority over the town in 1262, it banished the Dominicans from the town in 1287 for the first time, accusing them of having deprived individual citizens of their inheritance. The conflicts with the town council did not result in damaging the brethrens' reputation with the faithful, as can be demonstrated by the numerous gifts to the Strasbourg Dominicans and by the fact that many townspeople entered the order.[20]

II

Since the Dominicans began siding with the urban authorities, the number of entries of Basle citizens into the order increased. While at first brethren from outside, mainly from Strasbourg, acted as priors of the Basle convent, the priors of the years from 1290 to 1370 came mostly from the same Basle noble or civic families from which the town council was also recruited.[21] Family ties could considerably diminish the convents' usefulness as instruments in the service of papal policies, even in the first half of the fourteenth century. Thus, although Prior Gunther Münch did indeed publish the papal mandates in the episcopal election dispute between the candidates chosen by the pope and cathedral chapter respectively, as he was supposed to do, the Dominicans did not observe the interdict which had been imposed on the town by the pope to enforce the acceptance of the papal candidate. At the time, Prior Gunther's uncle was one of the most influential members of the cathedral chapter.[22] On the other hand, the Basle Dominicans kept the interdict which Pope John XXII had imposed on the supporters of Louis the Bavarian. In contrast to the events in Zürich or Strasbourg, the convent was not expelled from the town by the council for this decision. This is explained by the fact that there was not only

---

[20] W. Kothe, *Kirchliche Zustände Straßburgs im 14. Jahrhundert* (Strasbourg, 1903), pp. 67-70, 91-92; H. C. Scheeben, 'Der Konvent der Predigerbrüder in Straßburg. Die religiöse Heimat Taulers', *Johannes Tauler. Ein deutscher Mystiker. Gedenkschrift zum 600. Todestag*, ed. E. Filthaut (Essen, 1961), pp. 37-76, here pp. 42-50, 57 seqq.; F. Rapp, *Réformes et Réformation à Strasbourg. Eglise et Société dans la diocese de Strasbourg (1450-1525)*. Collection de l'Institut des Hautes Études Alsaciennes 23 (Paris, 1974), p. 111, cf. pp. 413-15.

[21] Boner, 33, pp. 277-92; Neidiger, *Mendikanten*, pp. 178-83; see also B. Neidiger, 'Dominikanerkloster Basel', here esp. 'Die Blütezeit des Konventes (1290-1370)' and the biographies of the priors, *Helvetia Sacra*, vol. IV/5: *Dominikaner und Dominikanerinnen in der Schweiz* (forthcoming).

[22] Boner, 34, pp. 196-98.

an imperial, but also a strong papal faction in Basle, which numbered two
mayors who were closely related to the Dominican convent. In this respect, the
internal civic policy of mediation turned out to be an advantage for the convent.[23]

Like other mendicant convents, the Dominicans started to accept memorial
and chantry foundations in their churches at the turn of the fourteenth century
and in turn received property and regular incomes. The faithful wished to secure themselves eternal salvation whereas the mendicants needed the incomes
mainly to finance their quite expensive study-system.[24] While this was a
general development which must have been discussed and co-ordinated by
provincial chapters,[25] the allocation of property to be conferred and their
opportunities to reinvest funds depended completely on the local situation. This
is sufficiently demonstrated by the completely different structure of properties
of Dominican convents in Basle, Zürich, Cologne, and Nuremberg.[26] Similarly,
it depended on local conditions whether the towns interfered using laws of
amortization or even as to whether they seized all the landed property of the
Dominicans within the town, as happened in Cologne in 1345.[27] In Basle, on
the other hand, there had been a broad agreement with the town council on the
property issue from the start. There was clear support by the mendicants when

---

[23] Wackernagel, vol. 1, p. 241; Boner, 34, pp. 202-4; M. Kaufhold, *Gladius spiritualis.*
Das päpstliche Interdikt über Deutschland in der Regierungszeit Ludwigs des Bayern
(Heidelberg, 1994), pp. 147 seqq. For Strasbourg cf. ibid., pp. 129-47; Scheeben, p.
162; Kothe, p. 68; for Zürich Wehrli-Johns, p. 81.

[24] Neidiger, *Mendikanten*, pp. 143 seqq.; I. W. Frank, 'Ordensarmut und missae speciales bei den spätmittelalterlichen Mendikantenorden', *Vorgeschmack. Festschrift für*
T. Schneider, eds B. J. Hilberrath, D. Sattler (Mainz, 1995), pp. 208-24.

[25] Corresponding decisions of provincial chapters have not survived. For the chapters
general and for the statutes see Neidiger, *Mendikanten*, pp. 51-66. Concerning the
Franciscans, it can be noted here that the assocation of their third order looked after
regular incomes for the brethren not only in Basle and Strasbourg (Neidiger, *Mendi-*
kanten, pp. 89-132), but for example also in Vienna (H. Hageneder, 'Die Minoriten in
den österreichischen Städten', *Stadt und Kirche*, ed. F.-H. Heye. Beiträge zur Geschichte der Städte 13 [Linz, 1995], pp. 57-68, at p. 62).

[26] Neidiger, *Mendikanten*, pp. 188-210; Wehrli-Johns, pp. 211-22; G.M. Löhr, *Beiträge*
zur Geschichte des Kölner Dominikanerklosters im Mittelalter, T. 1-2. Quellen und
Forschungen zur Geschichte des Dominikanerordens in Deutschland 15-17 (Leipzig,
1921-1922), vol. 1, pp. 11-31, B. Neidiger, 'Der Armutsbegriff der Dominikanerobservanten. Zur Diskussion in den Konventen der Provinz Teutonia (1389-1513)', *Zeit-*
schrift für die Geschichte des Oberrheins 145 (1997) 1-42, at pp. 10-11.

[27] Löhr, vol. 1, pp. 81-154, vol. 2, pp. 328-72.

the council extended the civic consumption (direct) tax, the *ungeld,* to the cathedral chapter in 1318.[28]

Whereas personal property was initially only conceded to individual brethren for the purchase of books and for their studies, this link between property and purpose was later lost and finally, at the end of the fourteenth century, it was even possible to have a fixed income which reverted to the family after the brother's death. Thus, the urban social structures were increasingly reproduced in the convents.[29]

The Basle town council as a secular authority had gained a far-reaching influence on ecclesiastical affairs by the fifteenth century. Whenever it was deemed to be necessary the town council intervened in the mendicant convents' temporal as well as spiritual concerns. However, it also supported them against third parties when economic or legal problems arose.[30] In practice the secular authority also decided whether a convent should be reformed by the Observant movement or not. Apart from spiritual considerations there were aspects of internal, foreign, and ecclesiastical policies which had to be taken into consideration by the town councils and territorial lords in these matters.[31] Observants, provincial officials, and the order's leading brethren alike had to accept the secular authorities' ecclesiastical regime while trying to influence the Basle town council.[32] However, there were two occasions in the fifteenth century when the order's general intervened energetically and enforced the obedience of the convent to his commands against the wishes of the town council. The reform of the Basle convent of the Dominicans had been unanimously agreed upon by the order's general and the town council in 1428. When the reform led to internal disturbances in the town, the town council asked the order's general to stop the reform. Nevertheless, with regard to the Council of Basle which was

---

[28] Boner, 34, p. 199.

[29] Neidiger, *Mendikanten*, pp. 183-87; Boner, 33, pp. 268-76.

[30] Neidiger, *Mendikanten*, pp. 211-28.

[31] B. Neidiger, 'Stadtregiment und Klosterreform in Basel', *Reformbemühungen und Observanzbestrebungen im spätmittelalterlichen Ordenswesen,* ed. K. Elm. Berliner Historische Studien 14, Ordensstudien 6 (Berlin, 1989), pp. 539-67; *idem,* 'Die Observanzbewegungen der Bettelorden in Südwestdeutschland', *Rottenburger Jahrbuch für Kirchengeschichte* 11 (1992) 175-96. For a survey on the research for single territories cf. M. Schulze, *Fürsten und Reformation. Geistliche Reformpolitik weltlicher Fürsten vor der Reformation.* Spätmittelalter und Reformation, Neue Reihe 2 (Tübingen, 1991), pp. 13-45.

[32] For Basle see e.g. Neidiger, 'Stadtregiment', p. 547.

soon to begin, the order's general persisted in the reform with papal help, even against the brethrens' resistance. In this situation the town council had to mediate between him and the convent.[33] The second intervention of the order's general was related to the attempt of Andrew of Carniola Zamometić to summon a general synod in 1482. The prior of the Dominican convent, Stephen Irmy, supported this attempt and thus followed the opinions which his brother Hans, a rich merchant, advocated in the town council. As a consequence, Stephen Irmy was deprived of his office and replaced by Matthew Fanckel from Cologne who had been authorized by the order's general to co-ordinate the measures against Andrew of Carniola. After Prior Fanckel had left for Rome for talks with the order's leading brethren, the Dominican convent did not observe the interdict which had been imposed on Basle by the pope to enforce the surrender of Andrew of Carniola, in spite of several admonitions by the order's general. It also remained faithful to the town in the following conflicts.[34]

III

The Basle town council saw itself as protector of the observance which had been introduced in the town's monasteries with its assistance. It approached the order's officials on its own initiative, for example to recommend a brother who seemed especially suited to become prior.[35] In 1453, the town council asked the order's general to allow the Basle Prior James Rieher to study in Italy to achieve the degree of Master in Theology. It argued that the learning which Rieher would thus acquire could prove of immense profit to his home town (*patria*). Rieher's studies were permitted but the gains for Basle which had been hoped for did not materialize. The order transferred him to Hungary to promote the order's reform.[36] When the town council founded the University of Basle in

---

[33] F. Egger, *Beiträge zur Geschichte des Predigerordens. Die Reform des Basler Konvents 1429 und die Stellung des Ordens am Basler Konzil (1431-1448)*. Europäische Hochschulschriften III 467 (Bern, 1991), pp. 63-76.

[34] Wackernagel, vol. 2/2, p. 883; R. Weis-Müller, *Die Reform des Klosters Klingental und ihr Personenkreis*. Basler Beiträge zur Geschichtswissenschaft 59 (Basle, 1956), pp. 188-89; *Registrum litterarum Salvi Casettae 1481-1483 et Barnabae Saxoni 1486*, ed. B. M. Reichert. Quellen und Forschungen zur Geschichte des Dominikanerordens in Deutschland 7 (Leipzig, 1912), pp. 52, 85-86.

[35] Neidiger, biographies of the priors Henry Schretz and Caspar Maner, *Helvetia Sacra* (forthcoming); Neidiger, *Mendikanten*, p. 225.

[36] Neidiger, biography of Prior Henry Rieher, *Helvetia Sacra* (forthcoming).

1459, it intended to employ a Dominican from the Basle convent for the faculty of theology whose lecture was to follow that of the ordinary professor, at the convent's cost. The first Dominican lecturers were Caspar Maner (from 1459) and, additionally, Henry Nolt (from 1469); in 1472, Nolt was even appointed ordinary professor. At the same time, from 1461 to 1464, Maner also acted as prior of the Dominican convent in Gebweiler which had been reformed by him, while Nolt was also spiritual adviser to the nuns in Strasbourg. After Maner's and Nolt's death in 1474, individual Dominicans continued to lecture at the Basle faculty of theology as part of the second phase of their studies. However, close ties were no longer maintained, mainly because the order's province which was directed by the Observants had decided to develop Heidelberg into its regional centre for studies in south-western Germany.[37]

In the thirteenth, fourteenth, and even in the fifteenth centuries, the decision as to when and where a member of the brethren studied or taught, and when a member of a convent was removed to another house, was exclusively in the hands of the order. The influence of secular authorities in ecclesiastical affairs had not extended into this area at all. The wishes expressed by single convents, towns, and territorial lords were taken into consideration whenever possible, but their compliance with the order's overall interests was paramount.[38]

Already in the early fourteenth century, the Basle brethren from prominent urban families were also acting – mostly as lectors or priors – in other houses such as Strasbourg or Colmar, and returned to their home convent afterwards. In the fourteenth century, brethren from Basle were mainly sent to other convents of the *Natio Alsatia*; moreover, after 1370, more often to the Swabian,

---

[37] Neidiger, 'Studienwesen seit 1429', *Helvetia Sacra* (forthcoming). For the 'regionalization' of the order's study-system in the second half of the fifteenth century cf. I. W. Frank, *Die Bettelordensstudia im Gefüge des spätmittelalterlichen Universitätswesens*. Institut für europäische Geschichte Mainz, Vorträge 83 (Wiesbaden, 1988).

[38] This is to be emphasized also in view of recent research on the ecclesiastical regime of the territorial lords; cf. *Lexikon für Theologie und Kirche* (3rd edn, Freiburg i.Br., 1995) vol. 3, p. 312; Schulze; D. Stievermann, *Landesherrschaft und Klosterwesen im spätmittelalterlichen Württemberg* (Sigmaringen, 1989), with further literature. Brethren who had the confidence of a territorial lord concerning, for example, the problems of monastic reform were not sent away. The wishes of the Basle town council, however, were neglected because the reforms in Hungary as well as the order's centre for studies in Heidelberg were more important for the order than the situation in Basle.

but not to the Franconian part of the *Natio Suevica*.[39] Evidently, this was determined by the linguistic frontiers between the different dialects. In the last
decades before the reform, in particular, several brethren from outside who
belonged to the cultural elite of the order's province acted as priors and lectors
in Basle.[40] At this point, the order's educational system, which was based on
regular transfers of suitable brethren from one convent or particular centre of
studies to another, was still working well, as can be shown by the records of the
provincial chapters from 1390 to 1410.[41] After the introduction of the observance in 1428, brethren from Basle participated in the reform of numerous
other convents and were to be found in houses all over southern Germany and
Austria, but – with the exception of Cologne – only rarely in the area of the
Low German dialect.[42] The transfer of brethren who were popular as pastors or
preachers to other convents often led to indignation in their towns of residence.
One well-known example is the complaints of the Nuremberg town council of
the absence of John Nider, who was first sent to bring about the reform in Basle
and subsequently took over as regent master in Vienna.[43] For the order and also

---

[39] Neidiger, biographies of the lectors and priors, *Helvetia Sacra* (forthcoming); for
brethren without the status of prior or lector cf. Neidiger, *Mendikanten*, appendix, pp.
508-35 (list of members of the Basle convent). After 1370, single priors and lectors
were transferred to Ulm, Constance, and Zürich or Chur. For brethren without the
status of priors or lectors promotions can only rarely be found. Perhaps this marks the
difference between the intellectual and administrative oligarchy of leading brethren and
the 'simple' brethren in the convents. Until 1290 they can be found in Zürich and Ess-
lingen, between 1290 and 1370 in Zürich, Freiburg i.Br., Strasbourg, and Gebweiler,
finally between 1371 and 1429 in Freiburg i.Br., Ulm, Koblenz, Colmar, and Bern. But
on the whole, the number of cases is small because nearly all records from the provincial chapters of the *Teutonia* are lost.

[40] Neidiger, 'Die Blütezeit des Konventes (1290-1370)' and 'Der Konvent von 1370-
1429', *Helvetia Sacra* (forthcoming); cf. also the biographies of the priors and lectors
involved.

[41] 'Aus den Akten des Rottweiler Provinzkapitels der Dominikaner vom Jahr 1396', ed.
B. Altaner, *Zeitschrift für Kirchengeschichte* 48 (1929) 1-15; 'Kapitelsakten der Dominikanerprovinz Teutonia (c. 1349, 1407)', ed. T. Kaeppeli, *Archivum Fratrum Praedicatorum* 22 (1952) 186-95; 'Akten der Provinzkapitel der Dominikanerprovinz Teutonia aus den Jahren 1398, 1400, 1401 und 1402', ed. B. M. Reichert, *Römische Quartalschrift* 11 (1897) 287-331.

[42] Egger, pp. 72-76; Neidiger, 'Bedeutung als Reformzentrum', *Helvetia Sacra* (forthcoming).

[43] F. Bock, 'Das Nürnberger Predigerkloster. Beiträge zu seiner Geschichte', *Mitteilungen des Vereins für Geschichte der Stadt Nürnberg* 25 (1924) 147-213, at p. 170.

for the Observants, on the other hand, it was important to have a sufficient number of suitable brethren in all convents at their disposal.

III

Nations, Regions, and the
Internal Structures of Religious Orders

10

Local Ties and International Connections
of the London Mendicants

Jens Röhrkasten

The mendicant orders provided the church with a new form of religious life, which was characterized not only by a common spiritual direction based on the gospel taking the apostolic life as a model for human existence, but also by its widespread popular appeal. Until the middle of the thirteenth century the Franciscans and Dominicans extended their organizations into Spain, the British Isles, Scandinavia, Russia, Cyprus, and the Holy Land, as well as establishing a close network of convents in virtually all other European territories.[1] This expansion coincided with the creation of internal structures, the subdivision of territories into provinces and other units, and the genesis of a system of regular meetings at different levels. These meetings involved the provinces as well as individual convents in the orders' government and decision-making processes. The orders' provinces formed and were integrated into extensive international organizations which were linked to the papacy and enjoyed a high degree of independence from the ecclesiastical hierarchy. Despite their entirely spiritual aims the friars soon became involved in the great ecclesiastical and also more general political issues of the day. In the long fight against heresy the education and the rhetorical skills of the most talented mendicants were powerful tools which were applied in different parts of Europe.[2] Another area which saw

---

[1] K. Elm, 'Bettelorden', *Lexikon des Mittelalters*, 1 (Munich and Zurich, 1980), cols 2088-93.

[2] A. Borst, *Die Katharer* (2nd edn, Freiburg im Breisgau, 1991), p. 102; L. Kolmer, Ad Capiendas Vulpes. *Die Ketzerbekämpfung in Südfrankreich in der ersten Hälfte des 13.*

From *Mendicants, Military Orders, and Regionalism in Medieval Europe*, ed. Jürgen Sarnowsky. Copyright © 1999 by Jürgen Sarnowsky. Published by Ashgate Publishing Ltd, Gower House, Croft Road, Aldershot, Hampshire, GU11 3HR, Great Britain.

a significant mendicant impact was the organization of new crusades in the thirteenth century. With their help, and based on their experience in addressing the crowds, crusade preaching was given a new impetus. In England the Franciscans and Dominicans were for the first time systematically employed as preachers in 1234 and 1235, following Gregory IX's crusading bull, and the friars were given similar roles in 1274 and 1291, gradually taking on an increasing workload as agents of crusade promotion.[3] Such tasks required strategic planning and careful co-ordination on an international scale.

The organizations which were created – most impressively in the case of the Dominicans – were well suited for these tasks. A hierarchical leadership ensured efficient government affecting even the remote branches both through regular visitations and by sending representatives from the branches to regular meetings at which decisions on all aspects of their existence were taken. The friars – wherever they happened to be located – wore the same habits, followed the same liturgy and the same course of study, adhered to the same electoral procedures, and the same constitutions and regulations were valid for all of them. In 1304 the Dominicans made sure that copies of their chapter general decisions were available in each province; the ordinations and admonitions were even required to be placed in each convent.[4] Integrated into this structure was a hierarchical system of education ranging from local *studia* and regional schools to the orders' general studies where the most promising friars from each province were sent. At least in theory these organizations were cosmopolitan, taking little or no account of existing political or even ecclesiastical boundaries. Their chapters general were gatherings of people from all over Europe brought together by a common purpose. The venues of these meetings changed from year to year, after 1245 when the Dominicans eventually abandoned the custom of alternating between Bologna and Paris, going further afield and also meeting at Cologne, Montpellier, Trier, Metz, Buda, Milan, and London.

Jahrhunderts und die Ausbildung des Inquisitionsverfahrens. Pariser Historische Studien 19 (Bonn, 1982) pp. 127, 150 seqq.; M. d'Alatri, *L'inquisizione francescana nell'Italia centrale nel secolo XIII* (Rome, 1954), pp. 14 seqq.

[3] S. Lloyd, *English Society and the Crusade (1216-1307)* (Oxford, 1988), pp. 19, 42, 51-54; C. Tyerman, *England and the Crusades (1095-1588)* (Chicago, 1988), pp. 86, 162, 168; C. T. Maier, *Preaching the Crusades. Mendicant Friars and the Cross in the Thirteenth Century* (Cambridge, 1994).

[4] *Acta capitulorum generalium Ordinis Praedicatorum,* vol. 2, ed. B. M. Reichert. Monumenta Ordinis Praedicatorum Historica 4 (Rome, 1899), p. 4.

However, the mendicants did not exist in a vacuum. At the time of their expansion they already had to adapt to local customs, and their advice was coveted by princes and influential groups, potentially involving them in political confrontation as well as social issues. As trusted supporters of the papacy they found themselves drawn into disputes between pope and emperor and there was more potential for conflict in the regions and localities. In this context it is important to emphasize that, like other orders, the mendicants consisted of a large number of small units, convents, each of which had its own functions and tasks, but which unlike the houses of other religious organizations depended on local society for their survival. Dependent on permanent and steady support from the communities around them they also had to focus on issues of relevance to these communities. It was crucial to remain in contact with the population on which they relied for support as well as for the recruitment of novices. This in itself required a degree of adaptation to local conditions and cultural norms. In addition the convents had to co-operate with urban authorities and the political élite. Thus arises the question of to what extent the friars were tied into the localities on which they depended for their existence while being at the same time members of truly cosmopolitan structures. From the combination of these roles – as contributors to the local spiritual life, and as part of a network of convents extending beyond the borders of territories and kingdoms with the concomitant involvement in international issues and controversies – bitter conflicts could ensue. The Dominicans were forced to leave their convent in Toulouse temporarily in 1235, only two years after they had been entrusted with the inquisition, because their methods of combating heresy were unpopular in the town.[5] When the Dominicans moved their convent into the city centre of Strasbourg in 1249 they had to overcome the resistance of the city government which promptly passed a law forbidding such action in the future. The already tense relations reached breaking point later in the thirteenth century when the city's Black Friars began to lay claim to their relatives' inheritance. Twice the Strasbourg Dominicans were forced into exile.[6] Whereas in this case it can only be assumed that the convent was following a centrally-directed policy there can be little doubt that the friars of Toulouse were acting on command. Unwelcome interference could occur both ways. In Basle lengthy

---

[5] Kolmer, Ad Capiendas Vulpes, pp. 129, 138.

[6] W. Kothe, *Kirchliche Zustände Straßburgs im 14. Jahrhundert* (Freiburg im Breisgau, 1903), pp. 67-68; A. Rüther, *Bettelorden in Stadt und Land. Die Straßburger Mendikantenkonvente und das Elsaß im Spätmittelalter*. Berliner Historische Studien 26 (Berlin, 1997), pp. 73, 234-35.

disputes between the town council and the Dominicans began when the order tried to implement reform from 1422. Although the town council itself had initially invited the Dominican prior general to go ahead with the reform, influential factions within the town later resisted changes which were regarded as excessive.[7] Wealthy families refused to contemplate a deterioration of living standards for their relatives who had joined the local Dominicans and their refusal prevailed. Although the Basle convents were part of a powerful international structure the local ties proved stronger.

Such international connections and their potential for conflict have never been studied for the eight London friaries which existed in the late thirteenth century, of which six survived the decisions of the Second Council of Lyons (1274) and were dissolved in the reign of Henry VIII. In this chapter it is intended to study the international links of the London mendicant houses and the effects they had on the convents' development, in order to assess their local roles in conjunction with their international importance. Even though not more than a local survey can be attempted here, the aim is to contribute to a more general picture, to determine the extent to which individual houses were shaped by their environment and the degree to which national or possibly even international issues influenced the friars in a particular location or a region.

I

The Dominicans were the first mendicants to arrive in England. Following their chapter general's decision to create an English province in 1221, a group of twelve friars set out for Oxford and arrived in July of that year, after having visited Canterbury and London. They were led by Gilbert de Fresney, an Englishman who has been identified as a master of canon law active at the University of Bologna.[8] It is likely that some of his companions were also English because this would have been in line with the order's policy to send native friars into areas where new provinces were to be created. The London friary was the order's second convent in England, founded between 1221 and 1224 when Hubert de Burgh, Earl of Kent, donated property in the parish of St

---

[7] B. Neidiger, 'Stadtregiment und Klosterreform in Basel', *Reformbemühungen und Observanzbestrebungen im spätmittelalterlichen Ordenswesen*, ed. K. Elm (Berlin, 1989), pp. 538-67.

[8] W. A. Hinnebusch, *The Early English Friars Preachers*. Dissertationes Historicae 14 (Rome, 1951), p. 3; E. Barker, *The Dominican Order and Convocation* (Oxford, 1913), p. 28.

Andrew Holborn.[9] While it is likely that the house was founded from Oxford, it is not known which friars were involved at that stage. The early London Dominicans only gradually emerge as individuals; for a long time they appear only as anonymous members of a group. The first known London Black Friar is Walter de St Maren', very likely an Englishman, who in *c.* 1232 acted as one of the executors of the London citizen Richard Renger.[10] He may have been identical with Prior Walter who is mentioned in 1244 but there is no further information. Another Englishman, William Rufus, who had fled the country after involvement in a killing, joined the Dominican order abroad and received a pardon in 1236 allowing him to return, but a link with the London convent cannot be established.[11] The London Dominicans of the later thirteenth century all appear to have been Englishmen, their names, e.g. John de Erdington,[12] Robert de Donewic (Dunwich),[13] John Balsham, John de Sevenhok,[14] or William de Norwico[15] reflecting the convent's wide recruitment area. Since the London Dominican house was not one of the order's international *studia* the absence of foreign friars at this time is only to be expected. However, by the late fourteenth century the composition of the London Black Friars had changed.

The convent had close links to the court and some of its members became figures of international standing. John of Darlington, conventual prior for several years, was King Henry III's advisor and confessor. In 1258 he was one of the king's representatives under the Provisions of Oxford, taking sides in a political conflict that eventually led to civil war. During these difficult years Darlington was prior of the London convent, and he appears to have maintained a connection with the London Black Friars throughout his later career. As close supporter of the Dominican Archbishop of Canterbury, Robert Kilwardby, he set his name to a declaration in November 1272, denying the possibility of papal provision to that see, a move which did not alienate Gregory X's curia because two years later Darlington was appointed collector

---

[9] Hinnebusch, *Early English Friars Preachers*, p. 20; PRO, DL27 59.

[10] British Library, Harl.Ch. 55 G 12.

[11] *CPR, Henry III, 1232-1247*, p.140, 439.

[12] PRO, E 403 3115 m2.

[13] Hinnebusch, *Early English Friars Preachers*, p. 30.

[14] R. Palmer (ed.), 'Monumenta Conventus S. Mariae et S. Ioannis Baptistae Londinensis', *Analecta Sacri Ordinis Fratrum Praedicatorum* 5-6 (1897-1898) 303.

[15] PRO, E 403 59 m1; E 403 64 m1; E 403 65 m2; E 403 72 m1.

of a papal tenth in England.[16] Darlington remained close to the court under
Edward I and was made Archbishop of Dublin in 1279.[17]

More prominent internationally was the next generation of London Dominicans. William de Hothum, another Dominican affiliated to the London convent
was active on the national and international scene, as scholar, teacher, and
administrator of his order. He participated in the sale of the first London
convent to the Earl of Lincoln in 1286, after the second site near Ludgate had
been acquired, and was elected provincial prior twice. The Dominican chapter
general of 1287 absolved him from his position as English provincial prior and
appointed him as teacher to the order's academic centre at Paris but it is unlikely that he obeyed this command with due diligence since he was severely
criticized for his failure to act by the subsequent chapter general at Lucca. De
Hothum had already taught at the Dominican convent at Paris as regent master
in 1280 and during this period he is thought to have become acquainted with
the most prominent members of the French royal court. His effectiveness as one
of Edward I's diplomats in France in 1297 was said to be due to his
acquaintance with the French king, an acquaintance going back to his teaching
days in the city. Although highly respected as a teacher, de Hothum's greatest
significance was in the field of diplomacy.[18] His mission in 1297 was by no
means the first diplomatic assignment since he was already in royal employment by 1282.[19] De Hothum was involved in at least four major affairs of
foreign policy. In May 1286 Edward I had arrived in France, and de Hothum
spent much of the year there, although he was not always in the king's company.[20] Edward I's intentions at the time were not just to do homage for his

[16] PRO, DL 25 137; DL 25 139; Hinnebusch, *Early English Friars Preachers*, p. 63; for
Darlington's intellectual work see R. R. Bennett, *The Early Dominicans* (Cambridge,
1937), p. 60; *CCR, Edward I, 1272-1279*, p. 39; Maier, *Preaching the Crusades*, pp.
131-32.

[17] D. Knowles, *The Religious Orders in England*, 1 (Cambridge, 1979), p. 167; *CCR,
Edward I, 1272-1279*, pp. 528, 563.

[18] *Acta*, 1, ed. Reichert, pp. 242, 246; H. Denifle, 'Quellen zur Gelehrtengeschichte des
Predigerordens im 13. und 14. Jahrhundert', *Archiv für Literatur- und Kirchenge-
schichte des Mittelalters* 2 (1886) 165-248, at p. 209; *The Chronicle of Walter of
Guisborough*, ed. H. Rothwell. Camden 3rd series 89 (London, 1957), p. 316; A. B.
Emden, *A Biographical Register of the University of Oxford to 1500*, vol. 2 (Oxford,
1958), pp. 970-71; Hinnebusch, *Early English Friars Preachers*, p. 387.

[19] Ibid., pp. 481-82; *Records of the Wardrobe and Household 1286-1289*, eds B. F.
Byerly, C. R. Byerly, vol. 2 (London, 1986), no. 335.

[20] M. Prestwich, *Edward I* (London, 1988), p. 325; *Records of the Wardrobe and Household*, nos 443, 481, 485, 573, 1740.

continental fiefs; the king had also taken on the role as mediator in the Franco-Aragonese dispute which had led to war in the previous year.[21] In 1289 Edward I sent de Hothum together with Otho de Grandison to Pope Nicholas IV in order to negotiate the conditions for England's participation in the next crusade. After their return to England they could report to the king that a grant of a tenth over six years had been conceded and Edward I did take the cross on 14 October 1290, a decision related to the papal curia by another embassy, consisting of William de Montfort, Dean of St Paul's, Robert Newmarket, a former Prior of the London Black Friars and the Franciscan John de Bekingham.[22] After his return from Rome, de Hothum, who in 1290 was reappointed Provincial Prior of England and Scotland, became involved in the question of the Scottish succession, an issue of particular urgency after the death of King Alexander III's heiress Margaret of Norway and the emergence of contesting claimants.[23] De Hothum had already tried to gain a papal dispensation for a marriage between Edward I's heir and Margaret when he was negotiating at the curia. In 1291 he prepared the legal and historical arguments for the English king's claims of sovereignty over the Scottish kingdom.[24] After the outbreak of the Anglo-French war in 1294 de Hothum acted as negotiator for Edward I. Neither the King of England nor Pope Boniface VIII, who was still hoping to launch a new crusade, had much to gain from this war and de Hothum's reply to two papal envoys in London in 1295 when he explained the English government's views of the affair must have met with approval.[25] In 1297, by now Archbishop-Elect of Dublin, he acted as mediator between the

---

[21] S. Runciman, *The Sicilian Vespers. A History of the Mediterranean World in the Later Thirteenth Century* (Cambridge, 1958), pp. 257 seqq.

[22] *Foedera, conventiones, litterae,* ed. T. Rymer, new edn by A. Clarke, F. Holbrooke, J. Caley, I, 2 (London, 1816), pp. 705, 708, 709, 714-15, 719, 741; C. F. R. Palmer, 'Fasti Ordinis Fratrum Praedicatorum: the Provincials of the Friar-Preachers, or Black Friars of England', *Archaeological Journal* 35 (1878) 140-43; Prestwich, *Edward I,* p. 313; *Calendar of Entries in the Papal Registers Relating to Great Britain and Ireland. Papal Letters,* vol. 1, ed. W. H. Bliss (London, 1893), pp. 511, 551; *Foedera,* ed. Rymer, I, 2, p. 746; Hinnebusch, *Early English Friars Preachers,* p. 435. De Hothum also brought back a list of papal complaints concerning infringements of ecclesiastical privileges in England.

[23] G. W. S. Barrow, *Robert Bruce,* (Edinburgh, 1988), pp. 29-49.

[24] *Chron. Walter of Guisborough,* ed. Rothwell, p. 235; Hinnebusch, *Early English Friars Preachers,* pp. 483-84; *Edward I and the Throne of Scotland 1290-1296,* eds E. L. G. Stones, G. G. Simpson, (Oxford, 1978), vol. 1, pp. 85, 112; vol. 2, pp. 213, 216.

[25] *Chron. Walter of Guisborough,* ed. Rothwell, pp. 256-57; Hinnebusch, *Early English Friars Preachers,* p. 485.

two kings and as English procurator when the dispute was submitted to papal arbitration. He died on his return from Rome and was buried in the London Dominican convent.[26]

English Dominicans became prominent on the international stage in the first decade of the fourteenth century when three Black Friars were created cardinals in quick succession. Among them were also friars with close links to the London house, a sign of the convent's prominence at the time. After the death of William of Macclesfield, a Dominican with no known link to the London Black Friars, who is unlikely to have received the news of his creation, Walter of Winterbourne was created Cardinal of Santa Sabina in 1304.[27]

Little is known about Winterbourne's background and early career. He may have studied at Oxford or Paris, but despite his description as *magnus in theologia magister*[28] it is not clear what kind of degree he held. He appeared at the royal court from 1282 onward and held the key position as royal confessor by 1289. In this capacity he must have spent much time at the royal court but he was also closely connected to the London Dominican house. This convent, in the last decades of the thirteenth century, was still in the process of construction, or more precisely reconstruction, after it had been relocated with the help of archbishop Kilwardby. Between 1289 and 1292 Winterbourne received considerable royal stipends on behalf of the London Dominicans, and still in 1302 he reminded Edward I of their requirements, having stayed in the house for long periods of time on many occasions and eventually choosing it as his place of burial.[29] Winterbourne not only accompanied the king abroad, he was also entrusted with important diplomatic missions. Following a journey to Guienne in 1289 he joined the inner circle of royal advisers in the following year, gaining access to patronage which was to benefit the English Dominican province and in particular the London Black Friars.[30] In October 1300 he witnessed the Bishop of Glasgow's oath of allegiance to the King of England, but his most important activity began after he had been created cardinal in February 1304.

---

[26] Ibid., p. 486.

[27] Knowles, *Religious Orders*, 1, p. 169; Palmer, 'Fasti', pp. 139-40; C. Eubel, *Hierarchia Catholica Medii Aevi* (Münster, 1913), 1, p. 13.

[28] J. Bale, *Scriptorum illustrium maioris Britannie catalogus* (Basle, 1559), p. 366.

[29] C. F. R. Palmer, 'The King's Confessors', *The Antiquary* 22 (1890) 116-19; PRO, E 403 59 m1; E 403 72 m1; *CCR, Edward I, 1296-1302*, p. 558.

[30] Hinnebusch, *Early English Friars Preachers*, p. 471; *CCR, Edward I, 1296-1302*, pp. 153, 158, 228, 248, 335, 348, 420, 434, 538, 558; the Franciscans also benefited; ibid. pp. 228, 425.

His departure for Italy was delayed because the king was unwilling to dispense with his counsel.[31] When he eventually left in the summer of 1304 it was in the capacity of royal envoy. He was accompanied by three other ambassadors, two of whom, Thomas Jorz and John de Wrotham, were also London Dominicans, who had spent time at the royal court. As one of the electors of Pope Clement V, the former Archbishop of Bordeaux, Walter of Winterbourne was chosen to convey the election results to that prelate but he died in Genoa, on his way to France. His confrère Thomas Jorz was the last of the English Dominican cardinals, being created in September 1305.[32] Jorz had taught at Paris, Oxford, and London and had succeeded William de Hothum as English provincial prior in 1297, an office he held until 1303. During this time he is known to have travelled abroad representing his province at the chapter general held at Marseille in 1300.[33] Whereas these activities appear to have been mostly concerned with the order's own affairs his role changed once he had obtained his new dignity. As cardinal he acted as one of the commissioners dealing with the Franciscan poverty dispute and was also involved in Clement V's confrontations with Philip IV of France. He died as papal ambassador on a mission to the German King and later Emperor Henry VII but throughout his career at the curia he maintained close links with England. In April 1306 Edward I sent a string of letters to the curia which dealt with a range of issues. The first text, sent to the pope as well as to a group of three cardinals, Thomas Jorz among them, dealt with the relations between the English king and Robert Winchelsea, Archbishop of Canterbury, who had antagonised the monarch on many occasions. Clement V had suspended the archbishop on the king's request in February 1306, and Edward was now keen to complete his victory, emphasizing the archbishop's malevolence, perhaps in the hope of a permanent removal.[34] At the same time the king was keen to promote the canonisation of Thomas

---

[31] *Foedera*, ed. Rymer, I, 2, p. 964.

[32] Palmer, 'Fasti', p. 145; Eubel, *Hierarchia Catholica*, 1, p. 14; Nicholas Trevet, *Annales sex regum Anglie*, ed. T. Hog (London, 1845), p. 406.

[33] W. Gumbley, 'Provincial Priors and Vicars of the English Dominicans, 1221-1916', *English Historical Review* 33 (1918) 243-51, at p. 245; *Acta*, 1, ed. Reichert, p. 294; the English provincial prior was absolved at the order's chapter general at Besançon in 1303, ibid., p. 322.

[34] *CCR, Edward I, 1302-1307*, pp. 430-31; J. Denton, *Robert Winchelsey and the Crown 1294-1313* (Cambridge, 1980), pp. 211 seqq., 228-29; *idem*, 'Pope Clement V's Early Career as a Royal Clerk', *English Historical Review* 83 (1968) 303-14; Prestwich, *Edward I*, pp. 540-41; G. L. Harriss, *King, Parliament and Public Finance in England to 1369* (Oxford, 1975), p. 59.

Cantilupe, Bishop of Hereford (1275-1282).[35] Whereas this plan came to a successful conclusion in 1320, another of Edward I's canonisation projects for which he invoked the assistance of Thomas Jorz in 1307, the sanctification of Robert Grosseteste, Bishop of Lincoln (1235-1253), eventually failed.[36] However, both Edward I and his son regarded Jorz's influence at the papal curia as invaluable. Even a few days before Edward I's death he was called upon to mediate in negotiations with the French government, and Edward II provided him with an annual pension of 100 marks for 'facilitating the king's business at the court of Rome'.[37]

The connection of the London Black Friars with international diplomacy in the late thirteenth and early fourteenth centuries became even more obvious under John de Wrotham, the convent's prior from 1309. In August 1297 he accompanied Edward I to Flanders where he was sent on a separate mission.[38] By 1300 he was *socius* of Walter of Winterbourne whom he accompanied on his journey to the papal court in 1304, from where he seems to have travelled on to Sicily.[39] He visited the curia again in 1311, this time as prior of the London convent, conveying Edward II's request to create John de Lenham, another Dominican and royal confessor, cardinal after the death of Thomas Jorz. This would have continued the presence of English Dominicans at the curia, but Lenham never became cardinal and after Clement V's death the chances of success were even more remote.[40] In 1313 and 1314 Wrotham again travelled abroad *in negotiis regis*.[41] While little is known about the nature of this assignment, another mission can be investigated more closely. Following the defeat of a large English army at Bannockburn in 1314 and the subsequent Scottish raids into northern England, the already volatile political situation in England deteriorated further. In 1317 two cardinals, Gaucelin of Eauze and

---

[35] *CCR, Edward I, 1302-1307*, p. 436.

[36] *Foedera*, ed. Rymer, I, 2, p. 1015; R. M. Haines, *The Church and Politics in Fourteenth-Century England. The Career of Adam Orleton c. 1275-1354* (Cambridge, 1978), pp. 8, 20, 25.

[37] *Foedera*, ed. Rymer, I, 2, pp. 1017-18; II, 1, p. 94; *CPR, Edward II, 1307-1313*, p. 105.

[38] Hinnebusch, *Early English Friars Preachers*, pp. 470-71; Prestwich, *Edward I*, p. 425.

[39] *Foedera*, ed. Rymer, I, 2, pp. 964-65; *CPR, Edward I, 1301-1307*, p. 238; *CCR, Edward I, 1302-1307*, p. 212.

[40] *Foedera*, ed. Rymer, II, 1, pp. 127-28; *CPR, Edward II, 1307-1313*, p. 324.

[41] PRO, E 403 167 m10.

Luca Fieschi, were sent as papal arbitrators not just for the internal conflict but also to negotiate a peace settlement between Robert Bruce and Edward II. Their negotiating attitude became more favourable to the English side when the strategic town of Berwick fell to the Scots in 1318.[42] On 3 September 1318 the Scottish king was excommunicated by the two cardinals in a ceremony in St Paul's Cathedral, and a version of the proceedings prepared by an unnamed Dominican friar was published in English.[43] This Dominican is very likely to have been John de Wrotham who is known to have left for Avignon at about that time 'delivering the sentence recently imposed against the Scots by cardinal Gaucelin to master Andrew Sapidi, royal proctor in the papal curia'.[44] It was this excommunication which led the Scottish aristocracy to reject claims of English overlordship in the Declaration of Arbroath in 1320.[45] Wrotham led yet another royal embassy to the papal curia, in 1320, and was subsequently appointed papal penitentiary.[46]

From the order's point of view this involvement in secular affairs was not always desirable. More than once the Dominican chapter general strictly prohibited the friars' meddling in political or legal affairs, categorically excluding them from embassies, and in 1334 this was extended to cover *guerris et guerrarum negociis directe vel indirecte*.[47] Eventually such commands appear to have been observed because the number of royal negotiators drawn from the London Dominicans dwindled in the course of the fourteenth century.

This involvement in diplomatic affairs resulted from the closeness between the Dominicans and King Henry III and his two successors, all of whom had Dominican confessors. Their presence in London may have been partly caused by the closeness of the court and the major institutions of government, but the

---

[42] M. McKisack, *The Fourteenth Century (1307-1399)* (Oxford, 1959), pp. 40, 52; Barrow, *Robert Bruce*, pp. 238-39, 246.

[43] *Annales Paulini, Chronicles of the Reigns of Edward I and Edward*, II, 1, ed. W. Stubbs. Rolls Series 76 (London, 1882), p. 283.

[44] *Fratri Johanni de Wrotham de ordine fratrum predicatorum London eunti pro diversis negotiis ad Curiam Romanam et deferenti processum sententie nuper contra Scotos lade per dominum Gaucelinum cardinalem et ibidem magistro Andree Sapidi procuratori domini regis in eadem curia liberandum et similiter litteras domini regis diversis in eadem curia predicta liberandas ... per manus proprias de dono regis 40 s.*, PRO, E 403 193 m5.

[45] A. A. M. Duncan, *The Nation of Scots and the Declaration of Arbroath (1320)* (London, 1970), pp. 23 seqq.

[46] *Calendar of Chancery Warrants 1244-1326*, p. 519.

[47] Padua 1308, *Acta*, 2, ed. Reichert, p. 33; Piacenza 1310, ibid., p. 48; Toulouse 1328, ibid. pp. 180, 220.

prominence of some friars was not the only aspect of the London Dominicans' international connections. For a long time the London convent also played an important role within the order. In 1250 the first of four chapters general was held in the city,[48] a sign of the English province's importance. Among the chapter's decisions was a decree to punish the prior of the English province *et de edificiis minus se intromittat*; the conventual prior of London was also disciplined.[49] When the next chapter general convened in London in 1263 the venue was still the old Holborn friary. The meeting occurred at a time of deep internal crisis in England where an armed opposition was trying to control royal government. Without doubt the Dominicans were preoccupied with internal matters, but even so the decision to hold a meeting in England may be interpreted as a sign of support for the royal faction which had also relied on the London Dominicans in its stand against Simon de Montfort's party. The inclusion of the feast of St Edward into the order's calendar may be a reference to this because Edward the Confessor was widely known to be Henry III's favourite saint and the rebuilding of his shrine and church was one of the monarch's principal projects.[50] The next Dominican chapter general was held in the new convent near Ludgate in 1314.[51] Again this was a meeting held at a time when royal government in England was in a crisis. After the Ordinances of 1311 and the subsequent execution of the royal favourite Piers Gaveston in the following year, an uneasy peace had been established between Edward II and his opponents. The mismanagement of government, and in particular the king's personal incompetence, led to further serious consequences with the English defeat at Bannockburn in June 1314. This conflict had a wider international dimension involving France as well as the papacy. The arrival of Dominican provincial priors from all over Europe may also have been intended as a show of solidarity with the young king. The Plantagenets had traditionally

---

[48] *Acta capitulorum generalium Ordinis Praedicatorum (1220-1303)*, ed. B. M. Reichert. Monumenta Ordinis Praedicatorum Historica 3 (Rome, 1898) pp. 49-55; G. R. Galbraith, *The Constitution of the Dominican Order (1226-1360)* (Manchester, 1925), p. 91.

[49] *Acta*, 1, ed. Reichert, p. 54.

[50] Ibid., pp. 117-21; it was without doubt that the choice of venue could have political implications, Galbraith, *Constitution,* pp. 88-89; F. Barlow, *Edward the Confessor* (New Haven, 1997), p. 286; M. Powicke, *The Thirteenth Century 1216-1307* (Oxford, 1953), p. 18; *Building Accounts of Henry III*, ed. H. M. Colvin (Oxford, 1971), pp. 190-287; D. Carpenter, 'King Henry III and the Cosmati Work in Westminster Abbey,' *The Reign of Henry III*, ed. D. Carpenter (London, 1996), pp. 409-26.

[51] *Acta*, 2, ed. Reichert, p. 69.

favoured the Dominicans, not only acting as founders of new convents[52] but also as sponsors of Dominican chapters general.[53] These payments, which can be regularly traced, were often channelled through the London convent. During the 1314 London chapter general when it turned out that the king wanted more than just prayers in return for this support, the show of solidarity, if such it was, threatened to turn into the reverse. There was an official request to investigate a rumour 'that many Scots have left the king's fealty at the persuasion of certain brethren of their order' followed by the strong demand that such brethren be punished.[54] There is no reference to this demand in the *acta* of that year's chapter general and the chapter may have been quite keen to adhere to a decision taken at Padua in 1308 not to get involved in political disputes and rivalries.[55]

The last Dominican chapter in London was held in 1335.[56] It convened in an atmosphere of irritation and tension between the English government and the papacy, although relations did not deteriorate noticeably until after the outbreak of the war with France.[57] This is not, however, reflected in the proceedings, which were entirely taken up by the order's routine business such as a reform of the system of provincial studies, a request for lives and miracles of saintly friars to be centrally collected at Paris, or a repetition of earlier warnings not to take on the leadership of religious lay groups. The chapter also addressed a number of problems within the English province, absolving eleven conventual priors and granting the licence for a new house at Thetford. The

---

[52] W. A. Hinnebusch, *The History of the Dominican Order* (New York, 1966), pp. 257-58.

[53] Such payments are recorded in the Issue Rolls of the Exchequer: PRO, E 403 90 m3 (1294), E 403 117 m3 (1303), E 403 134 m3 (1306), E 403 141 m8 (1307), E 403 144 m8 (1308), E 403 149 m6 (1309), E 403 155 m8 (1310), E 403 165 m1 (1313), E 403 179 m5 (1314), E 403 174 m1 (1315), E 403 178 m1 (1316), E 403 180 m2 (1317), E 403 187 m3 (1319), E 403 195 m1 (1321, for the chapter general in Florence), E 403 196 m6 (1321 for the chapter general in Vienna), E 403 200 m4 (1323 for the chapter general in Barcelona), E 403 204 m2 (1323 for the chapter general in Bordeaux), E 403 210 m12 (1325), E 403 218 m1 (1326), E 403 228 m1 (1327), E 403 232 m13 (1328), E 403 246 m13 (1330), E 403 259 m4 (1332), E 403 267 m7 (1333), E 403 282 m6 (1335), E 403 285 m21 (1336), E 403 291 m17 (1337). Generally £20 was paid.

[54] *CCR, Edward II, 1313-1318*, p. 101.

[55] *Acta*, 2, ed. Reichert, p. 33.

[56] Ibid., pp. 228-35.

[57] T. Eckert, 'Nichthäretische Papstkritik in England vom Beginn des 14. bis zur zweiten Hälfte des 15.Jahrhunderts', *Annuarium Historiae Conciliorum* 23 (1991) 116-359, at p. 171.

London convent itself was not mentioned. Since it was not uncommon for a chapter general to take a particular interest in the affairs of the province where it convened, the minutes show a state of normality, but this impression may be misleading. Only a few years later there are signs of tensions between the English province and the order, in which the French provinces gained greater weight after the outbreak of the Hundred Years' War when the priors general were French and the chapters general quite regularly met in French towns.[58] Gradually the English Dominican province lost its importance within the order, a loss of status caused indirectly by the long war with France. Even though this change occurred over a long period of time and does not appear to have been marked by any spectacular events, it did not go unnoticed by the English government, especially when the French prior general removed the English provincial from office at the chapter general of 1339 held at Clermont-Ferrand. The office was held by the London Dominican and future Royal Confessor Richard de Wynkele whose academic career had included a spell at the convent of Bologna to which he had been assigned in 1331.[59] His experiences abroad made him a valuable member to Edward III's embassy of May 1337, when diplomats led by the Bishop of Lincoln and the earls of Salisbury and Huntingdon began to form an alliance of continental rulers directed against France.[60] In October 1337 Wynkele was among those provided with a new set of credentials; this time the envoys were to conduct negotiations with the count of Flanders but it is not clear whether the Dominican provincial formed part of the embassy.[61] After Wynkele's removal from office in 1339 the English government sent a strong protest to the Dominican general reminding him of the many instances in which the Plantagenets had assisted the order and demanding amends at the forthcoming chapter general.[62] The response does not appear to have been satisfactory because, although prayers were still said for the King and Queen of England at the Milan chapter general of 1340, the year in which Edward III first styled himself King of France, the regular royal

---

[58] P. Mortier, *Histoire des maîtres généraux de l'ordre des Frères Prêcheurs*, vol. 3 (Paris, 1907), pp. 220.

[59] *Acta*, 2, ed. Reichert, p. 215. His transfer was known in England more than a year before the chapter general's decision, *The Register of John de Grandisson, Bishop of Exeter (1327-1369)*, vol. 1, ed. F. C. Hingeston-Randolph (London, 1894), pp. 107-08.

[60] *CCR, Edward III, 1337-1339*, p. 42; M. McKisack, *The Fourteenth Century 1307-1399* (Oxford, 1959), pp. 121-22; H. S. Lucas, *The Low Countries and the Hundred Years' War 1326-47* (Ann Arbor, 1929), pp. 204 seqq.

[61] *Foedera*, ed. Rymer, II, 2, p. 998.

[62] *CCR, Edward III, 1339-1341*, pp. 467-68.

payments to the Dominican chapters general were stopped. From now on the money was regularly paid to the English Dominicans as a subsidy for their provincial chapter. In effect the London convent received the money for its own use from 1354 onwards. Despite his dismissal from office by the chapter general, Wynkele's role as Edward III's ambassador continued. In 1339, 1341, and 1342 he received payments to conduct secret negotiations at the papal curia.[63] This move away from the Dominican chapter general also became apparent when Edward III requested perpetual prayers for his queen after her death in 1369. Her anniversary was to be celebrated at the provincial chapter, a tradition continued by Richard II, who, in addition to the prayers, made arrangements for obits.[64]

Richard de Wynkele was the last London Dominican whose international links developed in such a spectacular way. The London Black Friars remained important within the order's English province but this aspect of the convent's role remained hardly visible. However, it would be misleading to imagine the English province as isolated or independent[65] because the order's government made determined efforts to maintain its control over the province and affirm its authority over the London convent. For unknown reasons the Prior of the London Black Friars was removed from his office by the chapter general of Montpellier in 1350. At the same time the convent's lector was promoted master in theology. The resistance encountered when the prior general attempted a visitation of the province in 1376 certainly came as a surprise even though many English Dominicans were willing to accept the reforms and even denounced the rebels. While a certain reluctance to accept change imposed from above may have been expected, the secular authorities became involved, setting clear

---

[63] PRO E 403 436 m25. *Acta*, 2, ed. Reichert, p. 254 (Wynkele's deposition), ibid., p. 265 (prayers for Edward III and Queen Philippa); on Wynkele's travels see: PRO E 403 325C m1. Palmer, 'The King's Confessors', *The Antiquary* 22 (1890) 262-63; E 403 307 m5: *pro illis £20 quas fratres eiusdem ordinis habuisse debuerunt pro capitulo suo generali in partibus Francie nuper convocato*; E 403 314 m8, m12; E 403 321 m4, m5; E 403 327 m8; E 403 328 m11; E 403 330 m35: *quas fratres de eodem ordine percipere solebant de elemosina domini regis et antecessorum suorum pro celebratione capituli generalis sui in partibus transmarinis*; E 403 35 m26; E 403 336 m 30; E 403 338 m 27; E 403 340 m 18. *Fratribus ordinis praedicatorum London' commorantibus quibus dominus rex illas £20 de elemosina sua in auxilium sustentationis sue annuatim ad scaccarium percipiendas quas idem rex et progenitores sui nuper de elemosina sua dederunt et concesserunt capitulo generali ordinis praedicatorum ubicumque tentum fuerit ac postmodum* [20 May 1354] *occasione guerre Francie concessit idem dominus rex priori et conventui ordinis praedicatorum London'.*

[64] PRO E 403 512 m9.

[65] *Acta*, 2, ed. Reichert, pp. 336-37.

limits to outside interference. The use of the secular law against the unwelcome representatives of the order's central government led to the arrest of the prior general's vicar and of other foreign Dominicans. It was left to the chapter general of 1378 to deal with the affair and punish the rebels but the aftermath was overshadowed by the beginning of the Great Schism.[66] It is uncertain whether all subsequent chapters general were attended by representatives from the English province,[67] however, Raymond of Capua's surviving letter book provides an impressive testimony of his efforts to maintain the integration of the English province. Friar Raymond not only installed Thomas Palmer as visitor and later confirmed him as provincial prior, eventually removing him when his regime proved too harsh,[68] he also exerted direct influence on the London convent, assigning friars[69] and lectors[70] or granting privileges to individual members of the convent.[71] In April 1393 he appointed John de Pingh as visitor of the London Blackfriars with a special mandate to scrutinise the privileges enjoyed by the friars there.[72] Two years later Pingh found himself the subject of an enquiry, facing charges of dereliction of duty.[73]

Since the generals' or vicar-generals' registers survive only sporadically, the level and intensity of outside interference in the London convent cannot be precisely ascertained. Leonardus de Mansuetis (1474-1480), who was primarily concerned with the financial contributions due from the English province, appointed the head of the London house as one of two conventual priors who had to confirm the provincial's election, an arrangement which was continued by his successor Salvus Cassetta (1481-1483).[74] Both Leonardus de Mansuetis and Joachim de la Torre (1487-1500) granted a number of privileges to

---

[66] Mortier, *Histoire des maitres généraux*, 3, pp. 402-03; *Acta*, 2, ed. Reichert, pp. 450-54.

[67] No English diffinitor was present at the chapter general of Lyon 1431, *Acta*, 3, ed. Reichert, pp. 208-09. The London Friar Peter Eme was diffinitor of the English province at the chapter general of 1478, British Library MS Add. 32446 art. 21b.

[68] *Registrum litterarum Fr. Raymundi de Vineis Capuani magistri ordinis 1380-1399*, ed. T. Kaeppeli. Monumenta Ordinis Praedicatorum Historica, 19 (Rome, 1937), p. 175, no. 42; pp. 181-82, no. 91.

[69] Ibid., p. 171, no. 4; p. 177, no. 58; p. 183, no. 96; p. 192, no. 134; p. 193, nos 148, 150; p. 195, no. 171.

[70] Ibid., p. 172, no. 16; p. 173, no. 27; p. 175, no. 38.

[71] Ibid., p. 174, nos 33, 35, 36.

[72] Ibid., p. 177, no. 57.

[73] Ibid., p. 183, no. 93.

[74] British Library MS Add. 32446 art. 18d, 22g.

individual London Dominicans, allowing them to chose their own confessors or relaxing the strict regulations on diet and clothing,[75] but such references to individual friars become increasingly rare. Thomas de Vio Caietani (1508-1513) did not deal with the convent at all[76] and the last privilege for a London Dominican was granted in 1526 by the Master Franciscus Silvester (1525-1528).[77] The London Black Friars remained an important house within the English Dominican province, but by the mid-fourteenth century the political aspect of its international significance disappeared.

II

The first Franciscans who arrived in the city in 1224 belonged to a mixed group. Agnellus of Pisa, a deacon who had already gained experience as Custos of Paris, had been asked by St Francis himself to extend the order into England. Henricus de Treviso was another Italian who became the first warden of the London Grey Friars. There were other – most likely Italian – Franciscans among this first group, but after the disaster of the first mission to Germany, care had been taken also to include English friars who had joined the order abroad. Richard of Ingworth may have originally come from Norfolk, he was joined by Richard of Devon and William de Esseby.[78] In a very short period of time this group developed close ties with sections of the local population. These did not just consist of constant support during the convent's long phase of construction,[79] but also led to successful recruitment in the city. The first novice in England, Salomon, is known to have stayed in the London convent where he was soon joined by William de London and Philippus Londonia.[80] Salomon became the convent's second warden and *generalis confessor totius civitatis*, Philip de London later became warden of Bridgnorth and eventually moved on to

---

[75] Ibid., art. 18g (1474); 19e (1475); 19f (1475); 21e (1478); 23g (1489); 24b (1491); 25h (1500).

[76] *Registrum litterarum Fr. Thomae de Vio Caietani O. P. magistri ordinis 1508-13*, ed. A. de Meyer. Monumenta Ordinis Praedicatorum Historica 17 (Rome, 1935), pp. 226-27.

[77] British Library MS Add. 32446, art. 31c.

[78] *Fratris Thomae vulgo dicti de Eccleston Tractatus de Adventu Fratrum Minorum in Angliam*, ed. A. G. Little (Manchester, 1951), pp. 3-6.

[79] J. Röhrkasten, 'Mendicants in the Metropolis: the Londoners and the Development of the London Friaries', *Thirteenth Century England VI*, ed. M. Prestwich (Woodbridge, 1997), pp. 61-75.

[80] *De adventu*, ed. Little, pp. 12-15.

Ireland. The third Franciscan novice in London, Joceus of Cornhill, was a member of the city elite, his father Joceus FitzPeter being sheriff in 1221. Joceus of Cornhill's recruitment by the young order is another sign of the early Franciscans' attraction to a broad section of the population, but like Philip de London he did not stay in the convent. He later went to the Mediterranean and died in Spain.[81] John Iwyn was another London merchant who not only supported but soon joined the group. Other English friars joined the Franciscan convent in London, changing its initial cosmopolitan composition. Some of the friars' names are known from *c.* 1230 onwards, indicating that some at least came from a London background. William de Basinges, who appears in 1255, was a member of a prominent London family.[82] Other names – Adam of Hereford, Roger of Canterbury, John of Chichester, John Stanford, Peter of Tewkesbury – may reflect the pattern of migration to the capital. From the earliest time, when a London citizen sheltered the newly arrived Grey Friars, the local ties of the Franciscan convent emerge very distinctly.

Although the Franciscans also received generous royal support they were not as closely attached to the court as the Dominicans. Consequently London Franciscans hardly ever appear on diplomatic missions in royal service. William of Gainsborough's journey to the Franciscan chapter general at Assisi in 1294, financed by Edward I because he was also conducting *negotiis regis*, is an exception. This friar, who was also provincial minister, had already been in royal service in 1292.[83] Franciscan chapters general were also sometimes sponsored by English kings but such payments were not made on a regular basis. Records survive for 1306 and 1309 when Edward I and then his son made funds available for chapters general at Toulouse and Padua.[84] The money was received and transferred by Henry de Sutton, the warden of the London convent. Henry de Sutton also received £ 20 from Edward II in 1313 for the Franciscan chapter general in Barcelona and the same amount for the chapter general at Naples in 1316.[85] The next royal payment for a Franciscan chapter general was made

---

[81] Ibid., pp. 15, 21; Knowles, *Religious Orders*, 1, p. 134; he may be identical with the draper Joce de Cornhelle who held property in the parish St Benet Gracechurch, *The Cartulary of Holy Trinity Aldgate*, ed. G. A. J. Hodgett. London Record Society 7 (London, 1971), p. 61, nos 316, 317.

[82] C. L. Kingsford, *The Grey Friars of London* (Aberdeen, 1915), pp. 69, 159.

[83] PRO E 403 90 m3; A. G. Little, *Franciscan Papers, Lists and Documents* (Manchester, 1943), pp. 193-94.

[84] PRO E 403 134 m4; E 403 149 m6.

[85] 1313: PRO E 403 165 m1; 1316: E 403 176 m7.

early in Edward III's reign but it is not clear whether the London convent was involved.[86] In marked contrast to the Dominican order these royal stipends for the triennial chapter general of the Franciscans continued to be paid until 1344 after which they stopped to be resumed only in 1367.[87]

As a result of Benedict XII's measure to reform the Franciscan order, the London Grey Friars became a general study in 1336, a change of status which explains the presence of scholars like Roger Conway and William Woodford in the mid- and late fourteenth century.[88] In these decades and until the last quarter of the fifteenth century there appear to have been few significant influences from outside. Neither the Franciscans nor any of the other London friaries were much affected by the Great Schism because England was firmly integrated in the Urbanists' camp. Clement VII made various attempts to promote followers in Ireland; Benedict XIII even hoped to create a separate archbishopric in Wales during the wars of Owen Glendower; in England itself not even propagandists from the Avignon curia stood a chance. One of them, the Franciscan John de Woderone, was sent to England in May 1381 but he made no impact, his confrère William Buxton was soon unmasked, summoned to the royal council and imprisoned among the London Black Friars.[89] During these years some Franciscans were entrusted with delicate diplomatic missions by Richard II's government. This was not only a sign of the political control exerted over the English mendicant provinces but also a result of an overlap of interests, the support of the Roman pope, who could number the overwhelming majority of English friars among his adherents, a notion expressed in the treatise of Nicholas de Fakenham, the Franciscan prior provincial, who advocated a union of the church in 1395.[90] Already in 1377 the Franciscan Walter Thorp had

---

[86] PRO E 403 232 m13.

[87] The last recorded royal payment for the meeting *in partibus Tuscanie* was 1344, PRO E 403 332 m 14 but in 1367 sums were paid *quas dominus rex eisdem fratribus nuper concedit de triennio in triennium de elemosina sua (...) pro capitulo suo generali.* E 403 431 m15.

[88] C. Schmitt, *Un pape réformateur et un défenseur de l'unité de l'Eglise. Benoît XII et l'ordre des Frères Mineurs (1334-1342)* (Quaracchi, 1959), p.24.

[89] E. Perroy, *L'Angleterre et le Grand Schisme d'Occident* (Paris, 1933), pp. 69-71; K.Eubel, 'Zur Geschichte des grossen abendländischen Schismas', *Römische Quartalschrift* 8 (1894) 259-73; idem, 'Die *provisiones praelatorum* während des grossen Schismas', ibid. 7 (1893) 405-45, at pp. 424-25; idem, *Die Avignonesische Obedienz der Mendikanten Orden* (Paderborn, 1890), p. 20, no. 149.

[90] F. Bliemetzrieder, 'Traktat des Minoritenprovinzials von England Fr. Nicholas de Fakenham (1395)', *Archivum Franciscanum Historicum* 1 (1908) 577-600; 2 (1909) 79-91.

been sent to Lombardy to meet the English condottiere Sir John Hawkwood[91] and in 1379 the provincials from England and Ireland returned from a voyage to the continent with letters from the pope and the German king.[92] Among these ambassadors was also the prominent theologian John Welle from the London Grey Friars who, in September 1378 received his payments for being sent *in secretis negotiis regis versus curiam Romanam*.[93] This secret journey is the only sign of any involvement of the city's friaries in the negotiations at the beginning of the Great Schism.

In England the discussions beginning at the periphery of the general debate about church reform, the efforts to reform the Franciscan order, had no practical effect for a long time. The English Franciscan province showed little interest in the emerging Observant movement and the London convent was no exception. It may have been faced with the problem of finding new novices and it was difficult to replace the losses suffered in the various outbreaks of the plague. By the mid-fifteenth century the number of friars had been significantly reduced compared to the levels in the thirteenth and early fourteenth centuries. According to a list the convent had only thirty-three members in 1458, while the convent's precinct had now been extended to its full size. Already in 1440 John Kyrie, the warden, had accepted a tenant, the number of friars in his convent being reduced to little more than a third of those in 1336.[94]

The convent came to some prominence in the 1420s when one of its members, friar William Russell, interfered in a long-standing dispute between the parish clergy and the citizens about the payment of tithes. In the course of the affair not only the Archbishop of Canterbury but also the papal curia were approached. The dispute emerged from the settlement of a similar conflict according to which the London parishioners had to pay tithes on their income from trade and commerce as well as rent. The rates set in the arrangement found under Bishop Roger Niger (1229-1241) had become quite unrealistic by the second half of the fourteenth century because the level of rents charged in the city had risen significantly. Since the parish clergy's attempt to levy tithes

---

[91] PRO E 403 465 m3; E 403 468 m5; E 403 471 m12.

[92] Perroy, *L'Angleterre*, p. 140; PRO E 403 472 m11; they may have been the two friars who were paid 10 marks *eundo versus curiam Romanam* in 1377, E 403 461 m5.

[93] PRO E 403 468 m12; A. G. Little, *Studies in English Franciscan History* (Manchester, 1917), pp. 82-83.

[94] J. R. H. Moorman, *A History of the Franciscan Order* (Oxford, 1968), pp. 451 seqq.; PRO C 270/32/20; *Catalogue of Ancient Deeds*, 1 (London, 1890), p. 533, no. C1479; Little, *Studies*, pp. 69, 72.

on the increased incomes led to resentment among the citizens on the one hand and to legislation within the archdiocese of Canterbury on the other, William Russel's sermons, advocating the payment of personal tithes at will, were embarrassing. Russell, who had been warden of the London Franciscans, and two of his fellow friars were summoned before the Convocation in May 1425 and ordered to withdraw their statements in public. When Russell refused to submit, his opinions were declared to be heretical and he was excommunicated. He avoided arrest by taking his case to the curia in the summer of 1425, but instead of finding the expected support he suffered imprisonment. He escaped from Rome and returned to London and eventually ended up in the custody of Archbishop Chichele. Prosecuted in Rome as well as London Russell eventually submitted in March 1428.[95]

The accession of Pope Sixtus IV in 1471 marked a significant change for the four main mendicant orders. The new pontiff showed a great interest in the Observant movement and began a programme of legislation culminating in the general confirmation of their privileges. In London these bulls were not unknown, a clear reference to them was made in a letter of confraternity, granted by the Franciscan provincial minister in 1479. Yet the little effect they had on the London friaries and the attitudes of the Londoners towards them[96] is indicated as no changes in the patterns of devotion are expressed in the surviving late medieval London wills. However, the situation did begin to change for the London Grey Friars with the arrival of the Observants in 1482. Even though the second Franciscan house was not located in the city but at Greenwich, a site offered to the Vicar-General of the Observants by King Edward IV in 1481, the new convent soon began to attract the attention of the Londoners. By 1485 building work was in progress and the friars, the overwhelming majority of whom were not English, judging by their names, soon began to receive valuable bequests.[97] Among the first Londoners to turn their attention to the Observants were the fishmonger Robert Darlington and the painter Christian

---

[95] J. A. F. Thomson, 'Tithe Disputes in Later Medieval London', *English Historical Review* 78 (1963) 1-17; C. A. Robinson, 'The Tithe-Heresy of Friar William Russell', *Albion* 8 (1976) 1-16; Little, *Studies*, p. 54; Kingsford, *Grey Friars*, pp. 20, 22, 57-58.

[96] Moorman, *Franciscan Order*, pp. 488, 513; J. Smet, *The Carmelites*, 1 (2nd edn, Dariell, Illinois, 1988), p. 66. GL MS 21736.

[97] A. G. Little, 'Introduction of the Observant Friars into England', *Proceedings of the British Academy* 11 (1923) 1-17.

Colborne, who had migrated to London from Cologne.[98] Colborne was not the only member of the immigrant community who expressed a preference for the Observants in his will. Slightly later, Isaias Schenk, a canon lawyer working as a secretary for the Hanseatic merchants in the Steelyard, decided that the convent should be given one of his manuscripts after his death.[99] Other members of this group expressed similar sentiments.[100] A large group of tailors and textile workers gave legacies to and sometimes focused entirely on the Observants. Among them is Jacob van Zand who had migrated to London to work as a tailor. Clearly their appeal was not only to the more prominent citizens and expatriots but also to this section among the artisans.[101] This appeal to the large foreign communities in London is easily explained: there were a significant number of foreign friars among the Observants themselves. In April 1491 the first of them, Bernardus de Maclenia was ordained priest and until 1506 many more religious from the Rhineland, the Low Countries and southern Germany followed their vocation in the Greenwich convent.[102] The co-operation of foreign and English friars in the establishment of a reformed convent was successful and dozens of testators turned to the Observants as an alterna-

---

[98] GL MS 9171-7, fol. 50v-52r; fol. 56v-57r; A. F. Sutton, 'Christian Colborne, Painter of Germany and London, died 1486', *Journal of the British Archaeological Association* 135 (1982) 55-61.

[99] GL MS 9171-7, fol. 142v-143r.

[100] GL MS 9171-8, fol. 32v-33r (Fernand de Molonia, *doctor in medecynes*); ibid., fol. 79r (John Gyse *de Anwarp in Braband, merchaunt*); ibid., fol. 250v (Loye Devyle de London, hatmaker, born in the duchy of Normandy); GL MS 9171-9, fol. 94r-v (Gerardus Roest).

[101] GL MS 9171-8, fol. 203v (Jacobus van Zand, scissor); ibid., fol. 56v (Richard Croft, tailor); ibid., fol.80r-v (John Chylde, dyer); ibid., fol.67v-68v (William Grey, tailor); ibid., fol.100r (Richard Dacres, tailor); ibid., fol.117r-v (William Crosby, tailor); GL MS 9171-9, fol. 31v-32v (John Beld, dyer). S. Brigden, *London and the Reformation* (2nd edn, Oxford, 1991), p. 73.

[102] GL MS 9531/8, fol. 23r (2 April 1491); Raphael Antlernes, Willelmus Eliothis, Gabriel Plakmode *ordinis observancie minorum de Grenewico* (1 June 1493), fol. 28r; *frater* Andreas Zanter, fol. 28v, 32v; Barnardinus de Tinera munda, Florencius de Herndals (21 September 1499), fol. 61r; Andreas Zutphanie, Egidius de Veris (1500), fol. 63r; Willelmus de Meketunia, Arnoldus de Mekelinia (19 September 1500), fol. 65r; Hubertus Aquis, Ricardus Campis, Franciscus Campis, Franciscus Sand, Johannes Otmerzon, Fridericus Wricht, Cornelius Wurzerigie, Johannes de Monte, Johannes Guthnon, Nicolaus Wormatie (27 March 1501), fol. 67v; Petrus Magoncie (18 September 1501), fol. 77v; Nicholaus de Wormasia (19 February 1502), fol. 80r; Antonius Bolzverdie (24 September 1502), fol. 83v, 84r; Franciscus Emdis, Willelmus Machelynye, Johannes Kalkar, Johannes Leodie, Nicholaus Wormacie (2 March 1504), fol. 87v; Reynerus Limburgh (18 December 1506), fol. 94v.

tive to the Grey Friars' convent in the city. Although they were noticed and welcomed by sections of London's society, the Greenwich Observants were never integrated into the local ecclesiastical institutions: their close connections with the royal family under the Yorkists as well as under the Tudors gave them a special status which continued until they spoke out against Henry VIII's divorce.[103]

III

Much less is known about the first friars in London's other mendicant convents. In official records they emerge as groups rather than individuals. Two of the houses, the Friars of the Sack and the Fratres de Areno were founded from France. Both fell victim to the decisions of the Second Council of Lyons in 1274 which had been drafted with the intention of reducing the number of mendicant orders. Excepting the Franciscans and Dominicans and reserving the fate of the Carmelites and Austin Friars for a future decision, the orders were forbidden to recruit new novices and so were doomed to disappearance over a period. The council's decisions were also implemented in London but they did not affect the support given to the two houses by the population as well as the royal household which ensured that both survived into the fourteenth century and were still active more than thirty years after the council.[104] Equally little is known about the first Carmelites or the first Austin Friars in London. For both orders contemporary evidence relating to individuals is only available from the early fourteenth century. The surviving names indicate that the convents consisted mostly of English friars at that period.[105] In the case of the

---

[103] A. G. Dickens, *The English Reformation* (13th edn, Glasgow, 1983), p. 87; Brigden, *London and the Reformation*, p. 209.

[104] In March 1303 the *Fratres de Areno* or *de Pica*, on this occasion represented by a Londoner, Friar Gilbert de London, were still benefitting from royal alms, PRO E101/363/18, fol. 2r; the Friars of the Sack as well as the Friars *de Areno* still received royal alms in May 1304, PRO E101/369/11, fol. 7r-v, 33r.

[105] Among the Austin Friars there are Richard de Clare, PRO E 403 152 m1, E 403 176 m4; Thomas de Dunolm, conventual prior in 1322, E 403 200 m2; Nicholas de Morton, who several times collected royal donations between 1321 and 1330, E 403 195 m3, E 403 207 m10, E 403 213 m7; E 403 218 m7, E 403 249 m11; Thomas de Oxonia, E 403 122 m2; Robert de St Albano, who appeared between 1316 and 1335, E 403 178 m5-6, E 403 228 m4, E 403 259 m21, E 403 262 m16, E 403 276 m15, E 403 279 m26; Geoffrey de Scardeburgh, E 403 122 m2; an exception could be Guido de Fresingfeld, E 403 132 m4, E 403 184 m7. From the Carmelites only the names of English friars survive: John de Belegrave, E 403 200 m2; Richard de Fulmere, E 403 195 m5; John de Lacok, conventual prior in 1309, E 403 143 m3; E 403 174 m1, m4; Edmund de Norwich, E

Carmelites the importance of the English province for the order's development is reflected by the fact that some of the early chapters general were convened in London. The first such meeting appears to have been held in 1254, others followed in 1272, 1281, and 1312. In 1271 Ralph de Fryston, an English Carmelite, was elected prior general of the order and he stayed in office for several years.[106] By 1294 the London White Friars had become one of the order's *studia theologica*, receiving students from all provinces. By 1321 it was one of the three first *studia generalia*.[107] However, the Carmelites never again convened in London or in their English province after the end of the thirteenth century.

The English Carmelite province was visited by the prior general in 1376 and by Pope Urban VI's protegé Michael Aiguani in 1383 and 1384, after the attempts to stay united despite the schism had failed. Like all the other religious institutions in the kingdom it adhered to the Roman faction during the schism but in the case of the Carmelites the internal division was overcome earlier than in other orders. In the early fifteenth century the White Friars in Fleet Street were linked to events on a much larger scale, at least indirectly through Thomas Netter, who had joined the order in London. Netter was among the most prominent and articulate opponents of Lollardy whose writings were known throughout Europe and even played a role in the Counter-Reformation.[108] Furthermore he was a member of the royal household, combining his duties as royal confessor with those of diplomat. He attended the Council of Pisa in 1409 and it is very likely that he was sent as one of the English representatives to the Council of Constance in 1415. Four years later he acted as royal ambassador, travelling to Prussia as one of the mediators in the conflict between the Teutonic Knights and Poland, a conflict which Henry V

---

403 174 m1, E 403 176 m4, E 403 202 m6; Catalogue of Ancient Deeds, 2, p.514, no. C2387; William de Nottingham E 403 207 m11; Robert de Pershore, E 403 186 m2-3; John de Polstede, E 403 195 m5; Stephen de Seleby, E 403 128 m3; Thomas de Wytham, ibid.

[106] *Calendar of Liberate Rolls, 1267-72*, 6, p. 224, no. 2018; L. Saggi, 'Constitutiones Capituli Londinensis Anni 1281', *Analecta Ordinis Carmelitarum* 2 (1950) 203-45; J. Smet, *The Carmelites*, 1, pp. 16, 22; *CPR, Edward I, 1272-1281*, p. 158, safe conduct for *Ralph de Fryston*, Prior General of the Carmelite Order, 2 August 1276; R. Copsey, *The Medieval Carmelite Priory at London. A Chronology* (Rome, 1995), p. 4.

[107] F.-B. Lickteig, *The German Carmelites at the Medieval Universities* (Rome, 1981). pp. 29, 79; Smet, *Carmelites*, 1, p. 31.

[108] M. Harvey, 'The Doctrinale of Thomas Netter in the Fifteenth and Sixteenth Centuries', *Intellectual Life in the Middle Ages. Essays Presented to Margaret Gibson*, eds L. Smith, B. Ward (London, 1992), pp. 281-94.

and his ally King Sigismund were trying to solve.[109] The confessor, who had accompanied the king to France on earlier occasions, was sent by the royal council to Henry V in March 1422, at the time when the siege of Meaux, during which the monarch fell ill, was coming to an end. Netter was present when the king died and he also held the funeral sermon for the monarch whose attitude towards spiritual matters he had significantly influenced. Netter himself was to die in France, again in royal service, in November 1430.[110]

The English Carmelite province, which ranked third in the order after the Holy Land and Sicily, gave significant financial support to the order as a whole. Whereas in the fourteenth century, when the records began, the French province had been the largest provider of funds, followed by the *provincia Angliae*, this changed when the order split at the time of the Great Schism. By 1393 England was the largest contributor in the Roman obedience.[111] The demands regarding the routine sharing of expenses, reflecting the number of convents in the province, were repeated proportionately when old debts had to be paid or special expenses had been incurred. From this time onwards the English province consistently made the largest financial contributions for the prior general's expenses, for the order's procurator at the papal court and other, sometimes itemised, expenditures and it continued to be the largest contributor long after the schism had been overcome.[112] One could speculate that England eclipsed the French province in wealth, possibly as a result of decades of warfare in France but this line of enquiry cannot be pursued here. Instead it is important to note that these large contributions had no equivalent in the province's weight and influence in the order's government. England was again visited by the prior general in 1413 but the order's centre was in France and northern Spain. At two chapters general, Montpellier in 1420 and Asti in 1472, the English friars do not even seem to have been represented at all.[113] For most of the fifteenth century the office of prior general was held by French members

---

[109] J. Sarnowsky, *Die Wirtschaftsführung des Deutschen Ordens in Preußen (1382-1454)* (Cologne, 1993), p. 398. PRO E 403 640 m1; E 403 643 m8.

[110] C. Allmand, *Henry V* (London, 1992), pp. 304-5; PRO E 403 652 m19; *Fasciculi Zizaniorum Magistri Johannis Wyclif*, ed. W. W. Shirley. Rolls Series (London, 1858), p. LXXI.

[111] *Acta capitulorum generalium Ordinis Fratrum B. V. Mariae de Monte Carmeli*, ed. G. Wessels (Rome, 1912), pp. 111-12.

[112] Ibid., pp. 125, 128, 136, 138, 149, 150, 158, 159, 167, 174 (an exception here is the English contribution to the pension of the former Prior General John Grossi), 182, 190, 199, 200, 214-16, 222, 231, 238, 245, 281.

[113] Ibid., pp. 158, 271.

of the order,[114] not all of whom were very accommodating to their English confrères. In 1432 the English Provincial Prior John Kenynghale complained about the hostility shown him by the French prior general.[115] This lack of influence sets the context for a dispute which brought the London White Friars not only into conflict with the city's parish clergy and the local bishop but with the highest authorities. In this respect and as far as its outcome was concerned the affair is reminiscent of the scandal involving the London Grey Friars in the 1420s but the issue itself was different. The dispute was initiated by Harry Parker, a Carmelite friar, who in a sermon preached at St Paul's Cross on 16 September 1464 revived the claim that Christ and the apostles had been poor and survived by begging. At a time when the order's own chapter general punished the wrongful accusation of a Cologne Carmelite by a group of his confrères with heavy fines and ordered the money to be paid over to the victim, and when a retiring prior general was granted an annual pension for life, such notions must have seemed out of date even within the order. Since this was combined with an attack on the secular clergy the sermon was formally answered and the public debate was continued by Thomas Halden, regent of divinity in the Fleet Street convent. The Carmelites had a disputation in their convent which resulted in a citation before the Archbishop of Canterbury while the public exchange at St Paul's Cross continued. The affair became more acrimonious when on 23 December 1464 John Milverton, the Prior of the London convent and of the English Carmelite province, defended Parker and his supporters in a further sermon. Despite the Carmelites' privileged status, judicial proceedings against Parker and Halden were begun, and Halden as well as Milverton were excommunicated. In the spring of 1465 Milverton and two other friars from the London convent arrived in Rome only to be confronted with a letter from the Archbishop of Canterbury in which they were accused of heresy. Milverton was imprisoned in the Castel St Angelo for nearly three years, until 1468, when he made his submission to a committee of cardinals, acknowledged his errors and promised to withdraw his statements in public.[116]

---

[114] Smet, *Carmelites*, 1, pp. 29, 61.

[115] Ibid., 1, p. 62; *Concilium Basiliense. Die Protokolle des Concils 1431-1433*, ed. J. Haller, vol. 2 (Basle, 1897), p. 283; H. Müller, *Die Franzosen, Frankreich und das Basler Konzil (1431-1449)*, 2 (Paderborn, 1990), p. 720.

[116] F. R. H. Du Boulay, 'The Quarrel between the Carmelite Friars and the Secular Clergy of London', *Journal of Ecclesiastical History* 6 (1955) 156-74; Smet, *Carmelites*, 1, pp. 65-66; *Acta*, ed. Wessels, pp. 174, 203.

The London convent of the Friars of the Cross is supposed to have been founded by two citizens.[117] While there is no doubt that the first members of this order in London whose names survive in contemporary sources were English, possibly local,[118] the first houses of the English province were founded from abroad, most likely by foreign friars. Groups of foreign religious occasionally came to England, sometimes prompting the government to grant letters of protection. Royal protection was granted to a group of *Fratres ordinis Sanctae Mariae de ordine Cruciferorum* in 1244 whose links with the Friars of the Cross from the Low Countries cannot be established with certainty.[119] When the Friars of the Cross received papal approval in 1248 they had already established a house at Whaplode, in the diocese of Lincoln, where Bishop Grosseteste received a papal request to provide assistance to the community and about twenty years later a house was founded in London.[120] After the disappearance of the Friars of the Sack and the Friars de Areno this convent was the smallest mendicant house in London. In the fourteenth and early fifteenth centuries there are signs of internal conflict, possibly aggravated by recruitment problems and the Crutched Friars never managed to gain a status equal to that of the four main mendicant convents. However, the order had the strength to reform itself and this measure also affected its London house.

The order of the Friars of the Cross was clearly focused on its convent at Huy whose prior also customarily acted as prior general. For a long time, into the fifteenth century, the London convent does not seem to have maintained close connections with the centre, but this gradually changed after the chapter general of 1410 had taken the decision to reform the order.[121] At the time only a

---

[117] John Stow, *Survey of London*, ed. C. L. Kingsford, vol. 1 (Oxford, 1908), p. 147.

[118] John de Hurle, Westminster Abbey Muniments 13431.

[119] *CPR, Henry III, 1232-47*, p. 435; A. Franchi, 'Crocifissi', *Dizionario degli Istituti di Perfezione*, vol. 8 (Rome, 1976), p. 303. The historiographical debate is discussed by K. Elm, 'Entstehung und Reform des belgisch-niederländischen Kreuzherrenordens', *Zeitschrift für Kirchengeschichte* 82 (1971) 292-313.

[120] *Les registres d'Innocent IV*, ed. E. Berger, vol. 2 (Paris, 1887), no. 4155; H. van Rooijen, 'Crocigeri Belgi', *Dizionario degli Istituti di Perfezione*, vol. 3 (Rome, 1976), pp. 304-11; R. N. Hadcock, 'The Order of the Holy Cross in Ireland', *Medieval Studies Presented to Aubrey Gwynn S. J.*, eds J. A. Watt, J. B. Morrall, F. X. Martin (Dublin, 1961), pp. 44-53; H. F. Chettle, 'The Friars of the Holy Cross in England', *History* 34 (1949) 204-20; Knowles, *Religious Orders*, 1, p. 203; E. Beck, 'The Order of the Holy Cross in England', *Transactions of the Royal Historical Society* 3rd ser. 7 (1913) 191-208; J. Bulloch, 'The Crutched Friars', *Records of the Scottish Church History Society* 10 (1950) 86-106, 154-70.

[121] P. van den Bosch, 'Die Kreuzherrenreform des 15. Jahrhunderts. Urheber, Zielsetzung und Verlauf', *Reformbemühungen und Observanzbestrebungen im spätmittelalter-*

few priors from the order's heartlands were involved. England or even the London convent were not represented and they also did not participate in later chapters general, a lack of contact reflected in the difficulties encountered when an extension of the reform into England was attempted. The first friar from the Low Countries, who can be identified in the London convent in the same year, is likely to have been very young, being ordained subdeacon in September 1410.[122] The attempts to reform the English province began in 1428 when three friars, Conrad of Andernach and Herman Piddel led by the Prior of Huy, visited England.[123] Their efforts cannot have had a lasting success because the reform turned into a lengthy process. In the present context it is important to note that it was promoted entirely by friars from the Low Countries and the Rhineland where the order had its centre. Only gradually did the chapter general gain some influence in England, removing unsuitable friars to other convents, mostly in the Low Countries and sending its own representatives instead. In these years a number of friars from the Low Countries can be traced over longer periods of time in London.[124] A determined effort to extend the reform into the English province was begun in 1453, when the members of the chapter general decided to instruct and commission a group of friars for this purpose, an idea further developed in the following year when it was agreed to send twenty priests to England. Eventually only five friars were dispatched under William of Zutphen, who headed the group as *vicarius generalis*.[125] Although the group was small they seem to have made an impact, at least in the London convent, where friars from successfully reformed houses were transferred.[126] By 1459 a fraternity of the Holy Blood of Wilsnack was attached to the church, a sign that the presence of foreign friars facilitated the

---

lichen Ordenswesen, ed. K. Elm. Berliner Historische Studien 14 (Berlin, 1989), pp. 71-82.

[122] Walter Gouda was ordained subdeacon on 20 September 1410, GL MS 9531/4, fol.49v. In the following year he became subdeacon and priest, ibid., fol. 50v, 52v.

[123] *Definities der Generale Kapittels van de Orde van het H. Kruis, 1410-1786*, ed. A. van de Pasch (Brussels, 1969), p. 57, no. 19.

[124] Ibid., p. 62, no. 22; p. 69, no. 27; p. 78, no. 32. *Frater* Petrus Bloys, 1432, GL MS 9531/4, fol. 220v; *frater* Herbardus Zaliger (1433/1434), ibid., fol. 221v, 222r, 223v, 224v.

[125] *Definities*, ed. van de Pasch, p. 98, no. 44; p. 101, no. 45; p. 102, no. 46, confirmation of this decision in 1455; p. 103, no. 47.

[126] Ibid., p. 104, no. 47; p. 119, no. 54; p. 125, no. 56; p. 130, no. 58.

establishment of a steady link with the groups of foreign traders and craftsmen, in this case with the German community in London.[127]

Another attempt to implement a reform, again introduced from abroad, was begun in 1489 when a group of four German friars arrived in London, one of them, Christian Coloniensis, taking on the office of prior. It is likely that one of these four was the *informator in disciplina regulari* appointed in London by the chapter general of that year.[128] It cannot have been easy for the order's general to maintain close contact with the English province or its London convent which was never represented at the chapter general. The visitations of the English province were increasingly entrusted to friars from English convents, prominent among them the London Crutched Friars, after another five brethren had been transferred there in 1495. Between 1499 and 1507 new friars from abroad stayed in the London Crutched Friars where they introduced reform measures and some of them obtained the higher orders.[129] Gradually new arrangements were introduced for the English province. In 1502 the chapter general appointed the prior of the London convent visitor for all houses in England for the first time, a decision confirmed and repeated in 1504.[130] In the following year the prior was appointed vicar for the *Anglia* province and gradually the London convent, where discipline was monitored by a specially appointed subprior in 1512, obtained an important status in the country.[131] Between 1518 and 1529 the chapter general regularly appointed the London prior as visitor, often with far-reaching powers.[132]

It is difficult to say which measures were actually taken during the various attempts to bring about a reform, but the presence of foreign friars and a stricter discipline in the convent are likely to have been noticed in the neigh-

---

[127] H. C. Coote, 'The Ordinances of Some Secular Guilds of London', *Transactions of the London and Middlesex Archaeological Society* 4 (1871) 44 seqq.

[128] Henricus Russelius, *Chronicon Cruciferorum* (Cologne, 1635), pp. 132-33; *Definities*, ed. van de Pasch, p. 182, no. 80.

[129] Ibid., p. 200, no. 86. Johannes Duren', Albertus Hulsse, Johannes Makyn' (1499), GL MS 9531/8, fol. 61r, fol.62r, v; Augustinus de Casleto, Nicholaus Gronyngen (1500 or 1501), fol. 67r, v; Petrus de Haerlem, Cornelius de Sarflith (1503 or 1504), fol. 87r, 88r; Johannes de Roterdam, Jasper Ogershen (1506-1508), fol. 95r, 97r, 100r; Jaspar Meerson (1507), fol. 97r.

[130] *Definities*, ed. van de Pasch, p. 227, no. 93; p. 234, no. 95.

[131] Ibid., p. 235, no. 96; p. 254, no. 103.

[132] In 1518 and 1519 with the power *elocandi et relocandi*, ibid., p. 268, no. 109; p. 270, no. 110; cf. p. 272, no. 111; p. 273, no. 112; p. 276, no. 113; p. 278, no. 114; p. 281, no. 115; p. 284, no. 116; p. 286, no. 117; p. 289, no. 118; p. 292, no. 119; p. 294, no. 120.

bourhood. It cannot have been a coincidence that in the last decades of its existence the London Crutched Friars developed into a spiritual centre of some importance. This is reflected in the surviving wills from the London Commissary Court which show a notable increase in bequests as well as requests for burial. In the period 1460 to 1469 seven testators made bequests to the convent, a figure which almost doubled to thirteen in the decades 1470 to 1479 and 1480 to 1489 respectively while in the last decade of the fifteenth century ten bequests to the convent are recorded. The development over the following years is not clear because of a gap in the records between 1502 and 1515 but a dramatic change must have occurred in the early sixteenth century coinciding with the London convent's new role in the English province. Between 1515 and 1519 there were twenty-seven bequests. This must have been more than just a response to a fire which had caused severe damage in the church in 1514, because public interest remained at a high level. Between 1520 and 1529 the Crutched Friars appeared in thirty wills and even in the last years of the convent's existence, 1530 to 1537, there were still ten Londoners who entrusted the friars with their spiritual well-being. While it is difficult to explain the immediate connections between the reform attempts and the obvious increase in public interest it needs to be emphasised that there was also a qualitative development. The Crutched Friars, for almost two centuries merely the smallest of London's five male mendicant houses, came to be regarded as a religious community with its own distinct character. This is not just reflected in the number of legacies and the associated requests, but also by their nature. The majority of testators left legacies to all or at least more than one friary, only relatively few singled out a particular house and the Friars of the Cross were almost never given this preferential status. For the period between 1460 and 1500 there are only ten wills where pious bequests were focused on this particular convent. This number increased significantly after 1515. In the convent's last decades forty testators expressed their spiritual affinity in this manner and this trend is confirmed when the requests for burial in the precinct are included. The evidence suggests that not only did religious life in the house appeal to an increased number of people, it also affected them in a different way.[133] After a slow start a lengthy process of reform had led to tangible results.

---

[133] The first Londoner to request burial in the Crutched Friars in the sixteenth century was Edmund Sylver, a member of the adjacent parish of St Olave by the Tower, GL MS 9171/9, fol. 9r; other were John Waurost, ibid., fol. 40r; Robert de Aquisgrano, ibid., fol. 45v and Adrian Bloeme, ibid., fol. 46r, who had both chosen their confessors from among the community; Henry Harrison, ibid., fol. 48r-v; Herny Newys, ibid., fol. 83v-

The situation was different in the case of the last mendicant foundation in the city, the nuns of St Clare near Aldgate. Their convent was built by Edward I's brother Edmund of Lancaster and his wife Blanche in 1294. The first generation of nuns was brought from abroad,[134] still in 1308 a royal donation was received by Agnes of Arras.[135] Whether the presence of foreign nuns actually represented international ties is another question. English nuns began to enter the convent but the women who joined were often members of the aristocracy, and although the daughters of prominent London families were admitted as well, the character of the London Minoresses remained aristocratic for a long time.

IV

Whereas the Franciscans had established strong roots among the London population from the start, such connections were only developed (or became visible) much later in the case of the other orders. In the later fourteenth and fifteenth centuries the mendicant houses provided spiritual guidance to a sizeable part of the city's population who acknowledged this support in their wills. Between 10 per cent and 20 per cent of surviving London wills contain references to the city's friaries.[136] These texts do not just contain requests for prayers, masses and other spiritual services for the time after the testator's death, they also provide clear indications of relations between individuals and the convent, sometimes individual friars. One of the ways used to express a long term attachment to one of the friaries was the purchase of letters of confraternity which would enable the recipient to share spiritual benefits gained by the friars. The London widow Margaret Delowe, who died in 1457, described herself as a *suster* of the Austin Friars;[137] a London scrivener, Richard Grene,

---

84v; Elizabeth Aylmer, ibid., fol. 85r; Cornelius Johanes von der Zoune, ibid., fol. 87r-88r; Peter Rutter, another Dutchman, ibid., fol. 113r-v; Alice Spryng, who named Friar William Bowry, prior of the house, as one of her confessors, ibid., fol.135v-136r; Henry Atkin, ibid., fol. 154v-155r; Richard a Wode, whose will was witnessed by the prior, ibid., fol. 167r-v; William Cotton, GL MS 9171-10, fol. 56r; the brewer William Penreth, ibid., fol. 87r-v; Elizabeth de la Now, who also requested William Bowry's services as executor, ibid., fol. 114r, and Margaret Peters, whose will dated 20 January 1536 was the last recorded request for burial in the house, ibid. fol. 264r.

[134] A. F. C. Bourdillon, *The Order of Minoresses in England* (Manchester, 1926), p. 14; *CPR, Edward I, 1292-1301*, p. 24.

[135] PRO E 403 144 m2.

[136] J. Röhrkasten, 'The Londoners and the London Mendicants in the Late Middle Ages', *Journal of Ecclesiastical History* 47 (1996) 451.

[137] GL MS 9171/5, fol. 223v.

whose will was proved 4 September 1479 had obtained letters of confraternity from the London Franciscans.[138] These two examples of several show the extent to which the mendicants were rooted in the population even long after they had become part of established religious institutions. Numerous other pieces of evidence point in the same direction. Friars were entrusted with the office of executor, witness or supervisor, often having previously been advisers or confessors.[139] Friars received numerous personal bequests which were the fruits of patient work among the laity. Master William Swaffham, prior of the London Carmelite convent from 1456 and again in 1473 was mentioned in the will of the barber John Queldryk in 1456, again in 1466 by William Capon, a tailor, and by William Person, another tailor, in 1473.[140] Equally popular was the Franciscan Dr William Wolfe, who was asked to act as witness in 1450, became one of the executors of the will of Johanna Neumarch in 1452, and received a bequest from the London widow Elizabeth Rikill in 1456.[141] The Dominicans had an equally prominent and popular member of their convent in the mid-fifteenth century. Friar David Carne was repeatedly asked to act as supervisor, executor or witness and he also received numerous bequests. David Carne's popularity was more than just a reflection of the friars' pastoral work among the laity. He was the brother-in-law of a London citizen who named him executor and further requested that the remaining members of his family should also receive the friar's help.[142] Here was another type of local tie. By the late fourteenth century many London friars had relatives among local families and this trend was to continue into the fifteenth century. As the country's most important centre of population London had been an obvious recruiting ground from the start.

This survey indicates that all the London mendicant houses had international links and that their importance could extend far beyond the city at least temporarily. Prominent friars attended the royal court and were sometimes entrusted with new roles in this new environment, a feature emerging quite clearly in the case of the Dominicans, who were the order most closely affiliated to the royal family. Convents were used as venues for chapters general and functioned as centres of education. This pattern slowly changed when the English kingdom

---

[138] GL MS 9171/6, fol. 260v-261r.

[139] An example is the Austin Friar John de Bury, D. D., who was asked to be executor of the will of Connant Lassels in 1471, GL MS 9171/6, fol. 86r-v.

[140] GL MS 9171/5, fol. 193v-194r; 384r-385v; GL MS 9171/6, fol. 132v-133r.

[141] GL MS 9171/5, fol.13v; 110r-v; 197r.

[142] GL MS 9171/4, fol. 217r-v; GL MS 9171/5, fol. 29v; 118r; 140r-v; 314v-315r.

became more and more estranged from the papacy after the outbreak of the Hundred Years' War. The origins of this lengthy process can be traced back to Edward I's measures against alien priories which were renewed in the early stages of the war. This general climate of distance and suspicion also affected the friars. In April 1327 a government order prevented mendicant friars from leaving the kingdom unless equipped with a royal licence.[143] As England became more isolated in the conflict with France and Scotland, the government increasingly regarded the English mendicant provinces as local orders, not as parts of international organizations. In this context it is interesting to note that English provincial chapters were increasingly being described as chapters general in the records kept by government departments.

Although Benedict XII was preoccupied with monastic reform he could not ignore the fact that the English king had entered into an alliance with Louis the Bavarian, an avowed enemy of the papacy. The English government was aware that Clement VI was secretly backing the French king when it sent its ambassador to deal with *secretis et arduis negotiis*.[144] At home the English government showed ever greater suspicion possibly because of the knowledge that mendicants had been used as secret messengers in other conflicts, e.g. in Italy where financial aid was conveyed to towns besieged by the troops of Henry VII of Germany.[145] In August 1346 the warden of the London Grey Friars received an official order not to let alien friars into the convent.[146] Almost exactly a year later the government ordered the complete evacuation of Calais after the end of the siege. Among those exiled were also the town's Carmelites who were replaced by English friars, a process which was repeated with the Austin Friars.[147] Officially distinctions were now made between English and

---

[143] *CCR, Edward III, 1327-1330*, p. 107.

[144] PRO E 403 314 m7; PRO E 403 302 m4. The Dominican chapter general had been prominent in taking action against the emperor and his followers in 1328 and 1330, *Acta*, ed. Reichert, 2, pp. 178-79, 197; Eckert, 'Nichthäretische Papstkritik', pp. 182-83.

[145] R. Pauler, *Die deutschen Könige und Italien im 14.Jahrhundert* (Darmstadt, 1997), p. 82.

[146] *CCR, Edward III, 1346-1349*, p. 150.

[147] *Chronique latine de Guillaume de Nangis de 1130 à 1300 avec les continuations de cette chronique*, ed. H. Géraud, 2, (Paris, 1843), p. 207. In 1349 the Austin Friars of Calais received financial support from the English king, PRO E 403 344 m20.

foreign friars and from this point it was only a small step to suspect foreign friars studying at Oxford of espionage.[148]

Despite the deterioration in Anglo-papal relations after the accession of Clement VI neither the English mendicant provinces nor their London convents were completely isolated. Assistance from the papal curia was even sought in cases of urgent necessity. When the whole concept of mendicant religious life was called into question in a series of sermons preached in London by Richard Fitzralph, Archbishop of Armagh in 1356 and 1357, the London friars took up the challenge. The archbishop – a prominent Oxford theologian – had originally been a supporter of the friars, but by 1350 at the latest he had joined the ranks of their critics, contributing to the old debate about poverty and expressing public doubts about their purpose and sincerity. This change in attitude had probably been caused by his experiences in Ireland. His major concern was the influence of mendicant privileges on the work of the secular clergy.[149] Initially the dispute had no connection with the London convents because the archbishop expressed his views in a number of sermons and his treatise *De Paupertate Salvatoris*. This only changed when he visited London and preached the first of a series of anti-mendicant sermons in the city on 18 December 1356. According to Katherine Walsh this sermon, preached in the hall of Michael de Northburgh, Bishop of London, may have been answered at St Paul's Cross by the London Franciscan Roger Conway.[150] Certainly Fitzralph himself decided to use this public venue for his next sermon on 22 January 1357 when he rejected the concept of mendicant poverty as being without scriptural foundation. This was followed by a further sermon on 26 February when he attacked the friars' role as confessors in the city. These allegations, combined with the criticism of the mendicants' possessions and their fine buildings made in a later sermon in which the friars' sincerity was doubted, came at an awkward moment, only six years after a royal inquiry into the real estate holdings of the Dominicans, Carmelites, and Austin Friars in the city.[151]

---

[148] *CPR, Richard II, 1388-1392*, pp. 330-31; *CPR, Richard II, 1391-1396*, pp. 453-54; *CCR, Richard II, 1391-1396*, p. 5; R. D. Clarke, *Some Secular Activities of the English Dominicans during the Reigns of Edward I, Edward II, and Edward III* (M. A. thesis, London, 1930), p. 120.

[149] This passage is based on K. Walsh, *A Fourteenth-Century Scholar and Primate. Richard Fitzralph in Oxford, Avignon and Armagh* (Oxford, 1981), pp. 349-451.

[150] Ibid., p. 410.

[151] A. G. Little, 'A Royal Inquiry into Property Held by the Mendicant Friars in England in 1349 and 1350', *Historical Essays in Honour of James Tait*, eds J. G. Edwards, V. H. Galbraith, E. F. Jacob (Manchester, 1933), pp. 179-88.

On 7 March 1357 representatives of the four orders met in the chapterhouse of the Grey Friars where they drew up a list of twenty-one errors detected in Fitzralph's sermons. A written copy drawn up on the order of John of Arderne, the Prior of the Austin Friars' convent was presented to the archbishop in his London residence. The response came in a fourth sermon only two days later. By now the dispute had come to the attention of the government which, involved in its own delicate negotiations about a peace settlement did not want the involvement of the papacy. On 1 April 1357 a royal mandate was issued forbidding Fitzralph to leave the country unless he obtained the king's special licence,[152] a measure clearly designed to prevent the dispute from being taken to Avignon.[153] Despite royal intervention the archbishop arrived in Avignon in the summer of 1357 to be followed by John of Arderne in November. Pope Innocent VI sought to defuse the tension by ordering the enforcement of *Super Cathedram* in London, the bull dealing with the important aspects of preaching and burial fees and thus arranging relationship between friars and secular clergy. The document was reissued and sent to many parts of Europe. Meanwhile the dispute continued in Avignon. In spring 1358 a commission of English mendicants, among them Roger Conway, arrived in Avignon, petitioning the pope to order the English bishops to punish all those who spoke against the friars. It was Roger Conway, acting in his capacity as Prior of the English Franciscan province, who brought charges of heresy against the archbishop in 1358. The case against the increasingly isolated archbishop was then continued by the mendicants' representatives at the papal curia until Fitzralph's death in November 1360. The mendicants and their international network which had been vital in providing the funds for the procedures in Avignon had once again shown their resilience in the face of their critics.

Whether Fitzralph had only intervened in a dispute between the London friars and the city's secular clergy – as he claimed – cannot be established. There are signs of tensions between mendicants and parish clergy but these are counterbalanced by the equally strong indications of co-operation in the late fourteenth and fifteenth centuries. Numerous members of the secular clergy made bequests to mendicant houses and many testators requested the friars' involvement in their burial mass in the parish church. For a time this coexistence was threatened when the London Carmelites reopened the poverty debate

---

[152] *CCR, Edward III, 1354-1360*, p. 399.

[153] Walsh, *A Fourteenth-Century Scholar and Primate*, p. 421.

in the fifteenth century but there are no signs of further antagonism once this issue had been settled.

Even though the friars' attention was primarily directed towards the locality or at best the English provinces of their orders, this local perspective included an international dimension because the population of late medieval London was itself cosmopolitan. Foreign merchants and craftsmen were not only visiting but forming colonies. Many of them were turning to the mendicant houses for spiritual guidance because confessors and advisors who spoke their native languages could be found there. Attention has already been drawn to the development of closer connections between London's alien community, especially the merchants and craftsmen from the Rhineland and the Low Countries and the Friars of the Cross after the order's reform movement began to influence its English province. In a similar way the Observant Franciscans encountered a positive response from this group from the late fifteenth century onward. These two cases must not obscure the fact that foreign friars had long been members of the London mendicant communities. In the case of the Carmelites and the Franciscans their presence was caused by the status of these convents as *studia generalia* of their orders,[154] but in some form all friaries responded to the presence of members of the laity who formed no part of the parochial structure. The Austin Friars in particular had French, German, and Italian friars in their convent who kept close links to the communities of foreigners in the city. When in the late fourteenth century two Austin Friars, Johannes de Breda and Johannes de Saxonia, were mentioned in wills[155] their functions were not clearly defined, but sources from the fifteenth century clearly show that members of the convent acted as spiritual advisers. Thus Friar Georgius acted as confessor to the goldsmith Gisbert van Dist in 1431 and to the German merchant Arnold Soderman in 1441,[156] while his confrères Jacobus, Mathias van Prusen, Nicholas, and Alardus were acting as confessors to people from German-speaking regions.[157]

---

[154] J. R. H. Moorman, 'The Foreign Element among the English Franciscans', *English Historical Review* 62 (1947) 289-303; *idem*, 'Some Franciscans in England', *Archivum Franciscanum Historicum* 83 (1990) 405-20.

[155] GL MS 9171/1, fol. 21r, 459r.

[156] GL MS 9171/3, fol. 288r-v; S. Jenks, 'Hansische Vermächtnisse in London: ca. 1363-1483', *Hansische Geschichtsblätter* 104 (1986) 35-111, at pp. 87-89.

[157] Mathius van Prusen was confessor to Eva van Stybergh in 1445, Jenks, 'Vermächtnisse', p. 90; friars Jacobus and Nicholas both had contacts with the community of foreign goldsmiths, John Mone in 1434, GL MS 9171/3, fol. 396v, and Walter Eveldagh in 1445, GL MS 9171/4, fol. 179r, while Sebett Tierlott, whose confessor was Friar Alardus, is simply described as *ducheman*, ibid., fol. 233r.

In the second half of the fifteenth century other Austin Friars, e.g. Frederic Herbert and Heinrich Wydobak, played the same role.[158] In addition there was a *frater gallicus* and Italian merchants turned to the group of Italian friars in the convent. Friar Andreas de Alice received a bequest from an Italian merchant in 1391[159] and his compatriot Domenico de St Geminiano was mentioned by four testators – only one of whom was English – between 1465 and 1473.[160] The London Franciscan Géraud de Congiacha was referred to as confessor by Baillard Denbidam, a merchant from Bordeaux, who also requested him to act as executor,[161] while his confrère Henry Wodebox acted as confessor for two foreigners from central Europe in 1486.[162] Foreign friars among the London Dominicans appear from the late fourteenth century onwards, many of them being ordained in the city.[163] Their presence may explain why foreigners who made their testaments in the city requested burial in their convent.[164] The

---

[158] GL MS 9171/6, fol. 11r (Johannes Rerkys *de Andewarp in Brabantia, mercator*); GL MS 9171/7, fol. 38r-v (Lucas Ratenhole, *aurifaber*).

[159] GL MS 9171/4, fol. 25v; GL MS 9171/1, fol. 244r.

[160] GL MS 9171/5, fol. 376v-377r; GL MS 9171/6, fol. 13r; fol. 84r; fol. 171r-v; H. L. Bradley, *Italian Merchants in London* (PhD, London, 1992), pp. 17-21, 51, 288 seq.

[161] GL MS 9171/2, fol. 262v-263r.

[162] GL MS 9171/7, fol. 56v-57r (Christian Colborne); ibid., fol. 71v-72r (Harmannus Jonson).

[163] Henricus de Lovanio (28 May 1390), GL MS 9531/3, fol. 22v; Marchus de Saxonia (8 June 1392), fol. 30r; Jacobus de Saxonia (18 December 1395), fol. 41v; Johannes de Leodia (1398), fol. 49r; Mauricius Roche (19 March 1401), fol. 57r; Petrus de Argentina (1401), fol. 59v; Johannes de Argentina (22 September 1408), GL MS 9531/4, fol. 39v; Henricus Kaltyser (19 September 1411), fol. 55r; Theodoricus Beutem, Cornelius Arremueden, Hernestus de Lubeek , fol. 70r; Dominicus de Baiona, fol. 70v; Johannes de Anwerpia (22 December 1411), fol. 71r; Jacobus Kyppenheym (11 March 1419), fol. 85r; Johannes Dunnenheym, Johannes Brambache, Dominicus Pistoris, fol. 86r; Bernardus de Dulmen (21 September 1420), fol. 93v; Dionisius Breslave, fol. 94r; Reynerus de Lywardia (21 December 1421), fol. 95r; Hugo de Eslyngen (15 March 1432), fol. 218r; Cristophorus Deynart (14 June 1432), fol. 218v; Johannes de Colonia (20 September 1432), fol. 220r; Egidius de Flemalia, Nicholaus Theodorici (19 December 1432), fol. 220v; Paulus de Huyo, Eugenius de Soligia (18 September 1434), fol. 223v; Gerardus de Putten (21 September 1437), L MS 9531/6, fol. 155r; Jacobus Dyst (7 June 1438), fol. 157v; Lucius de Lapido (24 February 1442), fol.166r; Petrus Baerzelar (21 May 1442), fol. 167r; Habertus Moens (6 April 1443), fol. 169r; Dionisius de Sligia, Adrianus Aland (21 December 1443), fol. 170v; Nicholaus de Saxonia (20 February 1445), fol. 173v; Lucas Carnifares (23 September 1447), fol. 180v; Radulphus de Colonia (20 December 1495), GL MS 9531/8, fol. 32v; Cornelius Wissekert (1504), fol. 89r.

[164] GL MS 9171/1, fol. 42v (will of John Bachecot of Calais); fol. 408r (will of Henry Gerardson, *mercator Alemannie*).

fraternity of the Holy Blood of Wilsnack had moved to the Austin Friars from the church of the Friars of the Cross by 1490, and a partly German fraternity of St Katherine was founded in the Crutched Friars in 1495.[165] In London even the local ties had an international dimension. In this respect London was no exception. By 1344 English merchants had built a chapel of St Thomas in the Carmelite convent of Bruges[166] and by the fifteenth century merchants and artisans from the Iberian Peninsula had also formed close links with the friaries in the Flemish city, the Catalans with the house of the Carmelites, the Castilians and the people from the Bay of Biscay with the Franciscan convent while those from Navarra preferred the Austin Friars.[167]

From the time of their foundation the London mendicant houses had been forming a part of large international organizations. By the thirteenth century London had become a major urban centre in western Europe. The city's development into the country's capital, the proximity of the royal court over long periods of time and the presence of the administration all had an influence on the friaries and they created the preconditions for further international links. Henry III, Edward I, his brother Edmund, Queen Eleanor of Provence, Queen Eleanor of Castile, as well as Queen Margaret of France felt a close spiritual affinity to the mendicants which resulted in the support of – occasionally very ambitious – building projects but almost inevitably also led to the friars' involvement in political matters. Mendicants were used as royal ambassadors. Prominent among them were the London Dominicans because this convent had immediate contact with the royal court. The government's close relations with the papacy under Benedict XI and his successor found their echo in the creation of English cardinals, most of whom were associated with the London Black Friars. The links between the capital's Dominican convent and the royal household could potentially be a source of friction within the order if the friars involved did not restrict their work to spiritual matters. The English Dominicans in particular were affected by the problem of divided loyalties.

The effects of the Hundred Years' War on English mendicant provinces, on their relations with the papacy and their respective orders are as yet little studied. Whereas English friars had held very prominent positions in the

---

[165] Coote, 'Ordinances of Some Secular Guilds', pp. 47 seqq., 52 seqq.

[166] W. Simons, *Stad en apostolaat. De vestiging van de bedelorden in het graafschap Vlaanderen c. 1225-1350* (Brussels, 1987), p. 228.

[167] J. Maréchal, 'La colonie espagnole de Bruges, du XIVe auf XVIe siècle', *Revue du Nord* 35 (1953) 5-40, at pp. 10, 16, 30-31.

thirteenth and early fourteenth centuries it is difficult to find them later on. No more chapters general were held in England after 1335 and the entry of foreign friars who wanted to study in Oxford, Cambridge or London became difficult. Even among the Carmelites, who consistently obtained large financial contributions from their English province and who continued to send students to their general study in London, English friars rarely held prominent posts. The London Carmelite Thomas Netter is a famous exception.

Only on certain occasions, the dispute with Archbishop Fitzralph, the Franciscan involvement in the tithe controversy, or after the reopening of the poverty controversy in the fifteenth century, were London mendicant convents directly involved with the papal curia. Outside involvement also came from the orders' central organizations. In their daily lives the convents were occupied with their spiritual tasks, their liturgy, problems of internal discipline and recruitment, and more generally their relations with the London population. But even at this level the local ties could be significantly influenced by the convents' international connections. London not only attracted merchants but also artisans from all parts of Europe, many of whom eventually settled permanently. Their colonies formed a noticeable part of the London population and they were only superficially integrated into the city's complex parish structure. The spiritual services offered by the friars were ideally suited for them. The arrival of foreign friars could be sporadic but in the cases of the Observant Franciscans and the Friars of the Cross we are dealing with carefully-planned measures forming part of a wider reform movement. These initiatives came entirely from abroad and in the case of the Crutched Friars it required persistence on the part of the order's governing body to bring the attempt to a successful conclusion. Despite the difficulties, the reforms brought a reinvigoration of religious life which in the case of the Friars of the Cross lasted up to the time of their dissolution.

11

Change and Conflict within the Hospitaller Province of Italy after 1291

Anthony Luttrell

The Hospital of Saint John originated as a charitable body in Jerusalem before the capture of the city in 1099. It was already receiving endowments in the West before it began, perhaps in about 1130, to acquire a military character.[1] The new order's Syrian activities were partly dependent on men and money arriving from its Western possessions which were administered from houses known as commanderies or preceptories; these were gradually organized into priories, and from about 1170 the priories were for certain purposes being grouped in provinces.[2] These administrative divisions did not necessarily coincide with political or ecclesiastical boundaries, or with linguistic or other regions. In the Hospital's central headquarters in the East, known as the Convent, there were naturally disputes over matters of seniority, offices, incomes and benefices in the West, while some time before 1291, the year in which the Latins were expelled from Syria, the brethren in the Convent had been divided into *langues* which corresponded approximately to the western provinces of Provence, France, Auvergne, Italy, Spain, England, and *Alamania*. One func-

---

[1] The standard work is J. Riley-Smith, *The Knights of St John in Jerusalem and Cyprus: c. 1050-1310* (London, 1967).

[2] On provinces and their grand commanders, ibid., pp. 366-70; A. Luttrell, 'The Hospitaller Province of *Alamania* to 1428', *RR*, pp. 21-41.

From *Mendicants, Military Orders, and Regionalism in Medieval Europe*, ed. Jürgen Sarnowsky. Copyright © 1999 by Jürgen Sarnowsky. Published by Ashgate Publishing Ltd, Gower House, Croft Road, Aldershot, Hampshire, GU11 3HR, Great Britain.

tion of the *langues* in the Convent was the regulation of appointments within their respective provinces in the West.[3]

The way in which the Hospital's administrative boundaries were established sometimes led to conflict. Individual commanderies, which occasionally included one or more parishes, frequently crossed diocesan boundaries, while their exemption from the bishops' jurisdiction could cause frictions. In 1373 the commandery of Treviso near Venice included no less than four parishes inside, or in one case just outside, the town; none of them was subject to the bishop's control.[4] Four commanderies in southern Catalunya were allotted in 1319 to the Aragonese priory, and in 1350 part of the Aragonese commandery of Monzón was in Catalunya and subject to Catalan law.[5] Following the Catalan conquest of Athens in 1311 a newly-formed commandery of the duchy of Athens was separated from that of the Morea.[6] The transfer of the Templars' extensive properties to the Hospital after 1312 necessitated much reorganization. In Southern France for example, that part of the priory of Saint Gilles lying to the east of the Rhône, and therefore politically outside the kingdom of France, formed from 1317 to 1330 a separate priory sometimes called Petite Provence; the two regions were being taxed separately for their dues or *responsiones* in 1379 and at Rhodes the *auberge* of Petite Provence survived until

---

[3] On the *langues*, Riley-Smith, pp. 283-88, 296-97, 319, 328, 344; J. Sarnowsky, 'Der Konvent auf Rhodos und die Zungen (*Lingue*) im Johanniterorden: 1421-1476', *RR*, pp. 43-65; A. Luttrell, S. Fiorini, 'The Italian Hospitallers at Rhodes: 1437-1462', *Revue Mabillon* 68 (1996) 210-19. The provinces, in the West, are here distinguished from the *langues*, in the Convent in the East, though the Hospital's documents did not always follow that distinction. The *langue* of Auvergne was seldom mentioned. A *lengue d'Auvergne* was listed in 1302: *CGOH*, no. 4574 # 14. In 1330 the marshal, subsequently always from the *langue* of Auvergne, was Fr Ferry de Foucherolles who was prior first of Champagne and then of Aquitaine, both in the *langue* of France: J. Delaville le Roulx, *Les Hospitaliers à Rhodes jusqu'à la Mort de Philibert de Naillac: 1310-1421* (Paris, 1913), p. 278 n. 6. The *langue* of Auvergne appeared again in 1347: NLM, Arch. 317, fol. 233v.

[4] A. Luttrell, *The Hospitallers of Rhodes and their Mediterranean World* (Aldershot, 1992), XIV, pp. 762-63.

[5] *Idem*, 'The Structure of the Aragonese Hospital: 1349-1352', *APJC*, pp. 316-17; P. Ortega, 'Aragonesisme i Conflicte Ordes / Vassals a les Comandes templeres i hospitaleres d'Ascó, Horta i Miravet: 1250-1350', *Anuario de Estudios Medievales* 25 (1995) 151-78.

[6] The duchy of Athens was a commandery separate from that of the Morea by 1330: Delaville le Roulx, *Hospitaliers à Rhodes*, p. 201.

1440.[7] In Eastern Europe political changes led to a number of Pomeranian commanderies in the priory of Bohemia being transferred to that of *Alamania* in the mid-thirteenth century.[8] In 1330 when the Aragonese king was preventing the export of the Catalan and Aragonese responsions, the master of the Hospital sought to have the Hospital's dues from Mallorca and Roussillon, which were the separate kingdom of Mallorca, paid directly to the order's treasurer, thus escaping the Aragonese embargo.[9] A similar conflict arose from attempts begun in 1375 to arrange separate payments from the lands of the Scottish Hospital which were part of the priory of England.[10] After 1378 the papal schism and its reflection within the Hospital created widespread complications,[11] while the Anglo-French wars brought political changes and repeated devastation to the Hospital in France.[12]

Anomalies involving boundaries were frequent in Italy where there were numerous small bishoprics and many political divisions. The Italian province consisted of eight relatively small priories, those of Messina, Barletta, Capua, Rome, Pisa, Lombardy, Venice, and Hungary. The priory of Venice had a few German-speaking commanders in the Tyrol and some commanderies in Istria.[13] Brethren from Italian families, most of them Venetians such as the Querini and Crispi who ruled various small Aegean islands, also belonged to the Italian *langue*; Fr Fantino Querini, who was admiral of the order, Prior of Rome and Commander of Kos during the first half of the fifteenth century, was the outstanding example.[14] After the acceptance of an Angevin dynasty in Hun-

---

[7] Ibid., pp. 52-53, 143 n. 4, 216; B. Beaucage, *Visites générales des Commanderies de l'Ordre des Hospitaliers dépendantes du Grand Prieuré de Saint-Gilles: 1338* (Aix-en-Provence, 1982), pp. ii-iv, xi n. 13.

[8] K. Borchardt, 'The Hospitallers in Pomerania: between the Priories of Bohemia and Alamania', *The Military Orders*, vol. 2: *Warfare and Welfare*, ed. H. Nicholson (Aldershot, 1998).

[9] A. Luttrell, *The Hospitallers in Cyprus, Rhodes, Greece and the West: 1291-1440* (London, 1978), XI, p. 10.

[10] I. Cowan et al., *The Knights of St John of Jerusalem in Scotland* (Edinburgh, 1983), pp. xxv-vii.

[11] E g. Luttrell, *Hospitallers in Cyprus*, XXIII, pp. 30-48; *idem*, *The Hospitallers of Rhodes*, XIV, pp. 764-66; *idem*, 'The Hospitallers of Rhodes between Tuscany and Jerusalem: 1310-1431', *Revue Mabillon* 64 (1992) 135.

[12] R. Favreau, *La Commanderie du Breuil-du-Pas et la Guerre de Cent Ans dans la Saintonge méridionale* (Jonzac, 1986).

[13] A. Luttrell, 'The Hospitaller Priory of Venice in 1331', *MS*, pp. 134-36, 142-43.

[14] Luttrell-Fiorini, pp. 218-19, 230-31.

gary in 1308 that priory became part of the Italian province[15] and its priors and commanders were often Italian or Provençal, which repeatedly led to quarrels.[16] The priory of Rome was approximately co-terminous with the papal state, but early in the fourteenth century a number of commanderies in Northern Lazio were included in the Tuscan priory of Pisa.[17] Other conflicts arose in the north after 1405 as the Venetian state expanded into the *terraferma*. Venice had previously forbidden its citizens to enter the Hospital as knight-brethren, but as the mainland came under Venetian control its citizens soon saw the advantages of securing profitable benefices and even, after 1431, of holding the priory itself.[18]

Across much of the north and centre of Italy political control was fragmentary; commanderies were mostly rather small and their *responsiones* very low. In the thirteenth century the Hospitaller foundations in Calabria were being administered from the Sicilian priory of Messina.[19] There were Catalan-Aragonese priors of Messina such as Fr Martín Pérez d'Oros in 1311 and Fr Sancho de Aragón in 1319,[20] while the Sardinian commandery, which formed part of the priory of Pisa, passed back and forth between Aragonese and Italian commanders following the Aragonese conquest of that island in 1323.[21] There was a curious project in 1370 for the whole island to be given to the Hospital, which would have released lands in Italy to the Jutges d'Arborea in return for their claim to rule Sardinia.[22] Another such scheme was the complicated proposal, first mooted in 1346, for the transfer to the Hospital of the properties of the

---

[15] Luttrell, 'The Hospitaller Province', pp. 28-29.

[16] Delaville, *Hospitaliers à Rhodes*, pp. 71-72, 150 n.1, 174-75, 197, 335-36.

[17] Luttrell, 'The Hospitallers of Rhodes', pp. 120-21, 135-37.

[18] *Idem, Hospitallers of Rhodes*, XIV, pp. 768-69.

[19] E g. *CGOH*, nos 3358, 3424; cf. J. Delaville le Roulx, *Les Hospitaliers en Terre Sainte et à Chypre: 1100-1310* (Paris, 1904), pp. 373-74.

[20] Luttrell, *Hospitallers in Cyprus*, XI, p. 11.

[21] L. d'Arienza, 'Gli Ordini Militari in Sardegna nel Basso Medioevo', *APJC*, pp. 340-42.

[22] A. Luttrell, 'Gli Ospedalieri e un Progetto per la Sardegna: 1370-1374', *Società, Istituzioni, Spiritualità: Studi in Onore di Cinzio Violante*, vol. 1 (Spoleto, 1994), pp. 505-6.

Valencian order of Montesa which had been set up in 1319 with the lands of the Hospital and Temple in that kingdom.[23]

Until 1374 the Southern French brethren virtually monopolized the mastership and the powerful conventual office of grand preceptor, which became theirs by right; they also repeatedly secured the rich commandery of Cyprus and the priory of Navarre; a statute of 1357, passed on papal insistence, decreed the end of the practice by which the commanderies of Cyprus and Kos were 'appropriated' to the *langue* of Provence.[24] In Southern Italy the Hospital had flourished under a centralized monarchical regime, but the conquest of the *regno* of Naples and Sicily by the Angevins after 1266 and the subsequent loss of Sicily to the Aragonese after 1281 brought numerous changes, including many Provençal appointments in Southern Italy. The Hospital's own documents were seldom concerned to indicate the territorial provenance of individual brethren. The Southern French province of Provence comprised three distinct areas: Petite Provence, the lands to the east of the Rhône which were subject to the Angevin counts of Provence and Forcalquier who were also kings of Naples; those in Languedoc, to the west of the Rhône and within the priory of Saint Gilles; and, after 1317, the priory of Toulouse which stretched to the Atlantic. Technically, a Hospitaller belonging to any part of the province or *langue* of Provence could be appointed to any of its priories or commanderies. Furthermore, numerous Provençal families were permanently established in the Angevin kingdom of Naples where they became in effect Italian, while other Angevin subjects from Provence secured office in southern Italy.[25] The exploitation of Italian resources by Provençal Hospitallers was one aspect of a wider phenomenon; and if the Franco-Provençal nobility was generally absorbed,

---

[23] E. Louric, 'Conspiracy and Cover-up: the Order of Montesa on Trial (1352)', *Iberia and the Mediterranean World of the Middle Ages: Essays in Honor of Robert I. Burns S.J.* (Leiden, 1996), pp. 253-317.

[24] On Navarre, normally part of the Spanish province, Delaville, *Hospitaliers à Rhodes*, pp. 97, 101, 103 n. 4; on Cyprus and Kos, Luttrell, *Hospitallers of Rhodes*, IX, pp. 162-63, 177.

[25] This topic awaits thorough study; preliminary indications in Delaville, *Hospitaliers en Terre Sainte*, pp. 419-20; Riley-Smith, p. 266. The circumstances in which Fr Foulques de Villaret became Prior of Capua following his resignation from the mastership in 1319 were entirely exceptional: Delaville, *Hospitaliers à Rhodes*, p. 18. Except in so far as the province of Provence included lands to the west of the Rhône, the term Provence is here applied only to the area east of the Rhône, though contemporary texts normally left it uncertain whether brethren in southern Italy were from Italy, Provence, or Languedoc.

Provençal officials continued to provoke resentment in the Neapolitan kingdom. Many fourteenth-century priors of Capua and Barletta were Provençaux.[26]
One example was Fr Isnard du Bar from Grasse, Commander of Aix-en-Provence and then Prior of Capua;[27] his Hospitaller nephew, Fr Montréal du Bar,
acquired the priory of Hungary and became the powerful and brutal condottiere
known as Fra Morreale who was executed at Rome in 1354.[28]

One particular set of changes resulted from papal interventions which annexed to the Hospital a number of Benedictine monasteries which were in decline or collapse, or allegedly so. In 1300 Pope Boniface VIII transferred the
ruined and neglected Benedictine house of San Miguel de Burgo in Leon to the
Hospital, just as in 1299 he had granted the Hospitallers the house of the Friars
of the Sack in Bordeaux,[29] but most such transfers were made in Italy. An early
example was at Santa Eufemia on the Calabrian coast where between 1274 and
1280 the Hospital took over the Benedictine monastery and its estates. This was
said to have been done by force – *per violentiam* – but the crown and papacy
apparently favoured the move, hoping perhaps that it would strengthen the
coastal defences against pirates.[30] By 1294 the commandery there was independent of any priory, and by 1301 it was among those offices considered as
bayllis par chapitre general in a statute decreeing that in their case the monies
and properties of deceased officers were to be paid to the Hospital's central
treasury; in 1305 Santa Eufemia was held in addition to his priory by the Prior
of Messina, Fr Francesco de Pistania.[31]

An abandoned Benedictine house, again of some strategic importance, was
that at Alberese in the Tuscan Maremma where as early as 1280 the pope took

---

[26] The standard lists of priors and commanders in M. Gattini, *I Priorati, i Baliaggi e le
Commende del Sovrano Militare Ordine di S. Giovanni di Gerusalemme nelle Province
Meridionali d'Italia prima della Caduta di Malta* (Naples, 1928), are highly unsatis-
factory.

[27] Delaville, *Hospitaliers à Rhodes*, pp. 67, 140.

[28] É.-G. Léonard, *Histoire de Jeanne Ie, reine de Naples, comtesse de Provence: 1342-
1382*, 3 vols (Monaco, 1932-1936), 1, pp. 521-22; 3, pp. 83-86 and *passim*. Fra Morreale was Prior of Hungary and Commander of Esclavonia, according to J. Raybaud,
Histoire des Grands Prieurs et du Prieuré de Saint-Gilles, vol. 1 (Nîmes, 1904), p. 311.

[29] *CGOH*, nos 4450, 4497.

[30] A. Miceli di Serradileo, 'L'Ordine di San Giovanni di Gerusalemme in Calabria dal
XII al XV secolo', *Studi Meridionali* 10 (1977) 242-44; for the commanders and other
detail, F. Russo, *Regesto Vaticano per la Calabria*, 1-2 (Rome, 1974-1975).

[31] *CGOH*, nos 4259 # 1, 4549 # 2, 4705.

under his protection the Hospitallers who had already taken over the monastery there.[32] The Hospital seems subsequently to have lost control of Alberese. In 1299 Pope Boniface VIII was sending representatives and troops to occupy – *ad recipiendum et custodiendum* – the monastery,[33] and by 1303 he had granted it to Cardinal Teodorico Rainiero who administered it through a Benedictine monk; in or after 1305 Pope Clement V granted it to another cardinal, Riccardo Petroni.[34] Then in 1307, following an agreement between the commune of Grosseto and the Prior of Pisa, the Hospital took it over from the commune, which acquired part of the monastery's former properties and found an institution prepared to defend it.[35] Pope John XXII confirmed the Hospitallers' rights to Alberese in 1317[36] but they seem not to have secured possession of it, and then only after further troubles, until 1336.[37]

In 1297 the major Benedictine monastery of Santa Trinità at Venosa near Melfi, together with its very extensive estates, was transferred to the Hospital by the pope, who stated that its community had collapsed and made the provision that the order should maintain sufficient priests to conduct the services already established there.[38] In 1297 the lesser Benedictine house of Sant'Angelo at Palazzo just east of Venosa was granted to the Hospital in the same way.[39] By 1301 Venosa, like Santa Eufemia, was a *baylli par chapitre gen-*

---

[32] Ibid., no. 3722.

[33] T. Schmidt, *Libri Rationum Camerae Bonifatii Papae VIII* (Vatican, 1954), pp. 120, 127.

[34] E. Fedi, *L'Abbazia di S. Maria dell'Alberese presso Grosseto* (Naples, 1942), pp. 29-32, 43-44, 106-07; *Jean XXII (1316-1334): Lettres Communes*, 16 vols, ed. G. Mollat (Paris, 1904-1947), no. 64263. These events remain obscure.

[35] Fedi, pp. 32-33, 109-11.

[36] *Jean XXII*, no. 64263; the bull explicitly united Alberese to the Hospital's house of Santo Stefano Monopoli in Puglia but that apparently remained without effect.

[37] Fedi, pp. 35-39, 111-31.

[38] *CGOH*, nos 4387, 4399, 4406, 4433, 4588, 4644, 4672 # 5, 4741; further texts and references in G. Crudo, *La SS. Trinità di Venosa: Memorie storiche diplomatiche archeologiche* (Trani, 1899), pp. 312-57. Parts of the original monastic estates were eventually assigned to other commanderies: Crudo, p. 334. Excellent background in H. Houben, *Die Abtei Venosa und das Mönchtum im normanisch-staufischen Süditalien* (Tübingen, 1995). Note that in 1298 Fr Bonifacio de Calamandracen was not Commander or *preceptor* of Venosa but Grand Commander or *generalis preceptor* in the West and in that capacity he did homage for Venosa: texts in Crudo, pp. 320, 328-29.

[39] *CGOH*, nos 4386, 4566, 4903 bis.

eral.[40] In 1310 the priory of Barletta paid papal tenths not only for its own holdings but also for the monastery of Santo Stefano at Monopoli on the coast of Puglia,[41] and on 13 June 1317 Pope John XXII legalized the transfer to the Hospital of the Benedictine house, which had a long history of troubles and crimes. The monks had quarrelled among themselves and one faction called in the local Hospitallers, who already had a house at Monopoli; thereafter there were no monks left in the house. The pope was rewarding the Hospital for lands it had given him in Provence, and he may have exaggerated the Benedictines' problems in justifying his recognition of the Hospitallers' occupation at Monopoli, but he could point to the wealth of the monks' extensive possessions and to the advantages of a harbour which would allow the Hospital to ship horses, grain, and other supplies onto galleys and other vessels sailing to the East.[42] Eight days later an assembly of leading Hospitallers at Avignon, acting in gratitude for the transfer of the Templars' properties, for the monastery at Alberese, for Santo Stefano near Monopoli, and for the hospital at Varo near Vence in Provence, in their turn transferred to the pope various castles and extensive lands in the Comtat Venaissin just north of Avignon.[43]

John XXII wanted lands for his nephews in Provence where the Hospital had received much Templar property, and between 1322 and 1331 he acquired further extensive possessions there from the Hospital, in particular through an exchange made between 1322 and 1326 by which the Hospital acquired the county of Alife in the kingdom of Naples.[44] In later years the county was ruined

---

[40] Ibid., no. 4549 #2.

[41] ... *Tam pro capite quam pro membris et monasterio S. Stephani de Monopulo*: text in D. Vendola, *Rationes Decimarum Italiae nei secoli XIII e XIV: Apulia – Lucania – Calabria* (Vatican, 1939), no. 622.

[42] A. d'Ittolo, *I più antichi Documenti del Libro dei Privilegi dell'Università di Putignano: 1107-1434* (Bari, 1989), pp. cvii-xiii, republishing the text of 1317, correcting the error of 'Venosa' for 'Venaissin' and demonstrating the original to be genuine (Cosimo d'Angela most kindly provided a copy of this and other works). Note that the Master Fr Foulques de Villaret was at Monopoli in 1307 and for several weeks at Brindisi in 1310: A. Luttrell, 'The Hospitallers and the Papacy: 1305-1314', *Forschungen zur Reichs-, Papst- und Landesgeschichte: Peter Herde zum 65.Geburtstag*, 2 (Stuttgart, 1998), pp. 602, n. 30, 610.

[43] Text in C. Faure, *Étude sur l'Administration et l'Histoire du Comtat-Venaissin du XIIIe au XVe siècle* (Paris, 1909), pp. 204-07.

[44] Delaville, *Hospitaliers à Rhodes*, pp. 59-61, indicating much detail. There was a separate commandery of Alife: background and topography in D. Capolongo, 'Alife: un nuovo Insediamento templare in Terra di Lavoro', *Atti del XV Congresso di Ricerche Templari* (Latina, 1997).

by warfare and its town of Boiano was burnt. In 1361 Fr Isnard du Bar, Prior of Capua and also Commander of Santa Eufemia, began a series of three exchanges by which the Hospital secured rents and properties in Naples, Aversa and their territories which constituted the so-called exchange or *scambi d'Alife*; the order retained the commandery of Alife as it had existed before 1322. These arrangements were made with Goffredo di Marzano, Count of Squillace, and with two Neapolitan knights, Matteo Capuano and Cristoforo de Costanzo, and they were approved by the master at Rhodes, by the Queen of Naples and by the pope.[45]

The acquisition of these Italian houses threatened to disturb the normal balance of the priories of Capua and Barletta, partly because of their great wealth and partly because the Provençal brethren, at whose expense they had been acquired, logically had the right to hold them. The Western capitular commanderies were not under the jurisdiction of any prior: Santa Eufemia enjoyed such independence at latest by 1294 and Venosa by 1301,[46] Monopoli by 1317,[47] and Alife, and also Naples, by 1330.[48] A statute of 1320 which created conventual procurators made it clear that certain Italian *baylivi*, evidently the southern capitular commanderies, paid their responsiones directly to the Convent rather than to any local prior.[49] The status of capitular commanderies, whose commanders were appointed by chapter general or its representatives and whose dues were owed directly to the Convent, was confusing; they included those of Cyprus, Kos, Athens, and others in the East. Their commanders were capitular *baillis* but the term *bailli* and its innumerable variants meant little more than office or officer and was used by the Hospitallers in many varying senses.[50] The chapter general of 1330 appointed or confirmed numer-

---

[45] Russo, no. 7592; *Urbain V (1362-1370): Lettres Communes*, 11 vols, ed. M.-H. Laurent et al. (Paris, 1954-1986), nos 5921-22, 6521; G. Caetani, *Regesta Chartarum: Regesto delle Pergamine dell'Archivio Caetani*, 2 (Sancasciano, 1926), pp. 204-07.

[46] *CGOH*, nos 4259 # 1, 4549 # 2. A settlement reached at Rhodes in 1312 concerning the *pitancia* or dues owed by each Italian priory for the maintenance of the brethren of their Italian *langue* in the Convent involved the commandery of Venosa but not that of Santa Eufemia: text in Luttrell-Fiorini, pp. 220-22.

[47] *Jean XXII*, no. 4472.

[48] Text in C. Tipton, 'The 1330 Chapter General of the Knights Hospitallers at Montpellier', *Traditio* 24 (1968) 308.

[49] Paris, Bibliothèque Nationale, Ms. franç. 13531, fol. 62v.

[50] The confusions and anachronisms on this point which are endlessly repeated in the literature seem to stem from Giacomo Bosio. Crudo, pp. 351, 356, speaks of Venosa as being created a 'Baglio Conventuale' in 1330 and, contradictorily, as being 'elevata a

ous *bailiuij*, including Fr Bertrand de Malobosco or possibly Malbosc, probably a Provençal, to Venosa, Fr Foulques de Paucapalea to Santa Eufemia and Fr François Furoni, apparently also a Provençal, to Monopoli; it also set the separate responsions paid by the commandery of Naples; and it agreed that Naples and Alife, both capitular *baiulie*, be 'retained' or reserved to the master.[51]

The houses in Puglia were rich *latifundia* with an important agrarian production, part of which was exported to sustain the Convent at Rhodes.[52] The wealth of the capitular commanderies was considerable. In 1310 Venosa was paying 40 *uncie* of papal tenths in contrast to the 100 *uncie* paid by the whole priory of Barletta, whose contribution included a sum paid for the monastery at Monopoli.[53] Special impositions of 1317 taxed the priory of Barletta at 6000

Baliaggio' in 1419, but he cited Bosio's first edition which the second edition at least partly amended: G. Bosio, *Dell'Istoria della Sacra Religione et Illustrissima Militia di San Giovanni Gierosolimitano*, 2 (2nd edn, Rome, 1629), pp. 59, 116, 136-37. The text of 1330 (in Tipton, pp. 305-8) distinguished capitular commanderies from magistral *camere* and gives no justification for Bosio's anachronistic reference to 'otto Dignità di Gran Croce'. The situation before 1310 is clearly set out in Riley-Smith *passim*. Capitular commanders in southern Italy were capitular *baiulivi* but obviously differed from capitular *baiulivi* in the Convent who included the major conventual officers and the commanders of Cyprus and Kos. A statute of 1420 established that the master could, with the Convent's consent, create conventual *baiulivi*, priors and capitular commanders *supra anneam*, that is while the chapter general was not in session: Delaville, *Hospitaliers à Rhodes*, pp. 353-54. Only in the fifteenth century was the capitular commandery or baiuliatus *capitularis*, later known as the *baliaggio*, developed to provide a benefice for senior Hospitallers supposedly resident in the Convent. This involved a *miles* in the Convent expecting by virtue of his seniority a *baliaggio* with a seat in chapter general and council, the expectation of a priory and a 'grand cross'. Each *balì* would receive a designated commandery to support him in the Convent, for example Manosque (Provence), Caspe (Spain), Luriel (Auvergne), Egle (England), Santa Eufemia (Italy), and so on. On Santa Eufemia, L. Schiavone, *Pietrino del Ponte nella Storia dell'Ordine Gerosolimitano* (Asti, 1995), pp. 101-5, 132-34, 154-56. The *baliaggio* requires further clarification.

[51] Text in Tipton, pp. 301-8 [for *Fuxoni* read *Furonj*]. Fr Pierre Furoni was Commander of Aix-en-Provence in 1338: Beaucage, p. 588. In 1317 Paucapalea was Commander of Santa Eufemia and Malobosco was Prior of Barletta: *Jean XXII*, nos 4469-70. Raybaud, 1, p. 249, stated, without source, that the 1314 chapter general decreed that the priories of Capua and Barletta and the commanderies of Naples, Monopoli, and Venosa be common to the *langues* of Italy and Provence.

[52] Luttrell, *Hospitallers of Rhodes*, XII, pp. 113-18, 120.

[53] Vendola, nos 622, 1946; cf. H. Houben, 'La SS. Trinità di Venosa, Baliaggio dell'Ordine di San Giovanni di Gerusalemme', *Studi Melitensi* 2 (1994) 13.

florins and that of Capua at 4000, with Monopoli and Venosa at 1500 each and Santa Eufemia at only 100.[54] In 1330 the responsions due to the Convent were fixed at 800 florins each for the priories of Lombardy, Venice, Pisa, and Rome, a total of 3200, and at 2000 for Capua and 4000 for Barletta; in addition the five capitular commanderies were taxed at a total of 4700 florins, with Naples at 1800, Venosa 1500, Monopoli 800, Alife 500, and Santa Eufemia 100.[55] The responsions of Santa Eufemia stood at 200 florins a year in 1365 when it was granted to the Provençal Fr Bertrand de Boysson, formerly Prior of Barletta; those of Venosa were 1500 florins when it was granted to the Italian Fr Ruggero de Sansoniis in 1366.[56] These were notional figures. The incomplete accounts for 1373 to 1374 showed Naples and Capua each supposedly paying 692 florins as responsions alone and Venosa exactly half that sum at 346 florins; in 1374 to 1375 Venosa paid 342 and Monopoli 400, while Venosa owed a further 300, Santa Eufemia – for two years – 600, Naples 600 and Alife 500. If other payments to the Convent are included, in 1374 to 1375 these five commanderies paid a total of 1638 florins and owed a further 4451.[57] In 1373 the incomes of the *excambium* of Alife, whose commander, the Provençal Fr Guillaume de Montauroux, was then at Rhodes, were estimated at 1100 florins yearly in normal circumstances but its ruination had reduced this sum to about 130 florins, while its responsions were said to be 600 florins which had been paid for 1371 to 1372.[58] However, the accounts kept in Avignon showed that in 1373 to

---

[54] *Jean XXII*, nos 4455, 4469-72 [for '15,000' read '1500']. In 1294 the Commander of Santa Eufemia was allowed to travel with six horses, as were the priors of Rome and Pisa: *CGOH*, no. 4259 # 1.

[55] Text in Tipton, p. 304.

[56] NLM Arch. 319, fol. 246r-v, 250r-v. Fr Bertrand de Boysson belonged to the *langue* of Provence in 1373: NLM Arch. 347, fol. 42r-v.

[57] Text in A. Luttrell, 'The Hospitallers' Western Accounts: 1373/4 and 1374/5', in *Camden Miscellany*, 30 (London, 1990), pp. 8-9 and *passim* [for *Alife* read *scambi d'Alife*]; the figures given there do not include payments made or owed for tailles, arrears, mortuaries, and so forth, while the complications and details of the text are here simplified; R. Iorio, *L'Inchiesta di Papa Gregorio XI sugli Ospedalieri della Diocesi di Trani* (Taranto, 1996), p. 29, was confused by an earlier and misleading summary of this text in Luttrell, *Hospitallers of Rhodes*, I, p. 8. The sums demanded from the five Italian capitular commanderies as a special subsidy in 1374 are given in NLM Arch. 320, fol. 32r-v; the numbers of *milites* demanded from them in 1375 are given in Delaville, *Hospitaliers à Rhodes*, p. 188.

[58] Archivio Segreto Vaticano, Instrumenta Miscellanea, 2678. A Guillaume de *Monte Orosio* was a Hospitaller donat at Gap in 1338: Beaucage, p. 182.

1374 and 1374 to 1375 Alife paid nothing and that for 1374 to 1375 it owed 500 florins of responsions plus 229 for the taille and the cost of the masters' journey to Rhodes and another 653 florins of arrears.[59] For the three years 1378 to 1381 Naples paid 1800 florins or an average of 600 florins a year.[60] As everywhere else, disasters, devastations, and corruptions reduced the amounts actually paid,[61] but the general wealth of these commanderies was evident.[62]

The capitular commanderies were by definition at the disposition of the chapter general, but by 1288 there was another category of office, the magistral *camere* or chambers, which the chapter general granted to the master; they were directly under his jurisdiction, he appointed to them and they paid responsions directly to him rather than to their prior or, in the case of the capitular commanderies, to the treasurer.[63] These might include capitular commanderies; thus in 1330 the priories of Aragon, Castile, Catalunya, and Hungary, and the capitular commanderies of Naples, Alife, Armenia, and the Morea were all magistral *camere*.[64] These commanderies, like all Hospitaller lands, might be involved in local troubles. At Monopoli, for example, Gautier de Brienne, Count of Lecce and Conversano, usurped various possessions.[65] He returned these on his death, which took place in 1356, and they were received in 1358 by Fr Garin de Châteauneuf, Prior of Barletta, and by the future master of

---

[59] Luttrell, 'Hospitallers' Western Accounts', pp. 8-9. H. Sire, *The Knights of Malta* (New Haven, 1994), p. 166, wrongly presents the 1374 to 1375 figures as representing only responsions and as having all been paid.

[60] NLM Arch. 321, fol. 201r-204v. In 1373 the incomes at Naples were estimated at 2766 florins a year plus quantities of produce: Instrumenta Miscellanea, 2678.

[61] Examples in Miceli, pp. 246-52, and G. Sampietro, *Fasano: Indagini Storiche* (revised edn, Trani, 1981), pp. 159-61.

[62] The papal summonses of 1375 for the coming *passagium* against the Turks contained fantasy figures which none the less indicated relative expectations. Thus Santa Eufemia and Naples were each called upon to provide seven *milites*, Venosa and Monopoli five each, and the *excambium* of Alife three; by contrast, the priory of Barletta was to send sixteen, Pisa and Rome thirteen, and Venice and Lombardy twenty: *Lettres secrètes et curiales du Pape Grégoire XI (1370-1378) interessant les Pays autres que la France*, ed. G. Mollat (Paris, 1962-1965), nos 3634-35.

[63] Riley-Smith, p.352; Luttrell, *Hospitallers of Rhodes*, XV, pp. 107-08.

[64] Text in Tipton, p. 308. Naples was a magistral *camera* in 1319: Delaville, *Hospitaliers à Rhodes*, p.18.

[65] Sampietro, pp. 159-61, 173-76; d'Ittolo, pp. cxiii-xxvi.

Rhodes Fr Robert de Juilly, who at that time was Commander of Flanders in the priory of France.[66]

Fr Garin de Châteauneuf had been Prior of Navarre in 1346 when he was accused, falsely according to the pope, of offering bribes in order to secure the election as master of Fr Déodat de Gozon,[67] and in 1356 Pope Innocent VI sought to secure him a priory in France or, failing that, the commandery of Monopoli and other commanderies in the priory of Barletta 'as his predecessors had been accustomed to hold'.[68] In 1360 he was still Prior of Barletta and by then he held Monopoli;[69] in 1362 the master's *procurator* both in the priory of Barletta and in the *ecclesia* of Santo Stefano was the Provençal Fr Gautier de la Bastide, later Prior of Toulouse;[70] and in 1366 the Commander of Monopoli was again a Provençal, Fr Bertrand Flotte.[71] In 1373 Flotte held the commandery of Naples though he was absent at Rhodes. In that year the Neapolitan commandery housed various secular residents, including two Provençal priests, some Provençal *servitores*, and a French cook.[72] Some of these Provençal brethren, most of whom were knight-brethren and many of whom were absentees, later held important positions; Fr Bertrand Flotte became grand commander and governed Rhodes in 1378 and 1379 as lieutenant master. The Provençaux were in a position to secure the southern Italian capitular commanderies as convenient and lucrative benefices, while they regularly acquired capitular commanderies in the East.[73] These foreigners were frequently absent from their commanderies, often in service on Rhodes, and if some Provençaux were installed in the house at Naples in 1373, apparently not one of the fifty-seven brethren at Barletta, Trani, and Corato in the same year was from Provence.[74]

---

[66] NLM Arch. 316, fol. 267r-v.

[67] *Clément VI (1342-1352): Lettres closes, patentes et curiales se rapportant la France*, ed. E. Déprez et al., vol. 2, fasc. 3 (Paris, 1958), no. 2889.

[68] *Innocent VI (1352-1362): Lettres secrètes et curiales*, ed. P. Gasnault et al., vol. 4, fasc. 1 (Rome, 1976), no. 1897; Innocent acted at the request of *Lhancardus*, Lord of *Solemnaco*, to whom Fr Garin was *nepos*.

[69] Text in d'Ittolo, pp. 50-51.

[70] Text ibid., pp. 52-55; cf. Delaville, *Hospitaliers à Rhodes*, p. 207 n. 1.

[71] Text in d'Ittolo, pp. 59-63.

[72] Archivio Segreto Vaticano, Instrumenta Miscellanea, 2678.

[73] Luttrell, *Hospitallers of Rhodes*, IX, pp. 160-63, 176-77.

[74] Iorio, pp. 24-25, 100-106.

Provençal influence in the Neapolitan kingdom was waning but provisions made by French popes increasingly helped Provençal Hospitallers, who were well placed to exercise influence in the curia at Avignon, to secure the Neapolitan benefices. Popes had always interfered in the Hospital's affairs, often to protect the order or to resolve its internal disputes.[75] The growth of the system of provisions so financially advantageous to the papacy inevitably impinged on the Hospital, though for long the popes largely limited themselves to making requests or recommendations rather than direct provisions. The most notable exception was Fr Juan Fernández de Heredia who in 1355 secured two priories and in 1377 the mastership itself through papal intervention.[76] After 1362 Urban V and especially Gregory XI repeatedly interfered in Hospitaller appointments.[77] There was much trouble over the Provençal Fr Manuel Chabaut whom Urban V in 1370, and Gregory XI thereafter, insisted on imposing as Commander of Santa Eufemia in place of his deceased uncle Fr Bertrand de Boysson; Urban even freed Chabaut from the master's jurisdiction, making him directly subject to the pope.[78] In 1373 and 1374 Gregory ordered the master to have the Commander of Naples, Fr Bertrand Flotte, given the vacant priory of Hungary and have his nephew, Fr Jean Flotte, replace him in the Neapolitan commandery; the order resisted that but in 1375 Fr Bertrand Flotte became Grand Preceptor at Rhodes.[79]

The quarrels resulting from these Provençal pretensions were arbitrated at a Hospitaller assembly in 1373: the Provençal brethren were to retain rights to Alife, Monopoli, and Venosa while the Italians were in future to control of the priories of Capua and Barletta as also the capitular commanderies of Naples and Santa Eufemia, with the priory of Hungary being held by each party in turn.[80] None the less such disputes continued into the fifteenth cen-

---

[75] N. Housley, *The Avignon Papacy and the Crusades: 1305-1378* (Oxford, 1986), pp. 260-92.

[76] Luttrell, *Hospitallers in Cyprus*, XI p. 295, XXIII p. 32.

[77] Examples in P. Thibaut, 'Pope Gregory XI (1370-1378) and the Crusade', *Canadian Journal of History* 20 (1985) 326-30, and A. Luttrell, 'Del Carretto, Daniele', *Dizionario Biografico Italiano*, vol. 6 (Rome, 1988), pp. 394-97; the published registers of papal documents contain much further data.

[78] *Urbain V*, nos 25896, 26657; *Lettres secrètes et curiales du pape Grégoire XI*, nos 198, 515, 2204, 2287; Miceli, pp. 249-52 [with evident confusions].

[79] *Grégoire XI*, nos 1502-03, 2622-23; Delaville, *Hospitaliers à Rhodes*, p. 150 n. 1.

[80] Ibid., pp. 174-75.

tury,[81] though the Provençal claims were diminished by the sale in 1377 of the *excambium* of Alife.[82] Fr Manuel Chabaut, who was dead by March 1376, was apparently the last Provençal Commander of Santa Eufemia.[83] In 1373 Monopoli was held by the Neapolitan Fr Domenico de Alamania and Fr Ruggero de Sansoniis was Commander of Venosa; both belonged to the *langue* of Italy;[84] from 1378 Fr Domenico de Alamania was also Commander of Naples.[85] Thereafter the situation changed throughout Italy in consequence of the papal schism which from about 1381 onwards brought further conflicts and confusions of a different type.[86]

---

[81] For example, in 1434 the Italians protested unsuccessfully against control of Venosa by the *lingua parue Prouincie*: NLM Arch. 351, fol. 35r-36r, 119r-120v; cf. Luttrell-Fiorini, pp. 227-28. Fr Jean Romieu de Cavaillon was Commander of Manosque in Provence and of Monopoli in 1438, but with the Aragonese conquest of Naples in 1442 the Provençal *langue* began to lose control of Monopoli and Venosa: Raybaud, 1, pp. 378, 381. However, it was still claiming Venosa and Monopoli in 1466: NLM Arch. 376, fol. 42r. The two Provençal auberges at Rhodes were united in 1440: Arch. 354, fol. 52r-53r.

[82] NLM Arch. 48, fol. 170r-v.

[83] NLM Arch. 322, fol. 267v; cf. Miceli, pp. 251-52; Russo, nos 7877, 7895, 7906, 7909, 8077-80, 8110, 8312.

[84] NLM Arch. 347, fol. 42r-v; Sire, p. 167, gives Fr 'Dominique d'Alemagne' as of the *langue* of Provence. Fr Domenico seems to have restored the Hospital's church in Naples in 1386; his family in Naples was apparently related to the Merloto who were *de genere francorum* and may have had French or Provençal origins: M. Radogna, *Monografia di S. Giovanni a Mare Baliaggio del S. M. O. Gerosolimitano in Napoli* (Naples, 1873), pp. 36-42; A. de Rinaldis, *Santa Chiara: il Convento delle Clarisse – il Convento dei Minori – la Chiesa* (Naples, 1920), p. 161. Fra Giorgio Castriota Scanderbeg most kindly photographed the Alamania arms in the Merlotto chapel in Santa Chiara. An Alemagna went to Naples, apparently from Anjou in the second half of the thirteenth century: 'Alemagna, Guido d'', *Dizionario Biografico degli Italiani* 2 (Rome, 1960), p. 145.

[85] NLM Arch. 321, fol. 205r.

[86] Delaville, *Hospitaliers à Rhodes*, pp. 248-64; Luttrell, *Hospitallers in Cyprus*, XXIII, *passim*; idem, *Hospitallers of Rhodes*, XI, *passim*.

12

The Hospitallers, Bohemia, and the Empire,

1250-1330

Karl Borchardt

From the second half of the twelfth century the Hospitallers had two priories in central Europe, a western one usually called *Alamania*, and an eastern one usually called Bohemia. As a rule, the Hospitallers in the East sent men and money to the Holy Land via Venice, their brethren in the West via Genoa or Marseilles. From 1255 to 1325,[1] however, all known brethren who governed the priory of Bohemia were Germans from Swabia, Franconia, the Rhineland, or Thuringia. It had never happened before the middle of the thirteenth century and it never happened after the third decade of the fourteenth century that the

---

[1] Fr Michael von Tinz (since 1325) was from Silesia, but Fr Heinrich von Fürstenberg (mentioned 1255) came from Swabia; his predecessor Fr Clement (1249 to 1253) is of unknown origin. A. Wienand (ed.), *Der Johanniter-Orden, Der Malteser-Orden: Der ritterliche Orden des hl. Johannes vom Spital zu Jerusalem, seine Aufgaben, seine Geschichte* (3rd edn, Cologne, 1988), pp. 652, 654 [lists]; J. Delaville LeRoulx, *Les Hospitaliers en Terre Sainte et à Chypre 1110-1310* (Paris, 1904), pp. 392-402 and the lists pp. 428-31; R. L. Dauber, *Der Johanniter-Malteser Orden in Österreich und Mitteleuropa*, vol. 1 (Vienna, 1996), pp. 260-73 [lists]; B. Waldstein-Wartenberg, *Rechtsgeschichte des Malteserordens* (Vienna, Munich, 1969), pp. 69-74, 124-29; J. Riley-Smith, *The Knights of St John in Jerusalem and Cyprus c. 1050-1310* (London, 1967), pp. 341-71, especially pp. 358-59; A. Luttrell, 'The Hospitallers in Fourteenth Century Germany', *St John Historical Society Proceedings* 2 (1988/90) 20-26; K. Borchardt, 'Military Orders in East central Europe: The first hundred years', *Autour de la première croisade: Actes du Colloque de la Society for the Study of the Crusades and the Latin East*, ed. M. Balard. Byzantina Sorbonensia 14 (Paris, 1996), pp. 247-54; L. Jan, 'Die Würdenträger der geistlichen Ritterorden an dem Hof der letzten Přemysliden', *Böhmisch-österreichische Beziehungen im 13.Jahrhundert: Österreich (einschließlich Steiermark, Kärnten und Krain) im slawischen Großreichsprojekt Ottokars II. Přemysl, König von Böhmen*, eds M. Bláhová, I. Hlaváček (Prague, 1998), pp. 285-300.

From *Mendicants, Military Orders, and Regionalism in Medieval Europe*, ed. Jürgen Sarnowsky. Copyright © 1999 by Jürgen Sarnowsky. Published by Ashgate Publishing Ltd, Gower House, Croft Road, Aldershot, Hampshire, GU11 3HR, Great Britain.

two priories were placed under one grand preceptor and that both this grand preceptor and the Bohemian prior were Hospitallers from Germany. Later there are at least three cases when master and convent appointed a German to be Prior of Bohemia, but these Germans were never accepted in Bohemia.[2] The predominance of German knights in the eastern priory during the late thirteenth and early fourteenth centuries has sometimes been hailed as German colonizing and civilizing influence in an allegedly backward country, or it has been criticized as German imperialism. But in fact, as this paper seeks to demonstrate, this predominance was mainly caused by Bohemian involvement in the politics of the empire and by attempts of Bohemian kings to build a strong monarchy with foreign counsellors, among them German Hospitallers.

In order to understand the politics in central Europe between the 1250s and the 1320s, five main issues between Bohemia and the empire must be remembered: the quarrels over the empire with the Staufen party from 1245 (deposition of Frederick II) to 1273 (election of Rudolf von Habsburg) and with the Habsburg family from 1292 (election of Adolf von Nassau) to 1330 (death of Frederick the Fair), the attempts by Bohemian kings to expand in east central Europe, first by Přemysl Otakar II from 1253 to 1278 and then by his son and grandson Wenceslas II and Wenceslas III from 1283 to 1306, and finally the quarrel over the Přemyslid inheritance from 1306 (assassination of Wenceslas III) to 1318 (agreement between John of Luxemburg and the Bohemian nobles).

To trace the Hospitaller reaction to these issues it will be necessary to examine the regional divisions of the Hospitaller province for central Europe and the careers of their officers. This is, of course, difficult because the charters usually mention titles and seals but do not tell by whom, how and why the regional divisions were created or changed, and by whom, how and why the regional officers were appointed or deposed. Moreover, there were subdivisions of the two basic priories which were sometimes elevated to the status of priory themselves.[3] In fact, during the thirteenth century the Hospitallers instituted

---

[2] For Rudolf von Masmünster 1330 see below, pp. 227, 229-30. Fr Hesso Schlegelholz 1373: NLM Arch. 281, fol. 29v. Fr Eberhard Schenk von Erbach 1445 NLM Arch. 357, fol. 129v-130v.

[3] The chapter general of 30 September 1294 decreed that the Prior of *Alamania* should ride with ten horses, whereas the three priors of *Polonia*, Denmark, and *Starliche* = Bohemia should ride with eight horses. *CGOH*, 3, no. 4259, pp. 650-51. The priory of Hungary is missing. When the chapter general of 22 October 1301 decreed that no prior should have two priories, except the Prior of *Alamania*, *CGOH*, 4, no. 4549 # 13, p. 18, this meant that *Alamania inferior* and *Alamania superior* could be administered by the

several regional masters (*magistri*) or priors in central Europe that can be seen as analogous to the several *Balleien* of the Teutonic Order.[4] The western priory of *Alamania* was subdivided into *Alamania superior* in the south and *Alamania inferior* in the north-west. *Alamania superior* with houses in Swabia, the Breisgau, and Alsace remained the more important part, and in 1300 its prior – whose name the charter does not mention – was styled simply Prior of *Alamania*.[5] *Alamania inferior* had its centres at Cologne, Steinfurt, and Utrecht. In the second decade of the fourteenth century a third subdivision *Alamania media* was mentioned which comprised Thuringia, Franconia, and the Wetterau. In the 1320s a preceptor general began to administer the north-east, Saxony, the Mark of Brandenburg, and *Slavia* (i.e. Mecklenburg and western Pomerania). The far north formed the priory of *Dacia* which included the kingdoms of Denmark, Norway, and Sweden. The original central eastern priory developed four subdivisions in the thirteenth century, Bohemia itself, Moravia, *Polonia* (i.e. mainly Silesia), and *Austria*. The most important house in *Austria* was Mailberg, and its *magister* was sometimes responsible for Styria and Carinthia as well. Finally, the priory of Hungary was closely related with central Europe at this time.[6] The various regional *magistri* and *priores* were

---

same person. The prior for a region must not be confused with the prior of a single house, e.g. in Prague, who was the priest in charge of the priests living in that house.

[4] E. g. *magister et fratres in Boemia*, Lyons 21 December 1244: *CDB*, 4/1, no. 54, pp. 138-39; *magister* in Prague *frater Dvrata* and his successor *frater Petrus*, undated charter, probably after 1248: *CDB*, 4/1, no 155, pp. 256-57; Fr Heinrich von Toggenburg, *magister* for Alsace and Breisgau, 1252: *CGOH*, 2, no. 2599, pp. 724-25. Dauber, *Österreich*, pp. 270-71, has a prior for *Austria* and Styria in 1244, in 1263, and in 1277, a lieutenant of the prior in 1280, and a lieutenant of the *magister* [the master?] for *Austria*, Styria, Carinthia and Carniola in 1298. On the Teutonic Order K. Militzer, *Die Entstehung der Deutschordensballeien im Deutschen Reich*. QStGDO 16 (Bonn-Bad Godesberg, 1970).

[5] The prior and the brethren in *Alamania* issued the charter but their seal reads ✝ [*S(IGILLVM)] PRIORAT(VS) DOM(VS) HOSPITAL(IS) IH(E)R(OSO)L(IMITAN)I SV-P(ER)IORIS ALEMA[NIE]*, Würzburg 12 February 1300: *Monumenta Boica* 38 (Munich, 1866), no. 133, pp. 231-32; *CGOH*, 3, no. 4486, pp. 796-97. *Alamania inferior* is first mentioned in 1251: *CGOH*, 2, no. 2572, p. 715.

[6] J. von Pflugk-Harttung, *Die Anfänge des Johanniterordens in Deutschland, besonders in der Mark Brandenburg und in Mecklenburg* (Berlin, 1899); idem, 'Die inneren Verhältnisse des Johanniterordens in Deutschland, besonders im östlichen Niederdeutschland (bis zum Beginne der Herrenmeisterwürde)', *Zeitschrift für Kirchengeschichte* 20 (1900) 1-18, 132-58; Magdeburg 16 December 1317: F. Wilcke, *Geschichte des Ordens der Tempelherren* 2 (Halle an der Saale, 1860), pp. 499-502. In order to avoid confusion with modern Germany, Austria, Poland, or Denmark, the Latin terms *Alamania, Austria, Polonia*, and *Dacia* are retained throughout this paper.

not always mentioned with their names in the charters and other sources. Furthermore, the terminology of charters issued by local rulers or ecclesiastical dignitaries may be imprecise.

The grand preceptors and the priors may have been appointed and confirmed by the master and his convent on the chapter in the Levant. Whether this appointment was preceded by suggestions from the West or even by prioral elections in the West, is not clear. As a rule, the grand preceptor was in charge of the whole of central Europe, although the charters do not always enumerate all regions.[7] Usually, they name *Alamania*, Bohemia, Moravia, and *Polonia*. Hungary and *Dacia* might be added, and sometimes also Austria, Styria, and Carinthia.[8] Brethren from central Europe who came to the convent in the East were allotted to the German *langue*.[9] The grand preceptor ranked above the priors who owed obedience to him. Both the grand preceptor and the priors could be absent in the Levant, and during these absences lieutenants could be appointed. Even if present in Europe, both the grand preceptor and the priors could have regional lieutenants.[10]

This constitutional framework was essential for the careers of the Hospitaller officers. The other factor that influenced such careers were political quarrels, but the position of the Hospitallers in these quarrels is difficult to trace, since the sources usually just give names and titles. In some cases Hospitallers were actively involved as envoys and counsellors of princes, Fr Berengar von Laufen for Rudolf von Habsburg in 1275, Fr Gottfried von Klingenfels for Adolf von Nassau in 1295, Fr Hermann von Hohenlohe for Wenceslas II in 1297, Fr Berthold von Henneberg for John of Luxemburg in 1313, Fr Albrecht von Schwarzburg for Louis the Bavarian in 1323 and 1325. In most cases we must

---

[7] Beside the Grand Preceptor of *Alamania*, who should ride with not more than 10 horses in the priory of *Alamania*, because the Prior of *Alamania* himself was not allowed more than 10 horses, but outside that priory could have more horses, there were the grand preceptor of the Hospital (18 horses) and the two grand preceptors of Spain and Italy (20 and 12 horses): chapter general of 1294 *CGOH*, 3, no. 4259, pp. 650-52.

[8] Hungary and *Dacia* 29 April 1266: *FUB*, 1, no. 458, p. 220; *Dacia* 24 August 1269: ibid., 1, no. 467, p. 225; *Austria* 1 March 1271: ibid., 1, no. 475, p. 230; *Austria* and Styria 30 April 1290: ibid., 5, no. 248, p. 216.

[9] Seven *langues* 1303: *CGOH*, 4, no. 4574 # 14, p. 39-40.

[10] There were seals of the Grand Preceptor for *Alamania*, *Bohemia* and *Polonia* – 1258 (*CGOH*, 2, no. 2908, p. 865) – as well as of the Prior for *Alamania Superior* – 1289, 1298, 1299 and 1300 (*CGOH*, 3, nos 4042, 4435, 4457, 4486, pp. 537-38, 751-52, 764, 796-97) – but most officers used personal seals with their first name and their family coat of arms.

be content to determine the political position of the Hospitaller officers from the places where they issued their charters and from the business they conducted. The places can provide a hint because central Europe was torn by territorial strife and divisions, to a far greater extent than the big monarchies of France, England, or Castile. It can be said, for example, that if the Grand Preceptor Fr Clement held a meeting at Cologne in 1251 he must have been an opponent of the Staufen party at that time. The business the Hospitaller officers were conducting can also provide a hint. For example, if the Master of Mailberg – the regional officer for Austria and Styria – was rewarded by Rudolf von Habsburg immediately after the conquest of Vienna in 1276 with privileges and even received confiscated properties of citizens in Vienna, he must have favoured Rudolf against Přemysl Otakar. In other cases we can at least guess from the family background of the Hospitallers what their loyalties may have been. Fr Berengar von Laufen was certainly a Habsburg partisan, since he came from Habsburg territories in southern Swabia. Fr Friedrich and Fr Heinrich von Kindhausen, however, came from Thuringia and were probably close to the Archbishop of Mainz and to his ally, the King of Bohemia.

These problems of the sources and their interpretation must be born in mind, when we try to survey the political position of the Hospitallers in central Europe from 1250 to 1330. In the middle of the thirteenth century the two priories were faced with the struggle between the papacy and the Staufen family. Even after the deposition of Frederick II in 1245 the Hospitallers hoped that reconciliation would secure Staufen support for the crusade of Louis IX. Probably for this reason the Hospitallers appointed two grand preceptors for central Europe, Fr Clement for the papal territories (*Alamania*, Bohemia, Moravia, and *Polonia*)[11] and Fr Raimbaud de Voczon for the imperial territories (Italy, Hungary,

---

[11] Fr Clement, *magnus preceptor*, was present at [Schwäbisch] Hall and Würzburg 1249 [without day] and sealed an accord with the citizens of Hall who had petitioned previous *magistri et fratres* in *Alamannia* to take over a hospital in their town: *CGOH*, 2, no. 2493, p. 679; *CDB*, 4/1, no. 391, pp. 543-44; *Die Urkunden des Archivs der Reichsstadt Schwäbisch Hall*, ed. F. Pietsch, vol. 1 (Stuttgart, 1967), no. U 18, pp. 62-63. – In 1251 Fr Clement, *humilis preceptor*, and the preceptor of Cologne Fr Konrad and two brethren of that house, Fr Geldolf and Fr Cesarius, sold to Count Otto II of Guelders the Hospitallers' rights on the toll on the Rhine at Arnheim: Cologne 1251 [without day]: *CGOH*, 2, no. 2547, pp. 701-2. Among the witnesses *frater Albertus lector fratrum Predicatorum in Colonia*, possibly Albert the Great. – July 1251: *Hessisches Urkundenbuch*, I, *Urkundenbuch der Deutschordensballei Hessen*, ed. A. Wyss, 3 vols Veröffentlichungen der Staatsarchive in Preußen 3, 19, 73 (Leipzig, 1879-1899), here I, 1, no. 104, p. 88; *CGOH*, 2, no. 2568, p. 711, for Weißensee, perhaps when Fr Clement was present there.

Sclavonia, and Austria).[12] Fr Clement had a prior for *Polonia*, Fr Geldolf, who came from the house at Cologne and continued to be active under the next Grand Preceptor Fr Heinrich von Fürstenberg;[13] the *magister* in Prague Fr Johannes obviously acted as Prior for Bohemia.[14] The appointments of Fr Clement and of Fr Raimbaud may have happened in the autumn of 1248, perhaps on a chapter general, if the Grand Preceptor Fr Clement is identical with the Bailliff of Tripoli Fr Clement of August 1248.[15] On his journey to central Europe Fr Clement may have visited the papal curia at Lyons.[16] The family of Fr Clement is not known. A certain Clement, *palatinus* of Cracow, witnessed in 1244 a confirmation by Duke Boleslas V of Cracow and Sandomir for the Hospitallers in Zagost.[17]

Fr Clement and Fr Raimbaud disappear with Wenceslas I († 1253) and Konrad IV († 1254). The new Bohemian ruler Přemysl Otakar II (1253-1278) was vividly interested in the affairs of the empire and may even have hoped to be himself elected king of the Romans.[18] Under Přemysl Otakar Fr Heinrich

---

[12] Fr Raimbaud de Voczon, *magnus preceptor cismontanus* or *cismarinus*, 2 June 1247: *CGOH*, 2, no. 2445, pp. 656-59; 11 July 1248: *CGOH*, 2, no. 2481, pp. 672-73, and *CGOH*, 4 p. 350, note; *magister* for Italy, Hungary, and *Sclavonia*, 22 July 1250: *CGOH*, 2, no. 2526, pp. 689-90, by Bela IV; *preceptor* for Hungary, Perugia 25 February 1252: *CGOH*, 2, no. 2589, pp. 721-22, by Innocent IV; *magnus preceptor* for Italy, Hungary, and *Austria*, S. Germano August 1252 [without day]: *CGOH*, 2, no. 2638, pp. 732-33; Gravina February 1253 [without day]: *CGOH*, 2, no. 2638, p. 739; Foggia January 1254 [without day]: *CGOH*, 2, no. 2663, p. 751, all three charters by Konrad IV; without title, Györ 2 October 1254: *CGOH*, 2, no. 2694, p. 766 (*frater Remkaldus*) by Bela IV, and 1259: *CGOH*, 2, no. 2932, pp. 879-80 (*fratrem Remcaldum domuum Hospitalis Hierosolymitani per Hungariam et Sclavoniam tunc maiorem preceptorem*).

[13] On 27 June 1252 Fr Clement, styling himself in the same way as the year before and celebrating a *capitulum* of the order in Cologne, sold some villages to the Cistercians of Reinfeld (diocese of Lübeck); present were among others five named Hospitallers, among them Fr Geldolf *prior Polonie*: *CGOH*, 2, no. 2611, pp. 730-31.

[14] 1253: *CDB*, 5/1, no. 12, pp. 49-50.

[15] *Frater Clemens ballivus de Tripoli* and other leading Hospitallers as witnesses, when the Grand Preceptor and Vice-Master Fr Jean de Ronay received possessions from Santa Maria Latina, Acre 7 August 1248, vidimus 30 November 1248: NLM Arch. 16, no. 28; *CGOH*, 2, no. 2482, pp. 673-75.

[16] Papal letter to *magistro et fratribus* in *Alamania*, Moravia, Bohemia, and *Polonia*, Lyons 28 July 1249: *CDB*, 4/1, no. 389, pp. 542-43; *CGOH*, 2, no. 2505, pp. 682-83.

[17] *CGOH*, 2, no. 2325, p. 617.

[18] J. K. Hoensch, *Přemysl Otakar II. von Böhmen* (Munich, 1989); F. Graus, 'Přemysl Otakar II. – sein Ruhm und sein Nachleben', *Mitteilungen des Instituts für österreichische Geschichtsforschung* 79 (1971) 5-110; K. Richter, 'Přemysl Otakar II.', *Hand-*

von Fürstenberg and Fr Heinrich von Boxberg acted as grand preceptors for *Alemania*, Bohemia, *Moravia, Polonia*, and *Austria*. Fr Heinrich von Fürstenberg gave his consent in 1255, when a quarrel about tithes for Striegau and Lossen in Silesia (*Polonia*) was settled, and continued in his office to 1257.[19] In 1259 and in 1262, Fr Heinrich von Fürstenberg is known to have been in the Holy Land, as Grand Commander at Acre.[20] During these years Fr Heinrich von Boxberg was Grand Preceptor for *Alamania*, Bohemia, *Austria*, Moravia and *Polonia*.[21] Then the charters again name Fr Heinrich von Fürstenberg as Grand Preceptor for *Alamania*, Bohemia (1266 and 1271), *Polonia* (only 1266), Hungary (only 1266), *Dacia* (1266 and 1269), *Austria* (only 1271).[22]

---

buch der Geschichte der böhmischen Länder, ed. K. Bosl, vol. 1 (Stuttgart, 1967), pp. 272-78; O. Lorenz, *Geschichte König Ottokars II. von Böhmen und seiner Zeit* (Vienna, 1866); O. Redlich, *Rudolf von Habsburg: Das Deutsche Reich nach dem Untergange des alten Kaisertums* (Innsbruck, 1903; reprinted Aalen, 1965).

[19] For *Alamania*, Bohemia, *Polonia*, and Moravia, Ujest 4 February 1255: *Schlesisches Urkundenbuch*, eds H. Appelt, J. J. Menzel, vol. 1-5 ([Graz,] Cologne, Vienna, 1963-1992), here 3, nos 144-45, pp. 101-3; *FUB*, 2, no. 581, pp. 385-86, and 4, no. 483, pp. 437-38; *CGOH*, 2, no. 2713, pp. 771-72. The charter issued by Bishop Thomas of Breslau is still extant, the counter-charter by Fr Heinrich is lost but known from a fourteenth-century cartulary. It is not likely, as Riezler suggested, to read 1265 instead of 1255, especially since the witnesses come from the 1250s. – Fr Heinrich, without second name, *humilis preceptor* for *Alamania*, Bohemia, *Austria*, and Poland, Heimbach 13 June 1256: *Hessisches Urkundenbuch*, I, 1, no. 138, p. 109, for *Alamania*, Bohemia, *Austria*, Moravia, and Poland, 28 December 1257: *CGOH*, 2, no. 2908, p. 865; the charter gives the year 1258 according to the *stilus nativitatis*.

[20] Acre 24 and 25 October 1259: *CGOH*, 2, nos 2934-36, pp. 880-82, mentioning *frater Henricus Teotonicus, magnus preceptor* in Acre, and 19 December 1262: *CGOH*, 3, no. 3045, pp. 58-60, naming *frere Henry de Fer, grant comandeor de l'Ospital*. See *FUB*, 4, no. 483 n. 1, pp. 437-38. The next Grand Commander in Acre Fr Etienne de Meses is mentioned 16 September 1264: *CGOH*, 3, no. 3105, pp. 91-92.

[21] Fr Dietrich von *Vrislenheim* as his lieutenant for *Alamania inferior*, Cologne 13 January 1260: *Urkundenbuch für die Geschichte des Niederrheins*, ed. T. J. Lacomblet, vol. 2 (1840-1858; reprinted Aalen 1960), no. 499, p. 282. The second name of Fr Heinrich is not given here but should be clear from the next charter. – Fr Heinrich von Boxberg, *summus preceptor* for *Alamania*, 22 March 1260: *RB*, 4, p. 757; *CGOH*, 2, no. 2948, p. 886, for the house at Rothenburg. Although the charter merely mentions *Alamania*, the legend on the seal, however fragmentary, clearly includes Bohemia.

[22] Constance 29 April 1266: *FUB*, 1, no. 458, p. 220; *CGOH*, 3, no. 3219, p. 139, for Überlingen. – Degerfelden 20 April 1267: *FUB*, 4, no. 484, pp. 439-40, for Klingnau. – Roggweil 24 August 1269: *FUB*, 1, no. 467, p. 225, for Thunstetten. – 10 February 1270: *FUB*, 1, no. 469, p. 227; *CGOH*, 3, no. 3386, p. 218, for Nidda. – 10 February 1271: *FUB*, 1, no. 473, p. 229; *CGOH*, 3, no. 3412, pp. 240-41, for Klingnau. – 1 March 1271: *FUB*, 1, no. 475, p. 230, for Buchsee. – June 1272 [without day]: *FUB*, 2, no. 584, p. 387; *CGOH*, 3, no. 3455, p. 269, for Rothenburg. This charter apparently has the same seal Fr Berengar von Laufen used as *prior* or *magister*, 28 November

Probably he is identical with *frater Heynricus, magister per Boemiam*, as the Přemyslid chancery styles him, who received a privilege by Přemysl Otakar in 1272.[23] After that, Fr Heinrich von Boxberg is again mentioned as grand preceptor until 1277.[24] Throughout these years, priors or masters for Bohemia, Moravia, *Polonia*, and *Austria*, the regions under Přemyslid influence, continued to be mentioned,[25] though usually without their names. It is therefore impossible to decide whether there existed separate priories for all these regions or whether there was but one eastern prior under the grand preceptor for central Europe. After Přemysl Otakar fell from power, Fr Heinrich von Fürstenberg was only a brother without office, in 1279 at Hohenrain and in 1280 at Rottweil.[26] Usually this Fr Heinrich von Fürstenberg, grand preceptor in 1255, is thought to have been the otherwise unknown seventh child of Count Heinrich von Fürstenberg from a well-connected Swabian family. The father, however, was born in the 1220s, and was still a minor in 1239. A boy in his teens, then, is unlikely to have been grand preceptor. So perhaps the grand preceptor of 1255 was an uncle or other elder relation of the grand preceptor in 1266. The elder Fürstenberg may have secured the advancement of the younger Fürstenberg in the convent. After successful service as Grand Commander at Acre the younger Fürstenberg may have risen to be grand preceptor in central Europe.[27] Fr Heinrich von Fürstenberg and especially his successor Fr Heinrich

---

1274: *Urkundenbuch der Stadt Basel*, vol. 2 (Basle, 1893), plate 7, no. 83. – Fr Heinrich von *Vristenberg, humilis preceptor* for *Alamania*, 24 August 1272: *CGOH*, 3, no. 3470, p. 275 for Klingnau.

[23] Prague 19 January 1272: *FUB*, 2, no. 583, p. 387; *CDB*, 5/2, no. 651, pp. 279-80.

[24] Fr Heinrich von Boxberg, *magister* for *Alamania*, 28 May 1273: *CGOH*, 3, no. 3509, p. 292, by Přemysl Otakar for Laa; *summus preceptor in tota Alamania*, 16 March 1275: *CGOH*, 3, no. 3566, p. 319, for Count Wilhelm von Toggenburg; Vienna 20 May 1277: *CGOH*, 3, no. 3623, p. 347-48, Rudolf von Habsburg on Laa.

[25] The *magister* in Moravia, Lateran 18 January 1254: *CDB*, 5/1, no. 13, pp. 50-51. – The *magister* for Bohemia conducting business in Moravia, Znojmo (Znaim) 10 December 1255: *CDB*, 5/1, no. 58, pp. 116-118. – The Prior for *Polonia*, Viterbo 1 July 1267: *CDB*, 5/2, no. 510, p. 56, for Goldberg. – The Prior for Bohemia conducting business in Moravia, Viterbo 1 March 1268: *CDB*, 5/2, no. 549, pp. 111-12. – The Prior in Prague, 19 February 1273: *CDB*, 5/2, no. 695, pp. 334-35.

[26] 6 November 1279: *FUB*, 1, no. 538, pp. 262-63. – 13 June 1280: ibid., 2, no. 587, p. 389.

[27] K. Herquet, 'Zur Geschichte der deutschen Zunge des Johanniterordens, VII: Der Großpräzeptor Heinrich von Fürstenberg (1255-1272)', *Wochenblatt der Johanniter-Ordensballey Brandenburg* 19 (1878) no. 14, argued that Fr Heinrich was a brother of Count Heinrich. Riezler in *FUB*, 2, no. 581, pp. 385-86, suggests to redate the acts of

von Boxberg were clearly involved in negotiations about the empire between Bohemia and the rulers along the Rhine. The co-operation between Přemysl Otakar and the order was in the interest of both sides. The Hospitallers enjoyed the protection of the mightiest ruler in the empire, the king had trustworthy counsellors with important connections outside Bohemia and especially in Swabia. Both the Hospitallers and Přemysl Otakar supported Richard of Cornwall as King of the Romans, the Bohemian king because Richard recognized his conquest of Austria and Styria, the Hospitallers because they feared that Richard's rival Alfonso of Castile would not be interested in the Holy Land, and the Levant was then still the major concern of the military order.

Since the Hospitallers had many houses and commanderies in Swabia, they enjoyed good relations not only with the counts of Fürstenberg but also with other Swabian rulers, among them the counts of Habsburg. As lieutenant for *Alamania* the grand preceptors Fr Heinrich von Fürstenberg and Fr Heinrich von Boxberg appointed Fr Berengar von Laufen, who came from a family of lesser nobles in Swabia dependent upon the counts of Habsburg. In 1258 and in 1263 Fr Berengar was Vice Prior for *Alamania*, when the office of grand preceptor may have been vacant; in 1270 and in 1271 he acted as Vice Preceptor for *Alamania* under Fr Heinrich von Fürstenberg.[28] Count Rudolf von Habs-

---

1255 to 1265; ibid., 4, no. 484 n. 1, pp. 439-40, he suggests to assume that Fr Heinrich did not belong to the Fürstenberg family at all. Since no family coat of arms for Fr Heinrich is extant (the Fürstenberg having an eagle, his seals merely depicts St John the Baptist) and since his name is usually written like *Vristenberg* or in similar ways, not *Vurstenberg*, this cannot be excluded, but no such family is known. To distinguish between an elder and a younger Fr Heinrich von Fürstenberg seems to be the best solution, avoiding too young a grand preceptor in 1255 and explaining the steep career path and the good connections of the grand preceptor from 1266 to 1272.

[28] 5 [not 1] August 1258: *Hessisches Urkundenbuch*, II, *Urkundenbuch zur Geschichte der Herren von Hanau und der ehemaligen Provinz Hanau*, ed. H. Reimer, vol. 1. Publikationen aus den preußischen Staatsarchiven 48 (1891; reprinted Osnabrück, 1965), no. 338, pp. 249-50; *CGOH*, 2, no. 2899, p. 858, concerning Helfrich von Rüdigheim and his son Konrad von Ronneburg. There are several places called Laufen in or near the Habsburg territories of modern Switzerland. Fr Berengar did not come from Lauffen on the Neckar whose family of counts had died out *c.* 1220. – Klingnau and Olten 28 July and 1 September 1263: *CGOH*, 4, no. 3065bis, pp. 290-91, concerning Aarburg that was given to the Commander of Bubikon Fr Heinrich von Toggenburg. – Basle 2 February 1270: *Urkundenbuch der Stadt Basel* 2, no. 21 [with reproduction of the seal that showed his family coat of arms, an eagle, and the legend ...*RIS BEREN... DE LOVFFA...*]; *CGOH*, 3, no. 3385, pp. 217-18, for the house at Basle. – Fr Berengar, lieutenant of the *magister* in *Alamania*, Duisburg 26 May 1271: *CGOH*, 3, no. 3421, p. 253. Whether Fr Berengar was actually lieutenant of the master or merely of the grand preceptor as in 1270 is not clear.

burg († 1291) favoured Fr Berengar, who served as his *familiaris* and *consilia-rius*. When Rudolf was elected King of the Romans in 1273, Fr Berengar im-mediately rose to be Prior of *Alamania* and received a royal confirmation of the order's privileges.[29] Přemysl Otakar protested against Rudolf's election at the papal curia, and to his envoys Gregory X granted a privilege for the prior and brethren of the Hospital in *Austria*.[30] Apparently, the pope did not support Rudolf's attempt to expel Přemysl Otakar from Austria and tried to win round the Austrian Hospitallers. But the Austrian nobility, including the Hospitallers, resented Přemysl Otakar's strong rule. When Rudolf conquered Vienna, he rewarded the Hospitallers with property he confiscated from citizens in Vienna who had financed Přemysl Otakar.[31] In December 1274 King Rudolf sent Fr Berengar together with Duke Konrad von Teck, the Bishop-Elect of Basle Peter Reich von Reichenstein, the Royal Chancellor Rudolf von Hoheneck, and the Franciscan Fr Heinrich von Isny to Gregory X in Lyons to discuss the govern-ment of Italy and the imperial coronation. In the second half of the year 1275 King Rudolf sent Fr Berengar together with count Heinrich von Fürstenberg and the Royal Chancellor Rudolf von Hoheneck to Italy in order to secure his recognition by the *fideles imperii* throughout Italy, to negotiate with Charles I of Anjou, and to prepare his imperial coronation[32] which was thought to be the

---

[29] Fr Berengar as *prior* for *Alamania* and *dilectus familiaris* of Rudolf, Nuremberg 5 December 1274: J. F. Böhmer (ed.), *Acta imperii selecta* (Innsbruck, 1870; repr. Aalen, 1967), no. 401, pp. 322-23; *CGOH*, 3, no. 3562, pp. 316-17; *Regesta imperii*, 6/1, *Rudolf I.*, ed. O. Redlich (Innsbruck, 1898), no. 282.

[30] Lyons 27 June 1274: *CDB*, 5/2, no. 748, p. 411.

[31] One house at Laa, a suburb of Vienna, where the Hospitallers were to care for six poor and from which the Hospitallers were to maintain three knights in the Levant, Vienna 22 September 1277: *Regesta imperii*, 6/1, no. 2520. See also ibid., no. 643.

[32] Nuremberg 17 December 1274: *Monumenta Germaniae Historica, Legum Sectio IV, Constitutiones et acta publica et regum*, 3, ed. J. Schwalm (Hannover, 1904-1906), no. 75, pp. 63-64; Gregory X to Rudolf and others, Lyons 15 February 1275: ibid., nos 77-79, pp. 64-68. – Rudolf announces his three envoys, among them *frater B. magister hospitalis sancti Johannis per Alamanniam*, to his *fideles* in Italy, Zürich 9 July 1275: *Acta imperii inedita saeculi XIII et XIV*, ed. E. Winkelmann, vol. 2 (Innsbruck, 1885; reprinted Aalen, 1964), no. 101, pp. 86-87; *CGOH*, 3, no. 3580, p. 327. – The three envoys, among them *frater Berengerius*, Prior for *Alamania*, demand an oath of fidelity for Rudolf by the town of Piacenza according to treaties with Charles I of Anjou, Piacenza 10 October 1275: Böhmer, *Acta imperii selecta*, no. 998, pp. 698-99; *FUB*, 1, no. 507, p. 249; *CGOH*, 3, no. 3585, p. 331. – Gregory X congratulates the three en-voys, among them *fratri Berengario de ordine hospitalis sancti Johannis Jerosolimi-tani, familiaris* of Rudolf, for their successes, Pianoro 12 December 1275: A. Theiner (ed.), *Codex diplomaticus dominii temporalis Sanctae Sedis* 1 (Rome, 1861; reprinted Frankfurt am Main, 1964), no. 348, p. 196; *CGOH*, 3, no. 3591, p. 335. During the ab-

first step towards a crusade. The Hospitallers apparently hoped that King Rudolf would help the Christians in the Levant, as he had promised Gregory X, and it was probably also for this reason that they left the case of Přemsyl Otakar.

After the death of Přemysl Otakar both Fr Heinrich von Fürstenberg and Fr Heinrich von Boxberg disappear. The next Grand Preceptor Fr Hermann von Braunshorn came from the region between the Rhine and the Moselle. Like Fr Berengar von Laufen, Fr Hermann von Braunshorn was *consiliarius* of king Rudolf,[33] but his family background points to connections primarily with the Rhenish electors who began to be jealous of Rudolf's successes. The grand preceptor appears in the entourage of Přemysl Otakar's widow Queen Kunigunde and later of the Regent for Moravia Duke Albert II of Saxony. He held contact with Silesian princes[34] and was also lieutenant for Hungary and active in the Rhineland.[35] Despite some co-operation with the victorious Rudolf, Fr Her-

---

sence of Fr Berengar a vice-prior is mentioned, 9 November 1275: *CGOH*, 3, no. 3588, p. 333. On the embassies see Redlich, *Rudolf von Habsburg*, pp. 188-89, 199-200.

[33] Fr Hermann, *consiliarius noster dilectus*, [1278/79]: *Regesta imperii*, 6/1, no. 1044. – Fr Berengar *familiaris*, Vienna 5 March 1279: ibid., no. 1069, *unser henliger ratgeve*, 6 December 1281 and Weißenburg / Elsaß February 1282: ibid., no. 1627.

[34] At the request of Fr Hermann, *magnus preceptor* for Bohemia, *Dacia, Austria, Moravia*, and *Polonia*, Queen Kunigunde confirms a donation by the Bohemian Duke Sobeslav (1173-1179), Prague 9 October 1278: *CGOH*, 3, no. 3678, p. 375; *RBM*, 2, no. 2800, p. 1228. – At the request of Fr Hermann, *magnus preceptor* for Bohemia, Moravia, *Polonia, Dacia*, and *Austria*, Queen Kunigunde exempts possessions at Gröbnig and throughout the province of Troppau, Prague 11 February 1279: *Codex diplomaticus et epistolaris Moraviae*, 15 vols, ed. A. Boczek et al. (Olomunc, 1836-1903), here 4, no. 160, p. 221; *CGOH*, 3, no. 3689, pp. 380-81; *Codex diplomaticus Silesiae*, VII/2, no. 1595, p. 245; *RBM*, 2, no. 1166, pp. 500-501. – *Summus preceptor* for *Alamania*, Bohemia, Moravia, *Polonia, Austria*, and Hungary, Znojmo 22 [not 29] March 1279: *RBM*, 2, no. 1168, p. 501; *CGOH*, 3, no. 3692, p. 381. – In the presence of King Rudolf Fr Hermann, *magnus preceptor* for *Alamania* and *Polonia*, is given the parish church of the town Brieg by Duke Henry IV of Silesia, Vienna 4 March 1280: *CGOH*, 3, no. 3718, pp. 390-91; *Schlesisches Urkundenbuch*, 4, no. 387, pp. 256-57 [sometimes erroneously dated 1284]. – Fr Hermann, *magnus preceptor* for *Alamania*, Bohemia, *Austria*, Moravia, *Polonia*, and *Dacia*, receives exemption for the order from from Duke Albert II of Saxony, regent in Moravia, Brno 29 December 1280: *CGOH*, 3, no. 3774, p. 421. Albrecht calls Fr Hermann *dilectus noster consiliarius ac amicus specialis*. The charter has 1281 according to the *stilus nativitatis*. – Fr Hermann, *magnus preceptor* for *Alamania* and *Polonia*, receives donations made by Duke Bernhard of Silesia, Löwenberg 18 March 1281: *CGOH*, 3, no. 3744, pp. 409-10; *Schlesisches Urkunden-buch*, 4, nos 406-7, pp. 271-73. Among the witnesses the parson at Löwenberg Berthold and two Hospitallers, Fr Heinrich, *prior* at Heimbach, and Fr Konrad *dictus Thuringus*.

[35] Fr Hermann, *magnus preceptor* for *Alamania*, Bohemia, *Dacia, Austria, Polonia*, and Moravia, *gerensque vices summi magistri per Ungariam*, confirms a donation of relics

mann von Braunshorn primarily allied himself with those who had reason to fear Habsburg ascendancy. It is therefore no surprise that the Hospitaller possessions in Swabia were administered by a separate prior for *Alamania*, Fr Heinrich von Hermolsheim from Alsace and by his lieutenant for *Alamania superior* Fr Heinrich von Lichtensteig from Swabia.[36] Fr Berengar von Laufen was either indispensable as envoy for Rudolf, or opposition against the victorious Rudolf was so strong that his favourite Fr Berengar von Laufen had to wait until 1282 before he could succeed Fr Hermann von Braunshorn as grand preceptor.[37] Probably Rudolf himself secured this appointment when in 1281 he triumphantly returned from Austria, where he had spent almost three years in reorganizing the country, and when in 1282 he won the consent of the electors to enfeoff his sons with the duchy. The Habsburg dynasty may have had a very special reason for the advancement of Fr Berengar, because the new grand preceptor was not likely to make trouble when Rudolf's son invaded the castle of Aarburg in southern Swabia which had been bequeathed to the Hospital but which the Habsburgs coveted for their own territory. So in 1285 it was not Fr

---

and other treasure by Count Adolf VII of Berg and his wife Elisabeth, Neuberg 15 August 1280: *Urkundenbuch für die Geschichte des Niederrheins*, 2, no. 740, pp. 437-38; *CGOH*, 3, no. 3729, pp. 396-97.

[36] Fr Heinrich von Hermolsheim, Prior for *Alamania*, Basle 10 June 1278: *CGOH*, 3, no. 3665, p. 366; *magister*, Burgdorf 9 December 1279: *CGOH*, 3, no. 3714, p. 389, for Buchsee. – Fr Heinrich von Lichtensteig, 15 June 1279 and Hohenrain 6 November 1279: *Quellen zur Entstehung der Schweizerischen Eidgenossenschaft*, ed. T. Schieß et al., I: *Urkunden*, 3 vols; II: *Urbare und Rödel*, 4 vols (Aarau, 1933-1964), here 1/1, no. 1301, pp. 593-94; *maister in oberm tußem lande* and Commander of Hohenrain, Ottenhusen 23 March 1284: *CGOH*, 3, no. 3855, p. 460; *Quellen zur Entstehung der Schweizerischen Eidgenossenschaft*, 1/1, no. 1423, p. 652; Commander of Tobel, 26 December 1275: *CGOH*, 3, no. 3592, p. 335; Commander of Überlingen, Stockach 5 June 1299: *CGOH*, 3, no. 4465, p. 780.

[37] *Bruder Beringer, meister des spitals sancte Johannes ober Duthland, unser henliger ratgeve*, when King Rudolf confirmed a donation by the town of Colmar to the Hospitallers of Colmar, Weißenburg February 1282: *Acta imperii inedita*, 2, no. 135, pp. 108-9; *Regesta imperii*, 6/1, no. 1627; *CGOH*, 3, no. 3779, p. 423. The donation by the town, 6 December 1281: *CGOH*, 3, no. 3773, pp. 420-21. – *Magnus preceptor* for *Alemania*, Bohemia, Moravia, *Polonia*, and *Austria*, with a lieutenant for *Alamania inferior*, the Commander of Steinfurt Fr Lupert, 6 May 1282: *CGOH*, 3, no. 3786, p. 428. – On Rudolf's behalf Fr Berengar conducted business concerning the town of Mühlhausen together with Duke Albrecht of Brunswick and Duke Albrecht of Saxony, 20 August 1278: *Regesta diplomatica necnon epistolaria historiae Thuringiae*, ed. O. Dobenecker, vol. 4 (Jena, 1939), nos 1554-56.

Berengar, but the master himself, Fr Jean de Villiers (1284-94), who – vainly – protested against the Habsburg occupation of Aarburg.[38]

Meanwhile, Fr Berengar von Laufen had been removed from his office. The Hospitallers in central Europe saved their independence by the timely accession of Wenceslas II (1278-1305), the young son of the late Přemysl Otakar, who began his personal rule in 1283.[39] Wenceslas continued to employ as Hospitaller Prior for Bohemia a *consiliarius* of Rudolf, Fr Hermann von Hohenlohe, the illegitimate son of the Franconian nobleman Gottfried von Hohenlohe († 1254 or 1255).[40] As early as 1282, Fr Hermann von Hohenlohe, *summus magister* or *oberster meister* for Bohemia, Moravia, and Silesia, concluded a treaty with the town of Leobschütz concerning the commandery of Gröbnig.[41] His advancement must therefore have been favoured by Rudolf von Habsburg during the regency in Bohemia from 1278 to 1283. But as soon as Wenceslas himself took over, the quarrel about Aarburg offered an opportunity to replace Fr Berengar von Laufen as grand preceptor with Fr Friedrich von Kindhausen, a Thuringian, whose family was named after the village Kühn-

---

[38] *Regesta Habsburgica*, vol. 2/1: 1281-1298, ed. H. Steinacker (Innsbruck, 1934), nos 187-88, p. 43. In 1263 Count Ludwig von Froburg had given the castle to the Hospitallers: *Quellen zur Entstehung der Schweizerischen Eidgenossenschaft*, 1/1, no. 941, p. 426; *CGOH*, 4, no. 3065bis, pp. 290-91. The Bishop of Basle tried to mediate, but the quarrel led to open warfare in 1288, and in 1299 the Habsburg family bought the castle: Redlich, *Rudolf von Habsburg*, pp. 565-66.

[39] On 24 May 1283 Wenceslas II solemnly entered Prague: 'Continuation of the Chronicle of Cosmas', *Fontes Rerum Bohemicarum* 2 (1874), p. 366; F. Graebner, 'Böhmische Politik vom Tode Ottokars bis zum Aussterben der Přemysliden', *Mitteilungen des Vereins für Geschichte der Deutschen in Böhmen* 41/3 (1903) 333; J. Kadlec, 'Bischof Tobias und die Prager Diözese während seiner Regierungszeit (1278-1296)', *Regensburg und Böhmen: Festschrift zur Tausendjahrfeier des Regierungsantritts Bischof Wolfgangs von Regensburg und der Errichtung des Bistums Prag*, ed. G. Schwaiger, J. Staber. Beiträge zur Geschichte des Bistums Regensburg 6 (Regensburg, 1972), p. 134.

[40] Fr Hermann von Hohenlohe was first mentioned 12 December 1279: *Hohenlohisches Urkundenbuch*, 3 vols, ed. K. Weller (Stuttgart, 1899-1912), here 1, no. 400, p. 273, as *patruus* of Gottfried von Brauneck. On Fr Hermann von Hohenlohe see Redlich, *Rudolf von Habsburg*, p. 754; H. Hartmann, 'Die Komture der Mainzer Johanniter-Kommende', *Mainzer Zeitschrift* 76 (1981) 103-124, at pp. 103-04; L. Jan, 'Hermann z Hohenlohe, rádce a vyslanec českého krále Václava II.', *Sborník prací filosofické fakulty brněnské university* C 43 (1996) 17-35.

[41] Ratification by Nicolaus I of Troppau, 1282: *CGOH*, 3, no. 3775, p. 422; *Hohenlohisches Urkundenbuch*, 1, no. 650/2, p. 467; *Schlesisches Urkundenbuch*, 5, no. 38, pp. 38-39.

hausen near Erfurt, and who was active mainly in Franconia.[42] The connections of both Fr Friedrich von Kindhausen and Fr Hermann von Hohenlohe who co-operated closely[43] were used to form an alliance between Bohemia and the Rhenish electors, especially Mainz, that was not entirely favourable for Rudolf. Soon Fr Hermann became one of the favourite counsellors of Wenceslas. In 1286 Fr Hermann, Prior for Bohemia, *Polonia*, and Moravia and *dilectus fidelis* of King Wenceslas, received the parish church of Rouchovany.[44] In 1284 and again in 1293 Fr Hermann was concerned with a quarrel about tithes between the Hospitaller parish church at Přibice and the Premonstratensians at [Dolní] Kounice which was arbitrated by, among others, the Canon of Krems Master Heinrich of Bitĕs [Osová Bitýška].[45] That Wenceslas preferred these two German Hospitallers, Fr Hermann von Hohenlohe and Fr Friedrich von Kindhausen, reflects tensions between crown and nobility in Bohemia. Bohemian aristocrats frequently threatened possessions and liberties of religious orders, and as a consequence the Hospitallers as well as the Cistercians and other orders were glad to co-operate with the crown. Furthermore, the connections of Fr Hermann von Hohenlohe facilitated the rapprochement between

---

[42] For *Alamania*, Bohemia, *Polonia*, Moravia and *Austria*, 15 February 1283: *CGOH*, 3, no. 3810, p. 438 (extant only as sixteenth-century copy) for the Hospitallers at Würzburg. – Erfurt 19 February 1283: *Regesta diplomatica necnon epistolaria historiae Thuringiae*, 4, no. 2158. – For *Alamania*, Bohemia and *Dacia*, Rüdigheim 8 June 1285: *RB*, 4, p. 281; *CGOH*, 3, no. 3904, p. 480 for the Hospitallers at Würzburg. – For *Alamania*, Bohemia, *Polonia*, *Austria*, and Moravia, 6 March 1286: *CGOH*, 3, no. 3923, p. 487 (extant only as sixteenth-century copy) for the Hospitallers at Würzburg.

[43] As Prior for Bohemia, *Polonia*, and Moravia and *habito consilio et consensu magistri Fr de Kynthusen, magni preceptoris* Fr Hermann gave to the canon of Litoměřice Elias the village Tinc for life, because Elias had donated for his soul seven marks of silver. The text is extant only as fourteenth-century copy, was frequently misread *habito consilio et consensu magistri fratris de Kynthusen* and misdated to 1296 or 1297. Among the witnesses were Hospitallers from Prague, Fr C. the Commander, Fr Iar. the Prior, Fr Berth. the *camerarius*. *RBM*, 2, no. 2498, pp. 1075-76; J. Voigt (ed.), *Das urkundliche Formelbuch des königlichen Notars Heinricus Italicus* (Vienna, 1863) 117; *CGOH*, 3, no. 4298, p. 676. On the correct date see Jan, 'Hohenlohe', pp. 25-26.

[44] Ivanovice 23 October 1286: *CGOH*, 3, no. 3943, pp. 494-95. – 6 February 1289: *RBM*, 2, no. 1467, pp. 630-33; *Hohenlohisches Urkundenbuch*, 1, no. 650/4, pp. 467-68, as arbiter between Wenceslas II and Margrave Frederick of Meißen.

[45] Preceptor in Bohemia, *Polonia*, and Moravia, Brno 26 April 1284 and confirmation by Bishop Dietrich of Olomunc 14 October 1284: *Codex diplomaticus et epistolaris Moraviae*, 4, p. 293; *RBM*, 2, no. 1315, p. 568; *CGOH*, 3, no. 3861, p. 463; *Hohenlohisches Urkundenbuch*, 1, no. 650/3, p. 467. – 30 December 1293 [or 1292 because of the *stilus nativitatis*?]: *Codex diplomaticus et epistolaris Moraviae*, 5, p. 298; *RBM* 2, no. 1635, pp. 701-02; *CGOH*, 3, no. 4242, p. 642; *Hohenlohisches Urkundenbuch*, 1, no. 650/6 , p. 468, with consent by Archbishop Gerhard of Mainz in Aschaffenburg.

Bohemia and Rudolf. In 1287 at the council and diet in Würzburg, Fr Hermann appears as Rudolf's *consiliarius dilectus* and negotiated the arrival in Bohemia of Rudolf's daughter Jutta who had been betrothed to Wenceslas.[46] Whilst Fr Hermann remained Prior for Bohemia, Wenceslas dropped Fr Friedrich von Kindhausen and accepted the return of Fr Berengar von Laufen as grand preceptor.[47] But Fr Berengar had to admit as Prior for *Alamania superior* in 1289 the Commander of Würzburg Fr Helwig von Randersacker, from a local Franconian family without special Habsburg obligations.[48]

Under Adolf von Nassau (1292-1298) relations between Bohemia and the Habsburg dynasty remained extremely unstable. The recurring tensions saved the Hospitallers from the Habsburg domination imminent under Fr Berengar von Laufen. Contrary to Habsburg aspirations Wenceslas II supported the elec-

---

[46] *Regesta imperii,* 6/1, no. 2088.

[47] Vienna 1 December 1287: *Regesta Habsburgica,* 2/1, no. 295, p. 67, concerning Michelstetten, issued by Fr Berengar, *meister* for *Alamania*; among the witnesses Fr Hermann von Hohenlohe. – Prior for *Alamania,* 1 January 1288: *CGOH,* 3, no. 3983, p. 507, for the Hospitallers at Cologne. – Adenau 24 May 1288, extant as vidimus by the Commander of Adenau Fr Hermann von Virneburg about 1293: *Mittelrheinische Regesten,* ed. A. Goerz, vol. 4 (Koblenz, 1886; reprinted Aalen, 1974), no. 1550, p. 350; *CGOH,* 3, no. 4002, p. 317. – At the request of Fr Berengar the Bishop of Constance Rudolf von Habsburg permitted the Hospitallers to collect the tithes at Schlatt, 28 November 1288: *CGOH,* 3, no. 4023, p. 529 n. 4, for the Hospitallers at Freiburg im Breisgau. Consent to the donation by Otto von Staufen, the Commander at Freiburg being Rudolf von Staufen, 31 October 1288. – *Prior humilis* for *Alamania,* Mergentheim 29 March 1289: *Hessisches Urkundenbuch,* II, 1, no. 672, p. 486; *CGOH,* 3, no. 4033, pp. 532-33, for the Hospitallers at Rüdigheim, with the seal of Fr Berengar that depicts St John the Baptist. – Fr Berengar, *magnus preceptor* for *Alamania* with the seal of his priory (*sigillum nostri prioratus*), 26 June 1289, extant as vidimus by the official of Würzburg 26 November 1299: *CGOH,* 3, no. 4046, pp. 539-40, for the Hospitallers at Würzburg. – To Fr Berengar, Prior for *Alamania,* Kraft von Hohenlohe donated two houses and a garden, Weikersheim 4 December 1289: *CGOH,* 3, no. 4070, p. 552; *Hohenlohisches Urkundenbuch,* 1, no. 497, pp. 338-39.

[48] Hemmendorf 11 June 1289: *CGOH,* 3, no. 4042, p. 537. – Fr Helwig was Commander at Würzburg, 10 June 1289: *Monumenta Boica* 38, no. 7, p. 9; 28 July 1289: StAW Standbuch 245, fol. 498v; 21 January 1291: StAW WU 4912; *RB,* 4, p. 481; commander at Mergentheim, 25 January 1293: StAW Standbuch 522, fol. 27v; commander in Krautheim, 6 March 1294: StAW WU 4917; *RB,* 4, p. 557; 5 September 1294: StAW Standbuch 245, fol. 302v; again commander in Würzburg, 22 February 1296: StAW WU 363; *RB,* 4, p. 611; 17 September 1297: *Urkundenbuch der Benediktiner-Abtei St. Stephan in Würzburg,* vol. 1, eds F. Heidingsfelder, M. Kaufmann (Leipzig, 1912), no. 335, pp. 377-79. On Fr Helwig see U. Thomas, *Die Johanniterkomture in Mainfranken von den Anfängen bis zum Jahre 1500* ([manuscript] Würzburg, 1990), pp. 24-26.

tion of Adolf von Nassau in 1292. But then Adolf tried to subdue Thuringia,[49] and Wenceslas reacted by forming an alliance with Mainz and bringing the Habsburg candidate Albrecht to the throne of the empire in 1298. The appointment of Hospitaller officers not only reflects the changing political situation but the Hospitallers themselves played some part in bringing about new coalitions. Since Rudolf wanted to secure the election of his son as next King of the Romans by the electors of Mainz and Bohemia, he allowed Fr Berengar von Laufen to be replaced as grand preceptor in 1290[50] by Fr Gottfried von Klingenfels who, like Fr Helwig von Randersacker, came from Franconia and had no special Habsburg obligations. Their families had connections with Mainz and Hohenlohe, the Hospitaller Prior of Bohemia still being Fr Hermann von Hohenlohe. It cannot be a surprise, then, that Fr Gottfried von Klingenfels loyally served Adolf von Nassau who took him and his Hospitallers under his special protection in 1292. Fr Gottfried even went as Adolf's envoy to Edward I of England in 1295.[51] Meanwhile, the alliance between Wenceslas and Adolf

---

[49] F.-J. Schmale, 'Eine thüringische Briefsammlung aus der Zeit Adolfs von Nassau', *Deutsches Archiv* 9 (1952) 464-512. On the general situation A. Lhotsky, *Geschichte Österreichs seit der Mitte des 13. Jahrhunderts (1281-1358)* (Vienna, 1967), pp. 77-98 with further references.

[50] *Humilis preceptor* for *Alamania*, Bohemia, *Polonia*, Moravia, *Austria* and Styria, Villingen 30 April 1290: *FUB*, 5, no. 248, p. 216; *CGOH*, 3, no. 4091. – For *Alamania*, 13 December 1290: *CGOH*, 3, no. 4135, pp. 578-79. – *Magnus preceptor* for *Alamania*, Olmütz 17 January 1291: *RBM*, 2, no. 1530, pp. 658-59; witness for the oaths of allegiance by the dukes Mieszko and Boleslaw of Oppeln to Wenceslas II. – 2 June 1291: *CGOH*, 3, no. 4159, p. 594; *Mittelrheinische Regesten*, 4, no. 1901, p. 426, for Adenau. – *Humilis preceptor* for *Alamania*, Bohemia, *Polonia*, Moravia, *Austria*, and Styria, 11 November 1291: *CGOH*, 3, no. 4176, pp. 601-2. – *Humilis preceptor* for *Alamania*, Bohemia, *Polonia*, Moravia, *Austria*, and Styria, among the witnesses without special office Fr Helwig von Randersacker, 8 August 1292: *CGOH*, 3, no. 4192, p. 607. – *Magnus preceptor* for *Alamania*, Bohemia, *Polonia*, Moravia, *Austria*, and Styria, 13 May 1293: *Mittelrheinische Regesten*, 4, no. 2166, p. 484. – *Magnus preceptor* for *Alamania*, Bohemia, *Polonia*, Moravia, *Austria*, and Styria, 20 February 1296: *CGOH*, 3, no. 4305, p. 680, for Duisburg by his lieutenant Fr Hermann (Jude) von Mainz. – Former *preceptor*, [Klein-]Erdlingen 18 November 1297: *CGOH*, 3, no. 4394, pp. 726-27. – Fr Gottfried von Klingenfels Commander at Rexingen, Nuremberg 16 November 1298: *CGOH*, 3, no. 4435, pp. 751-52, and Wildberg 5 April 1302: *CGOH*, 4, no. 4559, p. 28. – Fr Berengar von Laufen is mentioned for the last time 21 January 1290: *CGOH*, 3, no. 4075, p. 553, as simple Hospitaller without any office.

[51] Protection for Fr Gottfried von Klingenfels, *magnus preceptor* for *Alamania*, Bohemia, *Polonia*, Moravia, *Austria*, and Styria, Landau 14 November 1292: *CGOH*, 3, no. 4200, pp. 612-13; *Regesta imperii*, 6/2, ed. V. Samanek (Innsbruck, 1948), no. 124. – Adolf confirms the privilege by Rudolf from 5 December 1274 for Fr Gottfried, *preceptor* for *Alamania*, Bohemia, and *Polonia*, Hagenau 11 March 1295: *CGOH*, 3, no. 4275, pp. 661-62; *Regesta imperii*, 6/2, no. 554. – King Adolf also sent the Provost

broke down and Wenceslas negotiated with the archbishops of Mainz Gerhard von Eppenstein (1289-1305) and of Cologne Siegfried von Westerburg (1275-1297) to replace Adolf von Nassau with Albrecht von Habsburg. During times of tension between Habsburg and Bohemia, the *magister* of Mailberg Fr Konrad von Hagenberg had controlled the Hospitaller possessions in Austria. That Mailberg had a mere commander in 1294[52] may indicate that these possessions were again under the Bohemian prior. This facilitated the alliance between Wenceslas and Albrecht which was publicly celebrated when Albrecht came to Prague for the royal coronation of Wenceslas by Archbishop Gerhard at Whitsun 1297. The coalition between Bohemia and Mainz led to the dismissal of Fr Gottfried von Klingenfels, who is last mentioned in 1296, when as *magnus preceptor* for *Alamania*, Bohemia, *Polonia*, Moravia, *Austria*, and Styria he had as lieutenants for the mostly pro-Habsburg *Alamania superior* Fr Gottfried von Staufen (formerly lieutenant for all *Alamania* under Fr Berengar von Laufen) and for *Alamania inferior* the Commander of Cologne Fr Hermann Jude von Mainz.[53] The coalition between Bohemia and Mainz was probably negotiated by, among others, Fr Hermann von Hohenlohe who in 1293 was in contact with archbishop Gerhard. Between 1293 and 1295 Fr Hermann von Hohenlohe resigned the Bohemian priory and was appointed Commander at Mainz,

---

of Utrecht Adolf von Waldeck, whilst King Edward sent to him Fr Simon, the Hospitaller Preceptor of Rossemalle and Alnetum = Aunay and a Templar, the Preceptor of Reims Fr Galcher. *Regesta imperii*, 6/2, nos 552, 554, 625. Edward to Adolf, Westminster 14 August 1295: *CGOH*, 3, no. 4294, p. 673; *Regesta imperii*, 6/2, nos 641-42, returning Fr Gottfried, the knight William of Ormesby and the Canon of Aachen *magister* Gerlach de Gardinis. F. Bock, 'Englands Beziehungen zum Reich unter Adolf von Nassau', *Mitteilungen des Instituts für Österreichische Geschichtsforschung, Ergänzungsband* 12 (1933), pp. 199-257, at pp. 237-39; F. Trautz, *Die Könige von England und das Reich 1272-1377* (Heidelberg, 1961), p. 139; M. Prestwich, *Edward I* (London, 1988), p. 391, on Gerlach and his brother Eustace.

[52] Wienand, p. 315; Dauber, pp. 270-71.

[53] Fr Gottfried von Staufen, Vice Prior for *Alamania*, 30 June 1281: *Urkundenbuch für die Geschichte des Niederrheins*, 2, p. 752; *CGOH*, 3, no. 3755, pp. 412-13; Neuenburg 21 November 1286: *CGOH*, 3, no. 3950, p. 497, for Neuenburg; *pfleger an des meisters stat in obern tütschen lande* and Commander of Neuenburg, Zürich 20 May 1294: *Quellen zur Entstehung der Schweizerischen Eidgenossenschaft*, 1/2, no. 73, pp. 30-31; *CGOH*, 3, no. 4250, p. 646, for Thunstetten. – 20 February 1296: *CGOH*, 3, no. 4305, p. 680. Fr Hermann Jude von Mainz must not be confused with Fr Hermann von Hohenlohe; see H. Hartmann, 'Bruder Hermann von Mainz, Meister der Johanniter in Deutschland', *Mainzer Zeitschrift* 63/64 (1968-1969) 76-78.

certainly with the connivence of the archbishop who sought the help of an intimate of the Přemyslid court.[54]

Then Wenceslas II sent his most experienced diplomats, his Chancellor Peter von Aspelt and Fr Hermann von Hohenlohe, to Rome to secure papal support for the deposition of King Adolf. But the mission failed, since Boniface VIII did not commit himself.[55] Fr Hermann took the opportunity to ask for papal dispensation from his illegitimate birth in order to obtain higher offices in his order. But this part of his mission failed as well; Fr Hermann only got a simple dispensation,[56] and therefore he lost any chance to regain the Bohemian priory or to succeed the pro-Nassau Grand Preceptor Fr Gottfried von Klingenfels. Instead, Fr Hermann von Hohenlohe had to be content as Commander of Mainz[57] and Fr Helwig von Randersacker returned as Prior for *Alamania superior*.[58]

---

[54] 1293 (or 1292?) see above, note 45. – *Frater Hermannus de Hoynloch*, Commander of Mainz, 18 December 1295: *Hohenlohisches Urkundenbuch*, 1, no. 650/7, pp. 468-69.

[55] The chronicle of Colmar relates – *Monumenta Germaniae Historica, Scriptores (in Folio)*, vol. 17, ed. G. H. Pertz et al. (1861, repr. Stuttgart, 1990), pp. 264-65 – that Boniface permitted the electors to depose Adolf. Later Boniface expressly declared that this was not true. On 4 April 1297 Boniface enfeoffed James II of Aragon with Sardinia and Corsica upon condition that neither James nor his successors would be elected kings of the Romans. On Boniface see V. Samanek, 'Studien zur Geschichte König Adolfs', *Sitzungsberichte Wien* 207/2 (Vienna, Leipzig, 1930), pp. 153-60, 234-48; Trautz, p. 143 with n. 195.

[56] Fr Hermann received dispensation from his illegitimate birth by the noble Gottfried of Hohenlohe (*coniugatus et soluta*) *ad omnes dignitates et administrationes ac officia prefati ordinis preterquam ad generale totius eiusdem ordinis vel provinciale alicuius regni sive provincie magisterium vel prioratum*, Vatican 21 April 1297: *CGOH*, 3, no. 4372, pp. 712-13; *Registres de Boniface VIII*, ed. G. Digard et al., 4 vols (Paris, 1884-1939), here 1, no. 1794, col. 679. – Peter von Aspelt was appointed Bishop of Basle: ibid., no. 1729, col. 654-55 (Vatican 31 March 1297), but King Wenceslas himself received only minor graces: ibid., nos 1744-46, col. 660-61. On Peter von Aspelt A. Gerlich, 'Die Machtposition des Mainzer Erzstiftes unter Kurfürst Peter von Aspelt (1306-1320)', *Blätter für deutsche Landesgeschichte* 120 (1984) 255-91, at pp. 257-61.

[57] Fr Hermann was Commander in Mainz, when on 20 October 1297 he witnessed the account given by the Commander of Weißensee Fr Thomas von Weimar for the house of Weißensee to the Master Fr Guillaume de Villaret. StAW WU 4927; *CGOH*, 3, no. 4392, p. 725. – He was probably identical with that Fr Hermann, Commander in Mainz, who was present at [Klein-]Erdlingen on 18 November 1297, when the commander of that house Fr Albrecht von Katzenstein made his account for the same master. *CGOH*, 3, no. 4394, pp. 726-27. With reference to Fr Gottfried von Klingenfels as former *preceptor*.

[58] At the request of Fr Helwig king Albrecht confirmed the order's privileges, Baden 5 April 1299: *CGOH*, 3, no. 4454, pp. 761-63. – Mergentheim 27 April 1299: *CGOH*, 3, no. 4457, p. 764. – Würzburg 11 November 1299: *CGOH*, 3, no. 4476, pp. 787-88. – 30 June 1300: StAW WU 4941; *CGOH*, 3, no. 4510, p. 807, with extant seal of the priory

The next Prior for Bohemia, Moravia, *Polonia*, and *Austria* was Fr Heinrich von Kindhausen, a relation of Fr Friedrich von Kindhausen.[59] His appointment had probably deepened and strengthened the co-operation between Bohemia and Mainz against Adolf von Nassau. Albrecht von Habsburg defeated and killed his rival at Göllheim on 2 July 1298. Now Fr Gottfried von Klingenfels was replaced as grand preceptor by Fr Heinrich von Kindhausen.[60] Whilst Fr Heinrich von Kindhausen was in Bohemia and controlled *Alamania superior*, Fr Hermann Jude von Mainz governed *Alamania media* and *Alamania inferior*: In 1300 he was the *summus magister* for the Commander of Lage, in 1302 and 1303 he was Commander of Maastricht, Herrenstrunden and Frankfurt and Lieutenant of the Grand Preceptor for *Alamania media* (Wetterau) and *Alamania inferior* (*Nydirland*).[61] Fr Hermann von Hohenlohe, who had done so much to bring about this diplomatic revolution remained mere Commander of Mainz,[62] being hampered by his illegitimate birth.

Soon after his victory Albrecht von Habsburg got into trouble with his former partisans: from 1300 to 1302 with the four electors on the Rhine, from 1301 to 1305 with Bohemia whose expansion into both Poland and Hungary threatened the equilibrium in east central Europe. The death of Wenceslas II in 1305 and the assassination of his sole son Wenceslas III in 1306 could have led to

---

for *Alamania superior*. – 14 September 1307: *CGOH*, 4, no. 4752, p. 145 n. 1. – Not prior, but Commander in Würzburg, 19 October 1303: Staatsarchiv Nürnberg RiU 143, Commander in Regensburg, 16 October 1306: StAW WU 8737; 9 May 1307 as vidimus 13 July 1329: StAW WU 5014, without office 13 September 1307: StAW WU 4960; *RB*, 5, p. 123.

[59] At the request of Fr Heinrich Wenceslas II renewed a privilege for the Hospitallers of Prague: Prague 27 July 1298: *RBM*, 2, no. 2812, p. 1232; *CGOH*, 3, no. 4427, p. 747.

[60] *Preceptor* for Bohemia, *Polonia*, and Moravia, November 1302: *RBM*, 2, no. 1942, p. 836; *CGOH*, 4, no. 4575, pp. 41-42, endowing the Hospitaller town of Ivanovice the rights of the town of Brno. – For *Alamania*, Buchsee 15 October 1303: *CGOH*, 4, no. 4610, p. 56. Fr Heinrich von Kindhausen gave his consent to the selling of estates by the house of Buchsee.

[61] 14 February 1300: *CGOH*, 3, no. 4487, p. 797. – 13 October 1302 accepting an arbitration for the Hospitallers of Neumarkt promulgated by Count Wilhelm von Berg 7 September 1302: *CGOH*, 4, no. 4569, p. 32 note 1. – Fr Heinrich von Kindhausen, *hoher meistir des Spitals sente Johannis von Jerusalem*, and his lieutenant in the Wetterau and *Nydirland* Fr Hermann von Mainz, 9 January 1303: *CGOH*, 4, no. 4583, p. 46, for the Hospitallers in Frankfurt. – Fr Hermann von Mainz Commander of Freiburg im Breisgau, 4 September 1313: *Regesten der Markgrafen von Baden und Hachberg 1050-1515*, vol. 1, ed. R. Fester (Innsbruck, 1892-1900), no. h 147; *FUB*, 5, no. 200/2, p. 170.

[62] Last mentioned 11 February 1302: *Hohenlohisches Urkundenbuch*, 1, p. 469.

Habsburg predominance in central Europe, but this was averted by the murder of Albrecht in 1308. For the time being, neither in the empire nor in Bohemia were the Hospitallers any longer likely to fall under royal control as in France, England, Castile, or Aragon. The Master Fr Foulques de Villaret and convent were preoccupied with the conquest of Rhodes from 1306 and with the Templar affair from 1308.[63] For central Europe Fr Heinrich von Kindhausen, a partisan of Mainz and Bohemia, was replaced as grand preceptor by the apparently less controversial Fr Helfrich von Rüdigheim between 1303 and 1305.[64] Fr Helwig von Randersacker led a group of knights to fight on Rhodes and was awarded with the lieutenancy for his native Franconia and Thuringia (i.e. *Alamania media*).[65] Although in central Europe the Hospitallers had to cope with the ever-changing regional alliances, this situation allowed them to maintain their independence from lay powers and to follow their own policy of territorialization. This had begun in the second half of the thirteenth century and sometimes, as in the case of Aarburg, had led to serious conflict. With the empire and Bohemia, the two great monarchies in central Europe, in crisis, the Hospi-

---

[63] A. Luttrell, 'The Hospitallers and the Papacy, 1305-1314', *Forschungen zur Reichs-, Papst- und Landesgeschichte*, eds K. Borchardt, E. Bünz, vol. 2 (Stuttgart, 1998), pp. 595-622; M. Barber, *The Trial of the Templars* (Cambridge, 1978).

[64] *Magnus preceptor* für *Alamania*, Bohemia, Moravia, *Austria* and *Polonia*, 1 September 1305: *CGOH*, 4, no. 4699, pp. 117-18, for Colmar. – 14 September 1307: *CGOH*, 4, no. 4725, p. 145 note 1 for Würzburg. – 25 October 1307: *CGOH*, 4, no. 4760, pp. 152-53. – 15 August 1308: *CGOH*, 4, no. 4813, p. 189, for [Nieder-]Weisel. – 22 February Striegau 1309: *CGOH*, 4, no. 4848, p. 206, for Striegau. – 23 June 1309: *CGOH*, 4, no. 4867, p. 217. – 6 February 1310: *CGOH*, 4, no. 4889, p. 230 for Würzburg.

[65] Lieutenant 6 February 1310: StAW Standbuch 245, fol. 233v; *CGOH*, 4, no. 4889, p. 230. Lieutenant and at the same time Commander in [Klein-]Erdlingen, 26 September 1313: *Oettingische Regesten*, ed. G. Grupp, vol. 2 (Nördlingen, 1899), no. 642, p. 184. – Rhodes: A. von Winterfeld, *Geschichte des ritterlichen Ordens St. Johannis vom Spital zu Jerusalem* (Berlin, 1859), p. 140; J. Friedlaender, *Die Münzen des Johanniter-Ordens auf Rhodos 1309 bis 1522* (Berlin, 1843), p. 2; J. N. Langenfeld, *Kurzgefaßte pragmatische Geschichte des hohen Malteserordens* (München, 1783), p. 55; Delaville, *Hospitaliers en Terre Sainte*, p. 282. – Commander in Würzburg, 15 June 1309 as vidimus 13 July 1329: StAW WU 5014; Commander in Regensburg, 12 March 1313: G. Neckermann, 'Beiträge zur Geschichte der Johanniter- (Malteser-) Ordenskomturei zu St. Leonhard in Regensburg', *Verhandlungen des Historischen Vereins für Oberpfalz und Regensburg* 54 (1910) 47-68, at p. 51; commander in Würzburg, 22 April 1314: StAW WU 8713; *RB*, 5, p. 279; commander in [Klein-]Erdlingen, 12 December 1317: A. v. Steichele (et al.), *Das Bisthum Augsburg, historisch und statistisch beschrieben*, 10 vols (1861-1940), here 3, p. 899; without office, 13 April 1318: T. D. von Popp, 'Urkunden, den vormaligen Templerhof zu Moosbrunn betreffend', *Archiv des Historischen Vereins von Unterfranken* 12/2-3 (1853) 243-48, at p. 246. His function as lieutenant is not regularly mentioned in all charters. Therefore he may have returned as lieutenant from Rhodes in 1309 and may have remained lieutenant until 1317.

tallers of central Europe now indulged freely in territorialization. Their *milites* no longer primarily fought the infidel in the Levant, but strove to build strong territorial commanderies.

The German Hospitallers were eager to acquire and colonize estates in the Slav countries of the East, in the Mark of Brandenburg and Pomerania, in Bohemia, Moravia, and *Polonia*. In 1309 the Franconian Fr Berthold [VI] von Henneberg was lieutenant in *Polonia*.[66] His brother Berthold [VII] († 1340) governed the meagre family estates in Franconia. So the brothers indulged in imperial politics as counsellors for the King and Emperor Henry VII (1309-1313). Together with some Bohemian Cistercians they favoured the marriage between John of Luxemburg and the Bohemian heiress Elisabeth in 1310 which was celebrated at the Hospitaller commandery of Heimbach near Speyer.[67] As his tutors and in order to re-establish a strong monarchy in Bohemia, the young John of Luxemburg brought foreign counsellors to his realm, among them the Henneberg brothers. In 1313 Fr Berthold von Henneberg was Prior for Bohemia, *Polonia*, and *Austria*.[68] For his advancement within the order he may have profited from his relations with his cousin Fr Albrecht von Schwarzburg who had helped to conquer Rhodes. In 1312 Fr Albrecht was sent by the Master Fr Foulques de Villaret and the convent to the papal curia to negotiate about the Templar estates. For this purpose he was given the rank of Grand Preceptor in the West. His companion Fr Leonardo de Tibertis followed him as visitor general.[69] During the next few years the Hospitaller comman-

---

[66] Lieutenant of the *summus magister* for *Polonia*, 1309: *CGOH*, 4, no. 4834, p. 200, for the commandery at Posen. On Fr Berthold see W. Füßlein, *Berthold VII. Graf von Henneberg: Ein Beitrag zur Reichsgeschichte des XIV. Jahrhunderts, Mit einem Urkundenanhang. Um den bisher unveröffentlichten 2. Teil erweiterter Nachdruck der Ausgabe von 1905*, ed. E. Henning. Mitteldeutsche Forschungen, Sonderreihe: Quellen und Darstellungen in Nachdrucken 3 (Cologne, Vienna, 1983), pp. 116-25, 127-31; Hartmann, 'Komture Mainz', p. 105; Thomas, *Johanniterkomture Mainfranken*, pp. 34-35.

[67] Chronicle by Peter von Zittau, c. 100, *Fontes rerum Bohemicarum*, 4, pp. 144-45: *in Heimbach, monasterio videlicet Cruciferorum hospitalensium, quod a Spyra distat spacio duorum milliarum*. F. Seibt, *Handbuch der Geschichte der böhmischen Länder*, p. 359.

[68] *Oberster maister ze Polan, ze Pehem, ze Osterreich und furbaz* or in Latin *preceptor per Boemiam, Poloniam, Moraviam, Austriam*, 1 March 1313: J. von Pflugk-Harttung, *Der Johanniter- und der Deutsche Orden im Kampfe Ludwigs des Bayern mit der Kurie* (Leipzig, 1900), p. 209.

[69] 17 October 1312: T. Rymer, *Foedera, conventiones, Litterae et cujusque generis Acta Publica*, vol. 2 (London, 1818), pp. 182-84; J. Delaville LeRoulx, *Les Hospitaliers à Rhodes jusqu'à la mort de Philibert de Naillac 1310-1421* (Paris, 1913; repr. 1974), pp. 7, 32-34. Fr Leonardo stayed on in Europe, whereas Fr Albrecht returned to Rhodes in

deries in central Europe were administered by lieutenants licensed by Fr
Albrecht, by Fr Leonardo, directly by the master, or by the master and the
convent. The former Grand Preceptor for central Europe Fr Helfrich von
Rüdigheim was among these lieutenants as well as the Italian Fr Paolo da
Modena, a companion of Fr Leonardo de Tibertis.[70]

The Hospitallers desperately needed the support of local rulers for securing as
soon as possible as many Templar possessions as possible. After 1314, however, the war in the empire between the Wittelsbach and the Habsburg kings
made the situation extremely difficult for them. Like the papal curia, the order
tried to maintain some kind of neutrality as long as no decisive battle occurred.[71] Apparently, both Fr Albrecht von Schwarzburg and Fr Berthold von
Henneberg supported Louis the Bavarian and his Luxemburg electors, John of
Bohemia and Balduin of Treves. For the Habsburg clientèle that was strong in
Austria, in Swabia, and on the lower Rhine, the three brethren Fr Hugo von
Werdenberg, Fr Hermann von Hachberg, and Fr Johann von Grumbach administered Hospitaller possessions.[72] In Bohemia, despite his royal backing Fr
Berthold von Henneberg was a controversial figure, because the native nobility
resented the Henneberg brothers and other foreign counsellors. Fr Berthold had
to leave and returned to Franconia. His Bohemian adventure may have yielded

the spring of 1315. He was granted the preceptory of Cyprus by Fr Foulques at only half
its proper *responsiones*, as the convent complained to John XXII in 1317: A. Luttrell,
'The Hospitallers in Cyprus, 1310-1378', idem, *The Hospitallers of Rhodes and Their
Mediterranean World* (Aldershot, 1992), no. IX, pp. 157, 159-61, 176-77.

[70] Fr Helfrich von Rüdigheim, Prior for *Alamania*, Mosbach 2 August 1312: *Regesten
der Erzbischöfe von Mainz von 1289-1396*, vol. 1/1, ed. E. Vogt (Leipzig, 1913; repr.
Berlin, 1970), no. 1504. – Consent of Fr Albrecht von Schwarzburg, *unsers grossen
gebieters*, and of Fr Helfrich von Rüdigheim, *meisters in tuschem land*, Luzern 9 May
1314: *Quellen zur Entstehung der Schweizerischen Eidgenossenschaft*, 1/2, no. 720, p.
362, for Hohenrain. – *Frater Paulus gerens vices magistri generalis per totam Alemaniam*, 25 November 1316: *Hessisches Urkundenbuch*, I, 2, no. 302, p. 228. – *Frater Hil-
phricus de Rudinkeim gerens vices per Alimaniam reverendi viri fratris Leonardi de
Thibertis generalis visitatoris in cismontanis partibus*, 22 December 1316: *Hessisches
Urkundenbuch*, I, 2, no. 304, p. 229.

[71] A Hospitaller from Treves, Fr Werner von Wintrich, was sent by Louis the Bavarian
to the Archbishop of Cologne to negotiate the royal coronation at Aachen, 18/20 November 1314: *Regesten der Erzbischöfe von Mainz*, 1/1, no. 1701-03; *Regesten der
Erzbischöfe von Mainz von 1289-1396*, vol. 1/2, ed. H. Otto (Darmstadt 1932-1935;
reprinted Aalen 1976), no. 3736. Since the archbishop had elected Frederick the Fair,
Louis may have feared that other envoys might not return safely. Pflugk-Harttung, *Der
Johanniter- und der Deutsche Orden*; H. Thomas, *Ludwig der Bayer (1282-1347): Kaiser und Ketzer* (Regensburg, 1993).

[72] Lenzkirch 28 February 1316: *FUB*, 5, no. 354, pp. 327-29.

some profit since in 1315 he bought from his brother the castle at Kühndorf, where he founded a Hospitaller commandery. Although in exile, he continued to style himself *meister und prior zu Behem und zu Polen*.[73] The Bohemian resistance apparently induced the Master Fr Foulques de Villaret to appoint the Commander of Tinz (Tyniec) Fr Michael to be lieutenant of the master in the eastern priory, *vices gerens magistri per Boemiam etcetera*.[74] Fr Michael came from a distinguished Silesian family[75] and had been godfather (*compater*) for Duke Boleslas of Liegnitz (Legnica), son of Duke Henry V (1278-1296).[76] His nomination may have been intended to suit both King John who pursued a policy of expansion towards Poland and the Bohemian nobility which loathed greedy foreign counsellors in their realm.

But Fr Michael was a nominee of Fr Foulques, and this was prone to breed trouble. When the convent deposed the master in 1317,[77] John XXII intervened

---

[73] Füßlein, *Berthold VII.*, pp. 116-25. On Kühndorf H.-J. Mrusek, 'Zur Baugeschichte der Johanniterburg Kühndorf in der ehemaligen Grafschaft Henneberg', *Wissenschaftliche Zeitschrift der Martin-Luther-Universität Halle-Wittenberg* 12 (1963) 663-92.

[74] Fr Michael was Commander of Tinz from 1312 to 1323: Schurgast 20 March 1312: Praha, SÚA, AVM, no. 606; Breslau 24 August 1318: ibid., nos 1112, 1118; Klein Oels 21 January 1319: ibid., no. 608; Brieg 30 July 1319: ibid., no. 746; Brieg 24 January 1320: ibid., no. 611; Brieg 5 June 1320: ibid., no. 610; Breslau 19 June 1320: ibid., no. 609; Brieg 6 February 1321: ibid., nos 612, 747; Schweidnitz 5 November 1323: ibid., no. 614. – Lieutenant of the master, Lossen 5 April 1317: ibid., no. 200.

[75] Even as prior, Fr Michael used his personal seal with the legend † *S(IGILLVM) FRATRIS MICHAHELIS* and his family coat of arms, three hunting-horns, that is extant 29 November 1331: Praha, SÚA, AVM, no. 754; 25 July 1332: ibid., no. 234; 24 April 1334: ibid., no. 618. Franz von Tinz, *comes* of *Wilchicz*, sold off an estate at Klein Tinz near Breslau in 1282, had two hunting-horns as his coat of arms in 1287, and belonged to the entourage of the dukes of Breslau in 1285 and 1288: Schweidnitz (Świdnica) 1282 [without day]: *Schlesisches Urkundenbuch*, 5, no. 36, pp. 32-33 [seal lost]; Oppeln (Opole) 13 April 1285 ibid., no. 197, pp. 161-62; Oppeln 23 April and 1 May 1285: ibid., no. 204, p. 166; 28 August 1287: ibid., no. 359, pp. 280-81; Breslau 25 January 1288: ibid., no. 369, pp. 291-92. The family must not be confused with the Wilczek who had a he-goat as their coat of arms: *Siebmacher 4/11: Der Adel von Österreichisch-Schlesien*, ed. K. Blažek (Nuremberg, 1885; repr. Neustadt / Aisch, 1977), pp. 102-04 and table 54; *Siebmacher 6/8: Der abgestorbene Adel der preußischen Provinz Schlesien und der Oberlausitz*, ed. K. Blažek, part 2 (Nuremberg, 1890; reprinted Neustadt / Aisch, 1977), p. 143 and table 85. The second name Tinz may refer to the family, not to the commandery as in the case of Fr Johannes von Tinz, Groß Tinz (Tyniec nad Ślęza) 29 May 1261: *Schlesisches Urkundenbuch*, 3, no. 354, pp. 231-32.

[76] Mentioned 5 November 1323: Praha, SÚA, AVM, no. 614, and 6 February 1331: ibid., no. 747.

[77] The convent first tried to assassinate Fr Foulques and then deposed him, electing in his place Fr Maurice de Pagnac. John XXII immediately cancelled this election in 1319 eventually appointed Fr Hélion de Villeneuve as new master. Report by Fr Maurice and

and himself appointed for ten years twenty-eight regional officers for the Hospital throughout Europe.[78] For the priory of Bohemia the pope nominated Fr Berthold von Henneberg, the Luxemburg and Wittelsbach partisan. For *Alamania superior* and *inferior* the pope appointed a Habsburg partisan from Swabia, Fr Margrave Hermann von Hachberg.[79] For *Dacia* Fr Eberhard von Kestenberg was appointed, for Hungary the Prior of Rome Fr Filippo de Gragnana. The deposition of Fr Foulques meant that lieutenants like Fr Helfrich von Rüdigheim, Fr Paolo da Modena, and Fr Michael von Tinz lost their function, unless they were reappointed e.g. by the *procurator generalis* and *visitator in partibus cismarinis* Fr Leonardo de Tibertis. Fr Gerhard von Hammerstein continued to administer *Alamania inferior* as lieutenant, but laid special emphasis on his licences from the master and the convent (who had deposed the master) or from Fr Leonardo.[80] A similar case was Fr Paolo da

---

the convent to John XXII, 8 July 1317: S. Riezler (ed.), *Vatikanische Akten zur deutschen Geschichte in der Zeit Kaiser Ludwigs des Bayern* (Innsbruck, 1891), nos 69-70, pp. 51-54; A. Luttrell, 'Notes on Foulques de Villaret, master of the Hospital 1305-1319', reprinted *idem, The Hospitallers of Rhodes*, no. IV, pp. 73-90.

[78] 21 July 1317: *Registres de Jean XXII, Lettres communes*, ed. G. Mollat, 16 vols (Paris, 1904-1947), nos 4450-72, especially no. 4451, Fr Leonardo de Tibertis for the priory of Venice with 4000 fl; no. 4454, Fr Filippo da Gragnana for the two priories of Rome and Hungary with 8000 fl; no. 4457, Fr Pierre de l'Ongle for the priory of Toulouse with 7500 fl; no. 4466, Fr Berthold von Henneberg for the priory of Bohemia, Moravia, *Polonia* and *Austria* with 1000 fl; no. 4467, Fr Eberhard von Kestenberg for the priory of *Dacia*, Sweden and Norway with 100 marks; no. 4468, Fr Hermann von Hachberg for the priory of *Alamania superior et inferior* with 1000 fl. Also Riezler, *Vatikanische Akten*, no. 71/4, p. 54.

[79] Fr Margrave Hermann was a brother of Margrave Heinrich. His brother's son Fr Rudolf was a Hospitaller, too. On behalf of his brother and his son Margrave Heinrich donated the church at Welschensteinbach to the commandery at Freiburg im Breisgau 4 September 1313: *Regesten der Markgrafen von Baden*, 1, no. h 147; *FUB*, 5, no. 200/2, p. 170. Soon Fr Margrave Hermann himself became Commander at Freiburg: 21 July 1315 and 30 December 1316: *Regesten der Markgrafen von Baden*, 1, nos h 153, h 159. Mentioned also 20 June 1315: ibid., 1, no. h 163 commentary.

[80] Lieutenant of the master, 21 March 1316 or 14 March 1317, dependent upon the *stilus annunciationis: Urkunden und Regesten zur Geschichte der Burggrafen von Freiherren von Hammerstein*, ed. E. Freiherr von Hammerstein-Gesmold (Hannover, 1891) no. 277, p. 143; anniversary for Fr Hermann von Mainz in Cologne; 1 June 1317: ibid. no. 279, pp. 143-44, for Cologne. – *Gerens vices in inferioribus partibus Alimanie venerabilis viri summi magistri ordinis beati Johannis baptiste hospitalis Jerosolimitani partium in transmarinarum* [referring probably not to Fr Foulques but to Fr Leonardo], 11 June 1317 ibid., no. 280, p. 144 for Borken. – *Per inferiores partes Alimanie magistri et conventus ultramarini locum tenens*, 17 June 1317: ibid., no. 281, p. 144 for Cologne. – *Gerens vices venerabilis viri fratris ac domini Fulconis de Vilareyt magistri transmarini, ac fratris Leonardi de Tybertis generalis visitatoris*

Modena in Thuringia and adjacent regions where his position was confirmed by the new Master Fr Hélion de Villeneuve (1319-46).[81] Since in the north-east Habsburg loyalties were scarce, Fr Margrave Hermann von Hachberg in *Alamania* had no influence there. Nevertheless, he survived in office as prior for *Alamania* until his death in 1321.[82] Fr Eberhard von Kestenberg faced serious conflict with the kings Erik VIII of Denmark and Hakon VII of Norway who had confiscated Hospitaller properties.[83] In the eastern priory the papal appointment of 1317 was almost thwarted by the barons' rebellion against John of Luxemburg in 1318. John may have been ready to enforce the acceptation of Fr Berthold as prior, whereas the native nobility probably stuck to Fr Michael von Tinz. At the same time the Hospitaller Fr Duke Mieszco of Beuthen (Bytom) challenged the papal appointment of Fr Filippo de Gragnana to the priory of Hungary.[84] When Louis the Bavarian saved his main ally John of

---

ordinis hospitalis beati Johannis Jerosolimitani, 31 October and 18 December 1317: ibid., no. 283, pp. 144-46, with personal seal; 17 December 1317: ibid., no. 284, p. 146. – Lieutenant of the master for *Alamania inferior*, 25 February 1321: ibid., no. 293, p. 149. – Fr Gerhard began and ended his career, as fas as we know, as Commander of Cologne: 17 January 1301: ibid., no. 203, pp. 100-101; 9 November 1336: ibid., no. 373, p. 190. His family had close connections with the Archbishop of Cologne.

[81] 20 July 1317: Roma, Archivio Segreto Vaticano, Reg. Vat. 66, ep. 4120. – 18 October 1317: Wilcke, *Tempelherren*, 2, p. 499. – 23 January 1318: Winterfeld, *Geschichte*, p. 660. – 12 April 1319: NLM Arch. 16, no. 10. – 16 December 1320: Roma, Archivio Segreto Vaticano, Reg. Vat. 71, fol. 75v, ep. 101. – Füßlein, *Berthold VII.*, p. 394 with n. 1.

[82] 12 April 1321 according to tombstone in the church of the commandery Freiburg im Breisgau destroyed in 1677, as recorded in a list of anniversaries in 1607: *Regesten der Markgrafen von Baden*, 1, no. h 163. – *Meister* for *Alamania superior*, 7 February 1318: *Regesten der Markgrafen von Baden*, 1, nos h 160, h 600; Preceptor General for *Alamania superior*, Freiburg 8 June 1318: *Quellen zur Entstehung der Schweizerischen Eidgenossenschaft*, 2/1, no. 931, pp. 473-74; lieutenant of the master for *Alamania*, St Urban 3 August 1319: ibid., 2/1, no. 994, pp. 513-14; with the Commander of Rheinfelden Fr Martin von Randegg as his lieutenant; *Hochmeister in deutschen Landen*, 13 February 1321: *Regesten der Markgrafen von Baden*, 1, no. h 162.

[83] John XXII to the kings of Denmark and Norway, Avignon 4 September 1320: *Registres de Jean XXII, Lettres communes*, nos 12002-03. Delaville, *Hospitaliers à Rhodes*, p. 70.

[84] John XXII to the Archbishop of Gran and to King Charles of Ungary, Avignon 10 March and 23 May 1318: *Registres de Jean XXII, Lettres communes*, nos 6549, 7284. Two brothers of Fr Mieszco governed the duchies of Cosel (Koźle) and Beuthen (Bytom), a third brother Boleslas became Archbishop of Gran in 1321; in 1322 Fr Mieszco is mentioned without office, whereas the Prior of Rome Fr Filippo da Gragnana had as his Vice Prior in Hungary Fr Gherardo da Gragnana. Delaville, *Hospitaliers à Rhodes*, pp. 71-72.

Luxemburg by mediating a compromise, the fate of the Bohemian priory was left open. Fr Berthold von Henneberg maintained his title but stayed on in Franconia. Only in 1319 did he briefly return to Bohemia.[85]

The decisive victory at Mühldorf on 28 September 1322 by Louis the Bavarian had important repercussions for the Hospitallers, because Louis immediately began a Wittelsbach expansion towards Brandenburg and Italy. By enfeoffing Brandenburg to his son, Louis estranged John of Luxemburg. By intervening in Italy, Louis sparked off open conflict with John XXII. Nevertheless, after the defeat of Frederick the Fair at Mühldorf no Habsburg partisan was possible as successor to the late Fr Margrave Hermann von Hachberg in the priory of *Alamania*. Before Mühldorf, the Master Fr Hélion de Villeneuve had appointed Fr count Albrecht von Schwarzburg, a relative of the Henneberg family and partisan of Louis and John, to be Prior for *Alamania* and visitor for Bohemia and *Dacia*. A few weeks after Mühldorf five pro-Habsburg commanders asked the master to recall Fr Paolo da Modena, whose administration had been ineffective because he had no local connections, and to nominate Fr Albrecht von Schwarzburg Preceptor for Thuringia, Saxony, and the Mark.[86] For Fr Albrecht von Schwarzburg a former lieutenant of Fr Paolo, Fr Gebhard von Bortfeld, acted as regional officer; he came from Brunswick, and his local duke was one of the first and staunchest Wittelsbach partisans in the Brandenburg question.[87] Meanwhile, Fr Albrecht was sent by Louis the Bavarian to Avignon in November 1323 to negotiate with John XXII.[88] Fr Paolo accompanied him and stayed

---

[85] 1319: Pflugk-Harttung, *Der Johanniter- und der Deutsche Orden*, nos 19-20, p. 212; Füßlein, *Berthold VII.*, p. 123 n. 1. On the internal situation in Bohemia Seibt, *Handbuch*, pp. 362-63; F. Palacky, *Geschichte von Böhmen*, vol. 2/2 (Prague, 1844-1867; reprinted Osnabrück 1968), pp. 109, 130-33; A. Gerlich, 'König Johann von Böhmen: Aspekte luxemburgischer Reichspolitik von 1310 bis 1346', *Geschichtliche Landeskunde* 9 (1973) 131-46, at pp. 133-34.

[86] 12 January 1323: NLM Arch. 16, no. 15. Fr Albrecht was thought fit for the office, because *infra terminos eiusdem preceptorie idem dominus frater Albertus de clariori sanguine principum, comitum ac nobilium traxerit originem, qui hodierno tempore dictas partes dominio regunt et potencia defendunt*. Fr Paolo was considered unfit, because *est in ipsis partibus inpotens et extraneus quoad amicos defensivos*.

[87] Pflugk-Harttung, *Anfänge*, pp. 18-23; Delaville, *Hospitaliers à Rhodes*, p. 75 with n. 1 and 2; Füßlein, *Berthold VII.*, p. 394 with n. 1, as the first Herrenmeister. On the regional alliances J. Schultze, *Die Mark Brandenburg*, vol. 2 (Berlin, 1961) pp. 26-27, 31-33; H. Assing, *Brandenburgische Geschichte*, eds I. Materna, W. Ribbe (Berlin, 1995), pp. 132-40. Berthold [VII] von Henneberg was named tutor and regent for the new Margrave of Brandenburg.

[88] Louis to John XXII, Nuremberg 12 November 1323: *Monumenta Germaniae Historica, Constitutiones*, 5, ed. J. Schwalm (Hannover, 1909-1911), no. 817, pp. 633-34. –

on at the papal curia,[89] whilst Fr Albrecht returned to Louis the Bavarian and did not leave him despite papal excommunication, interdict, and deposition. On the contrary, in September 1325 Fr Count Albrecht even went on an embassy on behalf of Louis to King Frederick of Sicily.[90] The alliance he was to negotiate was clearly directed against John XXII. Only after the death of Fr Albrecht,[91] did the papal curia secure the appointment of a Habsburg partisan, Fr Rudolf von Masmünster, as next Prior for *Alamania*. Fr Rudolf used his Swabian connections for intrigue on behalf of the pro-papal Bishop of Straßburg and sent intelligence to Avignon, with the express intention of being recommended to the master by the pope.[92] From 1328 to 1330 John XXII himself sent the

---

Avignon 7 January 1324: ibid., no. 839, pp. 661-62. – Avignon 9 and 13 January 1324: ibid., no. 840, pp. 663-64; Riezler, *Vatikan. Akten*, nos 342A and 345; *Regesten der Erzbischöfe von Mainz von 1289-1396*, vol. 1/1, nos 2501-02. – Avignon 23 March 1324: *Monumenta Germaniae Historica, Constitutiones*, 5, nos 881, 928, 944, pp. 692-99, 766-68, 779-88. – *Tunc magnus preceptor* for *Alamania*, Avignon 3 April 1327: *Monumenta Germaniae Historica, Constitutiones*, 6, 1, ed. J. Schwalm (Hannover, 1914-1927), no. 273, pp. 178-184. Fr Albrecht was accompanied to Avignon by *magister* Ernst von Seebach, Archdeacon of Würzburg, and by *magister Henricus de Throno*, canon of Prague. A. Schütz, 'Die Appellationen Ludwigs des Bayern aus den Jahren 1323/24', *Mitteilungen des Instituts für österreichische Geschichtsforschung* 80 (1972) 71-112 on the negotiations.

[89] 31 July 1324: Rome, Archivio Segreto Vaticano, Reg. Vat. 79, ep. 1888; Delaville, *Hospitaliers à Rhodes*, p. 73 n. 4.

[90] Munich 6 September 1325: *Monumenta Germaniae Historica, Constitutiones*, 6, no. 111, p. 78. Louis calls Fr Albrecht *preceptor* for *Alamania, amicus noster, secretarius noster dilectus*. – Messina 17 March 1326: ibid., no. 161, pp. 112-14. The treaty was concluded in the Hospitaller hospital at Messina. Among the witnesses was a Hospitaller, the Commander of Regensburg Fr Johannes de Spyra. – Ibid., no. 206, pp. 138-39, n. 1, a letter by Marino Sanudo informing a cardinal that he had met Fr Albrecht, *meus amicus intimus et dominus longo tempore tam Rodi quam in curia Romana Avinione*, on his return from Sicily in Venice.

[91] Fr Albrecht died 16 March 1327 and was buried in the commandery at Würzburg: *Die Würzburger Inschriften bis 1525*, eds K. Borchardt, F.-X. Herrmann. Die Deutschen Inschriften 27 (Wiesbaden, 1988), p. 34 no. 50†. Füßlein, *Berthold VII.*, pp. 392-93. Freiburg and Würzburg, 2 January and 2 June 1325: *FUB*, 2, nos 135, 137, pp. 91-92, *groz gebider vber mer, meister zu Deutschemelande*; 5 January 1328 [?]: Rome, Archivio Segreto Vaticano, Reg. Vat. 114, fol. 65r, ep. 1640.

[92] Mentioned as prior, 8 June 1328: *Urkunden und Regesten zur Geschichte der Burggrafen von Freiherren von Hammerstein*, no. 322, pp. 164-65; 18 June, 21 July, 17 September 1330: ibid., nos 334, 336, pp. 169-72; 15 August 1329: *RB*, 6, p. 302. His lieutenant for *Alamania inferior* was Fr Heinrich von Selbach. – On Straßburg, Avignon 21 January 1330: Riezler, *Vatikanische Akten*, no. 1256, p. 439. – Reports from Germany and recommendation to the master, Avignon 2 July 1330: ibid., no. 1342, pp. 468-69.

Hospitaller Prior of Toulouse, Fr Pierre de l'Ongle, to Germany with the task of winning over the electors and other princes to proclaim and accept a new King of the Romans.[93] Unfortunately, Fr Pierre was charged at the same time to sent to Avignon a huge amount of money due to the apostolic chamber from vacant benefices that Fr Gerhard von Bortfeld had collected,[94] a claim that certainly induced Fr Gerhard to back Louis the Bavarian. The mission of Fr Pierre de l'Ongle failed also with its main objective, the new royal election in the empire. Habsburg was now allied with Louis and kept this alliance even after the death of Frederick the Fair. So the Luxemburg family, Balduin of Treves, and John of Bohemia, had the keys for a new election in their hands. Balduin stayed with Louis because John XXII did not allow Balduin to unite Treves and Mainz after the death of the Mainz Archbishop Matthias von Buchegg.

The fact that John of Bohemia reluctantly followed his uncle decided the future of the eastern priory. Although Fr Berthold von Henneberg maintained his claims to the priory of Bohemia until his death on 21 August 1330,[95] the Bohemian nobility prevented him from returning to Bohemia. Since his family supported Louis the Bavarian, he also lost the favour of King John after 1323. When Louis the Bavarian was reconciled with his Habsburg cousin and rival Frederick the Fair, Fr Berthold was able to appear in *Austria* and Moravia in 1326.[96] In the Luxemburg territories Bohemia, Moravia, and *Polonia*, however, King John and the native nobility rallied behind Fr Michael von Tinz, the lieutenant of 1317, who was now made prior.[97] It was for the first time for

---

[93] 21 March 1328: E. E. Stengel (ed.), *Nova Alamanniae*, vol. 1/1 (Berlin, 1921), no. 187, p. 104. – 1 May 1328: ibid., no. 192, pp. 108-10. – 7 May 1328: ibid., no. 193, p. 110. – 14 July 1328: ibid., no. 199, p. 112. – 11 November 1328: Riezler, *Vatikanische Akten*, no. 1094, pp. 401-02. – Bonn 4 December 1328: Stengel, *Nova Alamanniae*, 1/1, no. 207, pp. 114-16. – 21 December 1328: Riezler, *Vatikanische Akten*, no. 1104, p. 404. – 4 April 1329: ibid., no. 1160, p. 417. – 2 June 1329: ibid., no. 1175, p. 421. – 21 July 1329: ibid., no. 1187, p. 423. – 22 April 1330: ibid., no. 1303, pp. 455-56. – 2 August 1330: ibid., no. 1370, p. 477. See Pflugk-Harttung, *Der Johanniter- und der Deutsche Orden*, pp. 254, 258; Delaville, *Hospitaliers à Rhodes*, pp. 74-75 with n. 3.

[94] Avignon 27 March 1329: Riezler, *Vatikanische Akten*, nos 1154-55, p. 416, calling for 953 marks. – Avignon 27 February 1330: ibid., no. 1275, p. 449, calling for 950 marks.

[95] Fr Berthold was buried in the commandery at Würzburg like his cousin Fr Albrecht von Schwarzburg: *Würzburger Inschriften*, no. 54, pp. 36-37 and photograph no. 30.

[96] *Perchtolt von Hennberch, maister zu Mawerperg* (Mailberg) for [Horní] Kounice, 1 February 1326: *RBM*, 3, no. 1179, pp. 458-59.

[97] Prior *per Boemiam, Poloniam, Austriam, Morauiam, Stiriam et Carinthiam*, 21 March 1325: *RBM*, 3, no. 1053, pp. 405-06; Tinz 28 October 1329: Praha, SÚA, AVM, no. 615; *per Boemiam, Austriam et Poloniam prior generalis*, Glatz 19 October 1331:

almost seventy years that a native took over the priory of Bohemia, Moravia, *Polonia* and *Austria*. The Luxemburg co-operation with the Czech nobility, grudgingly begun by King John († 1346) and willingly continued by his son Charles IV († 1378), dealt the final blow to the Hospitallers from Germany in Bohemia. In the autumn of 1330 the chapter general at Montpellier appointed the Prior of *Alamania* Fr Rudolf von Masmünster to hold the priory of Bohemia, as well, certainly in recognition for his pro-papal efforts in Swabia. As experts for central Europe, the Prior of Toulouse Fr Pierre de l'Ongle and the Prior of Venice Fr Leonardo de Tibertis were present at Montpellier. The former was rewarded with the priories St-Gilles and Provence, the latter with the priory of England. Fr Helfrich von Rüdigheim was nominated to the priory of *Dacia* and Norway. The chapter general expected more money to come from Bohemia than from *Alamania*, whereas in 1317 John XXII had expected the same amount from both priories.[98] Obviously trouble was feared in *Alamania*.[99] Cautiously, the chapter general did not appoint a new Preceptor General for Saxony, the Mark, and *Slavia* so that Fr Gerhard von Bortfeld and his Brunswick patron might still be turned against the Wittelsbach party. Both the appointment of Fr Rudolf von Masmünster for Bohemia and the huge amount of money expected from Bohemia reveal the hopes the pope and the chapter general set upon the anti-Wittelsbach King John. Neither the pope nor the order were aware of the impossibility for John to estrange his native aristocracy by intruding a foreign prior and to wage war on behalf of the papacy at the same time. Despite his backing by both the pope and the order, Fr Rudolf von Masmünster did not win Bohemia. Even when King John came to open warfare with the Louis the Bavarian and the Habsburg family, the Prior of Bohemia continued to be a native noble. The master and the convent had to respect the situation in the empire where Louis the Bavarian united with Luxemburg and Habsburg against Benedict XII. So the master and the convent nominated the

---

ibid. no. 616; *prior per Bohemiam*, Klein Oels 29 November 1331: ibid. no. 754; *prior per prioratum Bohemie*, Tinz 24 April 1334: ibid. no. 618. Delaville, *Hospitaliers à Rhodes*, pp. 70-71.

[98] *Alamania cum Thuringia* first 1360 fl and then annually 680 fl, Saxony, the Mark, and *Slavia* first 640 fl and then annually 320 fl, Bohemia first 2400 fl and then annually 1200 fl, *Dacia* and Norway 100 marks. 1317: 1000 fl Bohemia, 1000 fl *Alamania superior et inferior*, 100 marks *Dacia*, Sweden and Norway. C. L. Tipton, 'The 1330 Chapter General of the Knights Hospitallers at Montpellier', *Traditio* 24 (1968) 293-308, edition at pp. 301-8.

[99] As early as 5 September 1322 John XXII had asked Louis the Bavarian and other temporal lords in Germany not to exact military help at the expense of the Hospitallers: Riezler, *Vatikanische Akten*, no. 293, p. 151.

Commander of Würzburg and Biebelried Fr Berthold [XI] von Henneberg, nephew of the late Fr Berthold [VI] von Henneberg, as *locum tenens magistri et conventus per Alemaniam et Saxoniam* or in German simply *sant Johannis ordens meyster zu Teutzschen landen*. Regional lieutenants of Fr Berthold [XI] were accepted throughout the western priory[100] but not in the eastern priory. Instead, master and convent allowed Fr Michael von Tinz to be succeeded by Fr Gallus von Lemberg, from one of the leading families in the Czech aristocracy.[101]

Owing to the scarcity of our sources, many reconstructions suggested in this paper must remain hypothetical and many questions await further detailed study. Apparently, the office of Grand Preceptor for central Europe was created during the struggle between the Staufen family and the papacy in the late 1240s. With more or less success the high-ranking Hospitaller officers were then used both by the Bohemian kings Přemysl Otakar and Wenceslas II and by the Roman kings Rudolf von Habsburg and Adolf von Nassau for their political plans. Přemysl Otakar failed to secure his election as King of the Romans despite his Swabian friends Fr Heinrich von Fürstenberg and Fr Heinrich von Boxberg. Rudolf von Habsburg failed to gain control over the order with the help of his skilled diplomat Fr Berengar von Laufen. The order saw the danger in the Aarburg case and used the accession of Wenceslas II to counter-balance Rudolf von Habsburg and Fr Berengar von Laufen. Rudolf's successor Adolf von Nassau was not saved by the diplomacy of Fr Gottfried von Klingenfels. Wenceslas II in his turn used Fr Friedrich and Fr Heinrich von Kindhausen as well as Fr Hermann von Hohenlohe for his contacts with Mainz and as counsellors within his realm. The failure to build strong monarchies both in the empire and in Bohemia 1306 and 1308 left the Hospitallers free to try and acquire castles and estates. This, however, drew them into local quarrels. When the growing territorialization threatened the supply of men and money, the master and the convent sent lieutenants, especially after 1312, to secure the Templar heritage. These lieutenants had to cope with various instances of local resistance. In the Bohemian realm the native aristocracy prevented the appointment of foreigners either by their own king, thus expelling Fr Berthold von Henneberg, or by the order, thus preventing Fr Rudolf von Masmünster from winning the Bohemian priory. It was only under the native kings Přemysl

---

[100] Lieutenant of the master and the convent on Rhodes for *Alamania* and Saxony, 14 April 1336: StAW WU 7876; *RB*, 7, p. 145. Füßlein, *Berthold VII.*, pp. 127-31; Thomas, *Johanniterkomture Mainfranken*, pp. 41-42.

[101] Delaville, *Hospitaliers à Rhodes*, p. 71 with n. 5.

Otakar II and Wenceslas II that Hospitallers from abroad could serve as royal counsellors; under John of Luxemburg and his successors resistance in the country was too strong. Foreign counsellors were indispensable for building an effective, centralized monarchy. To hail or deplore the failure of German Hospitallers in Bohemia in terms of modern nationalism would be somewhat anachronistic. Two general points of this survey may be remembered for comparison with other countries or other orders. The Hospitallers reacted flexibly to political changes by regrouping their regional divisions and by appointing new officials. Secondly, the local Hospitallers changed their interest from the Levant to their native countries. The first point may be true for all orders that had a central administration and certainly deserves further study. The second point is connected with the decline of the crusades and therefore primarily affects the military orders.

13

King Wenceslas and the Dissolution of the
Teutonic Order's Bohemian Bailiwick

Libor Jan

By the last two decades of the fourteenth century, the inner stability which had characterized the states of the Bohemian crown under the reign of the Emperor-King Charles IV had disappeared. The Bohemian aristocracy, in pursuit of their own interests, rose up against the less able Wenceslas IV, Charles's son and heir, with the support of Wenceslas's younger brother Sigismund and his cousin Jost. Thus it is not surprising that Wenceslas twice found himself in captivity, first in 1394 thanks to the Bohemian lords and Jost and once more in 1403 at the hand of his brother Sigismund. In Moravia a war was raging between the elder Jost, the margrave and actual master of the land, and Prokop, who since the death of Wenceslas's brother John of Görlitz had become the former's most important supporter. Many members of the aristocracy took advantage of and even encouraged the state of anarchy which was spreading throughout the land, and armed force soon came to carry more weight than due process of law.[1]

At the end of the eighties and the beginning of the nineties King Wenceslas refrained from intervention in the empire. The Polish-Lithuanian union of 1386 had changed the face of the map, and the Teutonic Order, traditionally a rival of both states, was consequently thrown onto the defensive. Wenceslas's father, Emperor Charles IV, had failed to establish a clear and unambiguous

---

[1] F. M. Bartoš, *Čechy v době Husově*. České dějiny II 6 (Prague, 1947); J. Spěváček, *Václav IV. 1361-1419. K předpokladům husitské revoluce* (Prague, 1986); V. Štěpán, 'Osobnost Lacka z Kravař', *Časopis Matice moravské* 110 (1991) 217-38, 112 (1993) 11-41. English translation of the German version of this paper by Edith Pawlik.

From *Mendicants, Military Orders, and Regionalism in Medieval Europe*, ed. Jürgen Sarnowsky. Copyright © 1999 by Jürgen Sarnowsky. Published by Ashgate Publishing Ltd, Gower House, Croft Road, Aldershot, Hampshire, GU11 3HR, Great Britain.

relationship with the Teutonic Order.[2] As with the father, one would suspect an
analogous policy on the part of the son: King Wenceslas might pursue different
political goals in his dealings with the various branches of the order in the
empire, Prussia, Livonia, and the bailiwick of Bohemia-Moravia which belonged to the grand master's chamber, but one would not expect the relationships themselves to become fundamentally more complicated.

   The king's attitude towards the order began to change in the nineties. The
order's refusal to buy the Nova Marchia of Brandenburg, which was offered to
Grand Master Zöllner in 1390 not by the king himself but by his brother, John
of Görlitz,[3] likely played a role, but it was the dispute over the appointment to
the archdiocese of Riga which led to the decisive change in Wenceslas's policy
towards the order. Following the resignation of Archbishop John of Sinten,
King Wenceslas had his candidate, Otto, son of Svątibor, Duke of Stettin,
elected archbishop by the cathedral chapter at Riga, a number of whose members had fled to Prague. Otto, however, was unable to compete with the order's
candidate, John of Wallenrode, a relative of the now-deceased Grand Master
Konrad von Wallenrode. That same year, Pope Boniface IX incorporated the
Riga cathedral chapter into the Teutonic Order. In the two years which followed, and with the help of King Wenceslas, Otto prepared for the conquest, by
force if necessary, of the archdiocese of Riga.[4] Some chroniclers link this crisis
to a report that King Wenceslas temporarily confiscated the order's lands in
Bohemia and Moravia, gave some of them to his own partisans, and evicted all
the brethren from the lands.[5] Although it is impossible either to confirm or
entirely to dismiss this account of events, it seems clear that the dispute over

---

[2] M. Hellmann, 'Karl IV. und der Deutsche Orden in den Jahren 1346-1360', *Folia
diplomatica* 1 (1971) 103-12; U. Arnold, 'Preußen, Böhmen und das Reich – Karl IV.
und der Deutsche Orden', *Kaiser Karl IV. Staatsmann und Mäzen*, ed. F. Seibt (Munich, 1978), pp. 167-73; B. Jähnig, 'Der Deutsche Orden und Karl IV.', *Kaiser Karl IV.
1316-1378. Forschungen über Kaiser und Reich*, ed. H. Patze (Göttingen, 1978), pp.
103-49.

[3] H. Vetter, *Die Beziehungen Wenzels zum Deutschen Orden von 1381 bis 1411*. (Ph.D.
Diss., Halle, 1912), p. 15; J. Hemmerle, *Die Deutschordensballei Böhmen in ihren
Rechnungsbüchern 1382-1411*. QStGDO 22 (Bonn, 1967), p. 24; Z. H. Nowak, *Polity-
ka pólnocna Zygmunta Luksemburskiego do roku 1411* (Toruń, 1964), p. 50.

[4] B. Jähnig, *Johann von Wallenrode O.T.* QStGDO 24 (Bonn-Godesberg, 1970), pp. 10-
32.

[5] Hemmerle, p. 22; J. Voigt, 'Geschichte der Ballei des Deutschen Ordens in Böhmen',
Denkschriften der kaiserlichen Akademie der Wissenschaften. Phil.-hist. Klasse 12
(Vienna, 1862), p. 101.

the archdiocese of Riga led to considerable deterioration in king Wenceslas's relations with the Teutonic Order.

The Land Commander of the bailiwick of Bohemia-Moravia since 1393, Albrecht of Dubá, was a member of an influential northern Bohemian family of noble descent and a man of restless nature and unbounded ambition. Shortly after 1393, he initiated an armed conflict with the Margrave of Meissen from his base in Komotau (Chomutov). In 1396 and 1397 he granted the townsmen of Komotau, from whom he regularly borrowed money, a number of important privileges, including the right to create their own seals, and approved the construction of a town hall and a salt storage chamber, both of which had been completed beforehand.[6] It cannot be ruled out that the commander of the bailiwick's feuds in northern Bohemia, the strategic situation, and the economic potential of the city of Komotau combined to induce King Wenceslas to consider confiscating the commandery, including the fortresses at Platten (Blatno) and Neustein, the city, and the entire dominion. The grand master, informed of Wenceslas's intentions, sent word to the commander of the bailiwick that he should allow the king to take the city by force rather than give it up voluntarily. He also warned the superior of the bailiwick against signing the order's lands over to the king as payment for increased tax demands, as the situation might repeat itself in the following years. 'In this way, the bailiwick will in time be destroyed', concluded Grand Master Konrad von Jungingen on a realistic as well as prophetic note. Nonetheless, neither the Komotau commandery nor any of the order's other houses were confiscated at that time.[7]

At the end of the fourteenth century two other worldly powers, Přemek, Duke of Troppau, and Jost, Margrave of Moravia, attacked the order's lands and demonstrated what little protection either the church or the law could provide for the conflict-ridden country. Sometime in the second half of the year 1394,[8] Duke Přemek made a raid on the commandery of Troppau, destroyed the convent, its walls, and a mill, drove Commander Wenceslas of Deutschbrod and the brethren out of the city, and occupied three order villages near Leobschütz (Glubcyce). On 26 June 1398, Henry, Abbot of the Schottenkloster in Vienna and the order's conservator, along with other judges, demanded that the duke return the occupied lands and compensate the order for all damages and lost

---

[6] M. Millauer, *Der deutsche Ritterorden in Böhmen* (Prague, 1832), nos 29, 30, pp. 165-71; Hemmerle, pp. 25-26.

[7] Voigt, p. 103; Hemmerle, p. 26.

[8] In Pettenegg (see following n.), the letter in case is wrongly dated 14 June 1391.

income. Přemek, who lay claims to the before-mentioned manors, was bothered little by the ruling; hypocritically, he expressed to the grand master his desire to return those properties for whose ownership the order could provide legally valid testimony. Grand Master Konrad von Jungingen, unable to grasp the facts of the situation, instructed the commander of the bailiwick, Albrecht of Dubá, to end the dispute in accordance with the duke's suggestion so that the order might maintain its rights.[9]

It appears certain that by 1402 the commandery was once again in the hands of the order. Duke Přemek nonetheless remained in the order's debt for 520 *schock* and 40 (Prague) *groschen* for eight years' accrued interest and 252 *gulden* in costs to the commander of the bailiwick for the dispute, including 200 *gulden* for the order's proctor at the Roman curia.[10] A still more annoying mishap occurred for the order when Margrave Jost occupied the commandery of Austerlitz, the richest in Moravia. A letter written in 1397, in which the grand master, in a humble if not humiliating tone, appeals to the margrave for the return of the house of the order, as well as the city of Austerlitz and four nearby financially attractive villages, attests to the loss of the commandery. Jost had in all probability occupied the city of Austerlitz some time before, perhaps as early as the spring of 1393, in connection with the outbreak of a new series of struggles with his brother Prokop. It appears that strategic considerations, as well as mere greed, played a role in precipitating the margrave's act of aggression. Only after repeated efforts on the part of the new commander of the bailiwick Ulrich of Ústí, his brother John, and other aristocratic friends, was the commandery won back, reputedly in 1406, though in a devastated condition. Nonetheless, the order was able to retain the church patronage of Austerlitz even during occupation.[11] Albrecht of Dubá's position as the head of the bailiwick of Bohemia-Moravia had become untenable even before 1402; in the early months of that year he was relieved of his duties by the grand master and called to Prussia.[12] Only after the new commander of the bailiwick, Ulrich of

---

[9] E.G. v. Pettenegg, *Die Urkunden des Deutsch-Ordens-Centralarchives zu Wien*, vol.I (Prague-Leipzig, 1887), no. 1588, pp. 414-15; M. Wihoda, 'Stagnace a úpadek řádu německých rytířů na Opavsku ve 14. a na počátku 15. století', *Časopis Slezského zemského muzea* B 41 (1992) 203-04; Voigt, p. 104; Hemmerle, p. 26.

[10] Hemmerle, nos 197-98, 213, 222.

[11] Hemmerle, nos 173-74, 218, 221, 225, 315, 317; Voigt, pp. 102-03; L. Jan, 'Slavkov u Brna ve 14. a na začátku 15. století – rozmach a úpadek komendy řádu německých rytířů', *Časopis Matice moravské* 109 (1990) 54-55.

[12] Voigt, pp. 110-11; Hemmerle, p. 26.

Ústí, had assumed his position and the direction of the Komotau commandery did he realize that his predecessor had left behind 924 *schock groschen* in debt, including 446 *schock* and 5 *groschen* owed to local traders and workmen for goods which had been received but as yet not paid for.[13] Ulrich of Ústí established new account books, made efforts to correct mismanagement of the bailiwick's estates, and began to pay back the debt. In 1403 the commander was dealt a bad blow: on 9 June, Sigismund, King of Hungary, who was holding his brother Wenceslas prisoner in Vienna and had named himself Regent of Bohemia, ordered the commander to pay a *berna* (tax on property) for the amount of 400 marks within the next six weeks.[14] This *berna* (or *berna specialis*) was also required of other orders established by Bohemian rulers and royal cities. Apparently, this was double the usual sum required; according to *berna* schedules of the years 1418 and 1471, the bailiwick was obliged to remit only 200 *schock groschen*.[15] The commander of the bailiwick managed with great difficulty to collect the sum required in the following weeks by resorting to borrowing from Christians and Jews and collecting debts from the dependent population. In any case, he apparently gave the money to Ulrich of Neuhaus or Bernhard Schwarz, royal chancellor and Sigismund's representative, since the king himself had left the country.[16] After King Wenceslas had returned from captivity in the final months of 1403, he called together the representatives of the aristocracy, the orders, and the towns in order to secure their support. On this occasion he announced a *berna* of the same amount as Sigismund. Ulrich of Ústí was faced with a predicament and had no alternative but to lease the commandery of Miletín in north-eastern Bohemia to John Krušina of Lichtenburg, a loyal supporter of the king, for the amount of 700 *schock groschen* for life. Krušina, the king's steward and the highest-ranking burgrave of Prague, submitted only 212 *schock* of the agreed-upon sum as an advance on the *berna*. Not until 17 January 1404 was the estate handed over to Krušina.[17]

In May 1404, the king commanded the order to hand over its fortress at Platten, in the northern part of the Komotau dominion, to his officials, but the commander of the bailiwick was able to prevent this. Already in 1403, former

---

[13] Hemmerle, nos 131-32, 196-97.

[14] Ibid., nos 139, 159.

[15] *Codex iuris municipalis*, vol. 2, ed. J. Čelakovský (Prague, 1895), p. 901; K. Krofta, 'Začátky české berně', *Český časopis historický* 36 (1930) 471-76.

[16] Hemmerle, p. 162.

[17] Ibid., nos 139, 164-66, 263; Bartoš, pp. 218-19; Spěváček, pp. 346, 351-52.

Land Commander Albrecht of Dubá had, with the help of countless relatives and King Sigismund, forced his return to Bohemia. At that time he was commander of the same fortress at Platten which the king was the following year to demand. Before long, he was up to his old tricks, having begun, this time with the help of the villagers and retainers of Komotau, a series of raids in the margravate of Meissen. The grand master was forced to apologize to the margrave. Following this episode, on 17 February 1404, the commander of the bailiwick dismissed Albrecht of Dubá from his position as commander at Platten[18] and temporarily took the direction of the commanderies of Komotau and Býčkovice into his own hands. In the following year, he was able to buy back the village of Pesvitz in the Komotau dominion from the brothers Haugwitz, to whose father it had been pawned, for the sum of 190 *schock groschen*.[19]

The tax burden of the bailiwick of Bohemia-Moravia declined in the following years. Thus, a *berna* of 400 *schock* was required in 1406, and in 1410 *czwo summen berrn*. Of particular interest is the distribution of taxes among the various houses of the order. In 1406 114 *schock* had to be paid by the city of Komotau, while 40 *schock* were assigned to the commandery of Drobovice in each of the years 1408 and 1409. According to a regulation of the year 1402, the commandery of Komotau was required to contribute two-thirds of 100 marks to the tax, i.e., 71 *schock*, 6 *groschen* and 8 *heller*. The remaining third (35½ *schock*, 3 *groschen*, 4 *heller*) was divided between the commandery of Drobovice, which was assigned two parts (23½ *schock*, 12 *groschen*, 4 *heller*) and that of Řepín, which bore the remaining part (11½ *schock*, 21 *groschen*, 2 *heller*).[20] From the commanderies in Moravia, not including those in Troppau and in Jägerndorf, the commander of the bailiwick paid the margrave 163 marks *margrafengabe* in 1383.[21]

Albrecht of Dubá was not the only one with whom the commander of the bailiwick had problems in the second half of the first decade of the fifteenth century. A young brother of the order from Bohemia by the name of John of Egerberg (also known as of Pětipes, or Fünfhunden), whom Ulrich of Ústí had brought back from Prussia and appointed Vice-Commander of Komotau, was a further cause of concern. This high-living knight was careless with the order's funds, also began to launch warlike confrontations with Meissen from his base

---

[18] Voigt, pp. 111-13; Hemmerle, nos 267, 281, p. 27.

[19] Voigt, pp. 109, 119-20; Hemmerle, nos 131, 134, 171, 169-70, 309, 324.

[20] Hemmerle, nos 46, 149, 181-82, 192c, 194, 402-03.

[21] Ibid., no. 46.

in the region of the commandery of Komotau, and was generally damaging to the land commander's standing with King Wenceslas. At the end of 1408 the commander of the bailiwick relegated Egerberg to a position as commander in Hostěradice in southern Moravia, from where the troublemaker complained in writing of the unfair treatment accorded him by Ulrich of Ústí. The northern Bohemian cities, grateful for Egerberg's contribution to their defence during an attack by Meissen, took his side. Nonetheless, Egerberg was sent back to Prussia in May 1409,[22] after he had come into conflict with John of Lipá, whom the land commander was not keen on provoking due to his influence with the margrave of Moravia. By that time he had succeeded in plunging the commandery at Hostěradice deep into debt.

Taxes, in some cases financial mismanagement, and damages incurred in the course of armed conflict, as well as the high level of expense involved in the direction of the bailiwick forced the commander of the bailiwick to lease the commandery of Býčkovice near Leitmeritz to Hereš of Vrutice, a brother of Markold, the former Prior of the Order of the Knights of St John and a favourite of the king, who had been murdered in 1397. The painstakingly-negotiated terms of the agreement specified the lease of the commandery to Hereš for a period of six years at 70 *schock groschen* per year effective from 4 April 1409 and was approved by the king on 30 May of the same year, for which the royal chancellery received a tax of 3 *schock* 4 *groschen*, not 111 *schock*, as maintained by Josef Hemmerle.[23] Similar circumstances forced the commander of the bailiwick Ulrich of Ústí to lease the commandery of Miletín, which had reverted to the order as a result of the death of John Krušina of Lichtenburg in 1407 and was in any case in debt, to another of the king's favourites, the Chamberlain Beneš of Choustník and his wife, for life in exchange for the sum of 850 *schock groschen* and a yearly payment of 10 *schock* to the local priest.[24]

Before the battle near Tannenberg, the Bohemian lands had become a mercenary recruiting ground for both the order and Poland.[25] At that time King

---

[22] Ibid., nos 139, 164-66, 263; Bartoš, pp. 218-19; Spěváček, pp.346, 351-52.

[23] Hemmerle, no. 392, p.29; Voigt, pp. 120, 143-46.

[24] Millauer, pp. 175-82; Voigt, p. 120; Hemmerle, pp. 30, 82.

[25] E. Barborová, 'Češi a Moravané jako účastníci válek Polska s řádem německých rytířů v letech 1410 a 1414', *Sborník Matice moravské* 86 (1967) 191-201; V. Štěpán, 'Nové materiály k vývoji česko-polských vztahů počátkem 15. století', *Časopis Slezského muzea* B 30 (1981) 85-95; *idem*, 'Účast žoldnéřů z českých zemí (zejména Slezska a severní Moravy) ve "velké válce 1409-1411" zachycená prameny z velmistrovského archivu řádu německých rytířů', *Časopis Slezského muzea* B 39 (1990) 1-15.

Wenceslas co-operated with his brother Sigismund in supporting the Teutonic
Order. His verdict of 15 February 1410 in the Samaiten case in favour of the
order is further testimony to his stance.[26] After the battle, the order continued
to seek King Wenceslas's support, financial as well as otherwise. But it was the
order that ended up paying. Since he had failed to repay old debts by January
1411, Commander Czachwitz was forced to hand over the key commandery of
Austerlitz in Moravia to Wenceslas Hase from Brno, a creditor of the king, on
6 March 1411 shortly after the death of Margrave Jost.[27] On 20 September, the
land commander transferred the commandery of Drobovice to the possession of
two of the king's proxies, one of whom was the royal cupbearer Dietrich Kraa.
The commandery of Komotau was surrendered on 21 September to the armoury
captain of the Bohemian king, Stefan of Koberzheim, who in the following
year occupied the fortress at Platten as well.[28] Thus the economic strength of
the bailiwick had been severely undercut. Efforts to win back the commanderies in the following years were unsuccessful.[29] The fatal blow was dealt the
order's bailiwick at the beginning of the twenties by King Sigismund, who
distributed the lands which had been seized under Wenceslas to the nobility
with whom he was in league as security for his debts. The commandery of
Komotau was pawned to Botho of Ilburg in 1420, afterwards to Wilhelm of
Hasenburg, and finally to Jakub of Vřesovice in 1437, Drobovice to the Royal
Mintmaster Mikeš Divóček of Jemniště in 1422 and to Georg of Dubá in 1436,
Býčkovice to Sigismund of Wartenberg in 1422 and to Henning of Waldstein
in 1437, Řepín to Thobias of Harasov and Jakub of Maršov in 1426, and Aus-
terlitz to Henry of Plumlov (of Kravaře), Land Captain (chief administrator) of
Moravia, in 1420, and to Aleš of Sternberg in 1421.[30]

---

[26] S. M. Kuczyński, *Wielka wojna z zakonem krzyżackim w latach 1409-1411* (Warszawa, 1955), pp. 235-37; M. Biskup, G. Labuda, *Dzieje zakonu krzyżackiego w Prusach*
(Gdańsk, 1988), p. 364.

[27] Hemmerle, nos 416-17; Jan, p. 57.

[28] Hemmerle, nos 409-14, pp. 24, 31.

[29] Ibid., p. 31.

[30] *Archiv český*, vol. I, pp. 495, 501, 505, 545; II, pp. 192, 452, 176-77; A. Sedláček,
Zbytky register králův římských a českých z let 1361-1480. Historický archiv, 39 (Prague, 1915), nos 859, 890, 1003, 1048, 1358, 1407, 1457, 1504; *Regesta Imperii*, XI,
Die Urkunden Kaiser Sigmunds (1410-1437), ed. W. Altmann, 2 vols (Innsbruck, 1896-
1900; reprinted Hildesheim 1967), nos 4147, 5407, 5725, 6792, 11456, 11532, 11694;
E. Joachim, W. Hubatsch, *Regesta historico-diplomatica Ordinis S.Mariae Theutonicorum 1198-1525*, vol. I, 1 (Göttingen, 1948), no. 3119, p. 196.

The order continued to maintain some parishes in the fifteenth century (Pilsen, Neuhaus, Austerlitz, Křenovice, Hosterlitz, Hrotovice, Deblin, Troppau, Jägerndorf, Opavitz), while others were occupied by Hussite priests (Aussig, Königgrätz, Königstein, Lovosice, Býčkovice, Kolin, Čáslav, Deutschbrod, Polná, temporarily Pilsen, Kromau in Moravia, Osová Bitýška).[31] The Hussites ravaged the commandery of Prague near St Benedikt and in March 1421 Žižka's army captured Komotau, killing both the garrisoned troops and the town people there, including the Jews.[32] When, in 1534, the pontificals were given to the last commander of the bailiwick, the Pilsen priest Matthias Švihovský, it was but a sad epilogue;[33] the decline of the Teutonic Order's bailiwick of Bohemia-Moravia had begun more than a century before.

It is too simple to designate King Wenceslas a 'declared enemy of the order'.[34] He pursued his ruthless fiscal policy at the cost of other church institutions as well. The order's bailiwick was easy prey for him because it had become vulnerable due to the order's political position and inner unrest. When he seized the order's lands, Wenceslas asserted the so-called 'foundation rights', which were undisputed in medieval Bohemia and granted the king right of access to endowments which could be traced back to the monarchy. During the Hussite conflict, Sigismund followed Wenceslas's lead, pawned most of the lands of the religious orders, and thus ended up causing more damage than the Hussites themselves.[35] The dissolution of the bailiwick of Bohemia-Moravia is

---

[31] Millauer, pp. 187-90; *Fontes rerum austriacarum*, II: *Diplomataria et acta*, vol. XX, no. 70, pp. 81-82; Voigt, pp.136-37; Pettenegg, no. 2074, pp. 551-52; M. Bělohlávek, 'Řád německých rytířů v Plzni do válek husitských', *Sborník minulosti Plzně a Plzeňska* (Plzeň, 1958) 7-29; J. Balatková, 'K dějinám řádu německých rytířů v Miletíně', *Krkonoše – Podrkonoší* 7 (1983) 205-14; L. Domečka, 'Němečtí rytíři v Hradci Králové', *Časopis Společnosti přátel starožitností českých* 53 (1935) 29-34; E. Sloschek, 'Die Kromauer Kommende des Deutschen Ritterordens', *Zeitschrift für Geschichte und Landeskunde Mährens* 44 (1942) 166-73; L. Jan, 'Neznámá listina na deblínské panství', *Časopis Matice moravské* 114 (1995) 3-24; see also K. Beránek, V. Beránková, 'Částarchivu chomutovské komendy řádu německých rytířů ve Státním ústředním archivu v Praze', *Facta probant homines. Sborník příspěvků k životnímu jubileu prof dr. Zdeňky Hledíkové* (Prague, 1998), pp. 47-60.

[32] Jan, ibid.; F. Šmahel, *Husitská revoluce*, vol. 3 (2nd edn, Prague, 1996), p. 71.

[33] Millauer, pp. 196-98.

[34] Hemmerle, p. 22; E. Mirbach-Harff, 'Beiträge zur Personalgeschichte des Deutschen Ordens. Ballei Böhmen-Mähren', *Jahrbuch der k.k. heraldischen Gesellschaft 'Adler'* 11 (1911) 107.

[35] J. Čechura, 'Die Säkularisation der kirchlichen Güter im hussitischen Böhmen und Sigismund von Luxemburg', *Sigismund von Luxemburg, Kaiser und König in Mitteleu-*

a good example of the course of action taken by a number of secular rulers against a weakened church, and of their exploitation of church lands in their own interest.

ropa 1387-1437 (Warendorf, 1994), pp. 121-31; *idem, Die Struktur der Grundherr-schaften im mittelalterlichen Böhmen*. Quellen und Forschungen zur Agrargeschichte 39 (Stuttgart, Jena, New York, 1994), pp. 78-90.

14

The Mendicant Orders and their Architecture in Scotland[1]

Anneli Randla

I Introduction

The mendicant orders reached Scotland fairly early in the thirteenth century, some fifteen years after the papal recognition of the orders in case of the Dominicans and Franciscans, and had a substantial number of friaries by the end of that century. They were established in most towns of any importance and probably played a considerable role in the life of the towns, in the royal court, and the universities. They had an impact on the development of the Scottish townscape and their buildings were of major importance in the burghs.

The friars were responsible for a significant proportion of the architectural patronage of the later Middle Ages. However, the friaries have survived less well than the monasteries or collegiate churches. The reason for this was their location within the towns, which made them a ready target for the destruction of the Reformers, and also for the post-Reformation redevelopment, especially since they had no parochial function in the Reformed church, except in the few cases when they were converted to parish use.

---

[1] This article is based on my unpublished dissertation *The Architecture of the Mendicant Orders in Scotland*, including a full catalogue of the mendicant friaries and convents; it is available in the National Monument Record Office of Scotland in Edinburgh. I am grateful to Dr Deborah Howard (Cambridge University), Dr Richard Fawcett (Historic Scotland) and Dr Margaret Wilkes (National Library of Scotland) for their invaluable help with this article.

In spite of their importance very little interest has been shown in the mendicant orders either by historians or by art historians. It is especially surprising if compared to the significant amount of scholarship dedicated to the monastic orders in Scotland. Furthermore, the mendicant orders in England and Ireland have been thoroughly researched.[2]

The only general study on the history of the Scottish friaries is *The Scottish Grey Friars* by William M. Bryce dating from 1909[3] and there are occasional studies on individual friaries, all published before 1910. The only substantial exception is an article by Richard Copsey on the Carmelites in Aberdeen.[4] The friaries are also listed in Ian B. Cowan and David E. Easson's reference book on the medieval religious houses in Scotland.[5] General histories of Scotland make hardly any mention of the friars.

The architecture of the mendicants has been neglected for more obvious reasons, as only six of the forty-nine known friaries and mendicant nunneries have any architectural remains above ground. The remains were listed and briefly analysed for the first time as a group by Richard Fawcett as late as 1994.[6] Most earlier general architectural histories of Scotland have ignored the existence of the friaries completely. The remaining churches along with all other medieval structures are only described in David MacGibbon and Thomas Ross's compre-

---

[2] See for instance W. A. Hinnebusch, *The Early English Friars Preachers*. Institutum Historicum FF. Praedicatorum Romae ad S. Sabinae, Dissertationes Historicae 14 (Rome, 1951); A. R. Martin, *Franciscan Architecture in England*. British Society of Franciscan Studies 18 (Manchester, 1937); *Franciscan History and Legend in English Medieval Art*, ed. A. G. Little. British Society of Franciscan Studies 19 (Manchester, 1937); J. R. H. Moorman, *The Franciscans in England* (London, 1974), D.D.C.P. Mould, *The Irish Dominicans: The Friars Preachers in the History of Catholic Ireland* (Dublin, 1957); P. Conlan, *Franciscan Ireland* (Gigginstown, 1988), and various monographs on individual friaries.

[3] W. M. Bryce, *The Scottish Grey Friars*, 2 vols (Edinburgh, London, 1909).

[4] R. Copsey, 'The Carmelites in Aberdeen 1273-1560', *Carmelus* 42, 1 (1995) 44-111.

[5] I. B. Cowan, D. E. Easson, *Medieval Religious Houses, Scotland* (London, 1976).

[6] R. Fawcett, 'Scottish Architecture from the Accession of the Stewarts to the Reformation, 1371-1560', *The Architectural History of Scotland*, eds C. McKean, D. Howard (Edinburgh, 1994), pp. 128-41. Three paragraphs on the friars' churches are also published in R. Fawcett, *Scottish Abbeys and Priories* (London, Edinburgh, 1994), pp. 90-91. The short article by J. A. Stones, 'The Buildings of the Friars in Scotland', *Three Scottish Carmelite Friaries: Excavations at Aberdeen, Linlithgow and Perth 1980-1983*, ed. J. A. Stones. Society of Antiquaries of Scotland, Monograph Series 6 (Edinburgh, 1989), pp. 23-27, in spite of its title only lists the remains of the Carmelite friaries and does not give further analyses.

hensive work from the 1890s[7] and the RCAHMS inventories of the monuments. MacGibbon and Ross provide thorough descriptions and detailed drawings of those churches which still had some remains above ground – St Monans, Luffness, Aberdeen Greyfriars, St Andrews Blackfriars, Elgin and South Queensferry. These are particularly valuable as Aberdeen Greyfriars' kirk and part of Queensferry Carmelite church have been demolished since, and Elgin Observant Franciscan church and Queensferry church have been largely restored and rebuilt since these descriptions were made. The RCAHMS inventories provide more up-to-date information on individual buildings but the country is only partially covered by these volumes. St Monans Dominican church is the only one of the remaining six which has mostly preserved its medieval form.

The importance of archaeological evidence cannot be underestimated, as for most of the friaries this is the only source for the knowledge on the architecture of their buildings. Moreover, invaluable information about the daily life of the friaries can only be gained through archaeological investigation. In the 1970s and 1980s a series of excavations were undertaken in friaries: Aberdeen, Linlithgow and Perth Carmelite friaries, Roxburgh Franciscan friary, and Glasgow Observant Franciscan friary. The results of the three first mentioned friaries have been published in a monograph.[8] Further excavations on the sites of the Dominican friaries in Stirling and Perth, Jedburgh Observant Franciscan friary, and Aberdeen Carmelite friary have produced important information about the architecture of their buildings but the results of these excavations are still unpublished. The National Monuments Record of Scotland has a computerized database for the archaeologically investigated sites; this has been used for compiling the catalogue entries in cases where reports have not been published. Another less specific source is the series known as the Scottish Burgh Survey.

II Foundations and founders

There were probably urban settlements in Scotland at earlier times, but the creation of proper medieval towns (burghs) was a part of the reorganization of the country by David I (1124-1153). This development continued for nearly 160 years. The network of towns was vital for the promotion of regular trade

---

[7] D. MacGibbon, T. Ross, *The Ecclesiastical Architecture of Scotland from the Earliest Christian Times to the Seventeenth Century*, 3 vols (Edinburgh, 1896-1897).

[8] Stones, *Carmelite Friaries*.

and therefore the new chartered towns of the twelfth and thirteenth century were distributed all over the central Lowlands and along the eastern coast.[9]

The second half of the thirteenth century was a time of prosperity and peace for Scottish towns. Thus the first wave of mendicant foundations coincided with the 'good times' of the burghs. This development was cut short by the Wars of Independence and for nearly a century all aspects of town life declined. Very few bigger buildings were erected and the earlier ones were more likely to be destroyed than repaired.

The fifteenth century was more stable again and the burghs had their second flourishing time. If the earlier initiatives had been predominantly ecclesiastical or royal, now the lay people, and especially burgesses, were much involved in the major building projects. The trade and other contacts with France and Flanders are echoed in the architecture as well; the Flemish influence on burgh churches being especially noticeable.[10]

The mendicant friars reached Scotland fairly early after their establishment as orders. The Dominicans and the Franciscans are recorded as early as in the 1230s. Their expansion was rapid until the end of the thirteenth century, but new foundations appeared up to the eve of the Reformation (see Fig. 1).

The Dominican friars probably first appeared in Scotland in 1230. They were said to have been invited by Alexander II at the initiative of William Malvoisin, Bishop of St Andrews.[11] In less than thirty years houses were founded in Berwick-upon-Tweed, Ayr, Glasgow, Edinburgh, Stirling, Perth, Aberdeen, Elgin, and Inverness thus covering most of Lowland Scotland. Two more houses – Wigtown and Montrose – were added in the thirteenth century. There was only a single small foundation in the fourteenth century, in Cupar, which was already dissolved by the order before the Reformation. The late-fifteenth century foundations at St Monans and Haddington were also short-lived. The more permanent houses were established again in the early sixteenth century in St Andrews and Dundee.

---

[9] C. McWilliam, *Scottish Townscape* (London, 1975); R. J. Naismith, *The Story of Scotland's Towns* (Edinburgh, 1989); M. Lynch, M. Spearman, G. Stell, *The Scottish Medieval Town* (Edinburgh, 1988); I. H. Adams, *The Making of Urban Scotland*, (London, Montreal, 1978).

[10] R. Fawcett, 'Late Gothic Architecture in Scotland: Considerations on the Influence of the Low Countries', *Proceedings of the Society of Antiquaries of Scotland* 112 (1982) 477-96, *passim.*

[11] Cowan-Easson, p. 114.

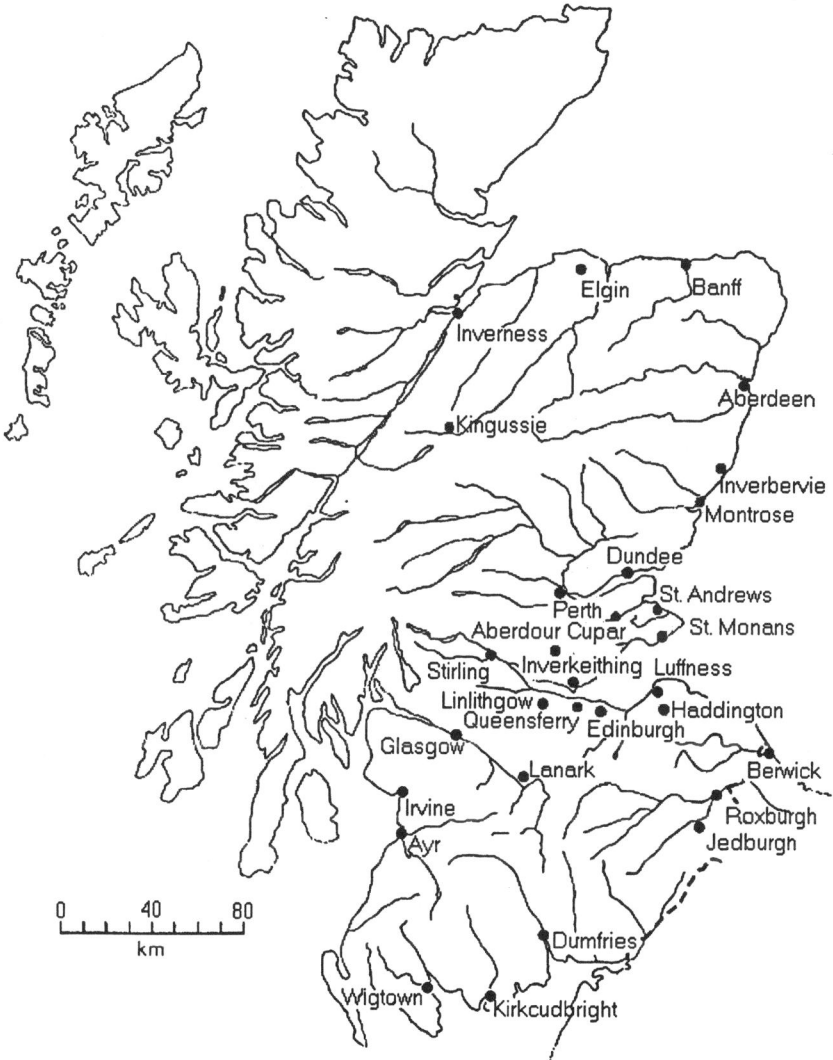

Fig. 1 The distribution of mendicant friaries in Scotland. All the marked towns had at least one friary or mendicant nunnery.

According to the Melrose Chronicle the Franciscans came to Scotland for the first time in 1231.[12] Their spread in Scotland was not as rapid as that of the Dominicans but by the end of the thirteenth century they were established in Berwick-upon-Tweed, Roxburgh, Dumfries, Haddington, Dundee, and possibly Inverkeithing. Unlike the Dominicans, the Franciscans continued to found lasting friaries in the later centuries. Two more Conventual friaries were founded in Lanark (1328 or 1329) and Kirkcudbright (between 1449 and 1456).

The reform movement in the Franciscan Order led to the formation of the Observant branch of this order. The Observant Franciscans were introduced to Scotland in or shortly before 1463 when the bull of Pope Pius II granted the right to found three or four houses of this branch. The first friaries founded were Edinburgh, Aberdeen, Glasgow, and St Andrews. In 1481 or 1482 the Bishop of Dunkeld received permission to found two or three further houses. During the reign of James IV (1488-1513) the friaries in Stirling, Ayr, Perth, Jedburgh, and Elgin were founded.[13]

The Carmelites probably arrived in Scotland in 1262 when they were recorded at Dunkeld and at Berwick-upon-Tweed.[14] Their first foundation was at Tullilum near Perth at the residence of the Bishop of Dunkeld. Soon followed the houses in Berwick-upon-Tweed, Aberdeen, Irvine, and Luffness. The fourteenth century saw only one foundation, that at Banff. The new houses became more numerous again in the fifteenth century when the friaries in Linlithgow, South Queensferry, Inverbervie, and Kingussie were established. There was one late foundation of the order, interestingly that of Edinburgh Greenside, in 1520 to 1525.

The spread of the orders in Scotland displays some interesting tendencies. It is not insignificant that the Dominican friaries were founded in episcopal centres (Aberdeen, Elgin, Glasgow, St Andrews). On the other hand there was no Conventual Franciscan friary in a cathedral town. The Observant Franciscans were located in episcopal centres and in all important royal centres. In spite of the tensions within the order they never came to a town where there was a Conventual friary already. The Carmelites did not show such clear tendencies, but the only cathedral town where they had a friary was Aberdeen. However, they had another friary at Tullilum near Perth, where, as mentioned, the Bishop of

---

[12] Cowan-Easson, p. 124.

[13] Cowan-Easson, p. 129.

[14] Cowan-Easson, p. 134.

Dunkeld was in residence. In general, mendicants inhabited nearly all Lowland towns of any importance (see Fig. 1).

Interestingly, both foundations in St Andrews were very late, and there was only a late Observant Franciscan friary in Jedburgh. No friary was ever founded at Dunfermline. This would lead to a conclusion that in the burghs with an extremely influential abbey there was no place for a mendicant friary.

It is also noteworthy that sixteen out of the thirty-three royal burghs by the end of the thirteenth century had at least one friary. With the exceptions of Dunfermline, Forres, Peebles, and Linlithgow, all the burghs founded by David I had a friary.

The choice of a burgh depended much on its importance and also on its wealth as the burghs had to 'feed' the friaries, which at the outset did not have other income than donations. Another important aspect was the population of the burghs – the larger ones attracted the mendicants more as they had large number of the poor and needy to whom their preaching was primarily aimed. The number of friaries in a given burgh corresponds well to the importance of the burgh. Berwick had the greatest number of friaries – five – all established in the second half of the thirteenth century when this burgh was the main trading town of Scotland. Aberdeen, Perth, and Edinburgh had three friaries each, and there was a nunnery in Edinburgh apart from the friaries. Dundee had two friaries and a nunnery. There were a number of burghs with two friaries: Ayr, Elgin, Glasgow, Haddington, St Andrews, and Stirling.

The mendicants were traditionally also attached to the centres of learning. Although it has been claimed that in Scotland the arrival of the Dominicans did not lead to the foundation of a university[15] it is clear that the Dominicans, and probably Franciscans no less, had a very important role in the universities, if not in the foundation then definitely later in teaching.

In the case of Glasgow where the first university building belonged to the Black Friars for a time and where the opening 'general chapter' of the university was held in the chapterhouse of the friary[16] it is difficult to overestimate their role in the foundation process of the university. The fifteenth century saw fresh stimulus to study in the Dominican Order generally and this was also reflected in Scotland.

St Andrews Dominican foundation (or re-foundation?) and Observant Franciscan foundation were both connected with the development of the university

---

[15] L. Butler, C. Given-Wilson, *Medieval Monasteries of Great Britain* (London, 1979), p. 126.

[16] J. Durkan, J. Kirk, *The University of Glasgow 1451-1577* (Glasgow, 1977), p. 9.

as were the Observant Franciscans of Aberdeen. Apart from the studies and teaching in the universities, the Dominicans had their own central study house in Perth.[17] The Observant Franciscans have been described as 'the most important stimulus of the age' including their role at the universities; they were also one of the channels of cultural and religious influences from the Continent, especially Flanders.[18]

Most of the friaries throughout the Middle Ages were royal foundations. Even if the king was not named as the founder of a friary, probably most of the friaries would have received at least part of their income through the exchequer. The friaries erected in the fifteenth century had other founders like bishops and even lay people. However, the Observant Franciscan houses were all established on the initiative of Mary of Gueldres and James IV, although in individual cases as in Aberdeen and St Andrews the bishops organized the practical foundation.

Identifying the founder in case of friaries can be complicated as several different people could be involved. Usually, the one who gave the land and first substantial grant for the friary was counted as the founder. Alternatively, this could be the person who initiated the idea of the foundation. Sometimes a later benefactor would be considered as the founder for a large donation towards building costs, etc. Whoever the founder was, his or her taste and ambitions as well as these of later benefactors could determine the architecture of the friaries greatly. In case of Aberdeen Greyfriars it is obvious that Alexander Galloway, who had the new Greyfriars kirk built (or the old rebuilt), had a great influence on its design.[19]

Most frequently the founder provided the friars with land and some income, and often with an existing chapel. This pattern was common throughout the period: the Carmelites in Perth were granted a chapel in 1262 and the Domini-

---

[17] A. Ross, 'Some Notes on the Religious Orders in Pre-Reformation Scotland', *Essays on the Scottish Reformation 1513-1625*, ed. D. McRoberts (Glasgow, 1962), pp. 195-196; A. Ross, *Dogs of the Lord: The Story of the Dominican Order in Scotland* (Edinburgh, 1981), pp. 4-5.

[18] Lynch, *Scotland*, pp. 109, 160.

[19] R. Fawcett, 'The Architecture of King's College Chapel and Greyfriars' Church, Aberdeen', *Aberdeen University Review*, 53 / 182 (1989) 117. For the life and patronage of Alexander Galloway see W. Kelly, 'Alexander Galloway, Rector of Kinkell', *A Tribute Offered by the University of Aberdeen to the Memory of William Kelly, LL.D., A.R.S.A.*, ed. W. D. Simpson (Aberdeen, 1949), pp. 19-33.

can nuns in Edinburgh one in 1517. Mainly, these were modest chapels which the friars enlarged considerably for their own use.

III Location

The mendicant friaries throughout Europe are mainly located on the edges of the towns, in the suburbs or just outside the towns. These locations were determined by a number of factors. Firstly, the mendicants usually moved into already well-established towns where the better (more central) plots were already occupied. Secondly, even if there were any plots left their cost would have been much higher and thus un-affordable for the mendicants who depended in their foundations on alms and donations. Thirdly, at least in the beginning, the friars preferred to have their houses among the poor and needy of the towns. Whatever the exact location, all friaries were close to busy streets.

The same pattern largely holds true for Scotland. Most of the friaries were on the edges of the burghs. Whether they were inside the fortifications or just outside seems to have been determined by the level of the development of the burghs. For instance, in Aberdeen all friaries were located within the town walls, whereas in Perth they were all outside the burgh bounds, presumably because the burgh had developed so intensively by the thirteenth century.[20]

However, there are two noticeable exceptions to the rule of the marginal locations of friaries. Firstly, some of the Carmelite houses – Linlithgow, Perth, Edinburgh, Luffness, Irvine – were situated fairly far outside the towns. Secondly, some of the Observant Franciscan friaries – Aberdeen, Dumfries – had very dominant locations.

The first phenomenon could possibly be explained by the eremitical origins of the Carmelite Order and therefore their probable tendency towards quieter locations. On the other hand, they were close to the main roads leading into the burghs and thus had strategically important positions. Another bias in these two cases could have been that the friars might not have been able to choose the site themselves because they were granted already existing chapels. This, however, should not have prevented the Carmelites from moving to a more desirable site some time later – a practice not unknown to the friars.

An extraordinary location was that of the Carmelite friary in Banff. Banff had an unusual located market area which extended from Old Market Place

---

[20] P. Yeoman, *Medieval Scotland: An Archaeological Perspective* (London, Edinburgh, 1995), p. 35.

along Carmelite Street and around into Low Street.[21] Therefore the friary was
located very close to the market area and town centre, being situated on the
south side of Carmelite Street which obviously bore a different name originally.
However, the friary was described as the priory 'of Bethlem of ye ordour of
Carmelits beside Banff' in 1543.[22]

The dominant locations of the Observant Franciscan friaries founded in the
fifteenth century – Aberdeen, Stirling – are harder to explain. By that time the
burgh centres were fully built up even if they had suffered during the wars.
Therefore, it seems more likely that the extremely close links with the royal
court could have played important role in obtaining these plots. Alternatively,
rich burgesses could have provided them with these plots to earn their salvation. The choice of the Observant Franciscans rather than other orders lay in
their reformed and thus higher standards of religiosity, and their general popularity. Interestingly, these were the Observant Franciscans who insisted upon
returning to the original poverty of the order, and yet enjoyed best funding and
other support at that time. The case of the Franciscan friary in Ayr reveals
another possible mechanism to account for the seemingly better locations of the
Observant Franciscan friaries. The friary in Ayr was founded in the second half
of the fifteenth century, and the brethren were given land closer to the town
centre than that of the Dominicans who had settled there around 1242. This
was caused by the fact that this land, which had been cultivated in the thirteenth century, had fallen out of use for some reason and thus this useless land
was given to the Observant Franciscans.[23]

The locations of those friaries that lay on the edges of towns were certainly
not insignificant. They were usually situated on the main roads into the towns
next to the gates, either inside or outside of these. The friaries outside the
towns, situated on the important roads leading to the town, were even more
prominent.

The position of the friaries near the 'ports' (gates) of the towns made them
stand out from a distance. The sumptuous stone buildings amongst the wooden
suburbs must have made them into landmarks for the burghs. This can be espe-

---

[21] R. Gourlay, A. Turner, *Historic Banff: The Archaeological Implications for Development*. Scottish Burgh Survey (Glasgow, 1977), p. 4.

[22] Cowan-Easson, pp. 135-36.

[23] W. J. Lindsay, 'Digging up Old Ayr', *Ayrshire Archaeological and Natural History
Society Collections* 14 (1985) 203.

cially well seen from an early map of St Andrews (see Plate 1).[24] Drawn some time around 1580 it still shows the medieval town although the destruction of the cathedral has already begun. This bird's-eye view of the town is very accurate in details although its perspective caused some obvious distortions. More importantly, it shows the attitude of the map-maker and his contemporaries towards the town and its buildings. The more important buildings are depicted larger and in more detail. These include the friaries, the cathedral, and the colleges. The friaries are located at the western end of the burgh near the ports of Market and South Streets respectively, forming a counter-balance to the cathedral at the eastern end. In a way they can be seen as welcoming houses of the burgh, the first step toward the more important cathedral at the other end of the town. It is also interesting that these more important ecclesiastical and academic buildings are lined along North and South Streets forming a circle around the burgh with the parish church in the middle.

Dumfries had neither walls nor a palisade and the friary was located at the north-western edge of the burgh near the bridge. There was a port in Friar's Vennel next to the friary (the friary was inside the port).[25] Thus the friary must have been the first landmark to be seen by any travellers crossing the river. Another interesting tendency can be observed in Dumfries: since the erection of the friary blocked the direct route to the bridge, the curved street, Friars' Vennel, was built.[26] Here, as in the case of some other early foundations, the location of the friary determined the later development of the burgh.

IV Reformation

The neglect of research into the mendicant orders can partly be explained by both Protestant and Catholic prejudice, which has led either to subjective study or to total neglect of the topic. Many reasons go back to the history of the Reformation and the twofold role of the friars in it. For the Catholic scholars the mendicants did not fit into the traditional monastic scheme and were not

---

[24] The accuracy, date, and some other aspects of this map are discussed by N. P. Brooks, G. Whittington, 'Planning and Growth in the Medieval Scottish Burgh: The example of St Andrews', *Transactions of the Institute of British Geographers* NS 2 (1977) *passim*; and M. Wilkes, *The Scot and His Maps* (Motherwell, 1991).

[25] R. Gourlay, A. Turner, *Historic Dumfries: The Archaeological Implications for Development*. Scottish Burgh Survey (Glasgow, 1977), p. 8.

[26] Naismith, pp. 47-48.

considered to be important.[27] The Protestant researchers in general considered the friars as one of the worst parts of the corrupt church, thus inheriting many of the views of the Reformers themselves.[28]

Mendicant historians like William M. Bryce[29] who are reasonably objective in other parts of their study become very biased when writing about the Reformation. Paradoxically though, one of the most neutral and objective accounts of the Reformation is written by a Dominican friar, Anthony Ross.[30]

The Reformation in Scotland is a well-studied subject,[31] but the fate of the friars and friaries during and after the Reformation is still partly unclear.[32] It is well known that they were one of the main targets of the Reformers and suffered much more destruction than the monasteries. The friaries were sacked in 1559 or 1560, although the actual amount of destruction is unknown (apart from the account by John Knox, who was by no means a neutral observer) and might have been less than is usually thought. The attitude towards friars from the 'Franciscanus' and the 'Beggars' Summons' is also often cited, but the problem seems to be a much more complex one.

The popularity of the mendicants had not declined by the sixteenth century. Not only were new friaries founded (five friaries and two nunneries), but the older ones were still, in the middle of the sixteenth century, increasing their property by bequest and gift, and it may be inferred that institutions which continued to attract fresh endowments must have been in a fairly healthy state.[33]

They were supported both by the lay people of the burghs and by the royal court. The Observant Franciscans as the most recent establishment and the strictest of them enjoyed particular favour in the royal court, producing a

---

[27] See for instance M. Dilworth, *Scottish Monasteries in the Late Middle Ages* (Edinburgh, 1995) who deliberately excludes the friaries from his study.

[28] Ultra-Protestant views have been expressed in G. Hay, *The Architecture of Scottish Post-Reformation Churches 1560-1843* (Oxford, 1957), pp. 3-20; and sadly also by G. Donaldson both in his *Scottish Church History* (Edinburgh, 1985) and *Scotland: The Shaping of a Nation* (London, 1974).

[29] Bryce, vol. 1, pp. 80-160.

[30] Ross, *Dogs, passim.*

[31] G. Donaldson, *The Scottish Reformation* (Cambridge, 1960) – this book is much more objective than his later writings on this topic; I. B. Cowan, *The Scottish Reformation: Church and Society in Sixteenth Century Scotland* (London, 1982).

[32] D. McRoberts, 'Material Destruction Caused by the Scottish Reformation', *Innes Review* X (1959) 126-72.

[33] Donaldson, *Reformation*, p. 9.

number of royal confessors. The mendicants in general were the most popular confessors of the time.

The friars were also known as preachers, and it seems that the full burden of preaching fell on them instead of being shared by the secular clergy. They were well-qualified preachers who preached in the vernacular, not only in their churches but also in the markets and on their tours in the remote villages.

There were reform movements within the orders towards the restoration of the original ideals of these orders; most noticeable was the Observant Franciscan establishment, but the reform of the Dominican Order also reached Scotland in the early sixteenth century.[34] They were critical towards their own fellow friars as well as secular and monastic clergy.

Although most friaries did well until the Reformation, their wealth was relatively small compared to that of the monastic institutions and cathedrals. Only scarce cases of moral laxity and corruption could be found even by the Reformers.

However, it was not only the Reformers (and the other clergy) who had trouble with the mendicants. The friars were most disliked by the paupers of the burghs,[35] but the miserable position of these people made them hate anyone with a higher social status anyway. Their probable attitudes towards the friars are expressed in the 'Beggars' Summons',[36] however, this text was not written by a pauper but by the leaders of the Reformers and could have had a deliberately-chosen topic for whipping up the masses against the friars. It is also unlikely that many of the paupers would have been literate enough to read this text.

Thus it can be concluded that what the friars were already doing was perhaps too close for comfort to what the Protestants wanted to do. The vision of those within the church who sought reform was often very close to the vision of those outside the church. They were also far more formidable opponents for they took on the Protestant preachers on their own ground. And this may have been the reason why so many friaries were targeted for sacking by the congregation in 1559.[37]

In this context it is hardly surprising that there were many friars who joined the Reformers. The earliest known mendicant convert to Lutheranism was

---

[34] On the Dominican reform see Ross, *Notes*, pp. 191-200; Ross, *Dogs*, pp. 6-9.

[35] Donaldson, *Reformation*, p. 48.

[36] For full text see Bryce, vol. 1, pp. 141-42.

[37] J. Wormald, *Court, Kirk, and Community. Scotland 1470-1625* (London, 1981), pp. 86-87, 115, 116; Lynch, *Scotland*, p. 192.

James Melvin or Melvil, an Observant Franciscan of St Andrews in 1526, who was prosecuted by his own order (not to be confused with the famous later Reformer Andrew Melville).[38] Several others followed, like Alexander Dick of Aberdeen Observant Franciscans in 1532, who fled to Dundee where the magistrates supported him,[39] or Alexander Seton, former Prior of the Dominicans of St Andrews, who had been the king's confessor and celebrated preacher, before he was exiled in 1537 for holding ideas that were considered too radical.[40] There were many others who joined the Reformers and three of them were burned for heresy in 1539.

On the other hand, the Dominicans and Franciscans were involved in the inquisition which led to the persecution of the early Reformers both within the orders and from outside.[41] As is only natural most of them stuck to their orders and defended the old faith from their own standpoint. Like the zealous preaching of the Reformers this fierce defence could lead to trouble. In 1543 John Routh, a Franciscan preacher, caused a riot in Ayr while preaching against the new law of reading of the Scripture in English. This led to a street disturbance and the arrest of the friar, but the town council seems to have been on the Franciscan's side.[42]

Neither the riot in Ayr nor the riots in Dundee and Perth in 1543, which were caused by the Reformers, were the first and only anti-mendicant demonstrations before 1559. In 1533 an image of the Blessed Virgin of the Grey Friars in Ayr was decapitated; an image of St Francis was hanged in Perth about 1543; and in 1544 two citizens of Aberdeen were imprisoned for hanging an image belonging to the Franciscan friary.[43]

However, these were only sporadic outbreaks of violence and most probably did not mirror a general hatred towards the mendicants in particular. Thus it can only be concluded that there were other reasons for choosing the friaries as the primary target of the attack of 1559. As already pointed out, they were too close in their aims to the Reformers and too powerful a force to be ignored.

---

[38] Bryce, vol. 1, pp. 104-6.

[39] Bryce, vol. 1, pp. 106-7.

[40] Ross, *Notes*, pp. 200-202.

[41] Bryce, vol. 1, pp. 98-103.

[42] W. J. Dillon, 'The Pre-Reformation Church', *The Royal Burgh of Ayr: 750 Years of History*, ed. A. I. Dunlop (Edinburgh, 1953), p. 102.

[43] Bryce, vol. 1, p. 103; Donaldson, *Reformation*, p. 29; I. B. Cowan, *Regional Aspects of the Scottish Reformation*. Historical Association Pamphlet, General Series 92 (London, 1978), pp. 13-14.

The revenues of the friars were derived largely from annual rents payable on tenements in the burghs. Moreover, the friaries being situated in burghs, their way of life was open to the constant observation of the burgesses. Thus even the slightest deviation from their professed ideals would arouse immediate criticism, and, whenever feelings ran high, their properties were ready targets for zealously Protestant burghers as well as for riff-raff in search of loot. The attacks on the friaries do not provide conclusive evidence either of grave delinquency within them or of a serious popular aversion towards them.[44]

The actual process of the sacking of the friaries gives further evidence of the provoked nature of this. Only the friaries in the burghs visited by the Lords of the Congregation were actually attacked. There numbered about half of the burghs where the friaries were located, and in the other half no harm was done to the friaries at that point. Furthermore, the amount of destruction seems to have varied from burgh to burgh: in Edinburgh, St Andrews, and Stirling the devastation was complete, whereas in Aberdeen the Franciscan church was left standing, as well as the Dominican churches in Glasgow and Ayr. The friaries in Jedburgh, Haddington, and Roxburgh had already been destroyed by the English in the 1540s. However, the urban mobs did demolish at least seventeen friaries. This might also have cultivated the later disrespect towards the surviving friaries, which were dissolved and their communities driven out, nominally in the interest of the poor. The buildings which were not used soon became dilapidated.

When the Reformation settlement was made, those friars who submitted to it received pensions of £16 a year and there were eighty-two friars receiving such a pension in 1562.[45] However, these pensions were not always paid regularly. There were a number of friars who left Scotland for the Continent and joined the friaries in the Catholic areas. Still others became ministers in the Reformed kirk. Two former Dominicans became very influential in the new church, John Willock, formerly of Ayr, and John Craig. John Willock was the more forceful preacher of the two, whereas John Craig was the author of the catechism and as a minister in Edinburgh concentrated on his pastoral duty and avoided entanglement with politics.[46]

There were also friars who remained in Scotland, wearing ordinary clothing and ministering as well as they could to those who held still to the old church.

---

[44] Donaldson, *Reformation*, p. 10; Ross, *Notes*, pp. 206-9.

[45] Bryce, vol. 1, p. 154.

[46] Ross, *Dogs*, p. 11.

A friar, James Johnstone, was charged with celebrating mass in Paisley in 1563.[47]

The fate of the buildings which physically survived the Reformation has been various. Only a few of their churches were converted into parish churches (Aberdeen Greyfriars', St Monans, South Queensferry, Kirkcudbright, and Dumfries – some of these temporarily). Even after all the destruction there was a surplus of ecclesiastical buildings after the monasteries, friaries, collegiate churches and the like had lost their function. Most of them were converted to other public use as hospitals, courts of justice, schools, etc. The remains of the buildings and income from the property of the friaries in all three university burghs – Aberdeen, Glasgow, and St Andrews – were given to the universities and they continued to carry out at least one of the former functions of the friaries, as places of learning.

In Aberdeen the newly-founded Marischal College used the conventual buildings of the Franciscan friary unaltered for the first fifty years of its existence. Marischal College also received the Dominican and Carmelite properties in Aberdeen, whereas King's College was granted the remaining buildings, revenues and lands of the Carmelites in Banff.[48]

Most of the other friaries fell out of use and were very soon dilapidated and their property redeveloped, which is also a reason why so few structures remain of the friaries' buildings.

V Mendicant architecture

There were two general factors which determined the architectural style of the mendicants: firstly, the rules and traditions of building followed by the orders; and secondly, the local architectural context.

The most precise rules for the architecture were set by the Dominicans. Their first extant constitution states that their houses had to be modest and humble, the height of the single-storey buildings not rising above 12 ft, the ones with a loft not more than 20 ft, and the church not more than 30 ft. Vaulting was not to be used except for the choir and sacristy.[49] In 1240 the chapter general passed legislation on the construction of screens between the nave and choir.

---

[47] Ross, *Notes*, pp. 227-30; Ross, *Dogs*, p. 10.

[48] Cowan-Easson, p. 136.

[49] R. A. Sundt, '*Mediocres domos et humiles habeant fratres nostri*: Dominican Legislation on Architecture and Architectural Decoration in the 13th Century', *Journal of the Society of Architectural Historians* 46/4 (December 1987) 394-407.

Several acts were passed on decorations, furnishings, vestments, etc. A regulation of 1245 stated that the churches were also not to be cluttered up with sepulchral monuments, especially those with notable sculptures, and the already existing ones were to be removed.[50]

The Franciscan General Constitutions of 1260 also have statutes on the architecture and decoration of the friaries. Elaboration of churches as well as excessive size was to be avoided; no vaulting was allowed, except for the chancel; bell-towers were strictly forbidden; and the windows had to be plain, except for the ones over the main altar, where a restricted number of saints could be depicted.[51]

However, these regulations were very soon exceeded in Italy and France and the repeated urging of the chapters general to 'repair the mistakes' was in vain. The churches of the friaries became large in scale, of high quality and lavishly decorated (as, for example, San Francesco in Assisi, Jacobin church in Toulouse, Regensburg Dominican church, and London Dominican church). Furthermore, the chapter houses, refectories, cloisters, and even individual cells were excessively decorated.[52] As the popularity of the friaries as burial-places for lay people grew constantly, the churches were filled with monuments.

Nothing like that happened in Scotland. As far as can be concluded from the scanty evidence, the friaries did not break the architectural rules even as late as in the sixteenth century. For example, no Observant Franciscans church is known to have had stone vaulting, and none of the surviving churches exceeds the height limit. This, however, was probably more due to modest means and small numbers than loyalty, although pious reasons, especially for the Observant Franciscans, certainly played an important role.

The matter of decoration is less straightforward as nothing survives of the furnishing or decoration of the friaries. The archaeological finds have confirmed that at least decorated, but mostly 'grisaille', window glass was used in Ayr, Linlithgow, Aberdeen, and Perth, and crumbled painted plaster testifies to the existence of wall paintings.[53] These remains are too scarce to make any firm conclusions about the decorations. The burials, however, were as popular

---

[50] Hinnebusch, pp. 126-27.

[51] Martin, p. 11.

[52] For the wall paintings and their iconography in the Italian friaries see W. Braunfels, *Monasteries of Western Europe: The Architecture of the Orders* (London, 1972), pp. 142-52.

[53] Lindsay, 'Digging up Old Ayr', pp. 213-15; Stones, 'The Small Finds: Summary Report', pp. 150-53.

in the Scottish friaries as they were elsewhere and the effigies could be elaborate.

Unlike the Cistercians, the mendicants most probably did not have their own
masons and depended on the local craftsmen for the actual process of construction. Whatever the intentions of the priors or the benefactors were, these were
carried out by people who most probably only knew the surrounding Scottish
architecture. Therefore it can be assumed that their buildings were basically
Scottish, and as will be shown below, most of them fit well into the Scottish
context. Nevertheless, it is unclear whether the similarity of the mendicant
churches with the parish churches was caused by the influence of the latter, or
vice versa.

VI Layout of friaries

Generally, the friars arrived in the burghs long after the layout of the original
town had been established, and therefore could not choose the most suitable
plots. However, in most cases the land obtained by them must have been large
enough to build a cloister and a church according to the conventual monastic
plan – their sites were spacious and prominent. In all cases where the layout of
the whole cloister (or most of it) is known – Jedburgh and Elgin Observant
Franciscan, Linlithgow and Aberdeen Carmelite friaries – it corresponds to the
typical quadrangular layout with the church forming one side of it and the
conventual buildings occupying the remaining three ranges (see Fig. 2). Most
of them also had a graveyard and household buildings scattered around the
cloister. Nevertheless, some aspects of the proper layouts have not been
followed. The churches were not always built in the northern range of the
building complex as would be expected from a traditional monastic plan. Out
of the seventeen friaries, where the position of the church and the conventual
buildings is known, ten had the church in the atypical southern range. There is
no difference between the orders in this matter. Certainly this arrangement was
partly caused by the restrictions of the sites like the water supply, topography of
the site, easy public access to the church (thus closest to the street), relative
quietness of the conventual buildings (thus further away from the street), etc.;
but it seems more likely that the mendicants were simply indifferent about the
traditional position of the church. The case of Luffness Carmelite friary, where
there were no other buildings or natural conditions hindering the erection of
the church in the conventional northern range, seems to be conclusive. Some of
the churches were also not properly oriented to the east – as the Franciscan

friary church in Aberdeen and the Dominican church in Stirling – but this was more likely caused by irregularity of the building sites than deliberate choice.

So far as is known the mendicants in Scotland held to the conventional monastic plan, unlike the friaries in some other parts of Europe where it had been quite freely interpreted. Most probably it was adopted as the most suitable for any closely related community (as later for the academic colleges). Multiple cloisters and irregular plans – so characteristic of the Italian friaries – which grew organically out of the necessity to accommodate increasing numbers of friars, were not relevant for Scotland as the friaries were neither big at the time of foundation nor did the number of the inmates increase dramatically.

Adoption of the conventional plan could also have resulted from the strong monastic tradition in Scotland. There were two extremely influential urban abbeys – Dunfermline and Holyrood – which probably acted as a local prototype for the friaries. These buildings probably influenced the expectations of the donors and the general public, as well as the friars, even if they contradicted some aspects of European mendicant tradition.

VII Churches

A great number of the friaries were given an earlier chapel for their use at their foundation: a pattern common from the first foundations of the thirteenth century (Perth Carmelites 1262; probably Stirling Dominicans c. 1233) until the late foundations of the sixteenth century (e.g. Edinburgh Carmelites, 1525). These chapels were gradually enlarged or rebuilt as the funds grew and necessity demanded, and obviously their shape influenced the design of the later churches. According to archaeological evidence, in Linlithgow Carmelite friary the founder's rectangular chapel was first used by the friars as their church and in the early fifteenth century converted into the nave of the enlarged structure.[54] In the Dominican church of Stirling, probably an earlier chapel with a semicircular apse was used as the chancel, and a nave was added by the friars.[55] The old masonry seems to have been retained as much as possible.

Whatever the earliest phases of the churches were, most of them acquired a simple rectangular ground plan with no separate chancel, no transepts or aisles.

---

[54] Stones, 'Buildings of the Friars,' p. 24.

[55] Alternatively, the chancel could have been a sixteenth-century addition with a polygonal apse. For discussion see R. Page, C. Page, *An Excavation at the Church of the Blackfriars, Stirling*, in press, and R. Page, C. Page, 'Blackfriars of Stirling', *Proceedings of the Society of Antiquaries of Scotland* 126 (1996) 881-98.

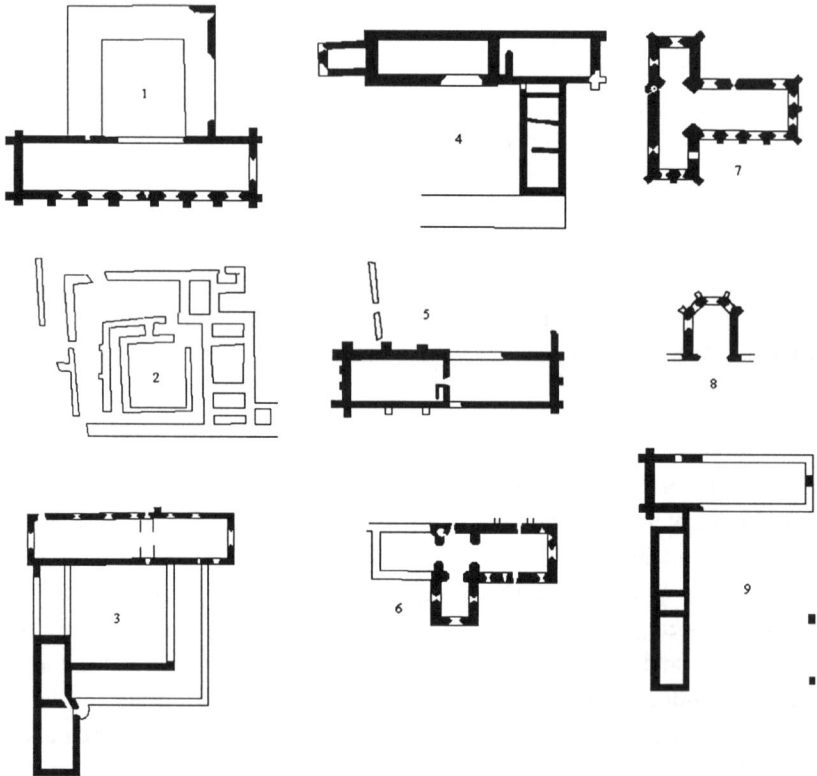

Fig. 2 Ground plans of the friaries. 1 Aberdeen Observant Franciscan friary, 2 Jedburgh Observant Franciscan friary, 3 Elgin Observant Franciscan friary, 4 Linlithgow Carmelite friary, 5 Luffness Carmelite friary, 6 South Queensferry Carmelite friary, 7 St Monans Dominican friary, 8 St Andrews Dominican friary, 9 Aberdeen Carmelite friary.

All these churches measured approximately 30 m by 10 m. Out of the twelve cases where at least the ground plan of the church is known, nine were of this type. Interestingly, even in the cases when the churches were considerably rebuilt, as in Linlithgow Carmelite church or Aberdeen Greyfriars' church,[56] they eventually resulted in the same plan (see Fig. 2).

This elongated rectangular church type was adopted in the thirteenth century and interestingly was not abandoned until the Reformation, probably because it proved to be the most practical for the friars. Luffness Carmelite church of the late thirteenth century is probably the earliest surviving example of this type and bears nearly all the typical features which recurred over three hundred years afterwards. Possibly the latest example of this was Aberdeen Observant Franciscan church, which was built in 1518 to 1532. There were, however, some more elaborate plans used in late foundations of the Dominicans and Carmelites such as St Monans and St Andrews Dominican churches and South Queensferry Carmelite church.

Luffness Carmelite church, of which the lower parts of the walls survive, is an oblong building. Its relatively thin walls are buttressed, but the structure is probably too insubstantial to have had stone vaulting. There is a buttress in the middle of the eastern wall which, if carried up to the full height of the wall, would have prohibited the construction of a central window – certainly an unsatisfactory solution. Alternatively, the buttress could stop under the window sill. Interestingly though, the same feature reappears at St Monans much later.

Internally the church is divided into the chancel and nave by a substantial stone partition wall – a feature frequently reappearing and in other cases later developing into a walking place. There was probably no walking place at Luffness[57] as the entrance into the chancel was further to the east just in front of the first of the two steps rising to the sanctuary, unless this door led from a sacristy and there was another entrance from the cloister. One more typical feature is the placing of side altars in front of the partition wall or screen. At Luffness only the foundations of the southern nave altar have survived, but most probably there was another one at the northern side as well. A fragment of a piscina has been found, but as it was not *in situ*, it is unclear whether it belonged to a nave or the main altar.[58]

---

[56] Fawcett, 'King's College Chapel', pp. 120-22.

[57] Fawcett, 'King's College Chapel', p. 119.

[58] *RCAHMS Inventory*, vol. 8, *East Lothian* (Edinburgh, 1924), no. 1, p. 1.

The late thirteenth-century effigy, possibly of the founder, in a recess of the northern wall of the sanctuary and another lay person's grave slab of the fifteenth century indicate the popular trend of lay burials in mendicant churches.

Linlithgow Carmelite church, another rectangular building, is likely to be the oldest where the traces of a walled-in walking place survive. The western of the two walls was the east wall of the original chapel, but the eastern one was specially constructed when the chancel was built. The walking place had a door into the cloister in the southern wall of the church and openings both into the chancel and the nave. Here, as at Luffness, the foundations of two nave altars were found in front of the screen walls – these can be identified from the written sources as dedicated to St John the Baptist and St Thomas the Martyr, respectively.[59] The walking place was probably surmounted by a bell-tower.

The Dominican church in Glasgow, which is only known from the view by John Slezer[60] seems to have had a similar structure as its substantial tower could not have been supported without firm masonry supports. Here also the church was an aisle-less rectangle with buttresses and large windows in between them (see Plate 2). Aberdeen Carmelite church which dates from the 1380s was of the same rectangular type with heavily buttressed corners.[61] As the central part of the church has not been excavated there is no information about the design of the partition of the nave and the chancel, but it is likely that there would have been a walking place.

While the Carmelites and the Dominicans probably became more relaxed about the design of their churches in the fifteenth and sixteenth centuries, the Observant Franciscans favoured the old scheme. The best-preserved or documented examples of the Observant Franciscan churches were in Elgin (see Plates 3, 4) and Aberdeen. The church in Elgin was probably begun in the last years of the fifteenth century and it survives having been considerably restored by John Kinross in 1896. The church in Aberdeen was dated by charter evidence as built in 1518 to 1532. Unfortunately, this building was demolished in 1902, but photographs and drawings of it at the time of demolition survive.

Both these churches were rectangular structures, the Elgin one being somewhat smaller and simpler. In Elgin the walls have no buttresses apart from the one at the partition of the nave and the chancel. Well-proportioned two-light

---

[59] W. J. Lindsay, 'Linlithgow: The Excavations', *Carmelite Friaries*, ed. Stones, pp. 75-77.

[60] The College of Glasgow in J. Slezer, *Theatrum Scotiae* (London, 1693).

[61] J. A. Stones, 'Aberdeen: The Excavations', *Carmelite Friaries*, ed. Stones, pp. 38, 51.

windows pierce the northern wall of the church. The large central windows of the eastern and western façade are more elaborate with interesting intersecting tracery. Although the tracery has been largely restored by John Kinross, he respected archaeological evidence.[62] The two smaller windows, one above the other, in the central part of the northern wall and a buttress testify to the existence of a screen with a loft at this place. Since across the church in the same place lies the entrance from the cloister with a window above it, there must have been a walking place. Unlike the earlier mendicant churches, the walking place was not a stone structure, but a wooden one, and did not carry a tower above. The walking place was lit by the lower window of the two, and the loft above by the higher windows in both walls. The loft may have contained a pulpit. As in the other mendicant churches there were two nave altars associated with the screen. In Elgin the piscinas of both of these altars survive. John Kinross recreated the wooden screens and altars in 1896, and although they do not represent their exact medieval form, the arrangement gives some idea of the spatial organization of the church (see Plate 4). The wooden pointed barrel-vault ceiling might well be close to its medieval predecessor, as there was obviously no stone vault, although the form of it could have been different, i.e. a wagon ceiling like that of Aberdeen Greyfriars' church.

The chancel in Elgin is subdivided into two parts by the elevation of the sanctuary with the main altar above the level of the choir stalls. Both the piscina and the aumbry of the main altar survive and are still used in their original function. Another interesting practical detail is a squint in the southern wall of the chancel. The celebration of the mass could be followed through it from the first floor of the conventual buildings by the friars who for some reason or other could not attend the mass.

It is also significant that neither in Elgin nor in Aberdeen was there a highly decorated stone sedilia as in South Queensferry Carmelite church or St Monans Dominican church. However, in the latter case it might date from the pre-friary period. At the Observant Franciscan churches the omission of this feature might have resulted from their desire for the humility of the church.

Aberdeen Greyfriars' church was very similar to the Elgin church only on a more elaborate scale in spite of its simplicity. The walls were here divided into seven bays by slender buttresses and horizontally articulated by the base course and a string course at the level of the window sills. Between the buttresses were wide four-light windows resembling the eastern window of Elgin. The western façade has not been preserved as the westernmost bay was removed in the

---

[62] Fawcett, *Architecture*, p. 136.

eighteenth century, but the magnificent eastern window survives having been incorporated into the new Greyfriars' church. The tracery of this window is a complex intersecting pattern, extremely sophisticated in its geometrical purity.

As in Elgin there were two smaller windows above each other in the middle of the southern wall with an associated piscina inside, testifying to the existence of a wooden screen with a loft above and altars in front of it. The nave altars here were dedicated to the Virgin and St John the Baptist, respectively. It seems that here there was only a screen and not a walking place dividing the liturgical parts of the church,[63] but as the northern wall, which was abutted by the cloister, had been demolished earlier to make way for an aisle, the possibility of a walking place cannot be excluded either. Furthermore, evidence was found below the modern floor level of a spiral staircase obviously leading to the loft and a doorway into the cloister.[64]

As can be seen from the 1661 view of New Aberdeen by James Gordon of Rothiemay,[65] the church had a small roof turret, in place of the towers of the earlier mendicant churches, but smaller and wooden as there was no construction to support it. Richard Fawcett has argued that the turret was rather an indication of the taste of the patrons and the carpenters than the choice of the friars.[66] It might well be so considering the general austerity of the Observant Franciscan churches.

The bird's-eye view of St Andrews of 1580 suggests that the Franciscans there had a similar church to those in Elgin and Aberdeen, only, it seems, with a peculiar free-standing belfry (see Plate 1). The late foundation of Jedburgh Franciscan friary also had the very conventional ground plan for the church.[67]

The rectangular church type was not unique to the mendicants – the majority of the parish churches from the twelfth up to the middle of the fifteenth century had similar design.[68] From the more general view of design it is unclear, however, whether it was the parish churches that influenced the mendicant ones or

---

[63] Fawcett, 'King's College Chapel', p. 120.

[64] Fawcett, 'King's College Chapel', p. 122.

[65] The view is published in: *Excavations in the Medieval Burgh of Aberdeen 1973-1981*, ed. C. J. Murray. Society of Antiquaries of Scotland, Monograph Series 2 (Edinburgh, 1982).

[66] Fawcett, 'King's College Chapel', p. 120.

[67] P. Dixon, 'Jedburgh Friary and the Border Burghs', *Current Archaeology* 97 (1985) 59-60; J. M. Clark, I. Banks, *Jedburgh Observantine Friary: Archaeological Assessment*. Archaeological Projects, MS [Glasgow, c. 1990].

[68] For parish churches see Fawcett, *Architecture*, chapters 6 and 7.

the other way round as in many parts of continental Europe and England. As the survival rate of the medieval Scottish parish churches is extremely low, a single conclusion on this matter cannot be drawn.

Three of the churches with more complex plans – St Monans, South Queensferry, and St Andrews Dominican church – deserve closer study, although they are less typical of Scottish mendicant architecture.

The church of St Monans (see Plate 5), which was built in 1362 to 1370 by David II as a votive church, was a T-shaped structure consisting of a chancel, transepts, and a tower over the crossing. The friars, most probably with royal support, largely rebuilt the church and adapted it to the needs of the friary just after 1471. The windows of the choir were rebuilt at that time and the chancel was vaulted (or re-vaulted). A rood-screen was presumably set up between the chancel and the crossing, if there was no earlier screen. Altars were set up in the transepts. Unusually, no nave was built but this could be explained by the modest scale of the foundation, or lack of funding. It is highly likely, though, that the nave was originally planned, but either never executed or has vanished without leaving any trace.

The windows of the choir were enlarged and new more fashionable tracery was inserted. This was of two different types, one of them being widely used in the Netherlands around the same time. It was probably not made by a Dutch stonemason but rather reflected a more general tendency of Netherlandish influence on the architecture of the Scottish eastern coast in the late fifteenth century.[69]

When the vaulting was built in the late fifteenth century (or rebuilt as vaulting had been at least planned in the 1360s) the currently popular pointed barrel vault could not have been built over the chancel. The walls were too thin and the windows too large, the buttresses had been designed to take only the directed weight of the groin vaults and not the massive weight of a tunnel vault. Even with the chosen pseudo-sexpartite vault problems occurred as the corbels of the short ribs are placed just above the window heads – into the weakest point of the wall (see Plate 6).

One of the typical mendicant features – a walking place between the chancel and nave – was missing at St Monans. There was no place for it inside the chancel and it could not have been accommodated in the triumphal arch separating the chancel from the crossing. Most probably there was just a rood-screen under the triumphal arch as separation of the chancel for the friars was

---

[69] Fawcett, 'Late Gothic', *passim*.

necessary. Unfortunately, later blocking and rebuilding of the triumphal arch has swept away any traces of the screen.

Interestingly, the two altars which were usually placed, in mendicant churches without transepts, in front of the screen or incorporated into it, were here placed in the transepts. The one in the northern transept was dedicated to Virgin Mary as in other mendicant churches. The piscinas and credence niches in the eastern walls of the transepts still testify to the existence of these altars.

South Queensferry Carmelite church was probably started in the 1440s and not finished until the early sixteenth century,[70] thus built roughly at the time of the rebuilding of St Monans, but it has nothing of the architectural splendour of the latter. The church had an irregular T-shaped ground plan consisting of a chancel, nave, and southern transept. The crossing is spacious and carries a sturdy tower. The nave was demolished by the 1850s, but drawings of it survive. The chancel is covered by a pointed barrel vault of stone and the crossing has also a stone vault. This low springing and heavy vault dictated the modest scale and low position of the windows.

South Queensferry church was in many ways unusual for the mendicants, resembling more the collegiate churches of the period. It can probably be explained with the ambition of the founder, James Dundas of Dundas, who might have wished to have a private chapel or a burial aisle for his family attached to the church, and therefore had the southern transept built. The transeptal aisle cannot be a later addition as one of the surviving six original consecration crosses[71] is on the wall of this aisle.

Another peculiar feature was the proportion of the nave and the chancel. The nave was considerably smaller than the chancel (c. 3 m shorter), which is very surprising in a purposely-built mendicant church. This would indicate that at the time of building South Queensferry was not a very populous place and there was no need for a bigger nave. The chancel is bigger than most chancels in the mendicant churches and a peculiar feature in the chancel – the corbels along the walls – has led to a conclusion that it also had a loft.[72] This seems unlikely as South Queensferry was not a big friary and there would have been plenty of room for the brethren in the chancel. It cannot be accepted that the two lower corbels in the eastern end of the chancel were for supporting some ceiling

---

[70] MacGibbon-Ross, vol. 3, p. 309; I. G. Lindsay, *The Friary Church of St Mary of Mount Carmel, South Queensferry* (South Queensferry, 1953), p. 7.

[71] See Lindsay, *Friary Church of St Mary*, pp. 11-12.

[72] MacGibbon-Ross, vol. 3, p. 306; *RCAHMS Inventory*, vol. 10, *Mid Lothian and West Lothian* (Edinburgh, 1929), p. 200.

structure as they were obviously meant for placing candles or lamps to light the aumbry and piscina, respectively. Richard Fawcett has suggested that the higher corbels were to carry a wooden ceiling within the vault[73] but it seems more likely that these were to carry the ornamental ribs of the vault. If these were to be of stone, as usual, they were never built as the plan must have been changed during construction. Alternatively, the ribs could have been wooden, as they did not have any constructional function, and therefore have not been preserved.

Interestingly, some archaic forms as round-arched doorways, sedilia, and aumbry appear in the chancel, all of high craftsmanship – seemingly a deliberate choice of the friars, although such tendencies were becoming exceedingly popular elsewhere in the ecclesiastical architecture as well. As a contrast, the southern window of the transept and the windows of the demolished nave had square heads with cusped tracery, which was the fashionable type in secular architecture of the late fifteenth century, thus underlining the difference between the lay and the friars' parts of the church.

The question of a walking place in this church is unclear. Traces of a screen are visible on the arch separating the chancel from the crossing, but no trace can be found on the arch between the crossing and the demolished nave. If there was another screen, it would have made the walking place extremely wide and dark as there is only one small window in the northern wall. Unfortunately, no trace of any nave altars has been recorded, thus the question about the walking place has to remain open.

The north chapel of St Andrews Dominican church (see Plate 7) is the latest of the surviving mendicant buildings, built in 1525. A new church was started here in 1514 and it could have been a rectangular structure as the projecting north chapel was originally not planned – permission was sought in 1525 to erect it partly on the street. The architecture of this chapel combines features from the Scottish local tradition with more cosmopolitan ideas.[74] A polygonal apse of a chapel or transept appears in a number of Scottish sixteenth-century churches – the closest to St Andrews being Ladykirk church – but the motif itself was taken over from the Netherlands. In St Andrews, however, the connection of the chapel to the nave is completely different from its Scottish analogics – instead of a very low arch, as in Ladykirk where the transepts are cut off from the nave, in St Andrews the high pointed arch opening into the

---

[73] Fawcett, *Architecture*, p. 137.

[74] Fawcett, *Architecture*, pp. 139-41.

nave made the chapel an integral part of the church, achieving a spatial unity comparable to that of St Monans church. While the pointed barrel vault with its decorative ribs is a very typical feature of the Scottish architecture of the period (see also South Queensferry church), the window tracery has strong connections with Netherlandish examples.[75]

One of the reasons why examples of design were sought in the Netherlands was the close link, established around 1510, between the Dominicans in Scotland and the reformed Congregation of Holland. The Netherlandish influence on architecture was not restricted to mendicants alone, but the role of the Dominicans in transmitting it could have been of considerable importance.[76]

VIII Conventual buildings

All of the Scottish friaries, where at least something is known about the layout of the conventual buildings, were ordered according to the traditional monastic plan. Although the function of the friaries differed considerably from that of the monasteries, their needs for conventual buildings were similar – every friary had a chapterhouse, a sacristy, a refectory, a kitchen and household buildings. But unlike the monastic orders, with the exception of the Carthusians, the mendicants had cells for individual friars rather than common dormitories. The cells had a dual function – they were used for study and sleeping. Usually a large room on the first floor of the eastern range was divided into cells by less substantial partition walls.

The Scottish friaries had most of their conventual buildings in their traditional location, with the exception that if the church was in the southern range the layout was a mirror-image of the usual. In general, the Scottish friary cloisters were relatively modest in scale, corresponding to the small numbers of inmates (see Fig. 2).

The chapterhouses were always located in the middle of the eastern range. The remains of these have been found in Linlithgow and Perth Carmelite and Jedburgh Observant Franciscan houses.[77] All of these were relatively small and simple, but could have been richly decorated as the finds of painted plaster and

---

[75] Fawcett, 'Late Gothic', *passim*.

[76] For general Dutch influence on Scottish liturgy see J. Galbraith, 'The Middle Ages', *Studies in the History of Worship in Scotland*, eds D. B. Forrester, D. M. Murray (Edinburgh, 1984), pp. 17-32.

[77] J. Todd, 'Jedburgh Friary', *Discovery and Excavation in Scotland* (1985) 2; Dixon, p. 60.

painted window-glass from Linlithgow suggest.[78] The chapterhouse of Glasgow Dominican friary must have been much bigger and probably more refined as it was large enough to house the university meetings.

Other rooms in the eastern range were the sacristy which was located between the chapterhouse and the church as in Linlithgow, Perth, and Jedburgh, and the parlour or warming-room on the other side of the chapterhouse.

Monastic dormitories were usually on the first floor of the eastern range and were accessed by a night-stair from the ground floor. The foundations of such night-stairs have been found in Jedburgh and Linlithgow where these were placed against the church wall in the eastern range. No dormitory has been preserved from a Scottish friary, but the foundations in Linlithgow, Perth, and Jedburgh friaries testify to the existence of the first floor in the eastern range which would have accommodated the dormitory.[79]

Associated with the dormitory was the reredorter which was usually located at the end of the eastern range opposite to the church. In Perth Dominican friary it was found at this location[80] and at Jedburgh there was not only a reredorter but also two garderobes in the eastern range.[81]

The range opposite to the church usually contained a refectory as was the case in Linlithgow and Jedburgh, and probably in other friaries. In both of these friaries a part of these large halls was elevated for the high table at one end of the refectory. No trace of a pulpit has been found, but there was a fireplace in Linlithgow and a lavatorium in front of the refectory in the cloister walk in Jedburgh.

The kitchen at the Carmelite friary in Aberdeen was in the middle of the western range adjoined by a storage room for wine and beer,[82] whereas the kitchens of the Linlithgow and Jedburgh friaries were in the southern range next to the refectory.[83] In Linlithgow this might have been caused by the fact that the western range was probably never completed; furthermore, there must have been a temporary kitchen in some other part of the friary before the southern

---

[78] Lindsay, 'Linlithgow: The Excavations', p. 93.

[79] The closest surviving example of a celled dormitory is in Gloucester Dominican friary, which dates from the second half of the thirteenth century. For the description and discussion see Hinnebusch, *Friars Preachers*, pp. 169-76.

[80] D. Hall, *Excavations at Kinnoull Street, Perth: Publication Draft*, MS. 1984 (Scottish Urban Archaeological Trust).

[81] Yeoman, pp. 41-42.

[82] Yeoman, p. 35.

[83] Lindsay, 'Linlithgow: The Excavations', p. 87; Dixon, p. 60.

range was built in the second half of the fifteenth century. The supposed warming-room or parlour in the eastern range with its large central fireplace[84] could have served for this purpose. There were substantial storage cellars in the northern range, presumably under a kitchen block, in Inverkeithing Conventual Franciscan friary.[85]

The different ranges were joined by cloister walks which in Scotland, as far as is known, were mainly insubstantial wooden corridors rather than arcaded and vaulted stone structures.[86] The traces of these corridors can still be seen at the churches in South Queensferry Carmelite friary and Elgin Observant Franciscan friary. In South Queensferry the excavations revealed no stone structures in the claustral area suggesting that not only were the cloister walks wooden, but probably most of the conventual buildings were as well.[87] However, in Jedburgh the foundations of the cloister walks on all four sides of the garth were substantial enough to carry stone structures.

If the western range was not entirely occupied by domestic buildings of the friars like kitchens, store rooms, etc., it could house guest rooms. The only surviving mendicant conventual building in Scotland is the guest house in Inverkeithing, where it occupies the central part of the western range. It is a large three-storey building which consists of two blocks: the larger one has a kitchen on the ground floor, a guest hall on the first floor, and possibly had smaller chambers on the second floor; the adjoining block has two storeys of small guest chambers with a fireplace in each, and two vaulted storage rooms on the ground floor. In other friaries the guest lodgings could have been outside the main cloister quadrangle, as in Perth Dominican friary. The modest scale of the friars' domestic buildings must have contrasted with the fine guest houses. The friaries were frequently visited by the Scottish kings and other lords with their households and had to provide lodgings of reasonable comfort and size for dozens of people. In Perth Dominican friary at least, and probably in some other friaries as well, there were separate king's lodgings, which were described by the contemporaries as extremely large and splendid buildings, including among other things even a tennis court.[88] The tradition of large royal

---

[84] Yeoman, pp. 38-39.

[85] *RCAHMS Inventory*, vol. 11, *Fife, Kinross and Clackmannan* (Edinburgh, 1933), no. 276, pp. 153-55.

[86] Yeoman, p. 39.

[87] J. C. Wallace, *Excavations on Site of Carmelite Priory, South Queensferry*, MS. 1971(?) (National Monuments Record of Scotland).

[88] Hall, *passim*.

guest houses in older religious institutions on urban sites in Scotland, especially Dunfermline and Holyrood abbeys, may have inspired the few documented fine guest lodgings of the Scottish mendicants.

It can be concluded that the conventual buildings of the Scottish mendicant friaries were traditional in layout and modest in scale, but they had guest houses which greatly surpassed these in grandeur.

IX Conclusions

The mendicant orders played an important role in the history of medieval Scotland and their influence in various forms extended beyond this era. Their architecture had a prominent role in the urban context not only because of their quantity – there were nearly fifty friaries and mendicant nunneries in Scotland – but also for their fine quality, which can be seen from the few surviving examples.

The research into the mendicant history has been unjustifiably neglected and their role in the Reformation has been understated. Although this article is not primarily devoted to the history of the mendicants, it has revealed that the part the friars played in the Reformation was much greater than formerly believed. They were prominent on both sides of it, and the closeness of the mendicant ideas to the reformers' ones made them the first target of the Reformation. They were too influential to be tolerated.

In general it can be argued that the architecture of the friaries was primarily Scottish as it fits well into the contemporary local architectural context, and secondarily mendicant. However, it is not clear to what extent the friaries influenced the course of late medieval Scottish architecture or to what extent they themselves were subject to its influence. Apart from its Scottishness, in later, especially Dominican, architecture the Netherlandish influence can be traced, if not in general style, then certainly in details.

The topic of the mendicants needs further investigation in many directions. A closer study of written sources and archaeological material is needed on the mendicant level, as well as of the local architectural context. Even more important would be to view Scottish mendicant architecture in its wider northern European context, to analyse its links to the Netherlands and Flanders as well as France.

This study is a part in a larger investigation of mendicant architecture in Protestant northern Europe. The fate of the buildings and the underestimation of their value in Scotland is similar to other northern European Protestant regions. Scotland exemplifies the transformation of the mendicant ideal into material architectural forms, and demonstrates how mendicant architecture interrelates with the local architectural context.

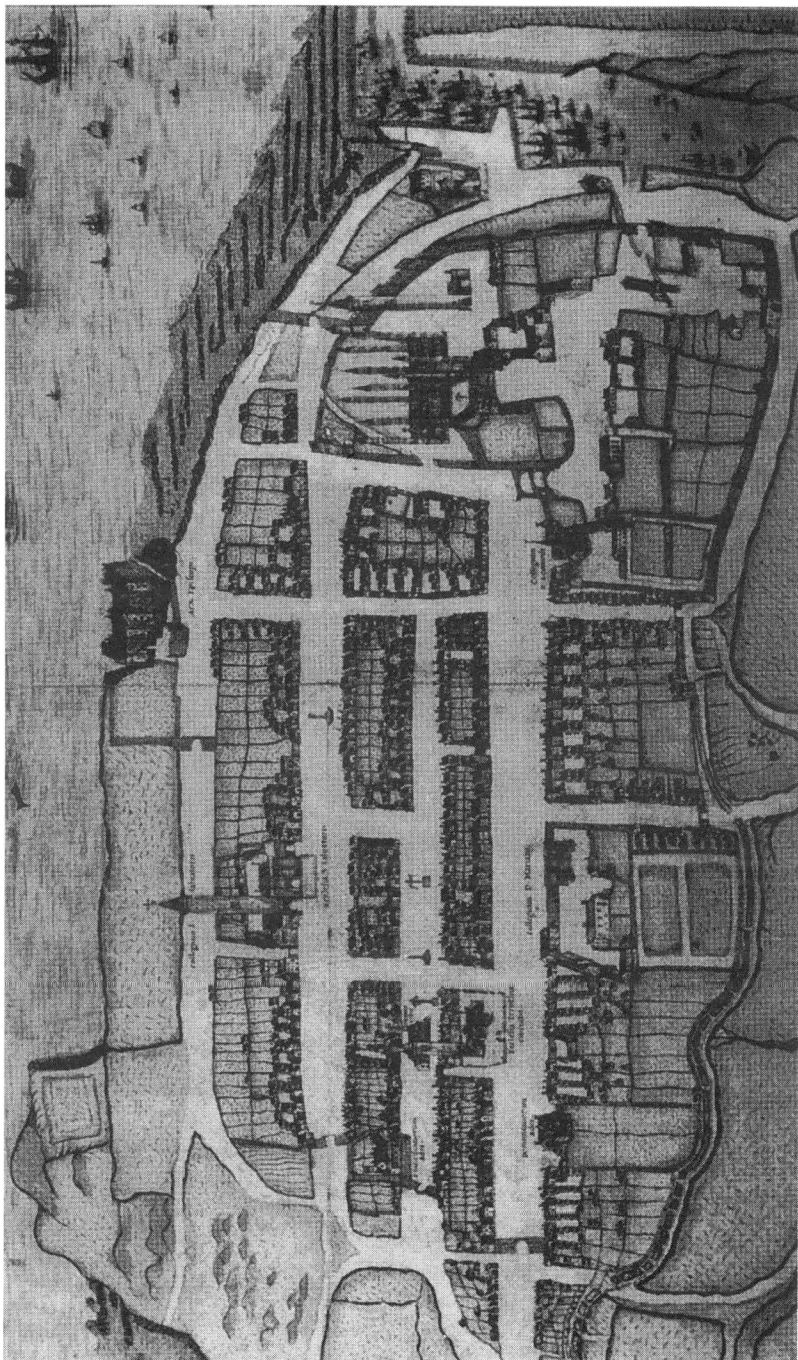

Plate 1 The anonymous bird's-eye view of St Andrews c. 1580. Reproduced by permission of the Trustees of the National Library of Scotland.

The COLLEDGE of Glasgow

Plate 2 The College of Glasgow. From: John Slezer, *Theatrum Scotiae* (London, 1693).

Plate 3   Elgin Observant Franciscan church from the north-west. Photograph: Richard Fawcett.

Plate 4 Elgin Observant Franciscan church. Interior looking east. Reproduced
         by permission of the Royal Commission on the Ancient and Historical
         Monuments of Scotland.

Plate 5 St Monans Dominican church from the south-east. Reproduced by permission of the Royal Commission on the Ancient and Historical Monuments of Scotland.

Plate 6 St Monans Dominican church. Interior looking east. Reproduced by
permission of the Royal Commission on the Ancient and Historical
Monuments of Scotland.

Plate 7   St Andrews Dominican church. The chapel from the north-west. Reproduced by permission of Historic Scotland.

15

Mendicants, Military Orders, and Regionalism

Jürgen Sarnowsky

The thirteen papers collected in this book have shown the variety of problems involved in studying the relations between international religious orders and regional influences. Of course, it has been possible to consider only a few examples and to give some impression of the 'mechanisms' which helped the orders to establish themselves, to expand their areas of influence, and to gain support from different social groups. The examples treated here concern very different regions – from Ireland, England, the Netherlands, and the French border area to Germany, Bohemia, and Silesia, from Scotland to Catalonia, Provence, and southern Italy – and different periods – from the early development of the military and mendicant orders in the twelfth and thirteenth centuries to the beginning of the Reformation in the early sixteenth century – and, as such, they may be taken as representative and some general observations can be drawn from them.[1]

1. The findings of Nikolas Jaspert, Helen Nicholson, Dieter Heckmann, Andreas Rüther, Jens Röhrkasten, Anneli Randla, and others, indicate that patronage by the leading social groups, especially rulers and rich townspeople, was an essential element in the early expansion of international religious

---

[1] This can only be an incomplete summary of the problems discussed in the papers collected in this volume; since I will refer to the articles in the text, there are no further references. Edith Pawlik and Caroline Cornish revised the first English versions of this text; the faults that remain are mine.

From *Mendicants, Military Orders, and Regionalism in Medieval Europe*, ed. Jürgen Sarnowsky. Copyright © 1999 by Jürgen Sarnowsky. Published by Ashgate Publishing Ltd, Gower House, Croft Road, Aldershot, Hampshire, GU11 3HR, Great Britain.

orders. The orders received large donations and strong support where their employment was expected to be useful. This is demonstrated in the cases of the Templars in Catalonia fighting the Moors, the Hospitallers in the frontier areas of the British Isles and the Teutonic Knights in episcopal towns of the empire stabilizing the position of the respective territorial lords, and the Crosiers of the Red Star in Silesia and the various mendicant orders in England and Scotland serving the spiritual needs of the ruling dynasties and of the townspeople. While the military orders – at least in the early phases of their development – were given lands, tithes, jurisdictional rights, and castles, the mendicants, with their strict regulations concerning the orders' properties, may have been given plots and funds for building their friaries, but generally received support on a smaller scale. The military orders thus succeeded in building up large rural centres with dependant populations and were able to supply men and money for their campaigns against the pagans in the east (and south) without ongoing financial contributions by the original donors, while the mendicants were required to pursue a continual programme of alms-collecting.

2. Since the main tasks of the military orders (and the mendicants) conformed to common Christian aims and goals, they were able to extend beyond political and linguistic frontiers – as has been shown by Helen Nicholson and Dieter Heckmann in the case of the Hospitallers in the British Isles and the Teutonic Knights in Lorraine – but not beyond religious boundaries – as becomes clear in Nikolas Jaspert's article concerning the Templars in Catalonia, who nevertheless relied at least in part on Muslim tenants. But even in the case of political and linguistic frontiers there are some exceptions: in Ireland (and to some degree also in south Wales) the Hospitallers were instrumental in the English predominance and were therefore confined to areas of Anglo-Norman influence, while the Teutonic Knights remained exclusively German where they had not been successful in receiving donations from the Romance-speaking population, as was the case in Liège. The success of the international religious orders' attempts to establish themselves in parts of Latin Christendom where they had not been present before and to cross political or linguistic borders depended therefore upon local and regional conditions at the time of their establishment. This is confirmed by the early history of the friaries in London, as discussed by Jens Röhrkasten: although these were founded by groups of brethren from the Continent, especially Italy and the Low Countries, from the beginning English brethren played an important role and in most cases the convents soon became predominantly English (although this changed – to some extent – when the Observant movement arrived in England).

3. Adaptation to the local situation did not interfere with integration into the orders' structures. Thus, the Templars' houses in Catalonia – which were transferred to the Hospitallers after 1312 and later formed their own Hospitaller priory – contributed to financing the campaigns of the Templars in the Levant (as in the case of Gardeny), and their commanders rose to influential positions within the order. Similarly, the commanderies of the Teutonic Knights at the empire's linguistic border in the west were recruiting points for the crusades against the Lithuanians and for the order's Prussian branch (as in the case of Metz). The London friaries also sent their brethren to the Continent, organized some of their orders' chapters general – as did Dominicans, Franciscans and Carmelites in the thirteenth and early fourteenth centuries – and were even assigned the rank of a *studium generale* (as the London Grey Friars were in 1336).

4. On the other hand, as becomes clear from all the papers, none of the international religious orders was able to neglect regional and local influences as they were dependant on them for new members and donations. When pressure was exerted by popes, emperors, kings, or other institutions, the orders' officials generally had to comply or at least to be very careful not to jeopardize their standing with the authorities in question. When two powers were in conflict this might even lead to faction-building, as in the case of the Teutonic Knights during the struggle between Frederick II and the popes, as has been pointed out by Klaus Militzer. On a secondary level, it was often inevitable that sides should be taken, as in the conflicts between the counts of Barcelona and Urgell in which the Catalonian Templars were involved, or in those between the bishop and the town of Basle, which were connected to the struggles between the emperor and the popes and which led to the problems of the Basle Dominicans (and Franciscans) described by Bernhard Neidiger. The latter case demonstrates that a shift in allegiance sometimes caused an increase in dependency, since the Basle Dominicans who turned to the town authorities were faced with growing efforts to interfere in the order's local affairs. Where regional and local influence was determined by the regional or local nobility, as with the Crosiers of the Red Star in Bohemia and Silesia or the Teutonic Knights in fifteenth-century Germany, whose situation has been analysed by Johannes Mol, shifting interests might even change the nature of the brotherhood. When the Crosiers of the Red Star, which had been founded as an association of hospitallers, over time increasingly concentrated on spiritual tasks and the cure of souls, they handed the control of their hospitals over to the towns; and the Teutonic Knights in the empire gradually restricted

admission to the order to noble Germans, while at the same time careers within the order became further differentiated between brethren serving in Prussia, in Livonia, or in the bailiwicks under the control of the German masters (Deutschmeister). In the fifteenth century, the conflicts between regional groupings of the nobility even influenced the orders' policies, especially in Prussia and Livonia.

5. The special nature of the international religious orders, in particular their exemption from episcopal jurisdiction, quite often caused problems. Where the military orders took over parochial churches, the bishops might lose part of their incomes (as has been shown for Tortosa and Lleida), while the local clergy suffered from the activities of the mendicants, who concentrated on preaching and the cure of souls, so that they became the primary targets of attacks by reforming movements, especially during the Reformation period (as, for example, in Scotland). It was therefore primarily the support of the higher spiritual and secular authorities, popes, kings, and other rulers, which allowed the mendicants and the military orders to maintain their position. In return, the orders were expected to support papal and royal policies. Thus the Basle mendicants sided with Innocent IV in his struggle against Frederick II, while the Provençal Hospitallers gave part of their estates to John XXII in exchange for the properties of monasteries in southern Italy, which led to the internal problems described by Anthony Luttrell. Brethren from mendicant and military orders also played important roles in the service of kings and other rulers: the Hospitallers in England, Germany, and Bohemia, and the Dominicans at the English court, for example. The Hospitaller priors of England were regularly summoned to parliament, at times formed part of the kings' entourage, and were sent on diplomatic missions. And the German Hospitallers, who took over as priors of *Alemania* and Bohemia between 1255 and 1325, helped to stabilize the rule of the Bohemian kings as well as that of Rudolph of Habsburg and other kings of the Romans, as has been demonstrated by Karl Borchardt. In this context it does not come as a surprise that the 'election' of officers was often manipulated by kings, who at least attempted to exert their influence on the outcome.

6. The different 'national' and regional settings also influenced the internal structures of the orders. This was always the case when provinces were to be formed, as becomes clear in the examples of the Hospitallers in the British Isles, in the empire, and in southern Italy discussed in this volume. While the priory of Ireland remained almost completely under the control of the English priors due to the Anglo-Norman origins of its brethren, the administrative

structures in the empire varied according to the current political situation. In east central Europe there were two grand preceptors primarily under the spheres of influence of Frederick II and the pope. The office of the grand preceptor and the priories of *Alamania inferior*, *Alamania superior*, and sometimes even of *Alamania media* (Franconia), of Bohemia, Moravia, Austria, and *Polonia* were then separated or united as seemed appropriate or necessary. A similar situation developed from the end of the thirteenth century in southern Italy, where Angevin and Aragonese interests overlapped with those of the local nobility. As the Angevins ruled in Provence as well as in southern Italy and (from the beginning of the fourteenth century) in Hungary, the Provençal brethren tried to exert some influence in these areas as well. As discussed by Anthony Luttrell, there were Provençal priors of Capua and Barletta and of Hungary, as well as several houses in southern Italy which had been granted to the order in exchange for properties in Provence: a circumstance which led to grave quarrels between the Provençal and Italian brethren. Although a treaty was signed in 1373 establishing spheres of influence, the conflicts continued well into the fifteenth century. On the other hand, the orders' provinces might face dissolution if national and economic influences worked together, as Libor Jan has shown for the Teutonic Knights' bailiwick of Bohemia, where nearly all property was lost to the king and the Bohemian nobility. Within most of the provinces where the orders were able to maintain their position, a kind of regional identity developed in the course of the later Middle Ages. This is confirmed here, for example, in the case of the Hospitallers and the Teutonic Knights in Germany and Bohemia as well as in that of the mendicants in Scotland. While the German and Bohemian Hospitallers turned their main focus of interest from the Holy Land to their native regions, the Teutonic Knights decided – after long internal struggles – to establish themselves in Prussia and to abandon the hope for a successful return to the Levant: a decision which finally led to the differentiation of the orders' branches in Prussia, Livonia, and Germany touched upon by Johannes Mol. There are also signs of regional identity in the orders' architecture: thus the architecture of the Scottish mendicants, who normally did not have their own masons, developed in close connection with the architecture of that region, as has been (cautiously) argued by Anneli Randla.

7. The central institutions were not always able to control regional developments, although they often succeeded in asserting their position in the long term, as is demonstrated by the case of the Hospitallers of England, who in the later fifteenth century succeeded in finding a working compromise with the

English kings. Sometimes regional and local influences might be stronger than those of central institutions, as in the case of the Basle town council, which was in competition with the south German provinces of the Dominicans. This was particularly the case when the orders were divided by internal quarrels, as when the mendicants split over the issue of reform. There were also informal divisions when provinces – backed by regional influences and probably encouraged by the limited strength of the order as a whole – reached a certain autonomy, as in the case of the Silesian Crosiers of the Red Star. However, these were exceptions; and in general, the orders' structures worked comparatively well in keeping their provinces together despite diverging interests.

All the examples of the influence of European regionalism on mendicants and military orders which have been examined in this volume require further research, especially from a comparative perspective, and there are other questions which remain to be answered, concerning, for example, the communications between the orders' central institutions and their provinces. It is hoped that this book will provide impulses for future studies. The history of 'international' medieval institutions and their regional settings may also contribute to a better understanding of today's problems. In the future, the gap between the individual and an expanding European political and economic community will likely be bridged not only by a new understanding of nations but also by a recognition of the growing importance of the various European regions. Our medieval ancestors developed several ways of settling conflicts of interest within 'multinational' communities, of which the international religious orders form an important example.

Select Bibliography

Printed Sources

Acta capitulorum generalium ordinis Praedicatorum, ed. B. M. Reichert. Monumenta ordinis fratrum Praedicatorum 3-4, 7-14 (Rome, 1898-1904).

Akten der Provinzkapitel der Dominikanerprovinz Teutonia aus den Jahren 1398, 1400, 1401 und 1402, ed. B. M. Reichert, *Römische Quartalschrift* 11 (1897) 287-331.

'Aus den Akten des Rottweiler Provinzkapitels der Dominikaner vom Jahr 1396', ed. B. Altaner, *Zeitschrift für Kirchengeschichte* 48 (1929) 1-15.

Beaucage, B., *Visites générales des Commanderies de l'Ordre des Hospitaliers dépendantes du Grand Prieur de Saint-Gilles: 1338* (Aix-en-Provence, 1982).

Die Berichte der Generalprokuratoren des Deutschen Ordens an der Kurie, vols 1-4, 2, eds K. Forstreuter, H. Koeppen. Veröffentlichungen der Niedersächsischen Archivverwaltung 12, 13, 21, 29, 32, 37 (Göttingen, 1961-1976).

Biskup, M., Janosz-Biskupowa, I. (eds), *Protokolle der Kapitel und Gespräche des Deutschen Ordens im Reich (1499-1525)*. QStGDO 41 (Marburg, 1991).

Bliemetzrieder, F., 'Traktat des Minoritenprovinzials von England Fr. Nicholas de Fakenham (1395)', *Archivum Franciscanum Historicum* 1 (1908) 577-600, 2 (1909) 79-91.

Bullarium Franciscanum sive Romanorum pontificum constitutiones, epistolas ac diplomata continens ..., eds J. H. Sbaralea, C. Eubel et al., 7 vols (Rome, Leipzig, 1759-1904); continued as: *Bullarium Franciscanum continens Constitutiones epistolas diplomata Romanorum pontificum*, vols 1-4, eds U. Hüntemann, J. M. Pou y Marti, C. Canci (Quaracchi, 1929-1990).

Bullarium ordinis fratrum Praedicatorum, ed. A. Bremond, 8 vols (Rome, 1729-1740).

Cartulaire de l'Ordre des Hospitaliers de S. Jean de Jérusalem, ed. J. Delaville Le Roulx, 4 vols (Paris, 1894-1906).

Cartulaire général de l'Ordre du Temple 1119?-1150, ed. M. d'Albon (Paris, 1913).

Casagrande, G. (ed.), *Chiese e conventi degli ordini mendicanti in Umbria nei secoli XII-XIV. Inventario delle fonti archivistiche e catalogo delle informazioni documentari*. Archivi dell'Umbria. Inventari e ricerche 14 (Perugia, 1989).

Codex diplomaticus ordinis Sanctae Mariae Teutonicorum. Urkundenbuch des Deutschen Ordens, ed. J. H. Hennes, 2 vols (Mainz, 1845-1861).

Cowan, I. B., Mackay, P. H. R., Macquarrie, A. (eds), *The Knights of St John of Jerusalem in Scotland*. Scottish History Society, fourth series 19 (Edinburgh, 1983).

Dondaine, A. (ed.), 'Documents pour servir à l'histoire de la Provence France', *Archivum Fratrum Praedicatorum* 22 (1952) 381-439.

L'Enquête Pontificale de 1373 sur l'Ordre des Hospitaliers de Saint-Jean de Jérusa-

lem; ed. J. Glénisson, vol. 1: *L'Enquête dans le Prieuré de France*, ed. A.-M. Legras (Paris, 1987).

Geer tot Oudegein, J. J. de, *Archieven der Ridderlijke Duitsche Orde, balie van Utrecht*, 2 vols (Utrecht, 1871).

Geer tot Oudegein, J.J. de, *Excerpten uit de oude rekeningen der Ridderlijke Duitsche Orde, balye van Utrecht, vóór de kerkhervorming* (Utrecht, 1895).

Gervers, M. (ed.), *The Cartulary of the Knights of St John of Jerusalem in England*, 2 parts (Oxford 1982-1996).

Hemmerle, J. (ed.), *Die Deutschordensballei Böhmen in ihren Rechnungsbüchern 1382-1411*. QStGDO 22 (Bonn, 1967).

Joachim, E., Hubatsch, W., *Regesta historico-diplomatica Ordinis S.Mariae Theutonicorum 1198-1525*, vol. I, 1-3; II; Register (Göttingen, 1948-1973).

Jordan of Saxony, *Libellus de principiis ordinis Praedicatorum*, ed. H. C. Scheeben. Monumenta ordinis fratrum Praedicatorum 16 (Rome, 1935).

'Kapitelsakten der Dominikanerprovinz Teutonia (c. 1349, 1407)', ed. T. Kaeppeli, *Archivum Fratrum Praedicatorum* 22 (1952) 186-95.

The Knights Hospitallers in England: being the report of Prior Philip de Thame to the Grand Master Elyan de Villanova for AD 1338, eds K. B. Larking, J. M. Kemble. Camden Society first series 65 (London, 1857).

Longo, C., 'I Domenicani a Cipro. Documenti (1451-1587)', *Archivum Fratrum Praedicatorum* 59 (1989) 149-211.

Papsturkunden für Templer und Johanniter, ed. R. Hiestand, 2 vols. Vorarbeiten zum Oriens Pontificius 1-2 (Göttingen, 1972-1984).

Pettenegg, E.G. v., *Die Urkunden des Deutsch-Ordens-Centralarchives zu Wien*, vol. 1 (Prague, Leipzig, 1887).

Preußisches Urkundenbuch, eds R. Philippi, A. Seraphim, M. Hein, E. Maschke, H. Koeppen, K. Conrad, vols 1, 1-6, 1 (Königsberg, then Marburg, 1882-1986).

Records of the Templars in England in the Twelfth Century: the Inquest of 1185, ed. B. A. Lees. British Academy, Records of the Social and Economic History of England and Wales 9 (London, 1935).

Regestenlijst der oorkonden van de landkommanderij Oudenbiezen en onderhorige kommanderijen, ed. J. Grauwels, 4 vols (Brussels, 1966-1969).

Registrum de Kilmainham: Register of Chapter Acts of the Hospital of St John of Jerusalem in Ireland, 1326-1339 under the Grand Prior, Sir Roger Outlawe, with additions for the times of his successors..., ed. C. McNeill (Dublin, 1932).

Registrum litterarum Salvi Casettae 1481-1483 et Barnabae Saxoni 1486, ed. B. M. Reichert. Quellen und Forschungen zur Geschichte des Dominikanerordens in Deutschland 7 (Leipzig, 1912).

Scriptores rerum Prussicarum. Die Geschichtsquellen der preußischen Vorzeit bis zum Untergange der Ordensherrschaft, vols 1-5, eds Th. Hirsch, M. Toeppen, E. Strehlke (Leipzig, 1861-1874, reprinted Frankfurt a. M., 1965), vol. 6, eds W. Hubatsch, U. Arnold (Frankfurt a. M., 1968).

Die Statuten des Deutschen Ordens nach seinen ältesten Handschriften, ed. M. Perl-bach (Halle, 1890).

Tabulae Ordinis Theutonici, ed. E. Strehlke (Berlin, 1869; reprinted [with an introd. by H. E. Mayer] Toronto, 1975).

Urkundenbuch der Deutschordensballei Thüringen, vol. 1, ed. K. H. Lampe. Thürin-gische Geschichtsquellen N. F. 7 (Jena, 1936).

Van der Eycken, M., *Inventaris van het Archief van de Balije Biesen van de Duitse Orde*, part II. Bijdragen tot de geschiedenis van de Duitse Orde in de Balije Biesen 3b (Bilzen, 1996).

Ypma, E., 'Les statuts pour le couvent des Augustins de Paris promulgués au XVe siècle', *Augustiniana* 33 (1983) 283-329.

Literature

Aarts, B., 'Bouw en verbouw van het kasteel van de Duitse Orde', *Commanderij Ge-mert. Beeldend Verleden*, ed. T. Thelen (Gemert, 1990) 43-64.

Aarts, B., *Die Kommende des Deutschen Ordens von Middelburg zwischen den Jahren 1248 und 1581* (unpublished M.A. Thesis, Free University, Amsterdam, 1990).

Alatri, M. d', 'A proposito dei più antichi insediamenti francescani in Sicilia', *Schede medievali* 12-13 (1987) 25-35.

Alatri, M. d', *L'inquisizione francescana nell'Italia centrale nel secolo XIII* (Rome, 1954).

Albersoni, M. P., *Francescanesimo a Milano nel duecento*. Fonti e ricerche 1 (Milano, 1991).

Albert i Corp, E., 'Els templers i la política de la Corona d'Aragó', *APJC*, pp. 219-26.

Alcoy Pedrós, R., 'El castell de Gardeny', *Lleida, la ciutat dels dos turrons* (Lleida, 1992), pp. 44-52.

Amato, A. d', *I Domenicani a Bologna*, vol. 1: *1218-1600* (Bologna, 1988).

Angelis, M. de, 'I conventi francescani della custodia viterbese fondati nei secoli XIII-XIV', *Laurentianum* 34 (1993) 227-43.

Arienza, L. d', 'Gli Ordini Militari in Sardegna nel Basso Medioevo', *APJC*.

Arnold, U., 'Der Deutsche Orden und Venedig', *MS*, pp. 145-65.

Arnold, U., 'Der Deutsche Orden zwischen Kaiser und Papst im 13. Jahrhundert', *RM*, pp. 57-70.

Arnold, U., 'Deutschmeister Konrad von Feuchtwangen und die "preußische Partei" im Deutschen Orden am Ende des 13. und zu Beginn des 14. Jahrhunderts', *Aspekte der Geschichte. Festschrift für Peter Gerrit Thielen zu seinem 65. Geburtstag*, eds U. Ar-nold, J. Schröder, G. Walzik (Göttingen, 1990), pp. 22-42.

Arnold, U., 'Die Ballei und das Land: Mittelalter', *Der Deutsche Orden in Tirol. Die Ballei an der Etsch und im Gebirge*, ed. H. Noflatscher. QStGDO 43 (Bozen, 1991), pp. 125-70.

Arnold, U., 'Entstehung und Frühzeit des Deutschen Ordens', *Die geistlichen Ritteror-*

den Europas, eds J. Fleckenstein, M. Hellmann. Vorträge und Forschungen XXVI (Sigmaringen, 1980), pp. 81-96.

Arnold, U., 'Europa und die Region – widerstreitende Kräfte in der Entwicklung des Deutschen Ordens im Mittelalter', *RR*, pp. 161-72.

Arnold, U., 'Preußen, Böhmen und das Reich – Karl IV. und der Deutsche Orden', *Kaiser Karl IV. Staatsmann und Mäzen*, ed. F. Seibt (Munich, 1978), pp. 167-73.

Ayala Martínez, C. de, 'Alfonso X y la Orden de San Juan de Jerusalén', *Estudios de historia medieval: Homenaje a Luis Suárez*, ed. V. Alvarez Palenzuela et al. Historia y Sociedad 18 (Valladolid, 1991), pp. 29-50.

Ayala Martínez, C. de, 'Origines de la Orden del Hospital en Castilla y León (1113-1157)', *Hispania sacra* 43 (1991) 775-98.

Ayala Martinez, C. de, 'Possessions and Incomes of the Order of Calatrava in the Kingdom of Léon in the Twelfth and Thirteenth Centuries', *MO*, pp. 283-87.

Ayala Martínez, M. de, Andrés Robres, F., Matellanes Merchán, J. V. et al., 'Las Ordenes Militares en la Edad Media peninsular. Historiografía 1976-1992, II: Corona de Aragón, Navarra y Portugal', *Medievalismo* 3 (1993) 87-144.

Ayala Martínez, M. de, Barquero Goñi, C., Matellanes Merchán, J. V. et al., 'Las Ordenes Militares en la Edad Media peninsular. Historiografía 1976-1992, I: Reinos de Castilla y León', *Medievalismo* 2 (1992) 119-69.

Baetens, D. J., 'Minderbroeders in de zuiderlijke Nederlanden', *Franciscana* 44 (1989) 3-62.

Balatková, J., 'K dějinám řádu německých rytířů v Miletíně', *Krkonoše – Podrkonoši* 7 (1983) 205-14.

Barber, M., *The New Knighthood. A History of the Order of the Temple* (Cambridge, 1994).

Barber, M., *The Trial of the Templars* (2nd edn, Cambridge, 1993).

Barborová, E., 'Češi a Moravané jako účastníci válek Polska s řádem německých rytířů v letech 1410 a 1414', *Sborník Matice moravské* 86 (1967) 191-201.

Barker, E., *The Dominican Order and Convocation* (Oxford, 1913).

Barquero Goñi, C., 'The Hospitallers and the Castilian-Leonese Monarchy: the Concession of Royal Rights, Twelfth to Fourteenth Centuries', *MO*, pp. 28-33.

Beck, E., 'The Order of the Holy Cross (Crutched Friars) in England', *Transactions of the Royal Historical Society* 3rd series 7 (1913) 191-208.

Bedford, W. K. R., Holbeche, R., *The Order of the Hospital of St John of Jerusalem. Being a History of the English Hospitallers of St John, Their Rise and Progress* (London, 1902).

Bělohlávek, M., 'Řád německých rytířů v Plzni do válek husitských', *Sborník minulosti Plzně a Plzeňska* (Plzeň, 1958), pp. 7-29.

Bělohlávek, P. V., Hradec, P. J., *Dejiny ceskych krizovniku s cervenou hvezdou* (Prague, 1930).

Bennett, R. R., *The Early Dominicans* (Cambridge, 1937).

Benninghoven, F., 'Zur Zahl und Standortverteilung der Brüder des Deutschen Ordens in den Balleien um 1400', *Preussenland* 26 (1988) 1-20.

Benninghoven, F., *Der Orden der Schwertbrüder*. Fratres milicie Christi de Livonia. Ostmitteleuropa in Vergangenheit und Gegenwart 9 (Cologne, Graz, 1965).

Berg, D. (ed.), *Bettelorden und Stadt. Bettelorden und städtisches Leben im Mittelalter und in der Neuzeit*. Saxonia Franciscana 1 (Werl, 1992).

Berg, D., 'Staufische Herrschaftsideologie und Mendikantenspiritualität. Studien zum Verhältnis Kaiser Friedrichs II. zu den Bettelorden', *Wissenschaft und Weisheit* 26 (1972) 26-51, 185-209.

Berg, D., 'Studien zur Geschichte und Historiographie der Franziskaner im flämischen und norddeutschen Raum im 13. und beginnenden 14. Jahrhundert', *Franziskanische Studien* 65 (1983) 114-55.

Berger, T., *Die Bettelorden in der Erzdiözese Mainz und in den Diözesen Worms und Speyer im 13.Jahrhundert. Ausbreitung, Förderung und Funktion*. Quellen und Abhandlungen zur mittelrheinischen Kirchengeschichte (Mainz, 1995).

Bertran i Roigé, P., 'Donacions de la comtessa Dolça d'Urgell als ordes religiosos (1184-1210)', *Analecta Sacra Tarraconensia* 49-50 (1976-1977) 41-50.

Bertran i Roigé, P., 'Gardeny, els Templers de Lleida', *Lleida, la ciutat dels dos turrons* (Lleida, 1992), pp. 11-42.

Bertran i Roigé, P., 'L'Ordre de l'Hospital a Catalunya: els inicis', *L'Avenc* 179 (1994) 22-27.

Bertran i Roigé, P., 'L'Orde de Sant Joan de Jerusalem i l'expansion de la Corona d'Aragó per la Mediterrània', *Ordes equestres militars i marítims i les marines menors de la Mediterrània durant els segles XIII-XVII* (Barcelona, 1988), pp. 27-34.

Bertran i Roigé, P., 'Les despeses del Gran Prior de Catalunya de L'Orde de Sant Joan de Jerusalem, 1419', *Miscellània de textos medievals* 6 (1992) 165-96.

Bertran i Roigé, P., 'Per un diplomatari d'Ermengol VII. Els ordres militars al Comtat d'Urgell', *Ilerda* 45 (1984) 147-74.

Bibliographie zur Geschichte der sächsischen Franziskanerprovinz, vol. 1, *Franziskaner in Westfalen*, ed. D. Berg. Saxonia Franciscana 4 (Werl, 1994).

Biget, J.-L., 'Autour de Bernard Délicieux: franciscanisme et société en Languedoc entre 1295 et 1330', *Revue d'histoire de l'Église de France* 70 (1984) 75-93.

Binding, G., 'Die mittelalterliche Ordensbaukunst der Franziskaner im deutschen Sprachraum', *Franziskanische Studien* 67 (1985) 287-316.

Biskup, M., 'Der Deutsche Orden im Reich, in Preußen und Livland im Banne habsburgischer Politik in der zweiten Hälfte des 15. und zu Beginn des 16. Jahrhunderts', *RM*, pp. 101-25.

Biskup, M., 'Der Deutsche Orden und die Freiheit der großen Städte in Preußen vom 13. bis zur Mitte des 15. Jahrhunderts', *SO*, pp. 112-28.

Biskup, M., 'Wendepunkte der Deutschordensgeschichte', *Beiträge zur Geschichte des Deutschen Ordens*, vol. 1, ed. U. Arnold. QStGDO 36 (Marburg, 1986), pp. 1-18.

Biskup, M., Labuda, G., *Dzieje zakonu krzyżackiego w Prusach* (Gdańsk, 1988).

Bladé i Desumvila, A., *El castell de Miravet* (Barcelona, 1994).

Blauth, C., 'Dominikaner und Dominikanerinnen in Metz. Ein Beitrag zur Entstehungs-geschichte der Konvente und zur Frauenseelsorge im 13. Jahrhundert', *Liber amico-rum necnon amicarum für Alfred Heit. Beiträge zur mittelalterlichen Geschichte und geschichtlichen Landeskunde*, eds F. Burgard, C. Cluse, A. Haverkamp (Trier, 1995), pp. 171-87.

Bock, F., 'Das Nürnberger Predigerkloster. Beiträge zu seiner Geschichte', *Mitteilungen des Vereins für Geschichte der Stadt Nürnberg* 25 (1924) 147-213.

Boner, G., 'Das Predigerkloster in Basel von der Gründung bis zur Klosterreform 1233-1429', *Basler Zeitschrift für Geschichte und Altertumskunde* 33 (1934) 195-303; 34 (1935) 107-259.

Bonet Donato, M., *La Orden del Hospital en la Corona de Aragón* (Madrid, 1994).

Boockmann, H., *Der Deutsche Orden. Zwölf Kapitel aus seiner Geschichte* (4th edn, Munich, 1994).

Boockmann, H., 'Der Deutsche Orden in der Geschichte des spätmittelalterlichen Ost-europa', *Deutscher Orden, 1190-1990*, ed. U. Arnold. Tagungsberichte der Histori-schen Kommission für ost- und westpreußische Landesforschung 11 (Lüneburg, 1997), pp. 11-32.

Boockmann, H., *Deutsche Geschichte im Osten Europas. Ostpreussen und Westpreus-sen* (Berlin, 1992).

Boockmann, H., 'Herkunftsregion und Einsatzgebiet', *RR*, pp. 7-19.

Borchardt, K., 'Military Orders in East Central Europe: The first hundred years', *Au-tour de la première croisade: Actes du Colloque de la Society for the Study of the Crusades and the Latin East*, ed. M. Balard. Byzantina Sorbonensia 14 (Paris, 1996), pp. 247-54.

Borchardt, K., 'The Hospitallers in Pomerania between the Priories of Bohemia and Alamania', *The Military Orders*, vol. 2: *Warfare and Welfare*, ed. H. Nicholson (Aldershot, 1998), pp. 295-306.

Börner, E., *Dritter Orden und Bruderschaften der Franziskaner in Kurbayern*. Franzis-kanische Forschungen 33 (Werl, 1988).

Bourdillon, A. F. C., *The Order of Minoresses in England* (Manchester, 1926).

Braasch-Schwersmann, U., 'Das Deutschordenshaus Marburg und seine Niederlassun-gen in hessischen Städten im Mittelalter', *Hessisches Jahrbuch für Landesgeschichte* 42 (1992) 49-85.

Bramato, F., 'L'ordine dei Templari in Italia. Dalle origini al pontificato di Innocenzo III (1135-1216)', *Nicolaus* 12 (1988) 183-221.

Brassens, J., 'Toulouse sous les Hospitaliers de Saint-Jean. De la Commanderie de Saint-Jean (1121) au Grand Prieuré de Toulouse 1315-1790', *Annales de l'Ordre Souverain militaire de Malte* 32 (1974) 87-95.

Braunfels, W., *Monasteries of Western Europe: The Architecture of the Orders* (Lon-don, 1972).

Brünjes, H. St., *Die Deutschordenskomturei in Bremen. Ein Beitrag zur Geschichte des Deutschen Ordens in Livland.* QStGDO 53 (Marburg, 1997).

Bryce, W. M., *The Scottish Grey Friars*, 2 vols (Edinburgh, London, 1909).

Bühler, B., 'Geschichte der Franziskaner in der Reichsstadt Hall', *Württembergisch Franken* 68 (1984) 23-62.

Bulloch, J., 'The Crutched Friars', *Records of the Scottish Church History Society* 10 (1950) 86-106, 154-70.

Bürger, Bettelmönche und Bischöfe in Halberstadt. Studien zur Geschichte der Stadt, der Mendikanten und des Bistums vom Mittelalter bis zur frühen Neuzeit, ed. D. Berg. Saxonia Franciscana 9 (Werl, 1997).

Burleigh, M., *Prussian society and the German Order. An aristocratic corporation in crisis c. 1410-1466* (Cambridge, 1984).

Burns, R.I., 'Religious Houses as Archives / Depositories. A "Letter of Credence" from the Majorcan to the Barcelonian Templars (1244)', *Estudis Castellonencs* 6 (1994-1995) 235-42.

Burton, J. E., 'The Knights Templar in Yorkshire in the twelfth century: a reassessment', *Northern History* 27 (1991) 26-40.

Butler, L., Given-Wilson, C., *Medieval Monasteries of Great Britain* (London, 1979).

Camao, P., 'Francescanesimo e cultura in Sicilia', *Quaderni medievali* 14 (1982), 169-96.

Capolongo, D., 'Alife: un nuovo Insediamento templare in Terra di Lavoro', *Atti del XV Congresso di Ricerche Templari* (Latina, 1997).

Carcenac, A.-R., 'L' élevage dans le Rouergue méridional au temps des Templiers', *Annales du Midi* 195 (1991) 293-306.

Castillon Cortada, F., 'Discusiones entre los obispos de Lérida y los templarios de Monzón', *Ilerda* 36 (1975) 41-96.

Chettle, H. F., 'The Friars of the Holy Cross in England', *History* 34 (1949) 204-20.

Cioffari, G., *Storia dei Domenicani in Puglia, 1221-1350* (Bari, 1986).

Cleve, H., 'Kaiser Friedrich II. und die Ritterorden', *Deutsches Archiv für Erforschung des Mittelalters* 49 (1993) 39-73.

Conlan, P., *Franciscan Ireland* (Gigginstown, 1988).

Copsey, R., 'The Carmelites in Aberdeen 1273-1560', *Carmelus* 42 (1995) 44-111.

Copsey, R., *The Medieval Carmelite Piory at London. A Chronology* (Rome, 1995).

Cowan, I. B., Easson, D. E., *Medieval Religious Houses: Scotland* (London, 1976).

Crudo, G., *La SS. Trinità di Venosa: Memorie storiche diplomatiche archeologiche* (Trani, 1899).

Czacharowski, A., 'Die politische Rolle der Johanniter im pommerschen Grenzgebiet im Mittelalter', *RM*, pp. 143-52.

Daris, J., 'Notes historiques sur les commanderies de l'Ordre teutonique au diocèse de Liège', *Bulletin de l'Institut Archéologique Liègeois* 17 (1883) 13-40.

Dauber, R. L., *Der Johanniter-Malteser Orden in Österreich und Mitteleuropa*, vol. 1 (Vienna, 1996).

Dedieu, H., 'Les ministres provinciaux d'Aquitaine des origines à la division de l'Ordre', *Archivum Franciscanum Historicum* 76 (1983) 129-214.

Delaville le Roulx, J., *Les Hospitaliers à Rhodes jusqu'à la Mort de Philibert de Naillac: 1310-1421* (Paris, 1913).

Delaville le Roulx, J., *Les Hospitaliers en Terre Sainte et à Chypre: 1100-1310* (Paris, 1904).

Delmas, J., Delmas, C., 'Les dominicains en Rouerge. Jean Capreolus et son temps', *Archistra* 117 (1994) 108-13.

Demel, B., 'Zur Geschichte der Johanniter und des Deutschen Ordens in Kärnten', *Symposium zur Geschichte von Millstatt und Kärnten (19.-20. Juni 1992)*, ed. F. Nikolasch (Millstatt, 1993), pp. 76-99.

Demel, B., *Das Priesterseminar des Deutschen Ordens zu Mergentheim*. QStGDO 12 (Bonn-Bad Godesberg, 1972).

Demurger, A., 'L'aristocrazia laica e gli ordini militari in Francia nel Duecento: l'esempio della Bassa Borgogna', *MS*, pp. 55-84.

Demurger, A., *Vie et mort de l'ordre du Temple* (2nd edn, Paris, 1989) [German translation: *Die Templer. Aufstieg und Untergang, 1120-1314* (Munich, 1994)].

Dilworth, M., *Scottish Monasteries in the Late Middle Ages* (Edinburgh, 1995).

Dittrich, P., 'Beiträge zur Geschichte des Fürstentums Breslau II; Die Kreuzherren im Fürstentum Breslau', *Zeitschrift des Vereins für Geschichte und Alterthum Schlesiens* 45 (1911) 201-56.

Dittrich, P., 'Beiträge zur Geschichte des Fürstentums Breslau III; Die Kreuzherren im Landkreise Breslau', *Zeitschrift des Vereins für Geschichte und Alterthum Schlesiens* 46 (1912) 124-58.

Dittrich, P., 'Die Besitzungen und wirtschaftlichen Verhältnisse des Matthiasstiftes bzw. der Kreuzherren mit dem Roten Stern', *Festschrift des Kgl. St. Matthiasgymnasiums zur Jahrhundertfeier 1811-1911*, pp. 5-95.

Dixon, P., 'Jedburgh Friary and the Border Burghs', *Current Archaeology* 97 (1985) 59-61.

Dobronič, L., 'The Military Orders in Croatia', *The Meeting of Two Worlds. Cultural Exchange between East and West during the Period of the Crusades*, ed. V. P. Goss (Kalamazoo, 1986), pp. 431-38.

Dola, K., 'Zakon joannitów na Śląsku do połowy XIV wieku', *Studia Teologiczny-Historyczne Śląska Opolskiego* 3 (1973) 43-86.

Domečka, L., 'Německti rytířů v Hradci Králové', *Časopis Společnosti přátel starožitnosti českých* 53 (1935) 29-34.

Du Boulay, F. R. H., 'The Quarrel between the Carmelite Friars and the Secular Clergy of London', *Journal of Ecclesiastical History* 6 (1955) 156-74.

Dygo, M., 'The German Empire and the Grand Master of the Teutonic Order in the Light of the Golden Bull of Rimini', *Acta Poloniae Historica* 61 (1990) 33-61.

Dzambo, J., *Die Franziskaner im mittelalterlichen Bosnien*. Franziskanische Forschungen 35 (Werl, 1991).

Easson, D., *Medieval Religious Houses in Scotland* (London, 1957).

Echarte, T., 'Huesca. Convento de predicatores (1254-1835)', *Argensola* 27 (1984),

315-32.

Edbury, P., 'The Templars in Cyprus', *MO*, pp. 189-95.

Egger, F., *Beiträge zur Geschichte des Predigerordens. Die Reform des Basler Konvents 1429 und die Stellung des Ordens am Basler Konzil (1431-1448)*. Europäische Hochschulschriften III 467 (Bern, 1991).

Eistert, K., 'Beiträge zur Geschichte des Ordens der Kreuzherren mit dem roten Stern vom Breslauer Matthiasstift', *300 Jahre Matthiasgymnasium zu Breslau 1638-1938. Eine Erinnerungsschrift* (Berlin, 1938), pp. 1-51.

Ekdahl, S., 'Die Schlacht von Tannenberg und ihre Bedeutung in der Geschichte des Ordensstaates', *Deutsche Ostkunde* 35 (1989) 63-80.

Elm, K., 'Die Spiritualität der geistlichen Ritterorden des Mittelalters. Forschungsstand und Forschungsprobleme', *MC*, pp. 477-518.

Elm, K., 'Entstehung und Reform des belgisch-niederländischen Kreuzherrenordens,' *Zeitschrift für Kirchengeschichte* 82 (1971) 292-313.

Elm, K., 'Gli ordini militari. Un ceto di vita religiosa fra universalismo e particolarismo', *MS*, pp. 9-28.

Elm, K., 'Les ordres monastiques, canonicaux et militaires en europe du Centre-Est au bas Moyen Age', *L'Eglise et le peuple chrétien dans le pays de l'Europe du Centre-Est et du Nord (XIVe-XVe siècles). Actes du colloque organisé par l'Ecole française de Rome avec la participation de l'Istituto polacco di cultura cristiana (Roma) et du Centre européen de recherches sur les congrégations et ordres religieux (CERCOR), Rome 27-29 janvier 1986*. Collection de l'Ecole Française de Rome 128 (Rome, 1990), pp. 161-80.

Elm, K. (ed.), *Stellung und Wirksamkeit der Bettelorden in der städtischen Gesellschaft*. Berliner Historische Studien 3. Ordensstudien 2 (Berlin, 1981) [*SWB*].

Englisch, E., 'Zur Geschichte der franziskanischen Ordensfamilie in Österreich von den Anfängen bis zum Einsetzen der Observanz', *800 Jahre Franz von Assisi. Franziskanische Kunst und Kultur des Mittelalters* (Krems, 1982), pp. 289-306.

Escobar Camacho J. M., 'Las Órdenes Militares en el reino de Córdoba durante el siglo XIII', *Andalucía entre Oriente y Occidente (1236-1492). Actas del V Coloquio de Historia medieval de Andalucía, celebrado en el Salón de Actos de la Exma, Diputación Provincial de Córdoba durante los días 27 al 30 de noviembre de 1986*, ed. E. Cabrera (Cordoba, 1988), pp. 113-21.

Estepa Diez, C., 'La disolución de la orden del temple en Castilla y León', *Cuadernos de Historia* 6 (1975) 121-86.

Eubel, K., *Die Avignonesische Obedienz der Mendikanten-Orden* (Paderborn, 1890).

Evertse, A. II, 'De stad Utrecht en de Franciscanen en de Dominicanen in de vijftiende eeuw', *Jaarboek Oud-Utrecht* (1986) 9-32.

Ewe, H., 'Die Franziskaner in der mittelalterlichen Ostseestadt Stralsund', *Recht und Alltag im Hanseraum. Festschrift für Gerhard Theuerkauf*, eds S. Urbanski, C. Lamschus, J. Ellermeyer (Lüneburg, 1993), pp. 145-62.

Ewig, E., 'Die Deutschordenskommende Saarburg', *Elsaß-Lothringisches Jahrbuch* 21

(1943) 81-126.

Failler, A., 'L' Occupation de Rhodes par les Hospitalliers', *Revue des études byzantines* 50 (1992) 113-35.

Farrero Isus, R., *Disputas entre los templarios y la mitra ilerdense en la diócesis de Lérida durante los siglos XII y XIII* (Tesis de Licenciatura, Universitat de Barcelona, 1982).

Favreau, M.-L., *Studien zur Frühgeschichte des Deutschen Ordens*. Kieler Historische Studien 21 (Stuttgart, [1974]).

Favreau, R., *La Commanderie du Breuil-du-Pas et la Guerre de Cent Ans dans la Saintonge méridionale* (Jonzac, 1986).

Favreau-Lilie, M.-L., 'Die Bedeutung der geistlichen Ritterorden für die Mission im östlichen Mitteleuropa (13. Jahrhundert)', *Auf den Spuren der Freiheit: Einheit Europas, was ist das?* Trigon: Kunst, Wissenschaft und Glaube im Dialog 7 (Berlin, 1997), pp. 56-69.

Favreau-Lilie, M.-L., 'The Military Orders and the Escape of the Christian Population from the Holy Land in 1291', *Journal of Medieval History* 19 (1993) 201-17.

Fawcett, R., *Scottish Abbeys and Priories* (London, Edinburgh, 1994).

Fernandez Conde, J. 'La orden franciscana en Asturias: origenes y primera época', *Archivum Franciscanum Historicum* 82 (1989) 306-59.

Ferrua, V., 'I frate predicatori a Torino. Dall'insediamento a tutto il secolo XIV', *Bulletino storica-bibliografico subalpino* 90 (1992) 111-65.

Field, P. J. C., 'Sir Robert Malory, Prior of the Hospital of St John of Jerusalem in England (1432-1439/40)', *Journal of Ecclesiastical History* 28 (1977) 249-64.

Fontette, M., 'Les Dominicaines en France au XIIIe siècle', *Les religieuses en France au XIIIe siècle*, ed. M. Parisse (Nancy, 1985), pp. 97-106.

Forey, A. J., 'A thirteenth-century dispute between Templars and Hospitallers in Aragón', *Durham University Journal* n.s. 49 (1988) 181-92.

Forey, A. J., 'Els Templers de la Corona d'Aragó i la reconquesta', *L'Avenc* 161 (1992) 24-27.

Forey, A. J., 'Recruitment to the military orders', *Viator* 17 (1986) 139-71.

Forey, A. J., 'Sources for the History of the Templars in Aragon, Catalonia and Valencia', *Archives* 21 (1994) 16-24.

Forey, A. J., 'The militarisation of the Hospital of St John', *Studia Monastica* 26 (1984) 75-82.

Forey, A. J., 'The Will of Alfonso I of Aragón and Navarre', *Durham University Journal* 73 (1980) 59-65.

Forey, A. J., *The Military Orders from the Twelfth to the Early Fourteenth Centuries* (Basingstoke, 1992).

Forey, A. J., *The Templars in the* Corona de Aragón (London, 1973).

Forstreuter, K., *Der Deutsche Orden am Mittelmeer*. QStGDO 2 (Bad Godesberg, 1967).

Fossier, R., 'Les Hospitaliers et les Templiers au nord de la Seine et en Bourgogne

(XIIe-XIVe siècles)', *OMVR*, pp. 13-36.

Franciscan History and Legend in English Medieval Art, ed. A. G. Little. British Society of Franciscan Studies 19 (Manchester, 1937).

Franciszkanie w polsce średniowiecznej, ed. J. Kłoczowski, vol. 1: *Franciszkanie na ziemiach polskich* (Kraków, 1983).

Frank, I. W., 'Ordensarmut und *missae speciales* bei den spätmittelalterlichen Mendikantenorden', *Vorgeschmack. Festschrift für T. Schneider*, eds B. J. Hilberrath, D. Sattler (Mainz, 1995), pp. 208-24.

Frank, I. W., *Die Bettelordensstudia im Gefüge des spätmittelalterlichen Universitätswesens*. Institut für europäische Geschichte Mainz, Vorträge 83 (Wiesbaden, 1988).

Franziskanisches Leben im Mittelalter. Studien zur Geschichte der rheinischen und sächsischen Ordensprovinz, ed. D. Berg. Saxonia Franciscana 3 (Werl, 1994).

Freed, J. B., *The Friars and German Society in the Thirteenth Century* (Cambridge, Mass, 1977).

Friedenthal, J.-F., 'Dominican Involvement in the Crusader States', *New Blackfriars* 75 (1994) 429-37.

Fuguet i Sans, J., 'Els Templers a Barcelona', *L'Avenc* 133 (1990) 6-14.

Fuguet i Sans, J., *L'arquitectura dels Templers a Catalunya* (Barcelona, 1995).

Galbraith, G. R., *The Constitution of the Dominican Order (1226-1360)* (Manchester, 1925).

Gancarczyk, K., 'Fundacja komendy joannickiej Bozego Ciała w Wrocławiu', *Acta Universitatis Wratislaviensis* 1112, *Historia* 76, pp. 155-63.

Gancarczyk, K., 'W kwestii początków zakonu joannitów na Śląsku', *Śląski Kwartalnik Historyczny Sobótka* 40 (1985) 191-201.

García Larragueta, S., 'La Orden de San Juan de Jerusalén en Navarra (siglo XIV)', *Las Órdenes militares en el Mediterráneo occidental, s. XII-XVIII. Coloquio celebrado los días 4, 5 y 6 de mayo de 1983* (Madrid, 1989), pp. 103-38.

García Larragueta, S., *El gran priorado de Navarra de la Orden de San Juan de Jerusalén, siglos XII-XIII*, 2 vols (Pamplona, 1957).

Garcia Oro, J., 'Páginas mindonienes de espiritualidad jacobea y franciscana. Los primitivos "freires" de la Tercera Orden Regular en Galicia', *Estudios Mindonienses* 1 (1985) 159-84.

García, J., Gonzàlez, J.-R., Markalain, J., 'La comanda templera de Gardeny', *APJC*, pp. 154-65.

Garcia-Guijarro Ramos, L., *Papado, cruzadas y órdenes militares XI-XII s.* (Madrid, 1995).

Gattini, M., *I Priorati, i Baliaggi e le Commende del Sovrano Militare Ordine di S. Giovanni di Gerusalemme nelle Province Meridionali d'Italia prima della Caduta di Malta* (Naples, 1928).

Gerbet, M.-C., 'Les ordres militaires et l'élevage dans l'Espagne médiévale (jusqu'à la fin du XVe siècle)', *OMVR*, pp. 79-106.

Gervers, M., '*Pro defensione Terre Sancte*: the Development and Exploitation of the

Hospitallers' Landed Estate in Essex', *MO*, pp. 3-20.

Gilmour-Bryson, A., *The Trial of the Templars in the Papal State and the Abbruzzi* (Città del Vaticano, 1982).

Goliński, M., 'Krzyżany czy Joannici? W sprawie rzekomej obecnosci Joannitów pod Wrocławiem w 1273r.', *Śląski Kwartalnik Historyczny Sobótka* 46 (1991) 341-44.

Goliński, M., 'Templariusze a bitwa pod Legnicą. Próba rewizji poglądów', *Kwartalnik Historyczny* 98 (1990) 3-16.

González Jiménez, M., 'Relaciones de las Órdenes Militares castellanas con la Corona', *Historia – Institutiones – Documentos* 18 (1991) 209-22.

Grana Cid, M. de Mar, 'Franciscanos y domenicanos en la Galicia medieval: aspectos de una poscion de privilego', *Archivo Ibero-Americano* 53 (1993) 230-70.

Grübel, I., *Bettelorden und Frauenfrömmigkeit im 13. Jahrhundert. Das Verhältnis der Mendikanten zu Nonnenklöstern und Beginen am Beispiel Straßburg und Basel.* Kulturgeschichtliche Forschungen 9 (Munich, 1987).

Gwynn, A., Hadcock, R. N., *Medieval Religious Houses in Ireland* (London, 1970).

Hadcock, R. N., 'The Order of the Holy Cross in Ireland', *Medieval Studies Presented to Aubrey Gwynn S. J.*, eds J. A. Watt, J. B. Morrall, F. X. Martin (Dublin, 1961), pp. 44-53.

Hageneder, H., 'Die Minoriten in den österreichischen Städten', *Stadt und Kirche*, ed. F.-H. Heye. Beiträge zur Geschichte der Städte 13 (Linz, 1995), pp. 57-68.

Hartmann, H., 'Bruder Hermann von Mainz, Meister der Johanniter in Deutschland', *Mainzer Zeitschrift* 63/64 (1968-1969) 76-78.

Heckmann, D., 'Wirtschaftliche Auswirkungen des Armagnakenkrieges von 1444 bis 1445 auf die Deutschordensballeien Lothringen und Elsaß-Burgund', *Zeitschrift für die Geschichte des Oberrheins* 140 (1992) 101-25.

Heim, P., *Die Deutschordenskommende Beuggen und die Anfänge der Ballei Elsass-Burgund.* QStGDO 32 (Bonn-Bad Godesberg, 1977).

Hellmann, M., 'Bemerkungen zur sozialgeschichtlichen Erforschung des Deutschen Ordens', *Historisches Jahrbuch* 80 (1961) 126-42.

Hellmann, M., 'Der Deutsche Orden im politischen Gefüge Altlivlands', *Zeitschrift für Ostforschung* 40 (1991) 481-99.

Hellmann, M., 'Der Deutsche Orden und die Stadt Riga', *SO*, pp. 1-33.

Hellmann, M., 'Karl IV. und der Deutsche Orden in den Jahren 1346-1360', *Folia diplomatica* 1 (1971) 103-12.

Hellmann, M., 'König Manfred von Sizilien und der Deutsche Orden', *Acht Jahrhunderte Deutscher Orden*, ed. K. Wieser. QStGDO 1 (Bad Godesberg, 1967), pp. 65-72.

Helvetia Sacra. Part V, vol. 1: *Die Franziskaner, die Klarissen und die regulierten Franziskaner-Terziarinnen in der Schweiz*, eds K. Arnold, G. Boner et al. (Bern, 1978).

Herquet, K., 'Zur Geschichte der deutschen Zunge des Johanniterordens, VII: Der Großpräzeptor Heinrich von Fürstenberg (1255-1272)', *Wochenblatt der Johanniter-*

Ordensballey Brandenburg 19 (1878) no. 14.

Heye, F.-H., 'Die Ballei an der Etsch und die Landkommende Bozen', *Der Deutsche Orden in Tirol. Die Ballei an der Etsch und im Gebirge*, ed. H. Noflatscher. QStGDO 43 (Bozen, 1991), pp. 329-58.

Hiestand, R., 'Templer- und Johanniterbistümer und -bischöfe im Heiligen Land', *Ritterorden und Kirche im Mittelalter*, ed. Z. H. Nowak. Ordines Militares IX (Toruń, 1997), pp. 143-61.

Higounet, C., 'Hospitaliers et Templiers: peuplement et exploitation rurale dans le sud-ouest de la France au Moyen Age', *OMVR*, pp. 61-78.

Hill, R. M. T., 'Fourpenny retirement: the Yorkshire Templars in the fourteenth century', *Studies in Church History* 24 (1987) 123-28.

Hinnebusch, W. A., *The Early English Friars Preachers*. Dissertationes Historicae, 14 (Rome, 1951).

Hinnebusch, W. A., *The History of the Dominican Order. Origins and Growth to 1500*, 2 vols (Staten Island, NY, 1966-1973).

Hlaváček, I., 'Zur Rolle der geistlichen und ritterlichen Orden am Hofe der böhmischen Luxemburger', *RM*, pp. 153-60.

Hofmann, H. H., *Der Staat des Deutschmeisters*, Studien zur bayerischen Verfassungs- und Sozialgeschichte 3 (Munich, 1964).

Houben, H., 'La SS. Trinità di Venosa, Baliaggio dell'Ordine di San Giovanni di Gerusalemme', *Studi Melitensi* 2 (1994).

Houben, H., *Die Abtei Venosa und das Mönchtum im normanisch-staufischen Süditalien* (Tübingen, 1995).

Iorio, R., *L'Inchiesta di Papa Gregorio XI sugli Ospedalieri della Diocesi di Trani* (Taranto, 1996).

Irgang, W., 'Beiträge zur *Silesia Franciscana* im 13. Jahrhundert', *Archiv für schlesische Kirchengeschichte* 47-48 (1989-1990) 218-47.

Izquierdo Tugas, P., 'Excavacions al Portal del Temple. Una aproximació a l'evolució del recinte emmurallat de Tortosa', *Acta arqueológica de Tarragona* 3 (1989-1990) 9-20.

Jähnig, B., 'Der Danziger Deutschordenskonvent in der Mitte des 15. Jahrhunderts', *Danzig in acht Jahrhunderten. Beiträge zur Geschichte eines hansischen und preußischen Mittelpunktes,* eds B. Jähnig, P. Letkemann (Münster, 1985), pp. 151-84.

Jähnig, B., 'Der Deutsche Orden und Karl IV.', *Kaiser Karl IV. 1316-1378. Forschungen über Kaiser und Reich*, ed. H. Patze (Göttingen, 1978), pp. 103-49.

Jähnig, B., *Johann von Wallenrode O.T.* QStGDO 24 (Bonn-Godesberg, 1970).

Jan, L., 'Neznámá listina na deblinské panstvi', *Časopis Matice moravské* 114 (1995) 3-24.

Jan, L., 'Die Würdenträger der geistlichen Ritterorden an dem Hof der letzten Přemysliden', *Böhmisch-österreichische Beziehungen im 13. Jahrhundert: Österreich (einschließlich Steiermark, Kärnten und Krain) im slawischen Großreichsprojekt Ottokars II. Přemysl, König von Böhmen*, eds M. Bláhová, I. Hlaváček (Prague,

1998), pp. 285-300.

Jaschke, F., *Die Entstehung, Bestimmung und Ausbreitung des ritterlichen Ordens der Kreuzherren mit dem roten Stern*. Programm des K. K. deutschen Gymnasiums in Kremsier 1902 (Prague, 1904).

Jaspert, N., 'Die Ritterorden und der Orden vom Heiligen Grab auf der Iberischen Halbinsel', *Militia Sancti Sepulcri. Idea e Istituzioni*, eds K. Elm, C. D. Fonseca (Rome, 1998).

Kłoczowski, J., 'Dominicans of the Polish Province in the Middle Ages', *The Christian Community in Medieval Poland. Anthologies,* ed. K. Kłoczowski. Polish Historical Library 2 (Warszawa, 1981), pp. 73-113.

Kadlec, J., 'Die Kloster der Eremiten des hl. Augustinus in Böhmen und Mähren', *Analecta Augustiniana* 56 (1993) 161-218.

King, E., *The Knights of St John in the British Realm*, 3rd edn by H. Luke (London, 1967).

Kingsford, C. L., *The Grey Friars of London* (Aberdeen, 1915).

Kleist, E. Frhr. v., 'Das Breslauer Matthiasstift des Ordens der Kreuzherren mit dem roten Stern', *Festschrift des Kgl. St. Matthiasgymansiums zur Jahrhundertfeier 1811-1911*, pp. 96-145.

Kleist, E. Frhr. v., *Beiträge zur Geschichte des Kreuzherrenordens mit dem roten Stern, besonders in Schlesien* (Theol. Diss., Breslau, 1911).

Klück, B., *De landcommanderij van de Duitse Orde te Utrecht* (Utrecht, 1995).

Kluger, K., *Hochmeister Hermann von Salza und Kaiser Friedrich II. Ein Beitrag zur Frühgeschichte des Deutschen Ordens*. QStGDO 37 (Marburg, 1987).

Knowles, D., *The Religious Orders in England*, vol. 1 (Cambridge, 1979).

Koch, E., *De kloosterpoort als sluitpost? Adellijke vrouwen langs Maas en Rijn tussen huwelijk en convent, 1200-1600*. Maaslandse monografieën 54 (Leeuwarden, Mechelen, 1994).

Kuczyński, S. M., *Wielka wojna z zakonem krzyżackim w latach 1409-1411* (Warszawa, 1955).

Laguesse-Plumier, N., 'Vestiging van de Duitse Orde in Luik (13de eeuw)', *De Duitse Orde in Luik (1254-1794)*, ed. M. Van der Eycken (Bilzen-Rijkhoven, 1991), pp. 21-25.

Laliena Corbera, C., 'Les ordres militaires et le repeuplement dans le sud de l'Aragon (XIIIe siècle)', *OMVR*, pp. 225-32.

Lange, W. T., 'Joannici na Pomorzu Gdańskim. Stan badan – interpretacje – próba syntezy', *Zapiski Historyczne* 59 (1994) 7-19.

Lawrence, C. H., *The Friars and the Impact of the Early Mendicant Movement on Western Society* (London, 1994).

Le Blévec, D., Venturini, A., 'Cartulaires des ordres militaires, XIIe-XVe siècles (Provence occidentale, basse vallée du Rhône)', *Les cartulaires. Actes de la Table ronde, 5-7 décembre 1991*, eds O. Guyotjeannin, L. Morelle, M. Parisse (Paris, 1993), pp. 451-67.

Lempfrid, H., *Die Deutschordenscomturei Metz*. Beilage zu dem Jahresberichte des Gymnasiums zu Saargemünd 1887 (Saargemünd, 1887).

Les Ordres Mendiants et la Ville en Italie centrale (v. 1220 - v. 1350). Melanges de l'École française de Rome, Moyen Age-Temps Modernes 89 (1977).

Les Ordres militaires, la vie rurale et le peuplement en Europe occidentale. VIe journées internationales d'histoire, 21-23 Septembre 1984, Centre culturel de l'Abbaye de Flaran (Auch, 1986) [*OMVR*].

Lickteig, F.-B., *The German Carmelites at the Medieval Universities* (Rome, 1981).

Ligato, G., 'Fra ordini cavallereschi e crociata: *milites ad terminum* e *confraternitates armata*', *MC*, pp. 645-99.

Limburg, H., *Die Hochmeister des Deutschen Ordens und die Ballei Koblenz*. QStGDO 8 (Bad Godesberg, 1969).

Lindsay, I. G., *The Friary Church of St Mary of Mount Carmel, South Queensferry* (South Queensferry, 1953).

Little, A. G., 'A Royal Inquiry into Property Held by the Mendicant Friars in England in 1349 and 1350', *Historical Essays in Honour of James Tait*, eds J. G. Edwards, V. H. Galbraith, E. F. Jacob (Manchester, 1933), pp. 179-88.

Little, A. G., 'Introduction of the Observant Friars into England', *Proceedings of the British Academy* 11 (1923) 455-71.

Lloyd, S., *English Society and the Crusade (1216-1307)* (Oxford, 1988).

Lock, P., 'The Military Orders in Mainland Greece', *MO*, pp. 333-39.

Logemann, S., *Die Franziskaner im mittelalterlichen Lüneburg*. Saxonia Franciscana 7 (Werl, 1996).

Löhr, G. M., *Beiträge zur Geschichte des Kölner Dominikanerklosters im Mittelalter*, p. 1-2, Quellen und Forschungen zur Geschichte des Dominikanerordens in Deutschland 15-17 (Leipzig, 1921-1922).

Loopstra, L. E., 'De Leidse commanderij van de Duitse Orde in de middeleeuwen', *Leids Jaarboekje* 76 (1984) 33-59.

Lopes, F. F., 'Franciscanos de Portugal antes de formarem Provincia independiente. Ministros provinciais a que obedeziam', *Archivo Ibero-Americano* 45 (1985) 349-450.

Lorenz, W., *Die Kreuzherren mit dem roten Stern*. Veröffentlichungen des Königsteiner Instituts für Kirchen- und Geistesgeschichte der Sudetenländer 2 (Königstein im Taunus, 1964).

Lourie, E., 'Conspiracy and Cover-up: the Order of Montesa on Trial (1352)', *Iberia and the Mediterranean World of the Middle Ages. Essays in Honor of Robert I. Burns S.J.*, vol. II (Leiden, 1996), pp. 253-317.

Lourie, E., 'The Will of Alfonso I el Batallador, King of Aragón and Navarre. A Reassessment', *Speculum* 50 (1975) 635-51.

Lourie, E., The Will of Alfonso I of Aragon and Navarre: A Reply to Dr Forey, *Durham University Journal* 77/2 (1984-1985) 165-72.

Lückerath, C.A., *Paul von Rusdorf. Hochmeister des Deutschen Ordens 1422-1441*.

QStGDO 15 (Bad Godesberg 1969).

Luttrell, A., 'Emphyteutic Grants in Rhodes Town: 1347-1348', *Papers in European Legal History: Trabajos de Derecho Histórico en Homenaje a Ferran Valls i Taberner*, ed. M. Peláez, vol. 5 (Barcelona, 1992), pp. 1409-16.

Luttrell, A., 'Gli Ospedalieri e un Progetto per la Sardegna: 1370-1374', *Società, Istituzioni, Spiritualità: Studi in Onore di Cinzio Violante*, vol. 1 (Spoleto, 1994), pp. 503-8.

Luttrell, A., 'Notes on Foulques de Villaret, Master of the Hospital 1305-1319' (1985), reprinted *idem, The Hospitallers of Rhodes and Their Mediterranean World* (Aldershot, 1992), IV, pp. 73-90.

Luttrell, A., 'Sugar and Schism: the Hospitallers in Cyprus from 1378-1386', *The Sweet Land of Cyprus. Papers given at the 25th Jubilee Spring Symposium of Byzantine Studies, Birmingham, March 1991*, eds A. Bryer, G. Georghallides (Nicosia, 1993), pp. 157-66.

Luttrell, A., 'The Economy of the Fourteenth-Century Aragonese Hospital', *Estudis Castellonencs* 6 (1994-1995) 759-66.

Luttrell, A., 'The Hospitaller Priory of Venice in 1331', *MS*, pp. 101-43.

Luttrell, A., 'The Hospitaller Province of Alamania to 1428', *RR*, pp. 21-41.

Luttrell, A., 'The Hospitallers' Western Accounts: 1373/4 and 1374/5', *Camden Miscellany* 30 (London, 1990), pp. 1-21.

Luttrell, A., 'The Hospitallers and the Papacy, 1305-1314', *Forschungen zur Reichs-, Papst- und Landesgeschichte*, eds K. Borchardt, E. Bünz, vol. 2 (Stuttgart, 1998), pp. 595-622.

Luttrell, A., 'The Hospitallers in Cyprus after 1386', *Cyprus and the Crusades*. Papers given at the International Conference of the same name, 6-9 September 1994, eds N. Coureas, J. Riley-Smith (Nicosia, 1995), pp. 125-41.

Luttrell, A., *The Hospitallers in Cyprus, Rhodes, Greece and the West: 1291-1440* (London, 1978).

Luttrell, A., *The Hospitallers of Rhodes and their Mediterranean World* (Aldershot, 1992).

Luttrell, A., 'The Hospitallers of Rhodes between Tuscany and Jerusalem: 1310-1431', *Revue Mabillon* 64 (1992) 117-38.

Luttrell, A., 'The Structure of the Aragonese Hospital: 1349-1352', *APJC*, pp. 315-28.

Luttrell, A., Fiorini, S., 'The Italian Hospitallers at Rhodes: 1437-1462', *Revue Mabillon* 68 (1996) 210-33.

Machilek, F., 'Die Přemysliden, Piasten und Arpaden und der Klarissenorden im 13. und frühen 14. Jahrhundert', *Westmitteleuropa, Ostmitteleuropa. Vergleiche und Beziehungen. Festschrift für Ferdinand Seibt zum 65. Geburtstag*. Veröffentlichungen des Collegium Carolinum 70 (Munich, 1992), pp. 293-306.

Machilek, F., 'Die selige Agnes von Böhmen und der Orden der Kreuzherren mit dem roten Stern', *Von der alten zur neuen Heimat. Vierzig Jahre Ackermann-Gemeinde in Bamberg*, eds F. Kubin, A. Rieber (Bamberg, 1986), pp. 23-34.

Machilek, F., 'Reformorden und Ordensreformen in den böhmischen Ländern vom 10. bis 18. Jahrhundert', Bohemia sacra. *Das Christentum in Böhmen 973-1973*, ed. F. Seibt (Düsseldorf, 1974), pp. 63-80.

Macquarrie, A., *Scotland and the Crusades, 1095-1510* (Edinburgh, 1985).

Magnou, E., 'Oblature, classe chevaleresque et servage dans les maisons méridionales du Temple au XIIe siècle', *Annales du Midi* 73 (1961) 378-97.

Marini, A., 'Le fondazioni francescane feminali nel Lazio nel Duecento', *Collectanea Franciscana* 63 (1993) 71-96.

Martin, A. R., *Franciscan Architecture in England*. British Society of Franciscan Studies 18 (Mancester, 1937).

Martin, H., 'Les prédicateurs franciscaines dans les provinces septentrionales de la France au XVe siècle', *I Frati Minori tra '400 e '500. Atti de XII convegno internationale, Assisi, 18- 20 ottobre 1984*, ed. R. Rusconi (Assisi, 1986), pp. 229-56.

Martín, J.-L., 'Ordenes Militares en la Peninsula Ibérica', *MC*, pp. 551-72.

Maschke, E., 'Die inneren Wandlungen des Deutschen Ritterordens', *Geschichte und Gegenwartsbewusstsein. Festschrift für Hans Rothfels zum 70. Geburtstag dargebracht* (Göttingen, 1973), pp. 247-77 [reprinted *idem, Domus Hospitalis Theutonicorum. Europäische Verbindungslinien der Deutschordensgeschichte. Gesammelte Aufsätze aus den Jahren 1931-1963*, ed. U. Arnold. QStGDO 10 (Bonn-Bad Godesberg, 1970), pp. 35-59].

Massip i Fonollosa, J., 'La carta de població del territori de Tortosa, i el Temple', *APJC*, pp. 42-66.

Matison, I., 'Die Lehnsexemtion des Deutschen Ordens und dessen staatsrechtliche Stellung in Preußen', *Deutsches Archiv* 21 (1965) 194-248.

Miceli di Serradileo, A., 'L'Ordine di San Giovanni di Gerusalemme in Calabria dal XII al XV secolo', *Studi Meridionali* 10 (1977) 241-60.

The Military Orders. Fighting for the Faith and Caring for the Sick, ed. M. Barber (Aldershot 1994) [*MO*].

Militia Sacra. Gli ordini militari tra Europa e Terrasanta, eds E. Coli, M. De Marco, F. Tommasi (Perugia, 1994) [*MS*].

Militzer, K., 'Auswirkungen der spätmittelalterlichen Agrardepression auf die Deutschordensballeien', *Von Akkon bis Wien. Studien zur Deutschordensgeschichte vom 13. bis zum 20. Jahrhundert*, ed. U. Arnold. QStGDO 20 (Marburg, 1978), pp. 62-75.

Militzer, K., 'Der Deutsche Orden in den großen Städten des Deutschen Reiches', *SO*, pp. 188-215.

Militzer, K., 'Die Aufnahme von Ritterbrüdern in den Deutschen Orden. Ausbildungsstand und Aufnahmevoraussetzungen', *Das Kriegswesen der Ritterorden im Mittelalter*, ed. Z. H. Nowak. Ordines Militares, Colloquia Torunensia Historica VI (Toruń, 1991), pp. 7-18.

Militzer, K., 'Die Einbindung des Deutschen Ordens in die süddeutsche Adelswelt', *RR*, pp. 141-60.

Militzer, K., 'Die Ritterbrüder im livländischen Zweig des Deutschen Ordens. Eine

Einführung in die Möglichkeiten und Grenzen der Auswertung des Ritterbruderkatalogs', *Ritterbrüder im livländischen Zweig des Deutschen Ordens*, eds L. Fenske, K.
Militzer. Quellen und Studien zur baltischen Geschichte 12 (Cologne, 1993), pp. 11-
70.

Militzer, K., *Die Entstehung der Deutschordensballeien im Deutschen Reich*. QStGDO
16 (2nd edn, Bonn, 1981).

Millauer, M., *Der deutsche Ritterorden in Böhmen* (Prague, 1832).

Miret i Sans, J., *Cartoral dels Templers de les comandes de Gardeny y Barbens* (Barcelona, 1899).

Miret i Sans, J., *Les cases de templers i hospitalers en Catalunya. Aplech de noves i
documents historichs* (Barcelona, 1910-1913).

Mol, J. A., *De Friese huizen van de Duitse Orde. Nes, Schoten en Steenkerk en hun
plaats in het middeleeuwse Friese kloosterlandschap* (Leeuwarden, 1991).

Mol, J.A., 'Nederlandse ridderbroeders van de Duitse Orde in Lijfland: herkomst, afkomst en carrières', *Bijdragen en Mededelingen voor de Geschiedenis der Nederlanden* 111 (1996) 1-29.

Molero García, J.M., 'Participación de la Orden del Hospital en el avance de la frontera
castellana (1144-1224)', *Alarcos 1195. Congreso internacional del VIII centenario
de la batalla de Alarcos* (Cuenca, 1996), pp. 331-51.

Moorman, J. R. H., 'Some Franciscans in England', *Archivum Franciscanum Historicum* 83 (1990) 405-20.

Moorman, J. R. H., 'The Foreign Element among the English Franciscans', *English Historical Review* 62 (1947) 289-303.

Moorman, J. R. H., *A History of the Franciscan Order* (Oxford, 1968).

Moorman, J. R. H., *The Franciscans in England* (London, 1974).

Morales Muniz, M. D.-C., 'Documentacion acerca de la administración de la Orden de
Santiago por el príncipe-rey Alfonso de Castilla (1465-1468)', *Hidalguía* 36 (1988)
839-68.

Mortier, P., *Histoire des maitres généraux de l'ordre des Frères Prêcheurs*, 8 vols
(Paris, 1903-1920).

Mould, D. D. C. P., *The Irish Dominicans: The Friars Preachers in the History of Catholic Ireland* (Dublin, 1957).

Mrusek, H.-J., 'Zur Baugeschichte der Johanniterburg Kühndorf in der ehemaligen
Grafschaft Henneberg', *Wissenschaftliche Zeitschrift der Martin-Luther-Universität
Halle-Wittenberg* 12 (1963) 663-92.

Müller, P., *Bettelorden und Stadtgemeinde in Hildesheim im Mittelalter* (Hannover,
1994).

Murray, A., 'Archbishop and Mendicants in Thirteenth-Century Pisa', *SWB*, pp. 19-75.

Neckermann, G., 'Beiträge zur Geschichte der Johanniter- (Malteser-) Ordenskomturei
zu St. Leonhard in Regensburg', *Verhandlungen des Historischen Vereins für Oberpfalz und Regensburg* 54 (1910) 47-68.

Neidiger, B., 'Der Armutsbegriff der Dominikanerobservanten. Zur Diskussion in den

Konventen der Provinz Teutonia (1389-1513)', *Zeitschrift für die Geschichte des Oberrheins* 145 (1997) 1-42.

Neidiger, B., 'Die Bettelorden im spätmittelalterlichen Rheinland', *Rheinische Vierteljahrsblätter* 57 (1993) 50-74.

Neidiger, B., 'Die Observanzbewegungen der Bettelorden in Südwestdeutschland', *Rottenburger Jahrbuch für Kirchengeschichte* 11 (1992) 175-96.

Neidiger, B., 'Stadtregiment und Klosterreform in Basel', *Reformbemühungen und Observanzbestrebungen im spätmittelalterlichen Ordenswesen*, ed. K. Elm. Berliner Historische Studien 14, Ordensstudien 6 (Berlin, 1989), pp. 539-67.

Neidiger, B., *Das Dominikanerkloster Stuttgart, die Kanoniker vom gemeinsamen Leben in Urach und die Gründung der Universität Tübingen. Konkurrierende Reformansätze in der württembergischen Kirchenpolitik am Ausgang des Mittelalters.* Veröffentlichungen des Archivs der Stadt Stuttgart 58 (Stuttgart, 1993).

Neidiger, B., *Mendikanten zwischen Ordensideal und städtischer Realität. Untersuchungen zum wirtschaftlichen Verhalten der Bettelorden in Basel.* Berliner Historische Studien 5, Ordensstudien 3 (Berlin, 1981).

Neitmann, K., 'Papst und Kaiser in den Staatsverträgen des Deutschen Ordens in Preußen, 1230-1466', *Archiv für Diplomatik* 33 (1988) 293-321.

Neitmann, S., *Von der Grafschaft Mark nach Livland. Ritterbrüder aus Westfalen im livländischen Deutschen Orden*, Veröffentlichungen aus den Archiven Preußischer Kulturbesitz, Beiheft 3 (Cologne, 1993).

Nicholson, H., 'The Military Orders and the Kings of England in the Twelfth and Thirteenth Centuries', *From Clermont to Jerusalem: the Crusades and Crusader Societies, 1095-1500*, ed. A. V. Murray (Turnhout, 1998), pp. 211-15.

Nicholson, H., *Templars, Hospitallers and Teutonic Knights: Images of the Military Orders, 1128-1291* (Leicester, 1993).

Nickel, R., 'Minoriten und Franziskaner in Westfalen vom 13. bis 17. Jahrhundert. Darstellung und Bibliographie', *Franziskanische Studien* 69 (1987) 232-360, 70 (1988) 3-43, and 71 (1989) 235-325.

Nowak, Z. H., 'Die imperialen Vorstellungen Siegmunds von Luxemburg und der Deutsche Orden', *RM*, pp. 87-98.

Nuyttens, M., 'De Tempeliers in Vlaanderen', *Handelingen der Maatschappij voor Geschiedenis en Oudheidkunde te Gent* n. s. 28 (1974) 47-57.

O'Carroll, M., 'The Educational Organization of the Dominicans in England and Wales, 1221-1348', *Archivum Fratrum Praedicatorum* 50 (1980) 23-62.

O'Callaghan, J. F., *The Spanish Military Order of Calatrava and its Affiliates.* Collected Studies Series (London, 1975).

Onorati, E., 'Die franziskanische Bewegung in Italien (1200-1500)', *800 Jahre Franz von Assisi. Franziskanische Kunst und Kultur des Mittelalters* (Krems, 1982), pp. 232-69.

Opsahl, E. P., *The Hospitallers, Templars, and Teutonic Knights in the Morea after the Fourth Crusade* (Ph.D. Diss., University of Wisconsin, Madison, 1994).

Ortega, P., 'Aragonesisme i conflicte ordes. Vassals a les comandes templeres i hospitaleres d'Ascó, Horta i Miravet: 1250-1350', *Anuario de Estudios Medievales* 25 (1995).

Otten, A., *De vestiging van de Duitse Orde in Gemert 1200-1500* (Gemert, 1987).

Pagarolas, L., 'Els senyorius templers de les Terres de l'Ebre. Significació i síntesi', *APJC*, pp. 54-66.

Pagarolas, L., *La comanda del Temple de Tortosa: primer periode, 1148-1213* (Tortosa, 1984).

Page, R. and C., 'Blackfriars of Stirling', *Proceedings of the Society of Antiquaries of Scotland* 126 (1996) 881-98.

Palmer, C. F. R., 'Fasti Ordinis Fratrum Praedicatorum: the Provincials of the Friar-Preachers, or Black Friars of England', *Archaeological Journal* 35 (1878) 134-65.

Parisse, M., 'L'implantation des ordres mendiants en Lorraine', *Annales de l'Est* 37 (1985) 132-38.

Paton, B., *Preaching Friars and the Civic Ethos: Siena 1380-1480*. Westfield Publications in Medieval Studies 7 (London, 1992).

Pellegrini, L., 'Territorio e città nell'organizzazione insediativa degli ordini mendicanti in Campania', *Rassegna storica salernitana* 5 (1986) 9-41.

Pellegrini, L., *Insediamenti francescani nell'Italia del Duecento* (Rome, 1984)

Pflugk-Harttung, J. v., 'Die inneren Verhältnisse des Johanniterordens in Deutschland, besonders im östlichen Niederdeutschland (bis zum Beginne der Herrenmeisterwürde)', *Zeitschrift für Kirchengeschichte* 20 (1900) 1-18, 132-58.

Pflugk-Harttung, J. v., *Der Johanniter- und der Deutsche Orden im Kampfe Ludwigs des Bayern mit der Kurie* (Leipzig, 1900).

Pflugk-Harttung, J. v., *Die Anfänge des Johanniterordens in Deutschland, besonders in der Mark Brandenburg und in Mecklenburg* (Berlin, 1899).

Pfotenhauer, P., 'Die Kreuzherren mit dem rothen Stern in Schlesien', *Zeitschrift des Vereins für Geschichte und Alterthum Schlesiens* 14 (1878) 52-78.

Pifarré Torres, D., 'L'esplotació dels bens territorials de la comanda templera de Gardeny', *APJC*, pp. 111-16.

Piper, R., *Die Kirchen der Bettelorden in Westfalen: Baukunst im Spannungsfeld zwischen Landespolitik, Stadt und Orden im 13. und frühen 14.Jahrhundert*. Franziskanische Forschungen 39 (Werl, 1993).

Pladevall i Font, A., *Guillem de Montrodon. Mestre del Temple i tutor de Jaume I* (Lleida, 1993).

Popp, T. D. v., 'Urkunden, den vormaligen Templerhof zu Moosbrunn betreffend', *Archiv des Historischen Vereins von Unterfranken* 12/2-3 (1853) 243-48.

Postles, D., 'The Austin canons in English towns, c. 1100-1350', *Historical Research* 66 (1993) 1-20.

Powell, J. M., 'Frederick II, the Hohenstaufen, and the Teutonic Order in the Kingdom of Sicily', *MO*, pp. 236-44.

Radogna, M., *Monografia di S. Giovanni a Mare Baliaggio del S. M. O. Gerosolimita-*

no in Napoli (Naples, 1873).

Rapp, F., 'Die Mendikanten und die Straßburger Gesellschaft am Ende des Mittelalters', *SWB*, pp. 85-102.

Rapp, F., *Réformes et Réformation à Strasbourg. Eglise et Société dans la diocese de Strasbourg (1450-1525)*. Collection de l'Institut des Hautes Etudes Alsaciennes 23 (Paris, 1974).

Raspi Serra, J. (ed.), *Gli ordini mendicanti e la città* (Milano, 1990).

Raspi Serra, J., 'Influenze arabe nella cultura architettonica degli ordini in Italia', *The Meeting of Two Worlds. Cultural Exchange between East and West during the Period of the Crusades*, ed. V. P. Goss (Kalamazoo, 1986), pp. 277-84.

Raybaud, J., *Histoire des Grands Prieurs et du Prieur de Saint-Gilles*, vol. 1 (Nîmes, 1904).

Rees, W., *A History of the Order of St John of Jerusalem in Wales and on the Welsh Border, including an Account of the Templars* (Cardiff, 1947).

Reese, W., 'Gesamtdeutsche und territoriale Zusammenhänge in der Geschichte des Deutschritterordens der Niederlande', *Blätter zur Deutschen Landesgeschichte* 83 (1936-1937) 223-72.

Reimer, H., 'Verfall der Deutsch-Ordensballei Koblenz im 15. Jahrhundert', *Trierisches Archiv* 11 (1907) 1-42.

Richards, M., 'The conflict between observant and conventual reformed Franciscans in fifteenth-century France and Flanders', *Franciscan Studies* 50 (1992) 263-81.

Riley-Smith, J., 'The Templars and the Castle of Tortosa in Syria. An Unknown Document concerning the Acquisition of the Fortress', *English Historical Review* 84 (1969) 278-88.

Riley-Smith, J., *The Knights of St John in Jerusalem and Cyprus, c. 1050-1310*. A History of the Order of the Hospital of St John 1 (London, 1967).

Ritoók, P., 'The Architecture of the Knights Templar in England', *MO*, pp. 167-78.

Die geistlichen Ritterorden Europas, eds J. Fleckenstein, M. Hellmann. Vorträge und Forschungen XXVI (Sigmaringen, 1980).

Die Ritterorden zwischen geistlicher und weltlicher Macht im Mittelalter, ed. Z. H. Nowak. Ordines Militares. Colloquia Torunensia Historica V (Toruń, 1990) [*RM*].

Ritterorden und Region – Politische, soziale und wirtschaftliche Verbindungen im Mittelalter, ed. Z. H. Nowak. Ordines Militares. Colloquia Torunensia Historica VIII (Toruń, 1995) [*RR*].

Robson, M., 'Notice about Bishop Moorman's Index of Franciscans in England, 1224-1539', *Antonianum* 66 (1991) 420-35.

Rödel, W. G., *Das Großpriorat Deutschland des Johanniter-Ordens im Übergang vom Mittelalter zur Neuzeit* (2nd edn, Cologne, 1972.).

Rodríguez Blanco, D., 'Las órdenes militares en la Frontera', *La banda morisca durante los siglos XIII, XIV y XV*. IIas jornadas de Temas Moronenses (Morón de la Frontera, 1994), pp. 149-56.

Rodríguez-Picavea Matilla, E., 'Frontera, soberanía territorial y órdenes militares en la

Península Ibérica durante la Edad Media', *Hispania* 52 (1992) 789-809.

Rodríguez-Picavea Matilla, E., 'Un ejemplo de aculturación cristiano-feudal en la frontera nazarí: la Orden de Calatrava en Alcaudete', *Actas del II Congreso de Historia de Andalucía* (Córdoba, 1994), pp. 49-61.

Rogers Rees, J., 'Slebech Commandery and the Knights of St John', *Archaeologia Cambrensis* 14 (1897) 85-107, 197-228, 261-84; 15 (1898), 33-53; 16 (1899) 220-34, 283-98.

Röhrkasten, J., 'Mendicants in the Metropolis: the Londoners and the Development of the London Friaries', *Thirteenth Century England* VI, ed. M. Prestwich (Woodbridge, 1997), pp. 61-75.

Röhrkasten, J., 'The Londoners and the London Mendicants in the Late Middle Ages', *Journal of Ecclesiastical History* 47 (1996) 466-77.

Ross, A., *Dogs of the Lord: The Story of the Dominican Order in Scotland* (Edinburgh, 1981).

Rudolf, V., *Křičovníci s červenou hveždou do r. 1419, rekonstrukce jejich činnosti.* (Ph.D. Diss., Prague, 1990).

Ruiz Mateos, A., Espino Nuño, J., Pérez Monzón, O., 'Architecture and Power: the Seats of the Priories of the Order of Santiago', *MO*, pp. 302-09.

Rüther, A., 'Ordensneugründungen und Anpassungsvorgänge im spätmittelalterlichen Klosterwesen Prags, Breslaus und Krakaus', *Wanderungen und Kulturaustausch im nördlichen Ostmitteleuropa des 15. und 16. Jahrhunderts. Tagung des Johann Gottfried Herder-Forschungsrates Marburg, 8.-10. Oktober 1997*, ed. H. Boockmann (Munich, 1999).

Rüther, A., *Bettelorden in Stadt und Land: die Straßburger Mendikantenkonvente und das Elsaß im Spätmittelalter* (Berlin, 1997).

Sans i Travé, J. M., 'Alguns aspectes de l' establiment dels templers a Catalunya: Barberà', *Quaderns d'Historia Tarraconense* 1 (1977) 9-58.

Sans i Travé, J. M., *Els Templers a Catalunya. De la rosa a la creu.* Els ordes militars 4 (Lleida, 1996).

Sarnowsky, J., 'The Teutonic Order confronts Mongols and Turks', *MO*, pp. 253-62.

Sarnowsky, J., 'Der Fall Thomas Schenkendorf rechtliche und diplomatische Probleme um die Königsberger Großschäfferei des Deutschen Ordens', *Jahrbuch für die Geschichte Mittel- und Ostdeutschlands* 43 (1995) 187-275.

Sarnowsky, J., 'Der Konvent auf Rhodos und die Zungen (*lingue*) im Johanniterorden (1421-1476)', *RR*, pp. 43-65.

Sarnowsky, J., *Die Wirtschaftsführung des Deutschen Ordens in Preußen (1382-1454)* (Cologne, 1993).

Sasse, B., 'Das Doppelkloster der Přemyslidenprinzessin Agnes in Prag', *Agnes von Böhmen 1211-1282. Königstochter – Äbtissin – Heilige*, ed. J. Polc. Lebensbilder zur Geschichte der böhmischen Länder 6 (Munich, 1989), pp. 219-42.

Scheeben, H. C., 'Der Konvent der Predigerbrüder in Straßburg – die religiöse Heimat Taulers', *Johannes Tauler. Ein deutscher Mystiker. Gedenkschrift zum 600. Todes-*

tag, ed. E. Filthaut (Essen, 1961), pp. 37-76.

Schiavone, L., *Pietrino del Ponte nella Storia dell'Ordine Gerosolimitano* (Asti, 1995).

Schickl, P., 'Die Entstehung und Entwicklung des Templerordens in Katalonien und Aragón', *Gesammelte Aufsätze zur Kulturgeschichte Spaniens. Spanische Forschungen der Görresgesellschaft* 28 (1975) 91-229.

Schmidt, H.-J., 'Die Bettelorden und ihre Niederlassungen in der Mark Brandenburg', *Beiträge zur Entstehung und Entwicklung der Mark Brandenburg im Mittelalter*, ed. W. Schich. Veröffentlichungen der Historischen Kommission zu Berlin 84 (Berlin 1993), pp. 203-25.

Schmidt, H.-J., *Bettelorden in Trier. Wirksamkeit und Umfeld im hohen und späten Mittelalter*. Trierer Historische Forschungen 10 (Trier, 1986).

Schmidt, R., *Die Deutschordenskommenden Trier und Beckingen 1242-1794*. QStGDO 9 (Marburg, 1979).

Schmitt, C., 'Les Franciscains en Alsace du XIIIe au XVIIe siècle', *Archives de l'Église d'Alsace* 44 (1985) 25-61.

Schmitt, C., *Un pape réformateur et un défenseur de l'unité de l'Eglise. Benoît XII et l'ordre des Frères Mineurs (1334-1342)* (Quaracchi, 1959).

Schuchard, C., 'Rom und die päpstliche Kurie in den Berichten des Deutschordens-Generalprokurators Jodocus Hogenstein (1448-1468)', *Quellen und Forschungen aus italienischen Archiven und Bibliotheken* 72 (1992) 54-122.

Sehi, M., *Die Bettelorden in der Seelsorgegeschichte der Stadt und des Bistums Würzburg bis zum Konzil von Trient*. Forschungen zur fränkischen Kirchen- und Theologiegeschichte 8 (Würzburg, 1981).

Selwood, D., *Knights of the Cloister. Templars and Hospitallers in central-southern Occitania c. 1100 - c. 1300* (Ph.D. Diss., Oxford, 1997).

Sensi, M., 'Gli ordini mendicanti a Spoleto', *Atti del 9o congresso internazionale di studi sull alto medioevo*, vol. 1 (Spoleto, 1981), pp. 429-85.

Simons, W., *Stad en apostolaat. De vestiging van de bedelorden in het graafschap Vlaanderen c. 1225-1350* (Brussels, 1987).

Sire, H., *The Knights of Malta* (New Haven, 1994).

Sloschek, E., ' Die Kromauer Kommende des Deutschen Ritterordens', *Zeitschrift für Geschichte und Landeskunde Mährens* 44 (1942) 166-73.

Smet, J., *The Carmelites*, vol. 1 (2nd edn, Dariell, Illinois, 1988).

Sommerlad, B., *Der Deutsche Orden in Thüringen* (Halle, 1931).

Sorelli, F., 'Predicatori a Venezia (fine secolo XIV - metà secolo XV)', *Le Venezie Francescane* 6 (1989) 131-58.

Sossalla, J., 'Przyczynki do historii krzyzowców z czerwoną gwiasdą', *Nasza Przeszłość* 23 (1966) 199-237.

Sossalla, J., *Die Säkularisation der Matthias-Stiftskommende Neuhof bei Kreuzburg OS. Ein Beitrag zur Geschichte der Säkularisation in Schlesien* (Theol. Diss, Breslau, 1936; Ohlau, 1937).

Starnawska, M., 'Krzyżowcy z czerwoną gwiazdą w Legnicy Średniowieczu', *Dzieje klasztorów i życia zakonnego w Legnicy*, eds M. Derwich, A. Niedzielenko (Legnica, 1997).

Starnawska, M., 'Nekrolog Krzyżowców z czerwoną gwiazdą: Źrodło do Poznania środowiska zakonu i jego kontaktów', *Klasztor w społeczeństwie średniowiecznym i nowożytnym*, eds M. Derwich, A. Pobóg-Lenartowicz (Opole, Wrocław, 1996), pp. 210-19.

Stenzel, G.A., 'Beiträge zur Geschichte des Ordens der Kreuziger mit dem rothen Sterne in Schlesien und des Hospitals der heiligen Elisabeth des Hauses des heiligen Matthias', *Übersicht der Arbeiten und Veränderungen der schlesischen Gesellschaft für vaterländische Kultur*, Beilage IV (Breslau, 1838).

Štěpán, V. 'Účast žoldnéřů z českých zemí (zejména Slezska a severní Moravy) ve "velké válce 1409-1411" zachycená prameny z velmistrovského archivu řádu německých rytířů', *Časopis Slezského muzea* B 39 (1990) 1-15.

Štěpán, V., 'Nové materiály k vývoji česko-polských vztahů počátkem 15. stoleti', *Časopis Slezského muzea* B 30 (1981) 85-95.

Stievermann, D., *Landesherrschaft und Klosterwesen im spätmittelalterlichen Württemberg* (Sigmaringen, 1989).

Stones, J. A. (ed.), *Three Scottish Carmelite Friaries: Excavations at Aberdeen, Linlithgow and Perth 1980-1983*. Society of Antiquaries of Scotland, Monograph Series 6. (Edinburgh, 1989).

Stüdeli, B. E. J., *Minoritenniederlassungen und mittelalterliche Stadt. Beiträge zur Bedeutung von Minoriten- und Mendikantenanlagen im öffentlichen Leben der mittelalterlichen Stadtgemeinde, insbesondere der deutschen Schweiz*. Franziskanische Forschungen 21 (Werl, 1969).

Sulowski, W., *The Hospital Orders in Bohemia, Poland and Hungary in the Thirteenth Century* (M.A. Thesis, Central European University, Budapest, 1994).

Sundt, R. A., '*Mediocres domos et humiles habeant fratres nostri*: Dominican Legislation on Architecture and Architectural Decoration in the 13th Century', *Journal of the Society of Architectural Historians* 46 (1987) 394-407.

Tandecki, J., 'Zalożenie i początki klasztori franciszkanów toruńskich w·XIII-XIV w.', *Zapiski Historyczne* 54 (1989) 7-21.

Ten. Haaf, R., *Deutschordensstaat und Deutschordensballeien. Untersuchungen über Leistung und Sonderung der Deutschordensprovinzen in Deutschland vom 13. bis zum 16. Jahrhundert*. Göttinger Bausteine zur Geschichtswissenschaft 5 (2nd edn, Göttingen, Frankfurt, Berlin 1954).

Terpstra, N., 'Confraternities and mendicant orders. The dynamics of lay and clerical brotherhood in Renaissance Bologna', *Catholic Historical Review* 82 (1996) 1-22.

Thomas, U., *Die Johanniterkomture in Mainfranken von den Anfängen bis zum Jahre 1500* ([manuscript] Würzburg, 1990)

Tipton, C., 'The 1330 Chapter General of the Knights Hospitallers at Montpellier,' *Traditio* 24 (1968) 293-308.

Tipton, C., 'The English and Scottish Hospitallers during the Great Schism', *Catholic*

Historical Review 52 (1966), 240-45.

Tipton, C., 'The Irish Hospitallers during the Great Schism', *Proceedings of the Royal Irish Academy* 69 (1970), 33-43.

Todd, J., 'Jedburgh Friary', *Discovery and Excavation in Scotland* (1985), p. 2.

Tommasi, F., 'Fonti epigrafiche dalla "domus Templi" di Barletta per la cronotassi degli ultimi maestri provinciali dell'ordine nel regno di Sicilia', *MS*, pp. 167-202.

Tommasi, F., *'Pauperes commilitones Christi.* Aspetti i problemi delle origini gerosoli-mitane', *MC*, pp. 465-75.

Ulpts, I., *Die Bettelorden in Mecklenburg: ein Beitrag zur Geschichte der Franziskaner, Klarissen, Dominikaner und Augustiner-Eremiten im Mittelalter* (Werl, 1995).

Valentini, R., 'Un capitolo generale degli Ospitalieri di S. Giovanni tenuto in Vaticano nel 1446', *Archivio Storico di Malta* 7 (1936) 133-68.

Van den Bosch, P., 'Die Kreuzherrenreform des 15.Jahrhunderts. Urheber, Zielsetzung und Verlauf', *Reformbemühungen und Observanzbestrebungen im spätmittelalterlichen Ordenswesen*, ed. K.Elm. Berliner Historische Studien 14 (Berlin, 1989), pp. 71-82.

Van der Eycken, M., 'Ridders, priesters en ambtenaren van de balije Biesen', *De Balije Biesen in het Maas-Rijngebied*, ed. U. Arnold (Gent, 1993), pp. 55-79.

Vatin, N., *L'Ordre de Saint-Jean-de-Jérusalem, l'Empire ottoman et la Méditerranée orientale entre les deux sièges de Rhodes, 1480-1522.* Collection Turcica 7 (Paris, 1994).

Vauchez, A., *Mouvements Franciscains et société française XIIe-XXe siècles* (Paris, 1984).

Vetter, H., *Die Beziehungen Wenzels zum Deutschen Orden von 1381 bis 1411* (Ph.D. Diss., Halle, 1912).

Vial, P., 'Les Templiers en Velay aux XIIe et XIIIe siècles', *Actes du 98e congrès national des Sociétés savantes, Reims 1970. Section de philologie et d'histoire jusqu'à 1610*, vol. 2: *Champagne et pays de la Meuse* (Paris, 1975), pp. 63-83.

Vilar Bonet, M., 'Actividades financieras de la orden del Temple en la Corona de Aragón', *VII Congreso de Historia de la Corona de Aragón* (Barcelona, 1962), vol. 2, pp. 577-85.

Virgili i Colet, A., 'Les relacions entre la Catedral de Tortosa i els Ordes Religioso-Militars durànt el segle XII, segons el "Cartulari de la Catedral de Tortosa"', *APJC*, pp. 67-79.

Voigt, J., 'Geschichte der Ballei des Deutschen Ordens in Böhmen aus urkundlichen Quellen', *Denkschriften der kaiserlichen Akademie der Wissenschaften. Phil.-hist. Klasse* 12 (Vienna, 1861) 87-146 (also separate: Vienna, 1863).

Voigt, J., *Geschichte des Deutschen Ritterordens in seinen zwolf Balleien in Deutschland*, 2 vols (Berlin 1857-1859).

Vones, L., '... *contra episcopalem auctoritatem multa praesumunt* ... Die Entwicklung des Verhältnisses des Templer- und des Johanniterordens zur Bischofsgewalt in den Ländern der Krone Aragón bis zum Ende des 12. Jahrhunderts', *Ritterorden und*

Kirche im Mittelalter, ed. Z. H. Nowak. Ordines Militares, Colloquia Torunensia Historica IX (Torun, 1997), pp. 163-92.

Wąs, G., 'Franciszkanie w społeczeństwie Śląska w średniowieczu i dobie nowożytnej', *Klasztor w społeczeństwie średniowiecznym i nowożytnym*, eds M. Derwich, A. Pobóg-Lenartowicz (Opole, Wrocław, 1996), pp. 105-37.

Wąs, G., *Klasztory franciszkanskie w miastach slaskich i luzyckich XIII-XVI w.* (Ph.D. Diss., Wrocław, 1996).

Walsh, K., 'The Augustinian observance in Siena in the age of S. Caterina and S. Bernardino', *Atti del Simposio internazionale Cateriniano-Bernardiniano, 17-20 Aprile 1980*, eds D. Maffei, P. Nardi (Siena, 1982), pp. 939-50.

Walter, E., 'Das Hospital zum Hl. Geist in Breslau und die Brüder vom Orden des Hl. Geistes', *Archiv für schlesische Kirchengeschichte* 49 (1991) 219-30.

Walter, E., 'Franziskanische Armutsbewegung in Schlesien. War die Herzogin Anna († 1265), die Schwiegertochter der hl. Hedwig, eine Terziarin des Franziskanerordens?', *Archiv für schlesische Kirchengeschichte* 40 (1982) 207-21.

Walter, E., 'Zu den Anfängen des Franziskanerklosters St. Jakob und des Klarissenklosters St. Klara auf dem Breslauer Ritterplatz', *Archiv für schlesische Kirchengeschichte* 53 (1995) 225-40.

Wehrli-Johns, M., *Geschichte des Zürcher Predigerkonvents (1230-1524), Mendikantentum zwischen Kirche, Adel und Stadt* (Zürich, 1980).

Weis-Müller, R., *Die Reform des Klosters Klingental und ihr Personenkreis.* Basler Beiträge zur Geschichtswissenschaft 59 (Basle, 1956).

Weiss, D. J., *Die Geschichte der Deutschordens-Ballei Franken im Mittelalter* (Neustadt a. d. Aisch 1991).

Zur geistigen Welt der Franziskaner im 14. und 15. Jahrhundert. Die Bibliothek des Franziskanerklosters in Freiburg / Schweiz, ed. R. Imbach (Fribourg, 1995).

Wessley, S. E., 'James of Milan and the Guglielmites: Franciscan Spirituality and Popular Heresy in late Thirteenth-Century Milan', *Collectanea Franciscana* 54 (1984) 5-20.

Wienand, A. (ed.), *Der Johanniter-Orden, Der Malteser-Orden: Der ritterliche Orden des hl. Johannes vom Spital zu Jerusalem, seine Aufgaben, seine Geschichte* (3rd edn, Cologne, 1988).

Wojtecki, D., 'Der Deutsche Orden im württembergischen Franken. Zur Entwicklung, Besitz- und Personalgeschichte der Kommenden Mergentheim, Heilbronn und Horneck', *Württembergisch-Franken* 60 (1976) 55-113.

Wojtecki, D., 'Der Deutsche Orden unter Friedrich II.', *Probleme um Friedrich II.*, ed. J. Fleckenstein. Vorträge und Forschungen XVI (Sigmaringen, 1974), pp. 187-224.

Wojtecki, D., *Studien zur Personalgeschichte des Deutschen Ordens im 13. Jahrhundert.* Quellen und Studien zur Geschichte des östlichen Europa 3 (Wiesbaden, 1971).

Zuidervaart, H., *Het Duitse huis te Schelluinen* (Schelluinen, 1988).

General Index